Churchmen and the Condition of England 1832–1885

Churchmen and the Condition of England 1832–1885

A study in the development of social ideas and practice from the Old Regime to the Modern State

G. KITSON CLARK

Methuen & Co Ltd

First published *1973*
by Methuen & Co Ltd
11 New Fetter Lane London EC4P 4EE
© *1973* G. Kitson Clark

Printed in Great Britain by
Richard Clay (*The Chaucer Press*), Ltd,
Bungay, Suffolk

SBN   416 13240 5

Distributed in the U.S.A. by
HARPER & ROW PUBLISHERS INC.,
BARNES & NOBLE IMPORT DIVISION

Dedicated to King's College London
and to
the Memory of F. D. Maurice

Contents

Preface

This book derives from three courses of lectures delivered at different dates for three different institutions. My warm thanks are therefore due to King's College London, to Trinity College, Cambridge, and to Leicester University for inviting me to lecture, and to King's College and Leicester University for very friendly hospitality while I was lecturing. Dr R. Robson of Trinity College, Cambridge, has read through the whole both in draft, and in proof, and Professor G. F. A. Best of Edinburgh University a large part of it, and I have gained much from their advice and criticism. I have also to thank Professor Chadwick for valuable assistance, and I owe much to Mrs Johnson for help in the laborious task of checking references. I am, however, alone responsible for what appears in this book, and all mistakes and mis-statements must be placed to my account.

I have gained permission to dedicate this book to King's College, and I wish to associate this dedication with the honoured name of F. D. Maurice. As things turned out he did not come to occupy the central position in the book which at one time I thought he would occupy, but my work throughout has given me some idea of his stature and significance.

G.K.C.
July 1971

NOTE

Where in the footnotes reference is made to a work which has been cited already, the page reference *within* the square bracket refers to the page in *this* book on which the first citation can be found, the number *outside and following* the bracket to the pages in the work cited to which reference is made. Where the place of publication is not cited, the work was published in London.

Introduction

As was said in the Preface, this book is the result of work originally begun when preparing for three successive sets of public
lectures: the Maurice lectures delivered for King's College
London in 1960, the Birkbeck lectures delivered for Trinity
College, Cambridge in 1967 and a course given in 1969 in
Leicester for the Centre for Victorian Studies in the University
of Leicester. But in each case after I had delivered the lectures
I became dissatisfied with what I had said and came to the
conclusion that more work on the subject was needed before I
could consider publication. For this reason not only was each
course substantially different from the one which preceded it,
but my text differs considerably both in the material used and
in its argument from what I said at Leicester.

From the beginning, however, my general objective has
remained the same. I wished to explore the attitudes of 'churchmen' – that is of the clergy of the Church of England and of
laymen who were consciously inspired by the principles and
teaching of the Church of England – to the social problems of
mid nineteenth-century England, to what Carlyle called 'the
condition-of-England question'. Where I think I gained in
perception was in seeing more clearly the nature of the relationship between the attitudes and actions of churchmen and the
history of the development of the social policy of nineteenth-
century England.

The period I have in mind stretches roughly from the First
Reform Act in 1832 till the end of Gladstone's Second Administration in 1885. Both dates are arbitrary; indeed it is part of the

thesis of this book that the development in social theory and practice from the traditional regime that existed before 1832 to the democratic collectivist State which was taking shape after 1885 was in some ways continuous and unbroken, and that this continuity gives its significance to the part played by members of the established Church, particularly by the parochial clergy. However, if there was continuous development there was also continuous change, and there are two points in the history at which the process of change seems to be more rapid, significant and decisive than during the rest of the century. Each is associated with an act reforming the methods of election to the House of Commons. In each case this not only altered the structure and methods of politics, but was ideally important as symbolizing a change in political philosophy. In each case, however, even more important than the act itself is the change in social conditions and in opinion which made the act necessary, and with the acts reforming Parliament should be considered other acts passed at about the same time which also demonstrate what was happening.

The first of these points of change is associated with the First Reform Act, passed in 1832. The impact of that act and the significance attributed to it by contemporaries made it appear to be the beginning of a new chapter in history, a conception which was of considerable importance at the time. Its provisions also made important alterations in the methods of politics though those alterations were neither as extensive nor as decisive as many contemporaries believed, nor as historians used to assert. But the full significance of what was happening can perhaps only be judged if the act reforming Parliament is seen as one of a series of fundamental reforms. In 1828 the Test and Corporation Acts, which imposed disabilities on Protestant dissenters, were repealed. In 1829 the Catholics were emancipated, largely as the result of pressure from Ireland. 1831 and 1832 were occupied by the crisis of parliamentary reform, but in 1835 the old municipal corporations were reformed, a measure which had wider social implications than are usually credited to it. After 1835 the pace slackened, and there followed about thirty years in which the old titled and proprietary classes, including the clergy of the established Church, still maintained both a decisive control over Parliament, and their tutelage over much of society.

Nevertheless other groups had established a permanent right to a place in the commonwealth which they had not possessed before, and that fact was practically and theoretically significant.

Throughout these years social, economic and demographic change was going forward, and the second turning point was not to be avoided. It can be associated with the Second Reform Act of 1867. That act, with its inevitable sequel the Third Reform Act 1884, effected a much greater change in the methods of politics, and the passing of the act of 1867 also signalized a general acquiescence in the principle of democracy. However, as was the case with the act of 1832 other measures passed at the same time are evidence of the social and ideological changes which were taking place. The acts passed between 1871 and 1876, establishing the legal position of trade unions and protecting their activities, were a sign of the increased import-ance of classes which had not hitherto possessed much power in society. The laws, such as the Public Health Act of 1866 and its sequels up to the act of 1875, and the Elementary Education Act of 1870, extending the mandatory powers of government, are a sign of the turn in social policy towards the modern col-lectivist State. It is not easy to give a date to mark the beginning of these changes. The passing of the Reform Act in 1867 was little more than a political accident. Perhaps a more significant date is 1865 when the landslide can be said to have started. In any case any precise date must be arbitrary.

With these provisos in mind the years 1832 and 1865 can be used to cut my subject up into three convenient sections, in the first of which I shall show the part played by churchmen in the traditional order that prevailed before 1832, in the second their part in the intermediate and transitional period that followed the First Reform Act, and in the third their part in the years between 1865 and 1885 when modern society, modern democracy and the modern State were beginning to take shape. Since in my view all this is part of a continuous process I wish to call my sections 'phases' not 'periods', since the word 'period' seems to suggest a decisiveness of ends and beginnings which I wish to avoid.

The society that passed through these phases was not only in constant transition, it was also constantly under strain. A

primary cause both for change and for strain was the continuous increase in the size of the population. This begins before
the end of the eighteenth century: in 1801 the population of
England and Wales had probably reached about 9 million, thirty
years later in 1831 it numbered just under 14 million, in 1861
it was well over 22 million, in 1891 it was a little over 29 million.
So great an increase would leave little unchanged in England,
and must threaten impoverishment and even starvation to many
unless large additions to the wealth and food in the country
were forthcoming. This increase helped to produce that crowded
urban society which provided some of the most intractable
problems that were to face Great Britain, and as a result of it in
large areas of the countryside there remained, in spite of
migration to the towns overseas, a larger population than could
be supported in reasonable comfort. This fact, combined with
the initial savagery and social neglect that still prevailed in
many country places, the isolation and backwardness of many
farm labourers, the decay of home industries, the lack in many
places of any occupation to compete with agriculture and the
effect of enclosures, created in many rural districts those bad
conditions among the agricultural labourers which were the
scandal of mid nineteenth-century England. Since more of the
clergy lived in the country than in towns and since a clergyman
was likely to exercise more power and incur greater responsibility when in charge of a parish in a village or a small town
than when lost in a great city, this rural poverty presented a
problem of peculiar significance to the established Church.

The additional wealth and food which the country needed
was provided for much of the population by the revolutionary
transformation of British commerce, industry and agriculture.
As a result there was a proportionate increase in wealth and an
improvement in the standard of life among the upper classes, in
that complex section of society which must be called the middle
class and, in due course, in a section of the working class.
However, there always remained a mass of abject poverty at the
bottom of society. Moreover improvements in technology could
exact a heavy price in human insecurity and distress. They
could mean the destruction of the value of those skills on which a
craftsman depended for his livelihood and self-respect; they
could replace him by the exploitation of the cheap labour of

women and children. They could place the workman at the mercy of the private capitalist, and leave both capitalist and workman at risk from the vagaries of an export trade which was subject to retrocessions that might bring ruin to the master manufacturer and starvation to those he employed.

The pressures which these developments created produced social problems of great urgency and difficulty. The forces which these pressures created were largely impersonal forces; they were not in general directed by any coherent human opinion, but the way in which their results were handled, or neglected, by society was necessarily largely controlled by the public opinion on social and political problems which prevailed at various points in the nineteenth century. Therefore with these developments must be considered the profound change in social and political philosophy that was going forward throughout the nineteenth century. Its progress was influenced by the results of the industrial and commercial revolution and by the population explosion, but it does not seem to have been caused by them. Its roots, indeed, can be traced far back into human history. In England the course it took cannot be understood without keeping in mind what had happened in the seventeenth century, and in particular the resultant difference between Church and Dissent, which provided the mould into which so much of the molten metal of nineteenth-century conflicts and animosities was poured. But in England the particular chapter of this revolution which concerned the nineteenth century may be held to start roughly with the accession of George III. From the time of the American Revolution, and the exploits of John Wilkes, there had been a steadily increasing challenge to the old ways of governing the country. This developed with growing success through the various reform acts till something like a democratic constitution was developed by the end of the century.

At the same time other things were happening to affect men's thoughts and actions. There was the great revival of religion which seems to have started with the Methodists in the eighteenth century, but fingered out into a number of religious fashions and movements in the nineteenth century. There was a rather mysterious movement which is often confounded with the revival of religion but seems to have affected many who were outside the main areas of religious ferment, an ever-increasing sense of moral responsibility and a growing sensitivity to the challenge of human suffering and the suffering of animals. There was also the development of what may be called rational liberal thought with its two important applications – utilitarianism and political economy.

These were the spirits that were moving the waters. They affected the way in which the social problems that the condition of England presented were handled. Sometimes they ran together in such a way that each added to the momentum of the other. Sometimes they were in conflict and there were confusions and cross currents, so that at some points it is not easy to see in which way things were going. Through it all, however, English society and government in fact developed in a progression which is marked by the three phases into which I have divided my subject. Indeed it is tempting to give each phase a nickname which claims to describe the way in which at that time society handled its problems; to call Phase I 'the phase of the old controls', Phase II 'the phase of *laissez-faire* and local initiative', Phase III 'the phase of incipient collectivism'. This however would be deceptive; it is important to remember that these are phases, not periods, that in each phase there are survivals from the past and anticipations of the future. Nor can any phase be characterized by one particular characteristic, in each phase there are contradictions and divergences. In order, therefore, to try to understand what happened it is necessary to look at the whole process as one and to trace what is continuous in it, as well as what is at any time novel or obsolescent.

It is the object of this book to consider the part played by churchmen, particularly the clergy, in this process. It is important to remember that in doing this the book is dealing with only one section of the community. The parts played by other sections were also significant. For instance, the part played by the medical profession in the development of public policy was of the greatest importance, and it awaits its historian. Nor should the Church of England be the only denomination to be considered. The contribution of the nonconformists, particularly the Unitarians, the Society of Friends and the Roman Catholics are important. It is also necessary to study what happened in cities where Anglicans were of little account. Nevertheless it seems legitimate to single out one section of the community for study, provided that it is always remembered that it is only one section of the community. If this is to be done the clergy and laity of the Church of England offer some points of special interest. They were probably the largest organized body of opinion in the country, in so far as they represented an organized body of opinion. Since the Church was an 'established Church' the ideas and practice of its clergy and laity were likely to bear a close relationship to the old theory of government and social ethics. Since the Church was an 'established Church' a parochial clergyman had a responsibility for everyone resident in his parish and not simply for the devout. The network of the parochial system covered the whole country in a way that was peculiarly important in periods when the country was inadequately equipped with local administrative institutions. For this reason many of the parochial clergy had important local tasks to perform both by virtue of their own office, as parish incumbents, and by taking part in the operation of the two other traditional administrative networks, the system of the justices of the peace and the system of the Poor Law.

The conditions of each phase, and the nature of the social problems of the country at any given time, necessarily dictate what aspect of the thought and activities of churchmen is relevant when that phase is under discussion. In general the things which are important in the *first phase* are the attitudes to the State and to society which men had inherited from the past, the general character of the clergy before the Reform Act, as far as that can be ascertained, and in particular the practical activities of the parochial clergy in dealing with social conditions in their local parish and its neighbourhood. The extent of this activity was no doubt limited by the abuses of the Church and by the number of neglected parishes, but it is clear that enough was done to establish important precedents for what was to follow. Another factor in the first phase which looks towards the second phase was the breakdown in certain circumstances, particularly in Ireland, of the old self-governing aristocratic methods of government and its replacement by centralized controls, working through paid officials, a tendency continued in the second phase partly under Benthamite inspiration.

The problems of the *second phase* are complicated by the fact that the middle of the nineteenth century was in England a period of survivals, anticipations and contradictions. Parliamentary elections had been partially reformed but the old titled and proprietary classes still dominated the electoral and political system. The political power of religious Dissent had increased; it was no longer possible for churchmen to rely on the assistance of Parliament as they had done in the past. To that extent the alliance between Church and State had been severed, but it was still formally intact and, what was more important, in those parishes where the incumbent was socially and administratively dominant secular and spiritual power might still be united in the same hand. The increasing realization of the clamant urgency of the country's social problems clearly pointed to the need for the State to extend its power to deal with them, but ancient principles and modern prejudices, reinforced by what was believed to be the teaching of the political economists, led men to suspect both the results of any government interference and the motives behind it. There was a particular dislike of any interference by the central government. Consequently the development of social policy was slow and partial, and in important matters it was still necessary to rely on the co-operation and initiative of locally important people. Where these were not forthcoming it was quite probable that nothing effective would be done.

For churchmen the years in the middle of the nineteenth century were years of spiritual revival. During this time more of the clergy and laity saw their religion in clearer outline and allowed its dogmas to exercise a more direct control over their lives than had possibly been the case since 1700. There was a considerable revival of parish life and there were probably fewer neglected parishes than there had been for many centuries. Clearly what is important in this phase is the attitude of the clergy to the problem of Church and State after the changes of the Reform Act and their attitude, as influenced by the spiritual revival, to the social problems of the country. But even more important in the development of social policy is their conception of their local secular responsibilities. Since the treatment of a number of important social needs depended on local initiative there was clearly an important part to be played by the men who staffed the network of parishes, particularly since they had inherited the tradition that spiritual office carried with it secular responsibilities. It is therefore important to examine the activities of the mid nineteenth-century parochial clergy in relation to education, to the functions of magistrates, particularly in relation to the Poor Law, to various schemes for mitigating the effects of poverty and to public health.

What the clergy, and others, did in these matters, what they failed to do and what they could not do, clearly led to the conditions of the *third phase*, in which local voluntary initiative working in co-operation with the central power tended to be replaced by a comprehensive mandatory authority imposing its standards on all districts alike. But the development of collectivism was not the only characteristic of the third phase. There was also the increased political and social importance of sections of the middle class and sections of the working class. Both parliamentary reform and the recognition of the legality of trade unions were signs of this, and also means by which the power of these sections of society was consolidated. Closely connected with this was a change in social doctrine which led not only to the conscious acceptance of collectivism but also to the socialist programmes which were being developed between 1880 and 1890. This revolution was of considerable significance for churchmen. A number of country clergymen came into contact with militant trade unionism in the movement among farmworkers between 1872 and 1874; of more importance, however, was the fact that secular collectivism and secular democracy, and the intellectual and economic climate of the time, would inevitably bring into being a society in which no religious body would be able to play the kind of role that religious bodies had played in earlier phases of English history.

However, the challenge to capitalism brings into prominence a religious issue the story of which runs back into the earlier phases of nineteenth-century history. As a Christian Church the Church of England professed a creed which taught values which should transcend the objects of secular society and by which the methods of secular society ought to have been judged and might have been condemned. Under the old regime the Church was so closely integrated with the pattern of secular society that any effective judgement on it was unlikely; indeed throughout the century many churchmen were too deeply committed to the old order of society to be adequate critics of its many shortcomings, though there were Church of England clergymen who were sufficiently independent to do their duty in this matter. But from the beginning of the century a new form of society began to come into existence to which they were not so deeply committed. It was largely an urban society with a large population, the great mass of which made nonsense of the old personal responsibilities on which the old system of social ethics purported to rest. Its mainspring was an industry which could be particularly ruthless in its treatment of those it employed, and its philosophy seemed to exalt the practice of unrestricted competition as the inescapable law of life and to teach that when confronted by social evils society could only allow things to take their course.

These conditions, this practice and this teaching seemed not only to defy the basic teaching of Christianity but also to be in contradiction with such ethical principles as the old system had possessed; and many churchmen combined to reform its results and resist its doctrine. The most practical movement of reform was probably the movement for the defence of the factory children. This was led by, among others, prominent churchmen such as Richard Oastler and Lord Shaftesbury, it was supported by many of the West Riding and Lancastrian clergy and by the appropriate bishops and the two archbishops. However, important as this was at the time it was probably not of such permanent importance as the attack in the name of Christian principle on the teaching of those political economists who had supplied industrialized capitalism with its apology and its ethics.

This attack started early in the century with the writings of such men as Coleridge and M. T. Sadler, it broadens with F. D. Maurice and the Christian Socialists into a general criticism of the whole of society and leads on to men who went further than Maurice was prepared to go. Together with the teaching of Carlyle and Ruskin and of the followers of Comte it helps to prepare the way for the socialist thought of the third phase. Indeed, as with the practical activities of many of the mid nineteenth-century clergy, it forms in some way a link between the old regime and what was to come. As it is an aspect of the way in which churchmen confronted the problems of the condition-of-England through most of the century it would have been proper to consider it in relation to each of the three phases, but it seems most convenient to take it when considering the general rejection of the absolute dictates of what had passed for political economy which characterized the third phase, and before the last chapter of the book which is concerned with the attitude of churchmen to the emergence of the New Leviathan – the modern omnicompetent, secular, necessarily agnostic, State.

Since this book is an attempt to treat this subject from a particular angle it would seem that a bibliography would be too eclectic and heterogeneous to be of much use. There are excellent bibliographies on the history of the nineteenth-century clergy in such books as C. K. F. Brown, *A History of the English Clergy 1800–1900* (1953), G. F. A. Best, *Temporal Pillars* (Cambridge, 1964), Desmond Bowen, *The Idea of the Victorian Church* (Montreal, 1968), Owen Chadwick, *The Victorian Church* (Part I, 1966; Part II, 1970). But beyond this literature there is the great mass of books, articles, contemporary articles, speeches, sermons, blue books and other forms of evidence which give relevant information on the history of political and social ideas and on the political and social history of the general period under discussion. This is so extensive and varied that it would be difficult to present a manageable list which would not be misleading; I trust, therefore, that my footnotes will supply sufficient warranty for what I say. However, my work for this book has impressed upon me how much more research there is to be done. For instance, too many of the statements still made about the nineteenth-century clergy are based upon impressions, or upon the unsupported assertions of contemporary observers, friendly or hostile; there is still much room for more research into the activities and available statements of individual clergymen. Even more pressing is the need for a history of medical practice, and for more knowledge of what was happening in a number of representative towns. Until these things are done it will not be possible to begin to consider writing the history of social ideas and practice in the nineteenth century.

The Old Regime
to 1832

I

The Old Order
of Society

A man or woman who wishes to make a spiritual and intellectual journey into nineteenth-century Britain is liable to make, in a greatly exaggerated form, a mistake resembling that which is sometimes made by Englishmen going to live for a period in the United States, or by citizens of the United States coming to live in Britain. At first the Englishman, or the American, finds a country which seems to be substantially the same as his own. The language resembles his, the way of life is not strikingly different or only different in rather amusing superficialities. The basic political and personal moralities appear to correspond. Then, sooner or later, he comes across a contrast in attitudes which does not appear to him to be superficial, that seems to suggest defective values on the part of his hosts, and he becomes angry and censorious. But in fact he made a cardinal mistake at the outset. Instead of starting from the assumption that the men and women he meets in the United States are English people who choose to use a slightly different accent and live in overheated houses, or, in England, are Americans who for reasons best known to themselves talk in a curious way and drink tepid beer, he should rather have realized from the beginning that he was confronting people of a different nation and a different tradition, and he should have started by trying to understand all that such a difference may mean.

If, as is likely, the hidden differences between modern Americans and modern Englishmen do not matter very much, this is not true of what is likely to confuse the judgement of the modern observer when he ventures into the middle of the nineteenth century. The people whom he will find, at least after about 1840, will in many ways seem to be not unlike his contemporaries. Their method of talking will be essentially the same as ours; their dress, though quaint, will not seem to be obviously fancy dress, like the dress of men and women at the beginning of the century. If they did not have the motor car and the aeroplane they had the railway train and the steamship. They were faced by the dire problems caused by industrialism and overpopulation, which are the source of many of our worst problems also, and if they did not live in a democracy, at least they had something like our parliamentary system, and newspapers resembling our newspapers. It is, therefore, easy to assume that they must have thought like us, or at least ought to have done so, and to mark it heavily against them when their scale of values was obviously different.

This is, I believe, a mistake, and to correct it it is necessary to put these people back into their proper historical perspective. I begin my period in 1832. An elderly man still active in that year might have been born during the war of American Independence, while Dr Johnson was still alive and before the trumpets of the French Revolution had been sounded to disturb the peace of mind of the old regime. He would have grown to manhood under the shadow of that revolution, and have shared the hopes and recurrent fears of the years that led up to, and followed, Waterloo. Even if the point of observation is moved to 1862, when Palmerston, who was elected to a seat in the House of Commons in 1807, was still prime minister, there will be a number of men about who are not yet really old, whose boyhood was passed during the war, and their early manhood in the unreformed, potentially unstable, Britain that existed before 1832. It is in fact a useful corrective to calculate in the terms of the ordinary span of the human life how long it took to leave the eighteenth century, and with it the old regime and the French Revolution, finally behind.

This is not only true in terms of the passage of years, it is true in terms of the development of men's minds, particularly in one article. Anyone who had lived in the country before 1832, and, though to an increasingly diminishing extent, anyone who lived in the twenty or thirty years that followed 1832, lived in a country largely dominated by a massive social hierarchy, which in one way or another went back to the middle ages. The monarch, the nobles and great landowners, the lesser landowners, or country gentry, the tenants of each group, the bishops, the rectors or vicars and the curates provided an ancient pattern which was still imprinted on a good deal of English life. That hierarchy had been for some time under attack, and after 1832 the vehemence of that attack redoubled, but its clamour should not make us forget how many people there were who grew up under this system and passed their lives on the terms it offered, who either did not question its legitimacy, or, if they thought at all, accepted the traditional justifications for its existence, and who tried to practise, or pretended to practise, its own peculiar form of social morality.

Of course those justifications would not satisfy the social philosophy of the twentieth century, and that social morality is different from the one we practise, or pretend to practise. But since both justification and morality were to a great or lesser extent accepted by a very large number of people who flourished between 1832 and 1885 it is of some importance to consider what they were.

The old conception of social morality took as its starting point the assumption that a rigid hierarchy in society was not only sanctioned by immemorial custom but was also necessary if that order, which made civilized life possible, was to be maintained. The point was an old one, indeed perhaps its best expression is in Ulysses' famous speech on 'degree' in Shakespeare's *Troilus and Cressida*. If, said Ulysses, 'degree' were 'taken away',

> Force should be right; or, rather, right and wrong –
> Between whose endless jar justice resides –
> Should lose their names, and so should justice too.
> Then every thing includes itself in power,
> Power into will, will into appetite;
> And appetite, an universal wolf,
> So doubly seconded with will and power,
> Must make perforce an universal prey,
> And last eat up himself. (I. iii. 116–24)

So Shakespeare had written, and so two hundred years later many men still believed. Indeed in the recent history of Europe the lesson seemed to be writ large. In France in 1789 'degree' had been taken away and matters had followed the dreadful course which Ulysses had predicted. There had been the September massacres, the execution of the king, the reign of terror and in the end the military despotism of Napoleon which had destroyed the liberties of France, and after ravening for unlimited conquests had finally destroyed itself. Probably not many people recalled Shakespeare's words, but there were quite enough articulate contemporary observers to make their own revealing comments on the terrible drama that was being enacted before their eyes. These ranged from comparatively sober statements through the passionate rhetoric of Edmund Burke to apocalyptic pronouncements in which the scriptural signs of the end of the world were clearly recognized in what was taking place, and Napoleon easily identified as the beast in *Revelations*. But whatever the form of the commentary, the lesson was apt to be the same: the chaos and suffering that awaited mankind if the ancient order of society were overthrown.

With a belief in this traditional order necessarily went a belief in the rights of private property and the propriety of wide differences in the amount of property different people in the different ranks of society possessed. This belief was in fact to survive when a belief in the inherent values of the traditional order of society was beginning to fade; it was indeed to be retained by many people who had attacked that order, but it was unavoidably implied by the old philosophy. And it was accepted even by men who recognized the absurdities and injustices which great accumulations of hereditary wealth occasioned.

There is an obvious example of this in the work on moral philosophy which Archdeacon Paley published in 1785, and which remained for some time the standard work on the subject. His chapter on property begins with his famous, if curious, image of ninety-nine pigeons seen in a field gathering corn for a single pigeon. This, said Paley, resembled what happened among men.

> Among men you see the ninety-and-nine toiling and scraping together a heap of superfluities for one (and this one too, often times, the feeblest and worst of the whole set – a child, a woman, a madman or a fool); getting nothing for themselves all the while,

but a little of the coarsest of the provision, which their own industry produces; looking quietly on, while they see the fruits of all their labour spent or spoiled, and if one of their number take or touch a particle of the hoard the others joining against him and hanging him for the theft.

It might have been expected that this would lead up to a condemnation of hereditary wealth, but it does not do so. He starts his next chapter by saying: 'There must be some very important advantages to account for an institution, which, in the view of it above given, is so paradoxical and unnatural.' He then goes on to describe what in his view these were, saying in conclusion:

> Inequality of property in the degree in which it exists in most countries of Europe, abstractedly considered, is an evil; but it is an evil which flows from those rules concerning the acquisition and disposal of property, by which men are incited to industry, and by which the object of their industry is rendered secure and valuable. If there be any great inequality unconnected with this origin it ought to be corrected.

The last sentence is enigmatic and may disclose some moral uncertainty, but Paley does not seem to have doubted the validity of the moral sanctions that justified society. His book also contains a section on the duties of obedience. It is therefore not surprising that when confronted by the Revolution he joined the chorus of warning voices. In 1792, in order to discourage 'schemes of hasty reform', he published a tract with the title *Reasons for Contentment addressed to the Labouring Part of the British Public*. In this tract he argued that: 'Providence which foresaw, which appointed, indeed, the necessity to which human affairs are subjected (and against which it was impious to complain) hath contrived, that, whilst fortunes are only for a few, the rest of mankind may be happy without them.' This tract is, however, only one example of a large literature the arguments in which are various, but which is generally directed to one object.[1]

[1] Paley, *Moral and Political Philosophy*, Bk. III, Pt. I, Chs. I and II; Bk. VI, Chs. II, III and IV (*Works*, ed. in 5 vols. by E. Lynam, 1828, Vol. IV, pp. 51-3 and 231-52). *Reasons for Contentment* (E. Lynam, ed., Vol. I, pp. 355-65). For the views of contemporary bishops both on the crisis of the Revolution and property, see R. A. Soloway, *Prelates and People: Ecclesiastical Social Thought in England, 1783-1852* (1969) pp. 19-84.

In this old conception, therefore, society depended for its ordered existence on the maintenance of a social framework in which everyone did his duty in that state of life into which it should please God to call him. Since the duties were different, and it was necessary for their proper performance that one human being should be subordinated to another, it was necessary that that order should be hierarchical. Since it was important that that order should be stable, and also that it should sustain inherited values, it was necessary that, to a large extent, particular places should be assigned in this order by hereditary succession. Since for the operation of the system it was necessary to accept the principle of private property it was necessary to permit a grossly unequal distribution of property, always accepting the proviso that property had its duties as well as its rights. And since it was God who had appointed these necessities, then the system which they imposed must be sanctioned by His law against which it would be impious to complain, and which, presumably, it would be still more impious to try to upset.

There is, of course, no need to emphasize the moral defects of this view of society, or the monstrous social injustices it could condone. The feeblest historical imagination should be able to envisage how wide and beyond calculation was the difference between the terms on which life was offered to the great nobleman living delicately in one of the gigantic country houses of the late eighteenth or early nineteenth century and all that was available for the potato-eating labourer living with all his family in one room in a fetid cottage not so far from the lodge gates. Nevertheless, while never forgetting the prevalence of such contrasts, it is important to recognize that this conception of the order of society was the framework of a system of social ethics which was to play its part in the progressive development of the State in Britain, and incidentally was to evoke from those who accepted it personal services which the adherents of a more egalitarian system might not have conceived as coming within the terms of their private duty.

For although the Reform Act of 1832 in many ways put an end to the old regime these ideas continued to be the commonplaces of a number of men and women, some of them eminent, some of them very obscure; and in these matters perhaps those who are obscure are the most significant, for what they say is most likely to represent the intellectual small change of the day. For instance, in 1838 the Reverend Marmaduke Prichett, once a chaplain of Trinity College, Cambridge, preaching in Bridlington a sermon on education, gave an earnest warning against over-educating a man, by which he meant giving a man 'knowledge uncalled for by that station of life in which the providence of God has placed him'. It was in fact his belief that, 'As we have every reason to believe that the order of human society is established by God – so we believe it to be a safe guide in our endeavour to ascertain that quantity of knowledge which is necessary for men in various ranks of life.'[1]

The implications of his doctrine are, of course, harsh, and it is to be feared they represent a view of the educational needs of the poor which had too much influence in the middle of the nineteenth century, but the form in which his case is made is evidence of the survival of the old view of society six years after the Reform Act. Four years later there is another example in a sermon which is a plea for charity for the sufferers from the trade depressions of the early 1840s. The preacher is Canon Parkinson of the Collegiate Church of Manchester. He says that it would be wrong to attribute the suffering in the country to the misbehaviour of any particular class, for:

> In considering *any* social evil, it is worse than erroneous, it is a sin, to lay the responsibility of such evil exclusively on whole classes of men. If inequality of rank and condition be an ordination of providence, no man is to be blamed for simply belonging to one class or another, but each is to be judged by the way in which he, as an individual, discharges his duty in that state of life into which it has pleased God to call him. Woe then be to him, whether ignorance or malice be his motive, who attempts to set master against man and man against master – who fails to see that both are as necessary in the economy of civil life as hill and valley in the economy of nature.[2]

The conception that an unequal order of society had been established by God, that inequality of rank and condition was

---

[1] The Rev. Marmaduke Prichett, M.A., F.S.A., *A Sermon on Christian Education for Subscribers to National Schools* (Bridlington, 1838).

[2] The Rev. R. Parkinson, *A Sermon preached in the Collegiate Church of Manchester on the 26th of June 1842* (Manchester, 1842).

an ordination of providence, is naturally both strange and repugnant to a modern thinker, but in order to understand its force and staying power it is important to recognize that there lay behind it a line of argument which is not easy to dismiss out of hand. But in order to recognize this it is best to move down the century to find something like the old argument in an extract from a sermon by a man whose thought is likely to be more sympathetic to men and women of our time.

As will be seen in a later chapter B. F. Westcott formed his social thought after an intensive study of Auguste Comte, who was an unusual authority for a Christian priest. Westcott was a leading member of the Christian Social Union, and at the end of his life bishop of Durham. He was deeply concerned about the welfare of a large mining population, and acutely conscious of the need for a policy of social reform in the country in general, and probably for some redistribution of wealth.

Yet Westcott envisaged a society in which there must be inequality of wealth and inequality of rewards. In a sermon preached in 1886 he said:

> There could be no true nation, even as there could be no true family without wide differences in power, in fortune, in duty among those who compose it. And the aim of the Christian patriot will be not to obliterate these differences but to harmonize them in their ripe development by shewing that they can minister to the vigour of one life.[1]

But the matter can be pressed beyond Westcott. It is pertinent to ask: how many people today really believe in an equality of reward or an equitable distribution of functions, and believe this in such a way that they will allow it adversely to affect their own standards and style of life? There is still an unresolved moral problem here. Any large society, and communist Russia is no exception, depends on the expert performance of a variety of services, some highly skilled and responsible, some humble, even menial. In certain very specialized circumstances – in a monastery, or in a Jewish kibbutz – the skilled and responsible tasks and the unskilled and menial tasks are done by the same people. But normally this is not so,

[1] Brooke Foss Westcott, D.D., D.C.L., *Social Aspects of Christianity* (1887), pp. 42–3.

and probably in any very large community it cannot be so, and where they are done by different people those who do the humbler, less skilled, jobs have less prestige and smaller remuneration than those who do the more skilled work. This is, I believe, the practice in the USSR; this is, I believe, the principle embodied in the 'differentials' upon which trade unions often insist.

It might therefore be suggested that rather than evading this issue it would be better to accept a theory which frankly takes account of it. But it is not the object of this book to comment on what are, or what ought to be, the principles of modern social ethics. The point of importance here is the continuing force of the logic of inequality underlying the social ethics of most of the men and women with whom I wish to deal. Of course the social ethics of most men are in fact largely the product of habit, environment and self-interest and only rationalized by ethical theories, if rationalized at all; and as habits, environment and the orientation of self-interest change, the code of social ethics will change also. Between 1832 and 1885 there were drastic changes in British society and considerable developments in the prevalent political and social philosophy, particularly in so far as this referred to the functions of the State. But there was no sudden social revolution. Old forms of property, old forms of social authority, continued to survive for a remarkably long time, and the new society which took shape alongside it was still an unequal society with great differences of function, and in the enjoyment of wealth, among its members. It is therefore not surprising that the old system of social ethics, recognizing as it did the logic of inequality, should play its part in developing what was to come.

The starting point of the old system of ethics was the claim that the order of society was divinely ordained. If this was so those who occupied positions in that order occupied them by divine ordinance, and must perform duties which were divinely ordained also. In general the more important and better rewarded were these positions the more extensive and inescapable were the responsibilities that were incurred. They were particularly heavy for those who owned land, or filled recognizably significant positions in the order of society, or who employed other men and women. But they bore heavily on anyone who

B

was endowed with any form of wealth. In 1740 Bishop Butler, preaching before the Corporation of London, had put the point clearly.

> And as rich men, by a right direction of their greater capacity may entitle themselves to a greater reward: so by a wrong direction of it, or even by great negligence, they may become *partakers of other men's sins*, and chargeable with other men's miseries. For if there be at all any measures of proportion, any sort of regularity and order, in the administration of things, it is self evident that *unto whomsoever much is given, of him shall much be required and to whom much is committed of him shall more be demanded.*[1]

There is one important difference between this system of social ethics and what is normally acceptable today. Modern public morality is inclined to be communal. Social obligations are seen to be incumbent on the community as a whole, the services which they impose are to be performed by the action of the community; indeed the organization of the community is the only organization strong enough, and the services it can command are the only services which are expert enough, to do what is known to be required. The old social morality was essentially personal. Public services were not performed by a salaried professional, nor were social obligations satisfied by the mere unavoidable payment of rates and taxes. Duties and services were performed by the individual himself. This meant that the way in which they were performed, indeed whether they were performed at all, was largely a matter for an individual's conscience; and consciences might be rather variable in their operations, even though their teaching was reinforced by a recollection of the punishment which Dives received for his negligence in this very matter.

The personal nature of these obligations led to a difference in approach to social problems, which not only had importance in determining the direction of the thought and the sphere of activity of a good many individuals, but also had an effect on the way in which social policy developed. In modern conditions a social problem is recognized as having a national, or even an international, relevance. Its treatment is therefore likely to call for action on a national scale. Under the old system any sense of

[1] W. E. Gladstone, ed., *The Works of Joseph Butler, D.C.L. Sometime Lord Bishop of Durham* (3 vols., Oxford, 1896) Vol. II, pp. 306-7.

obligation was likely to be confined to a particular locality, since being personal it was unavoidably limited by the personal capacity and natural perceptions of the individual involved. This point Bishop Butler also discussed in a sermon *Upon the Love of our Neighbour*. He pointed out that the conception of love towards mankind was too general for ordinary human beings, and that for the capacities of most men even love for all their fellow countrymen was too extensive. He said: 'The sphere of action of far the greatest part of mankind is much narrower than the government they live under.' And so he came to the conclusion that

> the scripture, not being a book of theory and speculation, but a plain rule of life for mankind has with the utmost possible propriety put the principle of virtue upon the love of our neighbour; which is that part of the universe, that part of mankind, that part of our country, which comes under our immediate notice, acquaintance, and influence, and with which we have to do.[1]

It was not a way of thought which excluded a sense of duty towards larger units than could come within a man's personal influence and comprehension. But it established an order of priority. Perhaps the position can be best made plain by recounting the views which Southey put into the mouth of the ghost of Sir Thomas More, in the strange *Colloquies* which he published in the next century, in 1829. Sir Thomas was made to say that a man was to do his duty first to his family, then to his neighbours and lastly to his country and his kind. He was to promote the welfare and happiness of those who were in any degree dependent upon him, or whom he had the means of assisting, and never wantonly injure the meanest thing that lived. It is significant that Southey believed that these principles had been violated in the treatment of the children in the factories and set at nought by the assembly of large uncared-for multitudes in the great cities.[2]

This narrowing of the sphere of a man's duty to his own immediate neighbourhood suited the conditions and habits of eighteenth-century England. Travel was difficult, the various

[1] ibid., Vol. II, pp. 210–11.

[2] Robert Southey, L.L.D., *Sir Thomas More or Colloquies on the Progress and Prospects of Society* (2nd edn. 1931, 2 vols.) Vol. I, p. 165, and Vol. II, pp. 107–15.

units of local government were practically autonomous within
the very wide limits set by the law of the land. For many men
the most important events in their lives happened in the neighbourhood in which they lived. Even in the House of Commons
an MP's local commitments were normally considered as the
most important part of his duties, and the vast mass of social
legislation was local legislation.[1]

All this emphasizes how personal the conception of public
duty in the eighteenth century was likely to be. It also means
that in order to judge the social policy at any time before 1830
it is probably more necessary to consider what local personalities, magistrates, landowners, the leading figures in the various
towns and possibly the parochial clergy, were doing in their
own neighbourhoods, than what seemed to be the tenor of
general legislation, or the actions of the central government.
If, however, this is so it makes it the more difficult to answer a
question which without this complication would be difficult
enough. How far was this traditional code of morality a reality
which effectively controlled men's actions and consciences and
how far was it a pretence, or completely inoperative? In most
social codes there is an element of truth and an element of
pretence. In a modern totalitarian State the proportions can
perhaps be judged by a comparison between the conditions
which actually exist within its borders and the claims made in
the official propaganda. In the England of the old regime it is
necessary to consider the working of the consciences of a large
number of different individuals in obscure situations.

Nevertheless a case against the old system is very easily made.
At its best it was the system of a social hierarchy in a savagely
unequal society. If it was the tradition that a man's position
imposed on him obligations towards his neighbours, tradition
also might give him intolerable privileges which might be enjoyed at their expense. A landowner who was also a magistrate
and a member of Parliament had very considerable opportunities for exploiting his position for his own pleasure and advantage at the expense of his poorer neighbours, and the nature and
administration of the game laws, the procedures sometimes
adopted in relation to enclosures, the tightness of the political

[1] E. and A. Porrit, *The Unreformed House of Commons* (2 vols., Cambridge,
1903) Vol. I, pp. 261–2.

controls which were often operated, suggest in what spirit these privileges could be used. Moreover, whether a man performed any of his duties to his tenants, neighbours and dependents, and the way in which he performed them, was certainly very much a matter for his own conscience. There was little else to control or check the absentee, the negligent, the callous, or the tyrannical. Before there was an effective Press, and before Cobbett, the check on public opinion must have been negligible. The law was inadequate. The ecclesiastical law seemed unable to make many of the clergy reside in their parishes. It is true that it was possible to carry a complaint against the justices of the peace to the judges of assize, or the Court of King's Bench, and that this restriction on their actions was a reality. But the discretion which the law permitted magistrates was great, and since their victims might well be poor and inarticulate, it seems probable that they often exceeded their powers, particularly apparently in the endeavour to put down poaching.[1] Many tenants and labourers had little or no protection against their landowners or employers.

Yet in spite of all this it seems clear that the traditional code of social morality was by no means altogether a pretence. If it had been so it is difficult to see that eighteenth- and early nineteenth-century England would have had any government at all. The existing system depended heavily on volunteers performing duties appropriate to their station. It is of course true that the justices of the peace, who were by far the most important of these volunteers, gained in return for their services prestige and power – power which they could use for their own purposes. It is also true that in preserving order, in so far as they did do this, they were protecting their own properties and the properties of their class, though it is important to remember that poor people can sometimes suffer more from the prevalence of violence and disorder than the rich, a fact which is sometimes forgotten. But the magistrate's time was by no means solely taken up with the business of keeping order. By the end of the eighteenth century in many counties they were transacting most of the important business of local government; in fact probably their most onerous and troublesome duties were

[1] Sir William Holdsworth, *A History of English Law* (12 vols., Vol. X, 1938) Vol. X, pp. 238–56.

supplied by the problem of destitution. Indeed the work which a number of magistrates did in relation to the administration of the Poor Law, in the very bad period with which the eighteenth century ended and the nineteenth century began, is a good example of the responsibilities which some men were prepared to assume to fulfil the duties of their station.

It would, of course, be quite meaningless to try to draw up a balance sheet weighing the many things which were bad under the old system against what was good in it. Nor is it necessary to try. What is important is that it embodies a living tradition which in different conditions was capable of growth and expansion, and which might act as a starting point for the development of social policy in the nineteenth century.

That development would, however, necessarily take place in drastically changing circumstances. Conditions would develop to which the old system was unsuited. The population would grow and become increasingly urban, and as a result cities would assume a size which was far beyond the capacity of any organization which might have sufficed for the small market towns and the closed and open villages which were normal under the old dispensation. There would be a greater diffusion of new wealth in the country, commercial wealth, industrial wealth in the hands of men who did not readily tolerate the pretension of the aristocratic and oligarchic groups which had played so great a part in the administration of the country under the old regime. The new wealth encouraged a new philosophy and a new hope, the hope that in the place of a hierarchical society based on hereditary wealth and status there should come into existence a new progressive society, based on enterprise, hard work, frugal living and free contract, determining its values and rewards by the operation of untrammelled competition.

In fact this conception fitted the tendency of British social and economic thought in the later eighteenth century. At that time men were becoming increasingly sceptical about the value and propriety of the attempts which their fathers had made to control the economic processes and social life of the country. Adam Smith attacked the usefulness of protective duties, bounties and the old colonial system. Magistrates tended to allow their control of wages and prices to fall into desuetude and Parliament began to repeal the laws which had been passed from time to time to regulate and protect labour in particular industries.

The social, indeed the ethical and philosophical, implications of what was happening, and still more of what men desired should happen, was of considerable significance. The society of the old regime was being transmuted into the moral reforming and progressive society which was taking shape in the middle of the nineteenth century. It was natural that anyone who was progressive and radical should wish to leave behind the rigidities, insolences and unearned privileges of a largely hereditary society and replace it by a system in which suitable positions were allocated to those whose usefulness and hard work had proved their worth. It was also true that a very cogent case had been made against the effectiveness and rationality of the regulative measures with which the men of an earlier period had cluttered the statute book and stifled trade. There was however another aspect to this development. To a man of business, prominent in commerce and industry, it might be of great advantage that his work should not be hampered by ancient and illogical trade regulations and that he should not have to yield place in society or politics to a lord or squire who had gained his position by the blind process of inheritance, and seemed to do little of any note to deserve it. But to a poor man or woman it might be of greater advantage to be considered as being even in the lowest rank of a divinely ordained hierarchical system which would attribute to him or her some rights, however meagre, than to be the loser in a competitive system which would allow them nothing, or to be judged to be examples of the undeserving poor whose moral failures were responsible for their condition.

The point is important. But it would not be easy to calculate its practical significance. It would not, for instance, be easy to say what had been the real value to a great many poor people of the old system of rights and duties. In a great many cases it would seem to have been negligible. It is true that in the middle and later nineteenth century a number of people were prepared to talk emotionally and at some length about the loss suffered by the poor through the decay of the network of personal responsibilities that had characterized the old system, but it would be hard to say to what extent they were relying on personal reminiscence, or to what extent on a conventionally idealized view of the past. The change after 1832 was not drastic. A large section of the nation remained in the control of authorities which had survived from an earlier period, and they in their turn were already influenced by the moralistic tendencies that had begun to influence social administration, and to some extent by contemporary economic thought. Where the new classes took possession, they were also often prepared to accept the traditions of the old regime. They also became unpaid magistrates. Many of them were prepared to accept the personal and local responsibilities which the old system enjoined. In several of the great provincial cities, notably where the leading denomination was Unitarian, there was to be much devoted and very intelligent social service on the part of wealthy manufacturers, and most particularly on the part of their wives and daughters. The activities of his man like Sir Titus Salt show a deep sense of responsibility for his workers, and he is not the only employer who behaved in this way; indeed it seems clear from a number of cases that the conscience and personality of an employer could affect the way in which his labour was treated.[1] Nor did the acceptance of a new economic philosophy inhibit a sense of responsibility for the casualties of the economic system. The last of the old labour laws had not been repealed before the first of the factory acts was passed, the beginning of a system which would become much more powerful and all-embracing than the old system could ever be.

In fact the large impersonal changes that took place in nineteenth-century society probably did more to make the old system impracticable than anything this change in doctrine effected in making it unaccountable. With the great increase in population the cities filled with refugees from Ireland, from the highlands of Scotland and from the English countryside for whom no one could be responsible in the old way. The new sensitiveness to human needs, and the conditions produced by very large populations living hugger-mugger in close proximity to one another produced problems and created tasks with which

[1] See J. H. Clapham, *An Economic History of Modern Britain*. Vol. I, *The Early Railway Age* (Cambridge, 1926) pp. 563–5.

the old authorities and the old systems were incompetent to deal. In certain areas economic conditions changed very rapidly. New men emerged as employers, who had inherited no social traditions and whose ethical standards were hardened by ruthless competition, or stultified by the hope of great profit or the fear of imminent bankruptcy. Meanwhile, men became aware of conditions prevalent in factories and mines, which had produced evils the control of which could not safely be left to the conscience of the employer, or the activities of local magistrates. Meanwhile, Jeremy Bentham was devising a more powerful system of government than had ever existed in these isles, a scheme which provided precedents for men who played an influential part in developing public policy after 1830.

It is, however, important to realize that the process by which the old system was displaced started in the eighteenth century, before the period of reform, before what is usually considered to be the beginning of the industrial revolution, perhaps before the beginning of the increase of population and certainly before Bentham's thought could possibly affect policy. As I have suggested, the reason for this is in fact simple, One of the reasons for the development of the new State in Britain was the failure of the old governmental system to cope with the problems presented to it. That failure was long dated, in fact in some respects the old system might be said never to have succeeded. The most elementary necessity for civil society is the maintenance of order within its bounds and the protection of its members from violence. In many parts of the country the eighteenth-century State noticeably failed to do either of these things. Armed highwaymen infested many of the roads and footpads and cracksmen the cities. Smugglers, using force where necessary, dominated long stretches of the coastline and the counties adjacent to the coast, particularly in the counties of the south-east corner of England. Rioting was endemic, and not easily controlled unless the military was called in. Brutal violence was a commonplace of life everywhere.

The situation in London was particularly significant because it anticipated the conditions which were to be reproduced in the nineteenth century elsewhere in Britain. London was the first of the really great cities in Britain. It had long overgrown its traditional institutions. In certain districts its parochial organization had been swamped and rendered meaningless by the numbers who swarmed in the old parishes. There was a large criminal class in no way kept in check by the recurrent harvest of human misery at Tyburn, and many districts in London did not supply what was the prerequisite of the old system – a local aristocracy or elite which would provide men to fill the office of justice of the peace with some sense of public responsibility. The justices were too often what were called 'trading justices', men who had taken on the job for the sake of the money they could wring from it, and police functions were too often in the hands of rogues like Jonathan Wild, the great thieftaker, who encouraged, succoured and sold criminals, as suited his private profit.

The sequel is important. The old system had failed and the government perforce gradually replaced it with a paid professional service. The process may be said to have started between 1740 and 1754 with the activities of Henry Fielding, the novelist, as a magistrate in London. Henry Fielding took a grant from the government for his services and also trained a small body of professional thieftakers. With these he opened up a systematic attack on crime, work carried on after him by his half-brother, the formidable blind Sir John Fielding. In 1792 regular stipendiary magistrates were instituted in various parishes in London, and in 1802 each of them was empowered to employ a small body of paid constables. A horse patrol was raised to police the roads round London. But there is no point in describing here the various steps which were taken to introduce into the metropolitan area paid and professional magistrates and paid and professional police, a process which culminated in 1829 with the institution of the Metropolitan Police. What matters is the tendency which this process reveals, the development in response to urgent public necessity of a form of administration and government which took the place of the old system of government by volunteers, or at least by non-professionals.

It is a characteristic of English predispositions that these precedents were not followed consistently or quickly. In 1813 an act was passed to make it possible to appoint stipendiary magistrates in Manchester. In 1835 the Municipal Reform Act enabled municipalities to appoint stipendiaries. A number of local acts gave municipalities power to raise police forces, and in 1839 a permissive act enabled justices at quarter sessions to create a paid constabulary for a county. But it was not till after 1856 that it was necessary for every county to appoint a paid police force. Since one would have thought that an effective police force is the minimum requirement for any government the process was extraordinarily piecemeal and slow.

The same tendency can be seen in an even more interesting example from Ireland. In many parts of Ireland the old system had no chance of success. The landlords were often the product of ancient conquest and oppression and divided by race and religion from their tenants. Under the old system a landlord was expected to reside on his estates, but many of the Irish landlords were permanent absentees. Miss Edgeworth's novel *The Absentee* is devoted to showing the dreadful results for his tenantry of the absence from his estates of an Irish peer, though in fact her more famous novel *Castle Rackrent* suggests that the presence anywhere of some Irish landlords would not have been of great value to anyone in particular. The established Church in Ireland was the Church of a small minority, and noticeably and cynically negligent at that. At the end of the eighteenth century Ireland had been the scene of armed revolt, in the early nineteenth century the smell of rebellion clung to much of Irish life and a turbulent nationalist movement was developing. In addition to this Ireland was overpopulated and very poor with little industry to remedy the situation. As a result it was troubled by endemic rural crime, often of a peculiarly revolting nature.

In 1814, in order to deal with this situation Robert Peel, at that time chief secretary, developed a scheme whereby paid police and paid magistrates with no local connections could be imposed on a disturbed district. By this scheme the central government in effect took direct control of the forces responsible for order, and this process went on until by 1836 all the Irish police were brought into one united system officered by an inspectorate of their own with their own training depots. Meanwhile, between 1815 and 1840 the Irish local authorities lost most of their powers, the chief county officers being appointed by the central government who fixed their salaries.

It was the same pattern of development as can be seen in London but on an extended scale and in a more drastic form. In Ireland, however, a new element made its appearance. Since one cause of Ireland's trouble was its poverty its condition was such that no class was likely to supply those services which local enterprise and charity might be expected to supply in England, and there did not seem to be enough native capital to supply the equipment which was necessary for economic growth. It thus seemed necessary for the State to step in and provide what no one else would provide. The result was a remarkable anticipation of what was to come elsewhere.

For instance, something like a public health service developed in Ireland in the early nineteenth century. In 1805 provision was made for public dispensaries for the treatment of the poor, half of the cost being provided by the State. By 1840 there were more than 600 of these; there were also a number of hospitals largely dependent on public funds. In fact it has been claimed that at that date Ireland possessed a more advanced system of State medicine for the benefit of the poor than existed anywhere else in Europe. A national system of education was also developed. From 1815 grants had been made to the Kildare Place Society to help provide undenominational schools for the people of Ireland, and in 1831 a body of commissioners was set up to give Ireland a centralized system of undenominational popular education under government control. Most remarkable of all the State took steps to stimulate economic growth. Loans, and in due course grants, were made to help provide roads, bridges, facilities for fisheries and even factories. In 1817 a central loan fund was established to finance Irish public works, and in 1831 the Irish Board of Works was created with a national inspectorate of engineers. In the next eight years this board spent over a million pounds in loans and grants. In fact in Ireland the direct action of the government was being invoked not only to perform the elementary tasks which the old system accepted as the duty of the State but also to perform new tasks which the social condition of Ireland seemed to have made necessary.[1]

---

[1] For Ireland, see N. Gash, *Mr Secretary Peel* (1961) pp. 138–236; Oliver MacDonagh, *Ireland* (*The Modern Nations in Historical Perspective*) (Englewood Cliffs, N.J., 1968) pp. 22–42.

After 1832, after the period of reform had started, these precedents were followed up in England, partly under the inspiration of Bentham and the guidance of Edwin Chadwick. However, even before 1832 there had been enough precedents to suggest three things. First, in certain circumstances the old system inevitably broke down. There were certain conditions in which it could not work, there were certain tasks it could not perform. Second, where this happened a new system working through professional agents was likely to take its place, and, Third, in order to maintain a standard of uniform efficiency it was probable that the new system would have to come under central control. However, in England, outside London, the old system had not been the complete failure that it was in Ireland and it proved to be possible for some local and voluntary agencies to expand their activities to meet the new demands. In the last resort this voluntary development was not universal or powerful enough to do what was necessary. But this expansion of the old system was a stage, a phase, in the creation of the system which would take its place.

As a result of this the development in large areas of England was not episodic but continuous. The same agencies and the same ideas tended to continue from one phase into another. This, however, raises another problem. The development of the power of the State raises not only the question of what agencies it will use, what objects it will pursue, but also the question of how far its rights extend and upon what moral justification its coercive powers are to be based. These questions will also be important in considering the development of the State in the middle of the century. Since there was this overlap, it is obviously important to turn back to the old regime and to consider what were believed to be the moral justification of the powers of the State under it. This raises the whole problem of the relations between Church and State before 1830.

2

Church and State
before 1832

Before 1830 a churchman might base his ideas about the nature of the State, if confusedly and remotely, on a very old line of thought. It went like this. The State was a Christian community. It was ruled by a king, who had been anointed and crowned and who had before the altar promised to do justice and observe the law. The members of the State were all members of Christ's Church, indeed Church and State were but aspects of the same society, either working in the uneasy partnership that prevailed in medieval Europe, or fused into the more complete unity described by Hooker. Therefore the moral content of the State was defined by the fact of its Christianity, the sanctions behind its claim to obedience were rooted in scripture and the Christian religion, and the law of God prescribed what must be the limits to its claims.

Probably in the early nineteenth century this theory was not likely to be produced in its most archaic form, and indeed the course of history had worked some changes in it. But, as has been seen, the central conception of an order of society ordained by God's providence and endorsed by His authority was firmly believed in; as much of the theory as was needed could be built on that without bothering about crowned and anointed kings. In saying this it is important to realize that the order so envisaged was more than simply a method for keeping the peace. It was an order which made possible the full richness of life that could be enjoyed by participating in the life of the nation. For this reason the State which provided that order must be considered as being, in the words of Edmund Burke used in his *Reflections on the Revolution in France*, 'a partnership in all science;

a partnership in all art; a partnership in every virtue, and in all perfection'. As such its existence and its power must be an expression of the will of God. To quote Burke again: 'He who gave our nature to be perfected by our virtue, willed also the necessary means of its perfection – He willed therefore the State.'[1]

The nature of Burke's book suggests the weakness of this position. It was a passionate defence of the existing order against the challenge of the French Revolution, and it was indiscriminating. In certain aspects and for certain people the contemporary State might be called 'a partnership in all ignorance, in all selfishness and in all oppression'; and it would be impious to say that that was according to the will of God. The same type of argument could be turned on those who claimed that an extremely unequal distribution of property was according to divine provision. Nevertheless, the conception that the nation was a Christian community and that the State existed to ensure the practice of Christian principles contained much more valuable and pregnant possibilities than the mere defence of existing conditions.

This older way of thought, however, had been compromised by what had happened in the sixteenth and seventeenth centuries. The unity between Church and State had led to the persecution of those whose views on Christianity differed from the beliefs of the rulers of either, and the theory that the authority of God endorsed the order of the State had been construed to mean that this authority required passive obedience to all the executive commands of the ruler, even if such commands threatened a man's fundamental liberties. The result had been civil war and much suffering, ending in a peace which was made possible by the fact that royalists and churchmen had abandoned their most extreme principles: religious persecution was seen to be wrong, and the divine right of kings was generally relegated to the dustbin.

From these struggles there had also developed another approach to the nature of the authority of the State. Those who could not conform to the Church were naturally anxious to repudiate the right of the State to control the religion of its

[1] Edmund Burke, *Reflections on the Revolution in France. Works* (1803 edn.) Vol. V, pp. 184 and 186.

subjects. Consequently there developed a tradition of noncon-formist thought which can be traced from Edmund Calamy's *Defence of Moderate Nonconformity* through the writings of men like Isaac Watts and Joseph Priestley to, for instance, Edward Baines, an eminent nineteenth-century nonconformist.[1] These men denied to the State any God-given right to control the religion of any man and consequently were prone to deny to the State the right to perform any duty which might lead to such control, such as, for instance, the education of children by the government, a point on which Joseph Priestley had been particularly insistent.

But though they had abandoned their extreme pretensions the leaders of the established Church in the eighteenth century had not accepted the nonconformist philosophy, many of them continued to believe that the union between Church and State was needed to guarantee and legitimize the order of society; indeed they were apt to assume that an established Church was one of the necessary constituents of any civilized community. For instance, in 1747 Bishop Butler said in a sermon in West-minster Abbey: 'A constitution of civil government without any religious establishment is a chimerical project of which there is no example', and in 1755 Bishop Warburton, in his curious book on *The Divine Legation of Moses*, summed up his argument thus: 'In a word *an established religion with a test law* is the universal voice of Nature. The most savage nations have em-ployed it to civilize their manners; and the politest knew no other way to prevent their return to barbarity and violence.' He had just explained that what he called a 'test law' was a law to prevent religious dissidents from occupying positions which would enable them to attack the established Church.[2]

At the end of the eighteenth century the kind of society which the Church was supposed to guarantee was violently threatened by the French Revolution, and in the early stages of the Revolution there was an assault on the ancient ecclesiastical establishment of France. This brought Burke out on the other side. In his *Reflections* he contrasted the views of the revolution-

---

[1] For Baines' opinions, see R. W. Dale, *A History of English Congregationalism* (1907) pp. 659–60.

[2] Gladstone, *Works of Butler* [op. cit., p. 12] Vol. II, p. 366. W. Warburton, *The Divine Legation of Moses* (1755) Vol. II, p. 27.

aries with those of the people of England who, so he said, 'do not consider their Church Establishment as convenient, but as essential to their State'. 'They consider it,' said he, 'as the *foundation of their whole constitution,* with which, and with every part of which, it holds an indissoluble union.' The sentiment did not disappear with the Napoleonic wars, and in 1824 it was given even more extensive and exuberant form by that much satirized man John Wilson Croker. Writing to Southey with reference to Southey's *Book of the Church,* Croker said that when he was talking about the union between Church and State,

> I do not mean the mere *political* connection of Church and State; but that mixture of veneration and love, of enthusiasm and good taste, of public liberty and self-control, of pride in our ancestors and hopes from our posterity, which affects every patriot and Christian mind at the contemplation of that glorious system which unites in such beautiful association and such profitable combination, our civil and ecclesiastical constitutions; our ambition and our faith; the one thing needful and all things ornamental; our well being in this world and our salvation in the next.

The words are probably too highly flavoured to appeal to ordinary individuals, but something of the conceptions behind them must have taken cloudy shape in the minds of those present when the toast of 'Church and King' was given at political banquets of the right complexion, at magistrates' dinners, or in Oxford common, or Cambridge combination, rooms, before the port took hold.[1]

In spite of Croker's profusion it might not be easy to say with precision what ends it was believed that the union of Church and State would serve, for men are not always able to analyse or rationalize their basic loyalties; but probably most men had three objects generally in mind. First, it is fairly often stated that the object of the establishment of the Church was to secure that Christianity was taught and mediated to the people. Secondly, it was probably hazily recognized that the establishment of the Church ought to be some sort of warranty that the

---

[1] Burke, *Works* [op. cit., p. 25] Vol. V, p. 188. Louis J. Jennings, ed., *Correspondence and Diaries of the late Right Honourable J. W. Croker* (3 vols., 1884) Vol. I, p. 277.

English nation was a Christian nation and ought to observe Christian principles in its laws and policy, a point much emphasized in the crusade against slavery. But the third object to be served by the union of Church and State was at least partly secular. It is best expressed in the words of Warburton. 'The sum of all is this, that whoever would secure Civil government must support it by means of Religion, and whoever would propagate Religion must perpetuate it by means of Civil government.'[1]

This statement was made long before the French Revolution, but the French Revolution gave it a new point. The challenge to society which the Revolution seemed to present, the crimes of which it appeared to be guilty, were believed to have had their origin in the ungodliness which it was believed had been rife in French society, and the repudiation by the French of those religious sanctions which in the view of Warburton were the only things which could 'secure Civil government'. If this had been so in France it might come to be so in England, therefore the friends of civil order tended to watch anxiously lest a rejection of religion, especially among the ill-instructed, should lead to a comparable catastrophe in England. The fear of revolution continued to darken the minds of many men and women after Waterloo, indeed it remained with greater or less intensity a factor in the situation till after the Chartist fiasco in 1848. Consequently there were in the first half of the nineteenth century those who still feared what might be done by those who rebelled against, or what was more probable had never learnt, the moral code that held society together. For instance, in 1844 Bishop Longley, at that time bishop of Ripon but subsequently archbishop of Canterbury, explained a Chartist incursion into his diocese in the following terms:

Now upon examining into the history of that popular movement it was clear that it was *not* the most destitute who were its leaders, that it was not prompted mainly by the urgency of temporal want, but that the principles of discontent and insubordination so sedulously instilled by the designing and too readily imbibed by hearts undisciplined by religious restraints were the springs that actuated it, while it was equally evident that just in proportion as the sound doctrine and discipline of the Church

[1] Warburton [op. cit., p. 26) Vol. I, p. 76.

were inculcated did respect for the law and a patient and exemplary submission to privations generally prevail.[1]

It is easy to recognize the moral dangers of this attitude. It is only fair to Bishop Longley to remember that he probably believed, as did most of his class, that popular disturbances would not bring relief to distress but only potential disaster to everyone. It is also important to remember that these beliefs could neither be held to cancel the duty of trying to relieve distress by private charity, nor of supporting legislation intended to abolish removable social evils. In fact Bishop Longley himself supported the legislation which was intended to protect the factory children. Nevertheless, the tendency of such teaching was to enlist the Church in the defence of the profits of an intolerably unequal economic system. It tended to convert Christianity into an instrument of oppression, and, to quote the words of Charles Kingsley in 1848, to reduce the bible to a 'mere special constable's hand-book, an opium dose for keeping beasts of burden patient while they were being overloaded.'[2]

According to the old theory of Church and State, however, not only was it the duty of the Church to legitimize and guarantee the order of society, but its members and ministers had duties to perform as occupying positions in that order, and therefore were subject to the obligations which those duties imposed. In order to understand the duties of the clergy of the Church of England under this dispensation it will be best to consider them as occupying positions simultaneously in three separate orders, each of which included the whole English nation. First there was the ecclesiastical order. They were ministers of a Church of which every Englishman was a potential member, be he devout, negligent, hostile or nonconformist. Then there was the social order. This was particularly important for the parochial clergy who owed the same kind of duty to their parishioners as a landowner did to his tenants, or a rich man to his neighbours, or any man to those he employed. Lastly there was the governmental order. Since the early middle ages the Church had been

[1] Charles Thomas Longley, D.D., lord bishop of Ripon, *A Charge addressed to the Clergy of Ripon at the Triennial Visitation in September 1844* (1844), p. 9.
[2] Quoted in C. E. Raven, *Christian Socialism, 1848–54* (1920. Reprinted 1968) p. 14.

integrated into the service of the secular government, the bishops had been the counsellors of the king and much of the machinery of the Church had been utilized in his service. In the late eighteenth and early nineteenth centuries, though the bishops no longer played any part in Cabinet government they were still in the House of Lords and were appointed by the king's ministers; and the ecclesiastical parish had been adapted to the purposes of secular administration. This was particularly important in relation to the administration of the Poor Law, in which the incumbent of a parish might play a leading part, though he did not always do so.

The social duties of the clergy had an important corollary. In the late eighteenth and early nineteenth centuries it was believed that the clergy could not play the part which they ought to play in the social order unless they were appropriately endowed. On 21 September 1782 Archdeacon Paley preached a sermon on the subject. He claimed that: 'The distinctions of the clergy ought, in some measure, to correspond with the distinctions of lay-society, in order to supply each class of the people with a clergy of their own level and description, with whom they could associate upon terms of equality.' In Paley's view the wealth and distinction of the higher clergy were needed to enable them to live on an equality with the rich and persons of high stations and so to influence them, whilst the clergy with small resources and in less exalted stations should live with and influence men and women in the lower ranges of society.[1]

Into this hierarchy, however, an important variant had been introduced by the turn of the century. It was considered that at the bottom of the social pyramid the poor and the uneducated should be served not by an equal but by a priest who had both the education of a gentleman and sufficient independence and adequate resources to do his duty as pastor and ruler of his parish. The theory was that if he had no more education than his parishioners, if he lived in the straitened circumstances in which they were likely to live, and above all, if he were financially dependent on their voluntary contributions as a nonconformist minister was dependent on the voluntary contributions

[1] Archdeacon Paley, *A Sermon preached in the Castle Chapel of Dublin*, in *Works* [op. cit., p. 7] Vol. V, p. 261.

of his congregation, he would not be able to guide them and help them as he ought to do.

Probably this argument would not have been convincing before the second half of the eighteenth century; but after about 1750 the resources of many of the clergy had begun to increase and their social status had begun to change. Tithe owners often gained handsomely from the results of enclosures, particularly when the tithe owner had taken his share in land. They also profited by the high prices of the war years, and in the early years of the nineteenth century from schemes for the commutation of tithe.[1] At the same time there was a marked change in the social status of many of the clergy. It is vividly described in the third chapter of Macaulay's history, and much of what Macaulay said has been borne out by more recent research. At the beginning of the eighteenth century many of the clergy seemed to have formed a class, rustic in manners, primitive in outlook, which did not rank higher than the neighbouring farmers and tradesmen or the upper servants of the great houses of the nobility. As the century went forward many of them gradually assumed the status of gentry. Their style of life changed, their standing in the county was enhanced, they were more often men with connections among the gentry or aristocracy, and they developed a culture which was a good deal more civilized, not only than that of their rustic predecessors but than anything that could have been understood by the more boorish country gentlemen of the past. Instead of concentrating, as their predecessors had tended to do, on rather crabbed theology, or on the cruder forms of sulky Tory politics, they began to take an interest in antiquarianism, or literature, in botany or scientific husbandry, or in local government and the very difficult social problems the country confronted at that moment.[2]

It should not be assumed that these changes necessarily affected all the clergy alike. Conditions clearly differed greatly

[1] See W. R. Ward, *The Journal of Ecclesiastical History*, Vol. XVI, No. 1 (April 1965) p. 67.

[2] Lord Macaulay, *History of England from the Accession of James II*, Vol. I, Ch. III. Cf. P. A. Bezodis' unpublished thesis in the library of Trinity College, Cambridge, on *The English Parish Clergy and their Place in Society*. For a discussion of the change in the social position of bishops, see R. A. Soloway, [op. cit., p. 7] pp. 7–18.

in different parts of the country. The economic conditions which had enriched many of the clergy were not to be found in all districts, and in many of the remoter areas a number of the clergy seem to have remained very rustic and savage, as some of the clergy in Wales seem to have been when Connop Thirlwall was bishop of St Davids in the middle of the nineteenth century. There were many poor livings and there were many poor curates who held a living for an absentee. Nevertheless the change was general enough to cause an important change in country society. Whether it was altogether an advantageous change for the clergy is open to question. Unfortunately the very processes that made many of the clergy richer, the rising prices and the enclosures, were those which pressed hardest on the agricultural labourer; and after the close of the Napoleonic wars during the long period of agricultural decline, between roughly 1813 and 1836, tithe became a burden to the farmers and a cause for the unpopularity of the clergy. Meanwhile the closer association of the clergy with the gentry, the change in their manners and habits of life, probably tended to divide them from their flocks as they had not been divided in the past; a change possibly symbolized by the fact that at this time many of the clergy became discontented with life in a cottage in a village street and either insisted on building more elaborate parsonages probably a little way away from the other houses, or made the fact that there was no suitable house in the parish an excuse for not residing there at all.

It is not clear that these disadvantages were necessarily cancelled by the fact that some of the clergy were becoming more presentable. It is not indeed certain that elevation from the hedgerow to the drawing room, or a change of habit from a concentrated study of the bible to the elegant pursuits of a gentleman, will necessarily lead to the deepening of religious experience or greater intimacy of pastoral care. It has in fact been suggested that Parson Adams in Fielding's *Joseph Andrews*, published in 1742, in spite of all the ludicrous and humiliating adventures his author heaps upon him, is in conception more truly a priest and a pastor than any of the agreeable young gentlemen whom Jane Austen described in the next century.[1]

[1] Sheila Kaye Smith in Sheila Kaye Smith and G. B. Stern, *Talking of Jane Austen* (1943) p. 112.

It is, however, very important not to generalize too easily in this matter, and it is also not desirable to detach what may have been happening to the clergy from other things which were happening to other groups in the countryside. Whatever the clergy did or failed to do there were powerful forces which would in any case have divided country society in many districts. Developments in agriculture meant that many farmers were learning to live in a style which was completely different from that in which the poorer clergy had passed their lives. Nor were the clergy the only people who were changing their habits and becoming more refined. The new parsonages have their parallel in the comfortable farmhouses and country houses which were being built at the same time, and the tendency of the clergy to move from the village street should perhaps be associated with the tendency on the part of farmers and the like to refuse to continue to live under the same roof and eat at the same board as their labourers. A new society was coming into existence, in which it was not clear that the old-style parson could find a suitable place.

Nor is it clear that if the parson's status and his economic position had remained what it had been in the earlier eighteenth century he could have done what the nineteenth century would call upon him to do, and it is by no means certain that the improvement in status and prosperity always resulted in spiritual loss. Sordid circumstances and economic anxieties do not always confirm religious faith, social equality and neighbourly propinquity do not always create love, and a slight elevation above the traditional habits of the countryside might elevate a parson a little above some very ugly things – above much grossness of life, above the enjoyment of such pleasures as bull baiting, badger drawing and cock fighting, above barbarisms and superstitions, such as the lingering belief in witchcraft.

It is, however, idle to try to draw up the profit and loss by summing up the results of the process of history, particularly when a great deal of the evidence is lacking and much of what exists has never been examined. What suffices for present purposes is that the improvement in status and wealth of many of the clergy encouraged a number of the clergy to put in hand services for their parishioners which were to be important precedents for what was to be done in the middle of the century.

I will deal with the nature of these services when I come to the mid nineteenth century; all that needs to be noted here is that they date back to before the Reform Bill and continued to carry the trade mark of the old regime, and that they were made possible by the changes which had been taking place in the economic and social life of the country.

The hierarchy of government was under the old regime closely integrated with the social order of society. From the great nobles at the top to the householders at the bottom, each rank in the social order, each gradation of wealth, carried with it its own peculiar duties, and thus it was natural that the improvement in status and economic standing of many of the clergy should bring with it a development of their functions in secular government. In the early seventeenth century there had been a few clerical justices of the peace, but after 1688 the practice of appointing them had fallen into abeyance. After 1760, however, the practice was renewed, and in due course a large number of clerical magistrates were appointed. This development does not seem to have been caused solely by the improvement in the status of the clergy. The Jacobitism of many of the inferior clergy, and the tendency of early eighteenth-century governments to use the appointment and dismissal of magistrates for the purposes of party warfare, seems to have prevented governments before 1760 from using the services of the clergy as magistrates, even if they had wanted to. After the accession of George III Jacobitism was dead, and there seems to have been less need to use the appointment of magistrates for the purpose of party politics and a conscious desire to appoint in every district those best qualified to provide reasonable standards of government. If this were to be done it would probably be necessary to call upon the local clergy, as there were not everywhere a sufficient number of suitable country gentlemen.[1]

In fact this development was, at least in part, the result of the change that was taking place in England in the late eighteenth and early nineteenth centuries. Bit by bit the country was moving away from the crudities, savageries and unashamed corrup-

[1] See S. and B. Webb (Lord and Lady Passfield), *English Local Government from the Revolution to the Municipal Corporation Act* (1906) Vol. I, Bk. II: *The County*, particularly pp. 350–64.

tion that had characterized the earlier eighteenth century towards greater decency and humanity and a more responsible
use of public offices. In this the appointment of clerical magistrates probably played an important part. They seem to have
made unusually good magistrates. They were assiduous at their
work and not open to corruption. They were fully literate, as
not all justices had been in the past; indeed, many of them had
trained minds and were able to assimilate the law required for
the work, instead of relying too much on the guidance of their
clerk. It is significant that the standard book on the office of
justice of the peace came to be written by a clerical justice,
Richard Burn, vicar of Orton in Westmorland, and that in a
number of ways clerical justices made their contribution to the
reform of local administration, particularly to the reform of the
filthy county gaols and the protection of poor prisoners against
the exactions and cruelties that had been habitually inflicted
upon them.

Whether this work was suited to their cloth as clergymen or
likely to help them with their tasks as parish priests is another
question. The law which they had to administer could be both
savage and unequal particularly when it related to the preservation of game, and at the end of the eighteenth century the
increase in self-conscious morality encouraged the pious and
respectable to believe that abandoned profligacy pervaded
much of English society and threatened its stability. This led
to an attempt to submit the poor for their own good to an
inquisitorial discipline, such as members of the middling and
upper classes would not have tolerated, and might not increase
the love in which a conscientious magistrate was held. Even
more serious was the fact that the turmoil and distress of the
last years of the eighteenth and the first thirty years of the
nineteenth centuries might involve magistrates in the repression
of popular disorders. It would be interesting to know how many
of the clergy became committed to this work, and what effect
this police service had on their other labours, particularly for
the years 1815 to 1830. But it is clear that these activities confirmed the impression, which was a commonplace among
Radicals, that the Church of England was simply an instrument
to be used by the government for the oppression of the people.

Probably the most important social work of a magistrate was

in relation to the administration of the Poor Law, which in the period between 1790 and 1834, and indeed afterwards, raised some of the most difficult social problems which confronted the country. A parish clergyman might become involved in these problems not only as a magistrate but also through the administration of the Poor Law by the vestry of his parish. Not every clergyman consistently attended his vestry when they were dealing with poor law matters. Some were in all probability too negligent or indolent to bother. Some apparently were too timid to intervene when the vestry contained hostile elements who would treat them with insults, and some are reported as being afraid that their teaching on the duty of charity would be compromised by association with the administration of relief which was likely to be restrictive. However, it is clear that a number of the clergy were not troubled by these fears or scruples. Either through their vestries, or as magistrates, they dominated the administration of the law in their neighbourhood, experimented with the problem of relief, and not only made important contributions to the literature of the subject but also developed a number of expedients which were intended to assist poverty, to tide over misfortune and generally to keep men and women off the rates.

The arguments which early nineteenth-century clergymen used when discussing the questions raised by the Poor Law and the policy they followed might not appeal to the humanity of a modern student, and he might be tempted to dismiss what they did outside the Poor Law as too inadequate to be taken into account. However, to take this line would be to fail to consider men's thoughts and actions in the context of their period. To judge men fairly they must be compared with their contemporaries, and in this case the ways of the poor law reformers among the clergy were certainly not less humane than the thoughts of Jeremy Bentham, and what they did was often more sensible and helpful to the poor than some of the things he proposed. But what is important here is the fact that commitment to local administration in general, and to this problem in particular, emphasized the fact that an incumbent of the established Church ought to be concerned with the secular problems of his flock, and not simply with their souls. Probably, in fact, under the old regime too many of the clergy were too exclusively preoccupied with what was secular, but in the nineteenth century, at the time of the religious revivals, the balance might very well have swung down to the other side, and clergymen might have come to think that they were exclusively concerned with the saving of souls and need not interest themselves in what happened to men's bodies. It was probably, therefore, of considerable importance at that time that many of them were inextricably committed to the problems of secular administration and that leading ecclesiastics had shown that they were concerned with the secular issues created by destitution.

To this commitment the relevant literature bears ample testimony. Not only were there the clergymen who wrote professionally about the Poor Law, but the list of the Church of England clergymen who made important contributions to the general economic problems of the day is impressive. There were Thomas Malthus, Edward Coplestone, Richard Whately and, in a rather later generation, William Whewell, Richard Jones and Adam Sedgwick. Of course to some extent the character of these men as clergymen was accidental. Most of the senior members of Oxford and Cambridge were of necessity in holy orders and therefore any contribution which should come from either of those universities was likely to be clerical in origin. But it would be as well not to press that argument too far. These men wrote as clergymen, and demonstrated the fact that these were matters in which it was proper for a clergyman to be interested. Even the much abused Malthus sincerely believed that the ideas he was promoting were in the best interest of the working class, and he eschewed a solution which he probably thought was contrary to the tenets of Christianity. Whately said that one of his reasons for turning to political economy was to prevent it from falling completely into the hands of those who were not Christians. Whewell, Jones and Sedgwick wrote, at least in part, to attack a mechanistic system of economics which seemed to undermine the possibility of more responsibility.

Therefore socially, magisterially and intellectually there were factors in the tradition of the Church of England which inevitably committed the clergy to the consideration of the secular social problems of their time, and it may be added that this was the result of their pastoral tradition as well. It is not easy to be sure, at any time, in what ways individual clergymen interpreted their duties. But certainly with some of the clergy in the early nineteenth century there was a tradition of visiting their parishioners, certainly of visiting the sick and dying, as is shown by the exemplary behaviour of the clergy in 1831 and 1832 when their parishes were stricken with cholera, the most terrifying of all nineteenth-century epidemics. Such visitations necessarily led to the administration of advice and help to those who needed it. It did not necessarily lead to the belief that Christianity demanded the adoption of a policy which would rectify the injustices of society or permanently reduce the sufferings within it. Inequality of wealth and extreme poverty had so long been the commonplaces of society that it was quite likely that even a humane man would never think that they might be remedied though he might spend himself freely to relieve individual cases. Late in life Cardinal Newman told Charles Marson that 'he had never considered social questions in relation to faith and had always looked upon the poor as objects for compassion and benevolence'.[1] It is worthwhile to remember that the exercise of compassion and benevolence might make greater personal demands on a man than the acceptance of an advanced social policy abstractedly considered. In his Anglican days Newman had been incumbent of Littlemore near Oxford, and he and his mother and sisters had served the secular needs of his parishioners with sympathy and generosity. This was a duty which he took for granted as no doubt did a number of his clerical contemporaries. And even though they might not use their experience as a basis for social theorizing or political planning, direct experience of the way the poor lived might very well affect their thoughts about social policy in practical matters.

Such pastoral work was essentially secular and the duties which derived from a clergyman's station in the social or governmental order were secular also. It might well seem, therefore, under the old dispensation as it had taken shape in the late eighteenth and early nineteenth centuries, that what pertained to the spiritual or ecclesiastical order had been so effectively pressed into the

[1] Charles L. Marson, *God's Cooperative Society* (1914) p. 71.

background as to be of very little general account. That is indeed the view taken by Dean Church in his famous description of the typical parochial clergyman of the period before about 1825. He wrote:

> The typical clergyman in English pictures of the manners of the day in the *Vicar of Wakefield*, in Miss Austen's novels, in Crabbe's *Parish Register* is represented, often quite unsuspiciously, as a kindly respectable person, but certainly not alive to the greatness of his calling. He was often much, very much, to the society round him. When communication was so difficult and infrequent, he filled a place in the country life of England, which no one else could fill. He was often the patriarch of his parish, its ruler, its doctor, its lawyer, its magistrate, as well as its teacher, before whom vice trembled and rebellion dared not show itself. The idea of the priest was not quite forgotten but there was much – much even of what was good and useful – to obscure it. The beauty of the English Church in this time was its family life of purity and simplicity; its blot was a quiet worldliness.[1]

Now the strange thing about this description is that, though there is no doubt much truth in it, the literary sources which are quoted do not really bear it out. *The Vicar of Wakefield* is not really of the same epoch as Crabbe and Jane Austen. Dr Primrose, if he can be conceived ever to have existed, existed in a period when a clergyman's economic position was more precarious and his secular influence less than it might well be at a later day. George Crabbe on the other hand was writing roughly between 1780 and 1820. He was himself a clergyman for much of his life, and he undoubtedly drew from nature. Indeed many of the clergy he describes do not present human nature in any very exalted form; there is the sporting parson who confines his duty to Sundays and fails to attend a dying pauper on a weekday, the easy-going parson who wastes his life on trivialities, the harsh parson who savagely mulcts his flock. Yet throughout there is the assumption that a parson's primary work is religious and not the secular functions of which Church speaks and of which Crabbe makes surprisingly little mention. Several of his parsons make trouble for themselves by excess of zeal. There is the Cambridge youth in the 'Parish Register' who gets across

[1] R. W. Church, *The Oxford Movement. Twelve Years 1835-45* (1891. New edn, 1966) p. 3.

with a large part of his congregation by turning over to extempore preaching and a rigorous version of the doctrine of justification by faith alone, or 'The Stern old Rector' in the tale of the 'Squire and the Priest' whose denunciations of sin and irreligion so antagonize the profligate squire of his village, or the squire's nephew who is put in to succeed him, yet still feels it his duty to denounce his uncle's way of life. In fact throughout Crabbe's poems, in spite of the materialism of his period, there is a firm realization of the spiritual values conveyed by the Church, and if several of its servants failed to live up to them, it was not, given Crabbe's general view of human nature, intrinsically likely that they would succeed.

With Jane Austen the problem is more complicated. She, too, should be a competent witness; she too was writing in the late eighteenth and early nineteenth centuries and she was a daughter of the parsonage and knew what she was writing about as Crabbe must have known, as Charlotte Brontë and George Eliot were to know it, and as Trollope did not; and since her young clergymen, with the exception of Mr Collins and Mr Elton, seem to have been agreeable young men with no obvious vocation for the priesthood and no obvious parish duties, even of a secular nature, there has been a tendency to generalize these characteristics into a judgement on the early nineteenth-century Church of England. There are, however, a variety of reasons why this should not be done. For one thing the clergy whom she describes are palpably a very small and largely homogeneous group selected from a large and various body of clergymen. In Jane Austen's time there were many poorer clergymen than any she draws, there were more grotesque clergymen, there were worse clergymen – for most of her clergy appear to reside in their parishes, and there were clergymen whose piety, real or ostentatious, would certainly have upset the balance of her novels.

But in her work the process of selection must have gone further than her choice of subjects. Her novels are essentially works of art, and in a work of art the subject matter must be subordinated to the artistic purposes of the author. Few artists have been so economical in their methods as Jane Austen. Little appears in any of her novels which has not a direct relevance to the interplay of character as revealed in the book. Other matters, which must have seemed of great importance to the actors, are rigorously excluded. There are no conversations between men. There is little about politics or war at a time when the letters and diaries of contemporaries are full of what was happening. There is practically nothing about the problems of agriculture and estate management, which must have occupied much of Mr Knightley's thought and time, and if a man's performance of his pastoral duties, or his personal religious beliefs, were not needed for her artistic purposes, it would not occur to her to mention them. Indeed, to a person of her up-bringing and temperament it would be natural for her to be reticent on such matters, and not to exploit them for the pur-poses of what were, after all, works intended for amusement.

In one of her novels, *Mansfield Park*, she does touch, if lightly, on the contrast between the life that the clergy ought to lead and the standards of the worldlings that surround them. Part of the argument of that novel is the danger of the attraction of the worldly Henry and Mary Crawford for Edmund Bertram who is intended for holy orders, and an important passage in the book is that in which Sir Thomas Bertram explains to Henry Crawford why Edmund will live and work in his parish all the week and not live at home and spend the stipend of his living on his '*menus plaisirs*'. It is true that Edmund was scandalously ill prepared for the cure of souls, a characteristic which he shared with many young clergymen of that period, and also, that the manner of his life before ordination, though innocent, was such that the Crawfords were not unreasonable in mistaking the seriousness of his intentions. But it is as well to remember that if the mythical Edmund Bertram can be conceived as being or-dained between 1811 and 1814, the real John Keble was ordained deacon in 1815 and the real Henry Venn, an evangeli-cal and the son and grandson of evangelicals, in 1819. It seems probable that if Mary and Henry Crawford had met either of these as ordinands they would not have been deceived.

It is worth while emphasizing the danger of misconstruction here since there is a tendency to underestimate the potency and significance of the spiritual element in the Church as it emerged from the eighteenth century. It is easy to do this, for not only was the Church at any time before 1836 and even after that a Church in which there were many corruptions, but it was a

Church whose ways of thought and practice were different from anything we know. The appearance of the parish church, with its box pews, its galleries, its great three-decker pulpit, would seem strange and singularly uninviting. The form of service, the dialogue between parson and clerk, the psalms sung in rhymed doggerel, the long sermon read from a manuscript, would seem to inhibit any normal religious feeling. Nor would the doctrines which were generally acceptable then seem tolerable nowadays to a reasonably intelligent and humane Christian, for they would almost certainly include a belief in the literal historicity of all the bible, some form of the doctrine of eternal punishment and also probably an implicit acceptance of a divinely ordained, or at least an ethically acceptable, social hierarchy of rich and poor. This strangeness, however, should not disguise the living reality that lies behind the not very attractive façade of the Georgian Church. To understand something of what was there it might be as well to look at some of the works it produced, at William Law's *Serious Call*, for instance, or at the works of the bishops Berkeley and Butler, or at some of the best of the printed sermons published by other divines, at the hymns of the two Wesleys, of Toplady or of Cowper and Newton, or at Dr Johnson's prayers. These are the products of a lively faith, and it was a faith which was accepted in one way or other by most Englishmen. There were of course exceptions. There was a certain amount of polite disbelief, or in some cases brutal scepticism. This was probably most often to be found at the top of society, but at the bottom there were unplumbed depths of barbarous ignorance. Where the faith was accepted it was no doubt often diluted by formality and indolence, or among the uneducated by some strange misunderstandings and stranger superstitions. Nevertheless it seems clear that in the eighteenth century most men and women in the country accepted the spiritual values which the Church claimed to represent. Of course if they were dissenters they might not believe that the Church itself did represent anything that was spiritual, and in all sections of society there were clearly many who did not allow what was spiritual to affect the tenor of their lives. But those values, and the faith that sustained them, were without question part of the background of English life.

The force which that faith could generate can be recognized

in the mission of the Wesleys and of Whitefield; the insensitive-
ness and unadaptability of the Church together with John
Wesley's refusal to abide by the rules of Church order caused
many of those they had inspired to move out of the Church, but
there were others inspired by the same spirit who remained
within the Church and developed the evangelical revival. This
was one of the most potent factors in shaping the characters of
Englishmen in the first half of the nineteenth century, and gave
leadership to one of the most important moral crusades there
has ever been, the crusade against slavery. Nor was the evangelical movement the only living movement within the Church.
There were also those inspired by the old high church principles
and discipline which had been inherited from the seventeenth
century, who were to play an important part before the Oxford
Movement developed. In addition to these named varieties
there was an incalculable number of men and women of no
definite religious party who were prepared to take their religion
seriously. All these groups combined to make the ecclesiastical
order of the old regime the expression of a living reality. Indeed
the behaviour of the English Church in the middle of the nineteenth century can never be understood without understanding
the nature of this spiritual legacy it had inherited from the
eighteenth.

Unfortunately it had also inherited from the past another
legacy of a very different sort. Since the early middle ages both
secular and ecclesiastical authorities had exploited the Church
for purposes which had nothing to do with its pastoral mission.
Offices in the Church had been given to reward secular service,
to offer a pleasant life to those who were well connected, or to
those who had used money or influence, or as the inherited
possession of an advowson, to gain preferment. As a result
unworthy men were entrusted with the cure of souls and mis-
behaved themselves, or at the least neglected their duties. Many
clergymen absented themselves from their livings, many held
pluralities, that is more than one living at the same time. When
a clergyman did not reside he sometimes arranged for a substitute, but sometimes he seems to have done nothing. During
the Middle Ages these abuses seem to have got steadily worse;
they were not, in England, redressed at the Reformation, and it

c

seems possible that during the eighteenth century the situation had deteriorated still further. There were several reasons for this. Although through the whole of that century there was an unbroken thread of true religion, through most of it the general standards of public morality were low. Much corruption was habitual and unashamed and both secular and ecclesiastical office were openly exploited as a source of revenue without much attention to the duties involved. Abuses tend to be cumulative; when usage has approved an abuse there is a tendency to extend it and follow it up with another which is more outrageous, and it seems probable that during the eighteenth century this tended to happen. Owing to the fierceness of electoral strife a great deal of ecclesiastical patronage was exploited to gain parliamentary interest, and the improvement in clerical incomes meant that more of the wealthy and well connected had taken holy orders in order to enjoy a well-padded livelihood.

It would be hard to say with any certainty how much of the Church was involved in these scandals and to what degree. From about 1810 till 1830, and later, the Church was under vehement attack both in pamphlets and oratory. This was clearly part of a general attack on the dominant social and political system and on the classes who ran it and profited by it. It is not therefore satisfactory to assume that it provides a reliable measure of the general popular feeling about the Church in particular, or an accurate judgement on the behaviour of the clergy. Some of the facts asserted in the literature which this agitation produced are certainly erroneous; but unfortunately they have at times been rather uncritically accepted by historians, who have also been rather too ready to suggest generalizations derived from the imputations of motive made by the opponents of the clergy. It is, as ever, necessary to try to listen to the other side, but it is not easy to know where to obtain a satisfactory statement of the case for the other side, or material upon which to base an independent quantitative judgement. There exist a number of returns purporting to record the residence of the clergy which were made for early nineteenth-century Parliaments; but they are also unsatisfactory, particularly so in relation to the very important question of whether a clergyman who was reported as being absent from his parish was really remote from it, or whether he lived possibly out of his parish, but like Henry Tilney in *Northanger Abbey*, near enough to serve it. Comparisons of the returns for one year with the returns for the next suggest that sometimes the same clergyman was placed in one category, sometimes in the other.

The only satisfactory procedure is to wait until a detailed enquiry has been made into the local records of enough districts to provide satisfactory samples for the whole Church and till that time to eschew generalizations and suspect most figures. It can, however, be said with confidence that in the Church as it existed before 1830 there were a large number of serious scandals. There were many clergymen who unashamedly occupied more livings than one, or if they only occupied one living were habitually absent from it. When the incumbent did not reside he might supply a curate to do duty, to whom he might pay only a small proportion of the income the living provided. There was a good deal of clerical negligence. There was much traffic in advowsons, much abuse of ecclesiastical patronage, and much nepotism on the part of important ecclesiastics such as the notorious Bishop Sparke, bishop of Ely from 1812 to 1832. There is no doubt that these things existed. The only question is how far they infected the whole body of the Church in the first thirty years of the nineteenth century.

In fact it seems probable that by that time things had to improve in certain directions. Men like Lord Liverpool and Sir Robert Peel were probably more conscientious in their use of Church patronage than previous politicians had been. It is likely that there was a general improvement in the character of the bishops appointed.[1] Eminent laymen who were not Radicals and not enemies of the Church were becoming anxious to correct its abuses, as indeed emerges in various parliamentary debates, particularly perhaps in a debate in the House of Lords in 1813.[2] There was an attempt to rectify matters by legislation in Parliament. Acts for this purpose were passed in 1795, 1813 and 1817.[3] The object of the first, and to some extent of the

---

[1] For the character of the bishops appointed in this period, see Soloway [op. cit., p. 7] passim.

[2] *Cobbett's Parliamentary Debates*, XXVI, 210–11 and 295–301.

[3] 36 Geo. III, c. 83; 53 Geo. III, c. 149; 57 Geo. III, c. 99.

second, was to enforce the employment of a properly paid curate when the incumbent did not reside, which might encourage residence, or at least make non-residence expensive. The act of 1817 was a more elaborate attempt to enforce attention to parochial duties. It limited the size of the farms which parochial clergymen might cultivate and tried to prevent them from engaging in trade. It attempted to put limits on non-residence, to make the clergy keep the parsonage in repair, and it gave the bishop the right to appoint a curate to serve those parishes in which he believed that owing to the age or infirmity of the incumbent the service was likely to be defective.

It is difficult to say what effects these acts had. In many ways influential public opinion was adverse. The abuses were ingrained and it was a period when men were morbidly anxious to protect vested interests. In the debates in Parliament it was often represented, particularly by the Whig opposition, that such acts as these were a gross and dangerous invasion of private property. Possibly also, what was needed for effective reform was more vigorous and less indulgent episcopal discipline than most dioceses were likely to receive for some time. Nevertheless, the acts clearly had some effect. The remuneration of curates seems to have improved, so much indeed in some cases that the amount the curate received was actually more than was earned by the incumbent, and private bargains with potential curates were made to escape the provisions of the act.[1] Clergymen who had hoped to evade duty were forced to reside, as in the case of Sydney Smith, who was forced in 1809, much against his will, to reside on his living at Foston-le-Clay in Yorkshire, where no parson had resided for 150 years and the parsonage was a 'hovel'.

But, whatever was accomplished, clearly much more remained to be done. Pluralities, absentee parsons, parsons intent on sport or secular activities continued to exist up to and after the Reform Bill. In the middle of the nineteenth century things improved, though even after 1860 there were some scandalous cases of non-residence, and the abuses that sprang from the sale of advowsons, family livings and the possible misuse of lay patronage remained. Till well on into the nineteenth century

[1] I owe information on this topic to Mr Peter Moore of Trinity College, Cambridge, who has been working on the subject.

the dead weight of the worldly cynical habits that had defiled the Church of England remained a serious encumbrance both to its ministrations and its reputation. Yet if the Church was a field which continued to yield a rich crop of weeds, healthy wheat was coming into maturity in it as well. In the first thirty years of the century the evangelical revival was at work. A steady trickle of evangelical ordinands passed through Cambridge, largely inspired by Charles Simeon, who from 1816 sought to stabilize the position of his party within the Church by renewing the policy initiated in the eighteenth century by John Thornton of purchasing livings.[1] The anti-slavery crusade extended through both clergy and laity over the whole country, and the evangelical revival seems to have begun to have a general effect on the manners and morals, even of those who were not technically converted, and even among the upper classes. At the same time men who were inspired by the old high church tradition, such as Joshua Watson, Charles Daubeny and H. H. Norris, were beginning a religious revival which emphasized the traditional principles of the Church. They put in hand an important programme of church extension to make spiritual provision for those multitudes for whom the Church did little or nothing. In 1817 the 'Hackney Phalanx', the group associated with Joshua Watson, founded the Church Building Society, originally the Church Room Society, and in 1818 they persuaded Parliament to hand over £1,000,000 to church commissioners for the building of churches in populous districts, and in 1824 to add another £500,000 for the same purpose, while the group themselves subscribed considerable sums towards the work. Men and women of both traditions vied with each other in supplying that influx of assistant curates which is reflected in Charlotte Brontë's *Shirley*. In 1830 the Church Pastoral Aid Society, which was inclined to be evangelical, was founded, to be followed in 1837 by the Additional Curates Society, which was high church.

Even more significant, however, was the development of greater religious seriousness among men who may have been influenced by the example and thought of one or other party, but could not be considered as clearly members of either. Possibly Lord Liverpool might be considered in this number,

[1] See Charles Smyth, *Simeon and Church Order* (Cambridge, 1940) pp. 243–7.

and more certainly the second Sir Robert Peel, a conscientious churchman, who was neither an evangelical – Lord Shaftesbury found him cold and worldly, nor a high churchman – he found Gladstone unintelligible, yet who did more for the Church of England than any other nineteenth-century statesman. Some of the bishops began to show an interest in Church reform, such as Bishop Porteus, bishop of London from 1787 to 1809, and Manners Sutton, archbishop of Canterbury from 1805 to 1828. It was such men as these who were behind the legislative attempts to enforce residence and to provide for the proper payment of those curates who were left to take charge of parishes and who, after 1835, were responsible for the work of Peel's Ecclesiastical Commission, which probably saved the Church.

Manners Sutton also became involved in an activity which was to have great importance in the future, the development of popular education. In 1808 the British and Foreign Society was founded, which provided non-denominational education; in 1811 this was followed by the founding of the National Society, which had as its object the provision of education according to the principles of the Church of England. Manners Sutton presided over the first meeting of the National Society. This society was to have an important future, particularly after its revival in 1838, but it was clearly not in these years the only agency through which popular education was provided by the Church. In 1832 the society produced a report on the state of education in the country. An enquiry was sent to every parish and chapelry to discover what provision the Church was making. 8,588 returns were received, and from these it appeared that of the places making returns 6,730 had some form of church school and 6,020 had daily and Sunday schools. Of these only 3,058 were in union with the National Society.[1]

Later in this book the provision of popular education by the clergy will become important as an anticipation of the services to be provided by the Welfare State, an anticipation initiated without the help of the State. But in this period the work only exists in embryo, and its significance is rather a sign of the awakening of the Church and of the development of its conception of the role it ought to play. Another sign of this was a changing attitude towards the training of the clergy. One of the

[1] H. J. Burgess, *Enterprise in Education* (1958) p. 43.

most notable symptoms of the easy-going secularism of so much of the English Church in the early nineteenth century had been the fact that most of the clergy received little special training for their work, and that the bishops had taken very inadequate steps to ensure that they were fitted for it. In many cases all the training that a clergyman received before he was entrusted with the cure of Christian souls was a degree taken at Oxford or Cambridge after study, if he had studied at all, in largely secular subjects – indeed there were those who had not even received so much; and many bishops were prepared to accept men for ordination after an extremely perfunctory examination, or what sometimes amounted to no examination at all. In the first thirty years of the nineteenth century this was ceasing to seem satisfactory.

The first developments had as their object the provision of a professional training for those of the clergy who could not go either to Oxford or Cambridge. In 1816 Bishop Law of Chester founded for such men a college at St Bees in Cumberland, and in 1822 Bishop Burgess of St David's founded St David's College at Lampeter. In 1826 the Church Missionary Society, which was on the whole evangelical, opened a training institution at Islington. Meanwhile both Oxford and Cambridge began to awaken reluctantly and confusedly to their responsibilities. In 1822 Charles Lloyd, a close friend of Robert Peel and later bishop of Oxford, became regius professor of divinity at Oxford and started classes in divinity, which were at the time a novelty. They were to have momentous consequences, for Lloyd believed in the importance of the Fathers and also expatiated on the pre-Reformation origins of the prayer book, and his classes were attended by several of the men who were to be the pioneers of the Oxford Movement. One of these was in fact Newman, who at that time still had leanings towards evangelicism; because of this Lloyd would stand in front of him and look at him 'with a satirical expression of countenance', and make playful feints as if to box his ears, or kick him on the shins. What he would have done if he could have foreseen the future it is difficult to say. Also in 1822 Professor Monk raised the issue of clerical education at Cambridge, but unfortunately it got entangled in the dilatory intricacies of academic politics and nothing was done till 1843. However, from the beginning of the century evangelical ordinands at Cambridge seem to have received some training from Simeon and others.[1]

It was likely to be some time before any new arrangements for the training of the ministry would have much noticeable effect except on a few select individuals like the men in Bishop Lloyd's class, or possibly some of the evangelicals. But the fact that men were coming to believe that it was necessary to provide a special training for the clergy seems not only to be a sign of the revival of life in the Church, but also a foretaste of a new conception of what the office of priest in the established Church might be held to mean. All but the dullest, most animal or most cynical, seem to have had a glimpse of the fact that a clergyman was a man who had spiritual duties to perform, but now it was beginning to be realized that a priest was a man who ought to be in some way separated from ordinary secular life, that the clergy were men who ought to receive special training and whose way of life perhaps ought to differ from what was proper for the laity more than had seemed to be necessary in the past. It was a tendency which is exemplified in the career of one who was going to play an important part in the second phase of nineteenth-century history. Charles James Blomfield seems to have been a man of both the old and the new dispensations, or rather he was a man moving, sometimes rather uncertainly, from the standards of one dispensation to those of the other. He was, significantly, of the same generation as Peel, he was in fact born in 1786 two years before Peel. He went to Trinity College, Cambridge, where he took his B.A. degree in 1808 and became thereafter a very distinguished classical scholar; his important editions of classical texts in fact continue till 1823, after which he published little fresh apart from a manual of family prayers, and printed sermons and charges. In 1810 he took orders and though a conscientious parish incumbent according to the ideas of that day he seems to have become a pluralist; in fact much later in his career, when he was bishop of London, he seems to have indulged in nepotism which bears an uncomfortable resemblance to the nepotism of the greedy bishops of the old

[1] See Owen Chadwick, *The Founding of Cuddesdon* (Oxford, 1954) pp. 1–26; D. A. Winstanley, *Early Victorian Cambridge* (Cambridge, 1940) pp. 168–75; Charles Smyth [op. cit., p. 47) pp. 98–143. On Lloyd and Newman see *Letters and Correspondence of J. H. Newman* (3 vols., 1891) Vol. I, pp. 109–12.

school. As a country clergyman he became heavily involved in county business. In 1813 he wrote to his friend Monk to tell him that he had become a justice of the peace, a commissioner of turnpikes and was likely to become a commissioner for the property tax. He added that he was afraid that work for these offices was likely to interfere with his Greek studies.

The change in Blomfield's life seems to have come after he became bishop of Chester in 1824. As bishop he tried to detach his clergy from their secular activities and to impose upon them a more spiritual way of life. Certainly in some cases this seems to have been desirable, for he is said to have found that 'one clergyman was postmaster in a large town, another was engaged in an extensive agency, and a third was, or hoped to become, Mayor of Macclesfield'. Their normal diversions were said to be fox hunting and heavy drinking. The discipline which he imposed seems to have been new to the clergy of Chester and they complained about it, but he persisted.

In 1828 the most important part of his career began. He was translated to London where as bishop he tried to build churches and create parishes to meet the terrible deficiencies of his teeming diocese. After 1835 he became the leading spirit in the ecclesiastical commission, which performed the necessary task of redeploying the resources of the Church so that they could be used to enable it to meet more effectively the heavy responsibilities which the condition of England imposed upon it.[1]

Blomfield's career is therefore doubly significant. It is significant because he was a leading actor in what can only be called the second reformation of the Church. It is also significant because of his progress from the pluralist editor of Greek plays to the committed Church reformer of the last years of his life. It was a progress which symbolized what was going to happen to the clergy of the Church of England. It foreshadows a change that no doubt was necessary if the Church was to survive but it also raises a question of importance in relation to the subject of this book. In his later years Blomfield came to disapprove of clergymen accepting duties as magistrates, since he believed

[1] The Rev. George Edward Biber, L.L.D., *Bishop Blomfield and his Times* (1857) pp. 27–64. Alfred Blomfield, *A Memoir of Charles James Blomfield with Selections from his Correspondence* (2 vols., 1863) Vol. I, pp. 38–9, 103–4.

that such secular duties were likely to interfere with their proper performance of their spiritual functions; and, his son adds, even when he was still a country clergyman he felt that the game laws pressed so heavily upon the poor 'that he could hardly bring himself to be instrumental in enforcing them'.[1] However, it was by playing the parts assigned to them by reason of their positions in the traditional secular orders of society and government that the clergy were most likely to be able to handle the social problems created by the condition of England. To what extent, then, would their activities be hampered by the fact that the rulers of the Church believed that secular duties interfered with their duties as servants of the spiritual order? And, further, to what extent could they usefully and suitably contribute to the solution of the problems of society as participants in a secular order which had some of the characteristics of the old regime? The game laws were later to be modified, but they continued to press heavily, if unevenly, on sections of the rural population and they were a symbol of class privilege. To what extent, therefore, would the clergy's activities be vitiated by the fact that they were acting by virtue of their positions in a regime that continued to maintain such laws, and in some ways was typified by them?

These were, however, problems for the future. Soon after Blomfield arrived in London there developed a situation which seemed to raise a more drastic question. Did the Church of England have any future? In the course of the eighteenth century conditions and ideas had developed which, with increasing force, demanded a revolutionary change in the order of State. New classes were developing power and selfconsciousness, and were inevitably dissatisfied with the position accorded to them under the old regime. At the same time new ideas about government, society and mankind developed which condemned the old order, based as it was on the rule of the few, hereditary privilege and prescription. The progress of reform was stopped by the outbreak of the French Revolution and by the force of the fears it excited, but in the early nineteenth century the process started again, and the traditional institutions of the country, and the people who governed the country through them and profited by

[1] Alfred Blomfield [op. cit., p. 51] Vol. I, p. 39.

them, came under attack by assailants with very various social positions and political ideas – by Whigs who were in opposition, by middle-class reformers, by intellectual reformers, by popular agitators and by revolutionaries.

The Church of England was a natural target for this attack and a peculiarly vulnerable one. It was closely integrated into the order of the old regime, its corruptions were an extension of aristocratic corruption, its tenets were repugnant both to the dissenter and the philosopher and it was exploited as an instrument to maintain the power of the oligarchies which were under attack. In Ireland the Church of Ireland was the Church of the Protestant Ascendancy, and the laws against Roman Catholics which secured that ascendancy were under increasingly massive assault by the forces of Irish nationalism under the leadership of Daniel O'Connell. In England in a large number of towns the effective government was in the hands of a small group of churchmen protected in their position not only by a traditional monopoly of corporate office but by the laws which prevented dissenters from participating. In due course these controls would certainly break, and in due course, also, the progress of reform would be resumed.

The positions on which the old regime based its power were, however, strongly held, and its influence was reinforced by the fears of revolution in the years that immediately followed Waterloo. After 1817, however, these fears got less and, to an increasing extent, reforming opinions began to pervade the country and even to gain entry into the House of Commons. The process was slowed down by the influence and adaptability of Lord Liverpool, who managed to maintain a Liberal Conservative government which partially satisfied the demands for reform, but maintained in essentials the old system of government. However, in 1827 Liverpool had a stroke and immediately the divergent elements he had held together fell apart. He was succeeded by Canning, under whom the Duke of Wellington and Robert Peel refused to serve. Canning died in 1827 and in 1828 the duke became prime minister with Peel as his chief lieutenant. They were unable to retain the Liberal Tories in the Cabinet, and in 1829 they mortally affronted the more traditional Tories by conceding Catholic emancipation. As a result they were defeated by a coalition of forces in 1830, and were succeeded by a ministry under Earl Grey pledged to parliamentary reform.

But before 1830 the process of decisive legislative reform had begun. In 1828 the Test and Corporation Acts were repealed. It was a symbol of what was to come, though in fact it was the Municipal Reform Act of 1835 which really transferred the power in the towns from the old rings into the hands of other groups in which dissenters very often predominated. In 1828, also, the Duke of Wellington and Peel were faced by the possibility of civil war in Ireland and in 1829 they pushed through the measures which emancipated the Catholics, against embittered opposition. In 1831 the bill for parliamentary reform was started on its course.

This started one of the most serious crises of the nineteenth century and a dark moment which seemed to many churchmen to mark the culmination of circumstances which would bring an end to the Church, and of much else besides. In 1830 there had been a new French revolution. In the winter of 1830 intense distress in the countryside had produced widespread disorders, which to the nervous seemed to be the result of revolutionary organization, or at least of revolutionary intention. On 1 March 1831 the government introduced what appeared to the conservative minded to be a revolutionary bill for parliamentary reform. The opposition to it was prolonged but unsuccessful and after lengthy debates and a general election a bill embodying the government's plan for parliamentary reform went up to the House of Lords. There it was rejected, a large majority of the bishops voting against it. As a result there was great indignation in the country. There were meetings and processions in London. Several of the bishops were rabbled in their coaches. There were riots in Derby, the castle in Nottingham was burnt down, and so were the Bishop's Palace, Mansion House and Bridewell at Bristol. And there seemed to be worse to come. Political unions which had come into existence at Birmingham and elsewhere seemed to promise a more effectively organized attack on the opponents of the bill, and it was prophesied of the Church that if the bishops obstructed the bill, to use the words of a contemporary orator, 'the haughty pinnacles of the Establishment will be buried in the dust with a nation's execration as its epitaph'.

In October 1831 it had been confirmed that there was a

serious epidemic of cholera at Sunderland. It spread rapidly, taking a tight grip on those towns which it had invaded, and killing swiftly and horribly a large number of those it infected. It was a new disease, it was obviously infectious but no one knew how it was communicated, and to many people, already frightened by the popular disturbances and the course which politics was taking, it seemed probable that it was the instrument of the wrath of God, who was justly offended by the sins and profligacy of the nation.

For churchmen therefore the winter of 1831 was a time of crisis and fear. It looked as if the enemies of the Church were closing in for the kill. Besides the anger of the mob there was the more persistent hatred of the Protestant dissenters and the Roman Catholics. To the Radicals the Church seemed to be no more than a rabbit warren of aristocratic privilege and abuse. Great publicity had been given to the Church's corruptions, which had been exaggerated, and moderate men had learned to look askance at it as an institution not worth preserving. Lord Grey had told the bishops to put their house in order, and many schemes for Church reform were being proposed. Not a few of these would fundamentally alter the character of the Church, but would it be possible to oppose them? To many churchmen all that was possible was a desperate resistance, more for honour's sake than with any hope of saving what they most cherished.

So in an atmosphere of fear and danger a new phase of nineteenth-century history began.

Mid Century – 1832 – 65

3

Church, State and Society
after 1832

1832 and 1833 were for any friend of the old order years of darkness and foreboding. After a sharp and menacing crisis in May 1832 the Reform Act was passed into law. At the end of the year there was a general election at which the Tories were reduced to a miserable 150 members, and at the beginning of 1833 the first Parliament of the new dispensation met containing a large majority of reformers, talkative, raucous and jubilantly intent on changing the world. Outside Parliament dissenters attacked the Church with venom, and confidently predicted that soon nothing of it would be left but a memory of its shame. In Ireland there was a general refusal to pay tithe and church dues to a Church which most Irishmen regarded as an heretical and alien intrusion. The Whig government were prepared to try to restore order in Ireland, but in 1833 they passed an act to remodel the Church in Ireland and to reduce the number of its bishoprics. To many churchmen this was sacrilege for it meant that a secular body, Parliament, was mangling the consecrated order of an ecclesiastical body. It was interpreted by some as a sinister portent of similar reforms in England.

The fear and anger which these events excited extended beyond the ranks of professional Tory politicians, old-fashioned squires and those churchmen who looked to the past, to men who were in fact going to play an important part in the future. Particularly significant was the effect of the shock of that moment on men who were connected with the two ancient universities. In Oxford it led to the important series of events that set in motion the Oxford Movement. In Cambridge the results were more complicated, and Cambridge opinion tended to move off at a tangent to the line taken by the Oxford apostles; for in Cambridge an important factor was the influence of F. D. Maurice. Maurice was the son of a Unitarian minister and had himself been a Unitarian. He had however joined the Church of England, and in 1823 he became a member of Trinity College. At Trinity, with the aid of his tutor Julius Hare and his friend John Sterling, he promoted the philosophy of Coleridge in place of that of Bentham which had been fashionable there. Both Maurice and Sterling left Cambridge before 1832; in fact in 1830, after a period as a journalist in London, Maurice had gone to Oxford with the object of taking orders. Meanwhile other able and interesting young men appeared at Trinity, such as Richard Chenevix Trench, James Spedding, Alfred Tennyson and his friend Hallam. The shock of the crisis was felt as severely by these men as it was felt at Oxford. This can be appreciated in the letters received by Trench, or in the poems which Alfred Tennyson wrote at this time. But Maurice's instincts led him in due course to seek a road which separated itself sharply from that which was to be followed by Newman, Manning or Pusey.[1]

It is as well to recognize the emotional intensity of men's feelings at that moment for, though they were to have important results in the future, it is difficult, in the light of what was to happen, to conceive that they were justified. At first, it is true, the impact of the Reform Act was considerable. Not only did it inspire much talk and rather feverish political activity but important measures were passed – the Irish Church Act, the act abolishing slavery in the British empire, a factory act (this last was the result of the agitation of Richard Oastler and Lord Ashley and gave a good deal less than Ashley wanted, but it was to be enforced by inspectors, which was an innovation). There was also an important legal reform which created the Judicial Committee of the Privy Council, and in 1834 the

[1] *Richard Chenevix Trench, Archbishop Letter and Memorials edited by the author of Charles Lowder* (2 vols., 1888) Vol. I, *passim*. The relevant poems of Tennyson are 'Hail Briton', 'You ask me why though ill at ease', 'Love thou thy land', 'Of old sat Freedom on the heights', 'I loving Freedom for herself'. See *The Poems of Tennyson*, ed. Christopher Ricks (1969) pp. 489, 613, 617, 619.

reform of the Poor Law. But by 1834 the flame was beginning to burn low. The ministry had not pleased those people who believed that reform would mean the wholesale reduction of taxes. It had disappointed the Radicals almost from the start. The ministry itself was divided on the subject of Irish tithes and Irish coercion, and began to break up. The House of Lords regained its courage and began to throw out government bills, and in November 1834 the king took the opportunity of a moment's weakness to replace the Whig Lord Melbourne by the Tory Peel. Peel dissolved Parliament, but did not gain enough seats to win a majority, so the Whigs returned in 1835 and passed at least one more important measure, the Municipal Reform Act of 1835. But the fire was dying, and their product had become little indeed by the time that Robert Peel won the general election of 1841 and became prime minister.

Peel came into power as the leader of a party which had been organized in opposition. It was a new kind of party, and it had a new name, the Conservative party. The name was suitable, for the party in large part represented those elements of the old regime who were united to prevent further change – the nobility, the country gentry and the Church. Many clergymen, in fact, played an active role in supporting Conservative candidates at elections, at most constituency dinners a local clergyman was normally found to respond to the appropriate toast, and in 1838 the Hampshire Conservatives announced their intention of celebrating an electoral victory by building a church which would be 'congenial with those Protestant and Christian principles which form the basis of true Conservatism'.[1] Since men on the other side were openly in favour of the destruction of the Church, and since so many clergymen were imbued with the ideas of the old regime, the action of the clergy is not altogether surprising. But it was unfortunate. In supporting the Conservatives the clergy were supporting much that was instinct with class selfishness and injustice, while several of the evangelical clergy openly encouraged that virulent popular hatred of Roman Catholicism which bedevilled England's relations with Ireland during most of the nineteenth century.

However, not all that the Tories supported between 1830

[1] R. L. Hill, *Toryism and the People 1831-46* (1929) p. 59.

and 1841 was of this order. A number of Tory members of Parliament representing West Riding or Lancashire constituencies supported Oastler, Sadler and Lord Ashley's crusade for the factory children. It has sometimes been asserted that this movement was primarily a factious manoeuvre, that it was in fact the landed interest's *tu quoque* to the assertions which the Anti-Corn Law League made about the treatment of the agricultural labourers. The facts do not bear this out. Most of the Tories involved had taken up the movement for factory reform five or six years before the Anti-Corn Law League started operations, and most of those who did get committed were not primarily agricultural Tories but Tories from the industrialized districts of the West Riding and South Lancashire. Their most significant organ was the *Leeds Intelligencer*. It is true that from the way that they wrote and spoke there was clearly a factious element in the activities of some of them, that sticks which were apt to the hands of those who wished to beat Liberal or Whig dogs were not unwelcome; and some, not all, became protectionists when that issue turned up. But there was clearly also a strong element of humane feeling behind this movement, which was largely enforced by a principle inherent in the traditional system of social ethics which as Tories and as churchmen they professed. In the old hierarchical system even a factory child had rights which the law should protect, and which might be denied to him in a society which took as its basic principle the inevitability and desirability of absolutely free competition.

For this reason it is significant that the movement for factory reform received very general support from the clergy of the Church of England, particularly from the clergy of the areas which were most affected. One of the most important organizers of the movement was the formidable G. S. Bull, the 'ten hours' parson. Among the many West Riding and Lancastrian clergy who supported it there stood out W. F. Hook, the most notable of the vicars of Leeds, and Fawcett his predecessor, the relevant vicars of Bradford, and Canon Wray of the Collegiate Church of Manchester. Among the bishops there were Bishop Ryder of Lichfield and Coventry, Bishop Longley of Ripon and the archbishops of Canterbury and York. Some of these men were in some way concerned with the Conservative party, many were not. Nevertheless the promise of factory reform, together with the determination to humanize the New Poor Law, became the earnest hope and expectation of the Conservative party in an important sector of industrial England, and to judge by the *Leeds Intelligencer*, as victory approached in 1841 their hopes rose very high indeed.[1]

They were bitterly disappointed. Factory reform and the reform of the New Poor Law were supported by a number of Conservatives in that Parliament. Disraeli based a social philosophy on the ideas that seemed to lie behind these demands, which he presented in his two novels *Coningsby* and *Sybil*, and they were adopted in a rather superficial form by the group that called itself *Young England*. But Peel would not do what was wanted. In his view, his function as prime minister was to pursue the general objects for which his party had been organized, but in individual matters he would only do as he thought best and would not be swayed by his party's prejudices. As a result, in many matters he disappointed his party's wishes, both good and evil; and in this matter he had convinced himself that restrictions on hours of labour such as Ashley demanded would create widespread unemployment and that a modification of the New Poor Law would recreate the chaos that had preceded 1834. He thus obstinately, and successfully, resisted what a large section of his party had very earnestly desired.

It would be hard to say what were the effects of his obduracy. Probably it did not much affect the progress of factory reform, which went forward, after Peel had retired, with the support of men of all parties. No doubt Peel's recalcitrance prevented the development of a party which might have remoulded the old concepts of social ethics as a new dynamic programme, but it may be doubted whether that was at any point a real possibility and, even though it did not have effective political expression, this conception of social ethics did not die; it remained

---

[1] J. T. Ward, *The Factory Movement* (1962), *passim*. On the *Leeds Intelligencer*, see Mildred Gibb and Frank Beckwith *The Yorkshire Post, two centuries* (The Yorkshire Conservative Newspaper Company Ltd., 1954), but the best record is in the columns of the *Intelligencer* itself. On the clergy, see, e.g., J. C. Gill, *The Ten Hours Parson* (1960); W. R. Stephens, *The Life and Letters of Walter Farquhar Hook* (2 vols., 1878) Vol. II, pp. 118–21.

a potent factor in mid nineteenth-century England. In any case the period of effective party politics which seemed to be beginning in 1835 came to an end in 1846. Peel drastically set on one side the prejudices of his party on the subject of the amount of protection which British agriculture needed. From his first budget he scaled down the protection it received from the Corn Laws and the other laws imposing duties on a number of agricultural commodities, and in 1846 he repealed the Corn Laws, which many of his party believed he had come into office to maintain. This was too much. He was driven from office. The Conservative party was fatally split, and for thirty years Whigs and Liberals were in a virtual majority. They did not, however, represent a single disciplined party and their governments were seldom in secure possession of power, or able effectively to control the House of Commons. Consequently, for thirty years the course of politics was indecisive and wayward.

There was, however, a profounder cause for the indecisiveness of mid nineteenth-century politics. For all the fears it had excited the First Reform Act had left power in the same hands as had controlled it before. Although the monopoly of power enjoyed by those whom Bright called the 'titled and proprietary classes' was not so complete and unquestioned as it had been before the Reform Act, nevertheless a large majority of the seats in the House of Commons remained in their hands. Many of these seats were held by men with Liberal instincts, but they did not receive a decisive impetus from the new forces that were shaping in society, and they were not likely to do anything that might endanger the control of power by men of their class, using the methods to which they were accustomed, for the objects which they favoured.

For this reason at least until after the Second and even till after the Third Reform Act, there was no real danger that Parliament would pass a measure disestablishing or disendowing the Church of England; and in fact between 1832 and 1867 it did very little to redress the grievances of dissenters. Even in the first reformed Parliament the attacks on the Church fell away to nothing and attempts to remove some of the main disabilities of the dissenters miscarried. After the dissolution of 1834 the friends of the Church were strong enough, with the help of the House of Lords, to ensure that nothing was done without their assent. In 1835, as prime minister Peel had instituted an ecclesiastical commission to redeploy the wealth of the Church. After his resignation the Whigs passed the legislation which implemented its work.[1] In 1836, with the approbation of many Conservatives, an act was passed to eliminate the troublesome business of the payment of tithes in kind. In the same year a new system of civil registration excused dissenters from the need to be married in church, but in this the Whigs followed a lead which Peel had given in his short ministry. In 1839 the government put forward plans which might have led to a greater secular control of education, but they had to come to terms with the bishops.

Taking into account all that had been threatened against the Church, and all that had been feared, this is but a meagre harvest of change and reform, and it was not to be added to in the years that followed. Most of the remaining dissenting disabilities remained unredressed till the third phase of nineteenth-century history. Indeed, the fact that such a bitterly resented grievance as the imposition of a compulsory church rate should remain a possibility till after 1867 is eloquent testimony to the real location of power between the Reform Acts.

In retrospect this prolonged anticlimax might suggest that men's fears in 1832 and 1833 had been unreasonable and irrelevant. This would be a mistake, however. They were not unreasonable, since no man knows what the morrow may bring, and they were not irrelevant because they were excited by forces in the country whose demands would not be for ever frustrated by the limitations of the electoral system.

In 1831 and 1832 the most poignant fears had been excited by the apparent threats posed by the crowded meetings, the rioting crowds and the political unions which had provided a threatening accompaniment to the crisis. In 1833 riots in London made it clear that the forces behind these disturbances had not been satisfied by the Reform Act. From 1834 to 1836 there was a period of prosperity and matters calmed down. Even so, as late as 1836 a man as able and sensible as Sir Robert Peel was still thinking in terms of revolution. From 1837 onwards industry, which had probably been developing too fast, declined into what became the most serious depression in the

[1] 3 and 4 Vict. c. 86.

nineteenth century. This inflicted severe suffering on a wide section of the working classes, and as a result there was a recurrence of popular agitation, amongst which were the agitation of the Anti-Corn Law League, which had at times a wilder appearance than is normally now remembered, and the working-class Chartist movement with its tragic, if futile, threats of violence.

These movements were calculated to renew the old fears. But fear is not a sufficient explanation of the emotions which haunted the minds of so many men in the upper and middle classes in the late thirties and early forties. Various factors had combined to bring before the minds of many men and women the depth, width and intensity of the unhappiness and neglect caused by the intolerable living conditions and oppression that existed in the country. A number of divines had come to realize how many people in the country lived beyond the reach of any form of spiritual ministration. The parliamentary enquiries which were occasioned by the issue of factory reform produced ugly facts which were endorsed by the written reports of medical doctors and others on the condition of children in the manufacturing districts. The agitation against the New Poor Law produced a good many accounts of the cruelties inflicted on paupers, a work in which *The Times* surpassed itself. Those engaged in the Anti-Corn Law agitation drew forcible attention to the oppression and deprivation suffered by many agricultural labourers, and *The Times* published a series of letters by Sidney Godolphin Osborne, who held the living of Durweston in Dorset, forcibly describing the bad conditions under which the poor lived in his neighbourhood. The suffering in the manufacturing districts in the early forties seems to have excited much general interest and pity, and in 1842 Edwin Chadwick produced the terrible revelations in his report on the sanitary conditions in towns. The report itself had a considerable circulation, and its lessons were driven home by much effective journalism.

The impact of all this may perhaps be judged from the more general literature it evoked, or which was itself inspired by conditions in the country. Disraeli's novel *Sybil*, published in 1845, was palpably based on a study of blue books. It was very successful, and it reveals the uneasy interest which people at that moment took in what might be going forward in the factory districts. So do novels by Mrs Trollope, by the evangelical Mrs Tonna (writing under the name of 'Charlotte Elizabeth') and by Mrs Gaskell. The revelations about factory conditions also inspired Elizabeth Barrett's well-known poem, 'The Cry of the Children', written apparently in 1844. But suffering in other parts of the country presented itself to the public in literature that it was not so easy to evade. An article in *Punch* by Douglas Jerrold on the miserable earnings of a poor needle-woman who had appeared in the courts in London inspired Tom Hood to write the 'Song of the Shirt' which appeared in the 1843 Christmas number of *Punch*. As a result the circulation of *Punch* is said to have trebled, the poem was translated into a number of languages, and in 1844 a play at the Haymarket was based upon it. Dickens, possibly the most powerful influence in the nineteenth century, had started to write, and there was a large mass of contemporary journalism, vigorous commentary enforced by the direct verbal reports of such occasions as trials and inquests which revealed without mercy what could happen in contemporary England. The commentary was not confined to the newspapers. In 1840 Lord Ashley contributed an important article to *The Quarterly Review*.[1] During these years Thomas Carlyle published his three great tracts, *Chartism* (1840), *Past and Present* (1843), *Latter Day Pamphlets* (1850), and therein were two evangelical comments on the situation, of which the first achieved considerable notoriety, these being *The Perils of the Nation* (1843) and *Remedies suggested for the Perils of the Nation* (1844). Both were anonymous. Their publisher was R. B. Seeley, the father of Sir John Seeley, the historian, but their probable author was Mrs Tonna.

Some of these publications excited anger in some quarters. As was to be expected, Osborne's letters incensed his Dorsetshire neighbours, as did his brother-in-law Charles Kingsley's descriptions of rural life published in *Fraser's Magazine* in 1848. Indeed, in the latter case the indignation was so great that the proprietors brought the series to an end lest it should damage

---

[1] On the novels with a social interest, see Louis Cazamian, *Le Roman Social en Angleterre* (Paris, 1904); for Lord Ashley's article, see *The Quarterly Review*, CXXXIV (1840), Article V, pp. 171–81. The article was, of course, anonymous.

the future of the magazine, a fate which later overtook the articles which Ruskin contributed to the *Cornhill* in 1860, and to *Fraser's* in 1862 and 1863. And no doubt as the fear of revolution became less and as prosperity became established there developed not a little self congratulatory complacency. Mr Podsnap is a reflection of reality, though it should be noted that his author exhibited him as the subject of severe satire. Unfortunately the best-known flesh and blood example of complacency – the eulogy on existing conditions by J. A. Roebuck in 1864 with which Matthew Arnold made such play in his *Essays in Criticism* – is not satisfactory, since it turns out that Arnold partially misrepresented the purport of, and indefensibly misquoted, Roebuck's speech.[1]

What is clear is that rising prosperity did not stifle the interest which many people felt in what might be wrong with society, and this interest seems to have continued after any peril of revolution had faded. Chartism collapsed after the failure of their monster meeting on 10 April 1848 and many people seem to have developed that mood of relief and confidence which is echoed in Macaulay's history; but in 1849 and 1850 Henry Mayhew produced his articles in *The Morning Chronicle* which ultimately became the core of his book on London life and London labour, which was published in four volumes in 1861–2. When they first appeared Mayhew's articles excited considerable and painful interest; but he quarrelled with *The Morning Chronicle* and set up on his own, and in due course his output fell off. However, his activities were imitated in the years that followed by a good many journalists. Much of this work is of inferior quality, and is rather inspired by a desire to describe the strange and the sensational than to probe social evils. This seems to be largely true of the 'pilgrimage' to London in 1869 by Gustave Doré and Blanchard Jerrold, which produced the famous pictures. But even at its lightest this work was not compatible with a belief that everyone in the country was prosperous and happy.[2]

[1] *Review of English Literature* VIII (1967) G. Watson, 'Arnold and the Victorian Mind', pp. 37–9.
[2] See E. P. Thompson and Eileen Yeo, eds., *The Unknown Mayhew* (1971) pp. 11–95. London. *A Pilgrimage by Gustave Doré and Blanchard Jerrold* (reprinted with an introduction by Millicent Rose, New York, 1970).

With Kingsley, Dickens, Mrs Gaskell and Charles Read the spate of social novels continued. In addition to these there was the technical literature dealing with the problems of the day. There was a large range of books of varying merit and there were also the proceedings of various societies interested in social problems – medical societies, local statistical or sanitary societies, the proceedings of the Social Science Association founded under the auspices of Brougham in 1857, and the reports of the appropriate sections of the British Association. Above all there were government publications, the reports of royal commissions or of select committees of either House of Parliament, or the reports of such public servants as Dr John Simon, from 1858 the medical officer attached to the Privy Council and of the various government inspectors, such as the factory inspectors.

Government publications seem to have been mediated to a larger public through the serious reviews. It is, for instance, interesting to notice how faithfully between 1860 and 1866 *The Quarterly Review* followed the run of them. To take as examples only those which deal directly with social conditions, in 1861 it is discussing spiritual destitution and social conditions in London following a report of a select committee of the House of Lords, in 1861 and again in 1862 it deals with the education of the poor relating its report to the findings of a royal commission, in 1865 it has an article on the sanitary reform of the metropolis using Simon's reports from 1858 to 1864, and in 1866 there is an elaborate report on child labour based on the report of the Children's Employment Commission. It would almost seem as if a section of the more serious-minded public received from government publications a continuous education in some of the realities of the conditions then prevalent. This does not appear in all cases to have led to complacency. In 1865 *The Quarterly Review* said of London:

> With all our elaborate apparatus backed by our national wealth there is much which might well make us blush in matters affecting the intellectual moral and physical well-being of the inhabitants of the metropolis. Notwithstanding our Revised Code, our New Poor Laws and our Metropolitan Management Acts there is really no adequate provision made for the education of the people, the relief of the poor or the maintenance of our thoroughfares

and it went on to talk of 100,000 children without schools, of reports in the newspapers of men and women dying of starvation 'at our very doors', and of the dirt and desolation of the streets in which the poor lived.[1]

It would not be possible to say with any certainty what effects all the literature, journalism and disquisitions had on the minds of contemporaries, and it is clearly undesirable to supply this lack of information with speculations based on assumptions about the effects on ways of thought of the class structure of the period. But it does suggest that a consciousness of the social problems of the country was a permanent factor in the minds of most literate people from about 1830 if not before, till 1870, and certainly afterwards. The ways in which they responded clearly differed greatly. It seems clear that in many cases the response was flaccid and spasmodic leading to little more than sentimental self-indulgence, or at best a momentary agitation on one particular point, or a flood of ill-organized charity. No doubt descriptions of existing social evils made a number of people angry and unwilling to listen. Dickens' works frequently excited indignation, though it is noteworthy that what is on record as having made men angry was in each case republished and consequently made an impression on part of the public. At any rate it seems to be beyond doubt that the response of not a few educated men and women to what was wrong in the country was both serious and practical. This response often naturally tended to be personal and local, though in such matters as public health many men drew their inspiration from a national figure like Edwin Chadwick. In the last resort, however, the most important issues could not be left to the vagaries of local initiative. This raised a problem which Victorian England found peculiarly difficult to solve, and even to discuss with reasonable clarity. A uniform national policy could only be imposed by the State. What, then, should be the functions of the State and what the extent of its powers?

Here then were two issues, the challenge of the condition of the country, and the problem of the functions of the State. In

[1] *The Quarterly Review*, Vol. 109, pp. 414–63; Vol. 110, pp. 485–516; Vol. 111, pp. 73–115; Vol. 118, pp. 254–80; Vol. 119, pp. 364–93. The quotation is in Vol. 117, p. 430.

what ways were the different brands of churchmen going to approach them?

Of the various distinguishable schools of churchmanship probably the evangelicals were inclined to be the most primitive in their approach to secular problems. Their morality was rigid and unaccommodating. The evangelical revival had a long history and taught that form of Christianity which had made the fewest concessions to the intellectual currents of the nineteenth century. There was some advantage in this. The letter of the Authorized Version of the Bible, which provided the staple of their thought, was on a number of points a sounder guide to the understanding of the needs of society than some of the doctrines attributed to the classical economists. But it meant that evangelicals were apt to be encumbered by a good deal of unreasoning fanaticism. They tended to be extremely intolerant in their attitude to those whose religious convictions differed from their own. They often tried to impose their own code of conduct on other people, to whom it did not seem to be reasonable or necessary, and they were apt to entertain a fanatical hatred of the Roman Catholic Church and of those in the Church of England whom they believed were betraying the Church of England to the Roman Catholics. As a result of this vein in their make up the same man might perform the most valuable services to society and at the same time disclose the most disastrous prejudices. For instance, Hugh Stowell was the much-loved pastor of a difficult area in Manchester, for which he developed not only a formidable array of services, lectures and prayer meetings but also day and Sunday schools, an adult school, ragged schools, a refuge for the fallen and a staff of district visitors to seek out the poor. In many ways a bigoted old goose, he was for many years president of the Manchester and Salford Operative Association, which seems to have been a strongly Protestant body, and his references to Roman Catholics were calculated to ferment the already sufficiently strong working-class hatred of the Irish. Or there was J. C. Miller, vicar of St Martin's, Birmingham from 1846, who among other things founded very successful working-class clubs in Birmingham and was a warm advocate of a halfday holiday on Saturday, partly it is true to enable working men to go to church on Sundays, but also to protect them from overwork.

Yet the fierceness of his views on the Church of Rome and Puseyism can be judged from the sermon he preached in Oxford to celebrate the martyrdom of Ridley and Latimer.[1]

Evangelical fanaticism at its most intolerant can be seen in the ruthless destruction of a promising educational experiment at Liverpool by a formidable Ulster-born clergyman, Hugh MacNeile.[2] On the other side of the scale can be placed the work of William Champneys, rector of Whitechapel from 1837 to 1860. In Whitechapel Champneys built three churches. He founded schools both for boys and girls, and a ragged school for those who could not go to an ordinary school for want of proper clothing. He founded a provident society. He helped to start the shoeblacks' brigade as a source of relief for vagrant boys, with a refuge and an industrial home for the boys. He joined with others to build the Whitechapel Industrial Foundation. He also introduced a local association for the health and comfort of the working classes, and was instrumental in providing for the coal whippers of London a hiring office where previously they had had to hang about in public houses. Taking into account the general standard of social services at that time, this is obviously a very important contribution; and to the work of the evangelical clergy can be added the ministering activities of the evangelical laity, and the network of ragged schools, soup kitchens, refuges, scripture readers and missions of one sort or another, that they brought into being. It was not always very wise work and too often the spirit was narrow and fanatical, but they knew human suffering when they saw it and they were prepared to spend themselves and their resources to help those whom no one else was likely to reach.[3]

[1] The Rev. J. B. Marsden, incumbent of St Peter's, Birmingham, *Memoir of the Life and Labours of the Reverend Hugh Stowell* (1868). On J. C. Miller, see D. E. Mole, *Journal of Ecclesiastical History*, Vol. XVII, No. I, and the article in the *Dictionary of National Biography* (*D.N.B.*) by G. C. Boase. See also a printed sermon, *The Martyr's Candle: a sermon preached at the commemoration of the Tercentenary of the martyrdom of Ridley and Latimer on Tuesday Oct. 16 1855* (1855).

[2] On the experiment at Liverpool, see James Murphy, *The Religious Problem in English Education* (Liverpool, 1959).

[3] On Champneys, see article in *D.N.B.* by G. C. Boase. On evangelical work in general, see Kathleen Heasman, *Evangelicals in Action. An Appraisal of Social Work in the Victorian Era* (1962).

In their general proposals for the country the evangelicals showed the same mixture of dynamic benevolence, spiritual integrity and oppressive and intrusive intolerance. On the credit side there are the suggestions for factory reform proposed by the evangelical Lord Shaftesbury and supported by many evangelicals, and the careers of evangelicals such as Fowell Buxton show that there was still work to be done in the crusade against slavery and for the protection of the primitive tribes with whom British expansion came into contact. Moreover, the country would have done well to heed the evangelical condemnation of the opium wars. On the other side must be placed the laws which promoted the awful solemnity of the English Sunday, mainly at the expense of working people whose one day of recreation it was.

Theirs was an unfortunate mixture. Their intolerance nullified much of the good they did at the time, and has damaged their reputation with historians, where they might have deserved more praise. Their simplicity and fanaticism had a further significance, for it seems to have prevented them from understanding the difficult problem of the nature of the authority of the State to which I referred before. As the social needs which the condition of the country had created became the more fully revealed it became increasingly clear that to secure the standards of civilization which nineteenth-century susceptibilities demanded the State must increase its powers and interfere with men's lives and properties as it had not done before. To do this it must assume a wider-ranging moral authority than it had previously possessed. But in the period after 1832 the tendency had been not to increase men's conception of the moral authority of the State, but to reduce it. The political results of the Reform Act had been to loosen the ties between Church and State. It had increased the power of dissenters who denied to the State all but the minimum of moral authority. It had increased the power of a school of thinkers who thought that in many matters it was inexpedient for the public power to do anything at all. Where then should be found the generally acceptable moral authority which should endorse the action of the State, indeed direct it to those actions which humanity required that it should take? The evangelicals' answer to this was naïve. The generally acceptable moral authority was to be found in the bible. As the writer on the *Remedies Suggested for the Perils of the Nation* made clear, in God's word there were general and sufficient directions 'for legislators, for statesmen, and for men of wealth and influence, the tenor of which is directly opposed to that of a set of philosophers "falsely so called" of our times, have conspired to dignify with the name of "Political Economy"'.[1] That might be so, but it was unlikely that the bible as interpreted by earnest evangelicals would oust the influence of the political economists from the minds of a sufficient number of legislators, statesmen and men of influence to enable it to direct the policy of the country.

The evangelicals recognized the urgency of the moral challenge created by the condition of the nation, but their dogmatic assurance was such that they could not recognize the difficulties presented by the varieties of religious beliefs in the country or the strength of secular opinion nor did they realize the problem posed by the power of the State. It is interesting, therefore, to compare them with a clergyman who was so impressed by the urgency of that challenge that he would not take account of the divisive power of mens' dogmatic convictions. Thomas Arnold became headmaster of Rugby in 1828, but the school did not occupy the whole of his attention. He was an uneasy, emotional man deeply preoccupied with the social and political situation of the moment. The rural disturbances of the autumn of 1830 moved him deeply. He was strongly aware of the social wrong and the harshness and cruelty that had characterized life in the English countryside. He was also darkly apprehensive about the future. As the crisis went forward his gloom increased, and when cholera broke out he began to see signs of the end of the world. When the Reform Act was passed he began to fear lest the cry for Church reform should lead to the destruction of what he believed the Church to stand for. He therefore published his pamphlet on the *Principles of Church Reform*.

This is a strange production. Roughly speaking it suggests that the task of the national Church should be taken over by an amalgam of the principal Christian denominations; and

[1] *Remedies suggested for the Perils of the Nation* [op. cit., p. 67] p. 51.

indeed it has been usual to dismiss it as the ill-considered aberration of a man of impracticably latitudinarian principles. There is, however, much more to it than that. Arnold was troubled by the fundamental question that confronted the country: supposing you dissolve the union between Church and State, upon what foundation will you base the moral authority of the State and what will men believe to be the scope of its activities? He feared that if men lost sight of the moral content of the idea of the State they would lose sight of the extent of its moral responsibilities. He feared that the view was becoming increasingly predominant according to which:

> Society has been regarded as a mere collection of individuals looking each after his own interests, and the business of government has been limited to that of a mere police whose sole use is to prevent these individuals from robbing or knocking each other down.[1]

This view, he said, was 'alike unphilosophical and unchristian.' Its evil effects could be seen in the state of the poor. 'For their physical distresses, their ignorance and their vices are the true fruits of the system of "letting alone".'

The remedy was to use the resources of the Church. There were churches everywhere, 'even in the most unattractive districts of the country'. In many villages the church was the only building not devoted to getting or spending, and it was in the power of the Church to place a man of education in every parish. What in Arnold's view hindered the proper use of these resources was what he called 'sectarianism'. He therefore produced his carefully thought out scheme for making these resources available to the various denominations, who would all have a part in the same establishment. He feared that if nothing was done:

> The end of all this will be what the godless party are earnestly labouring to effect, that dissolution of the Establishment altogether, that is, in other words, the public renouncing of our allegiance to God; for without an Establishment, although it may happen that the majority of Englishmen may still be Christian, yet England will not be a Christian country – its government will be no Christian government.

[1] T. Arnold, D.D., *Principles of Church Reform* (3rd edn., 1833) p. 7.

D

As was to be expected his proposals had no results. Men were not prepared to surrender principles which they valued to enter an unworkable coalition which denied their validity. Arnold did not retreat from his position. He continued to be anxious, he continued to fear the results of the neglect of the labouring population 'by one of the falsest maxims which ever pandered to human selfishness under the name of political wisdom – I mean the maxim that civil society ought to leave its members alone, each to look after their several interests, provided they do not employ direct fraud or force against their neighbour'.[1] And he continued to demand a co-operation between the Churches, which was in his view hampered by such claims as the claim to the independent authority of a divinely inspired priesthood which the Oxford Movement was making.

As he could not eradicate that or other beliefs which he found inconvenient, his proposals had no future. In actual fact he was going to influence the future in quite a different way. All this time he was doing the great work of his life and moulding his school, Rugby; and there his restless spirit, acutely sensitive to what was going on around him, and tempting him to dramatize things, communicated its message to the élite among his pupils. It gave them a heavy sense of social responsibility, which crushed a delicate character like the poet Clough, but gave to others a purpose in life. As a result Rugbeians, and those educated by masters inspired by Rugby, were among the most important architects of mid-Victorian society. It was largely their spirit, often reinforced by training at Balliol, which gave its tone to the Victorian civil service, both in England and in India. Thus with some stretching of language it might be said that he begat what in the end became the undenominational priesthood of a State that was to assume the functions of a Church and reverse the conception of the functions of the State which he detested.

That, however, was in the future; moreover it was a solution which Arnold himself would have been unable to accept, for he was a sincere Christian and it is unlikely that he could have accepted a moral authority which could be separated from

---

[1] *The Miscellaneous Works of Doctor Arnold, D.D.* (1845) pp. 452–3. *Letter on the* 'State of the manufacturing population' *to the Hertford Reformer*, published on 1 December 1838.

Christianity. What matters here is not the end to which Arnold's activities tended but the significance of his perceptions in the decade after the reform, and it is clear he perceived two things of great importance. He perceived that if it were to do its duty the State must assume far greater moral authority than men were at that moment prepared to accord it, and he finally realized that an obstacle to this was the multiplicity of contending beliefs in the country.

The evangelicals and Arnold had this in common, however. They neither of them accorded much importance to the historic doctrine of the Church: the belief in a divinely ordained society whose task it was to define Christian dogma and instruct in Christian morals. This conception, however, was important to many churchmen, and as soon as it entered the calculations it introduced two new problems. What would guarantee the safety and integrity of the Church? And what should be the relationship of a Church, particularly of an established Church, to the State? Of those on this more ecclesiastical side of opinion probably the nearest to Arnold was F. D. Maurice. If he was in his way a strong churchman he was also one who believed in comprehension, and one whose theology would be repudiated by evangelical and high churchman alike. He also tended to look forward to the challenge and possibilities of the future, rather than turn backward to the fathers of the seventeenth century, or the middle ages. In 1832 he told Chenevix Trench that, though while they lasted he would feel it to be his duty to fight for the institutions which were in peril, if they were destroyed he would 'wash his face and eat bread, assured that out of this evil a greater good shall come'.[1] He clearly felt that if this moment was probably an end, it was also certainly a beginning, for the spiritual cannot end. In his poem 'Love thou thy land', his friend Tennyson wrote of this moment:

> Ev'n now we hear with inward strife
> A motion toiling in the gloom –
> The Spirit of the years to come
> Yearning to mix himself with Life.

For Maurice it was possible that that Spirit came from God.

[1] *Trench* [op. cit., p. 60] Vol. I, p. 120.

However, Maurice was much more deeply committed than Arnold to specifically clerical work, though not to the service of an ordinary parish. After ordination in 1834 he had a brief spell in a country parish, and then in 1836 he moved to London to become chaplain at Guy's Hospital. In London he gathered round him a band of devoted young men who tended to regard him as their prophet, attracted, it would seem, by the strong sense of the reality and supreme significance of what was spiritual in his teaching, and by his readiness to understand the problems of the troubled generation that was trying to find its bearings in the 1830s and 1840s. He was certainly concerned about the situation of the Church, and in 1837 he began his series of letters to a member of the Society of Friends to explain the problem of the establishment of the Church, and the principles of the Catholic Church as he understood them. These were published in 1838 in what became an influential book, his *Kingdom of Christ*.

His letters IX to XII deal with the relations of Church, State and society. He ends the eleventh letter by saying:

> I mean to make the statesman perceive, that his province is a most sacred one, and yet, that if it is a province at all there must be one beyond it, on which it is dependent for its most important resources; . . . . one which is ruled over, not by a vague abstraction called a religious principle – not by a set of wavering notions, but by a body which God has established and with an order permanently fixed by His Word [endued] with living powers and energies, proceeding every moment from his spirit.[1]

This body was the Catholic Church. Maurice was aware of the objections contemporaries might urge against what he calls the 'Theocratic Principle', and he starts his next lecture by discussing the doctrine of Rousseau and natural rights, and of Bentham and the rule of the majority. With them he deals reasonably effectively. He discusses the uncertain moral authority of the word 'natural' and he suggests that the rule of the majority may perhaps represent the *will* of the majority but not the *right* of the majority. Being the man he was, he blurs the edges a little by trying to prove that the exponents of each

[1] The Rev. F. Maurice, *The Kingdom of Christ* (1838) Vol. III, pp. 106–7.

theory were feeling towards his conception of the divine law. But his own belief is clear. The State needs to go to the Church to teach it subjects to be 'free men'. And by the Church he means, as far as England was concerned, the Church of England; indeed he devotes much of his tenth letter to answering the arguments of those who wished to take away the revenues of the Church.

This was a view which in one way or another Maurice held to the end of his life. It was going to cause him much trouble and frequent misunderstandings with some of his friends and allies, for it contained two unresolved problems. What should be the action of the Church if the State and society habitually disregarded its admonitions? And if it was the duty of the clergy to teach men to do good freely, what should be their attitude supposing that widespread coercion were necessary to remedy intolerable social conditions? These issues were, however, only really to trouble Maurice when he began to turn to social problems. At the moment he was faced by two pressing ecclesiastical issues: the threat of disestablishment, and the problem of popular education.

The threat of disestablishment was still felt to be a reality in the late thirties. In 1838 the great Scottish Presbyterian divine, Dr Chalmers, delivered a series of lectures in vindication of established Churches. They were not satisfactory to Anglicans, for Chalmers got over the problem of the diversity of the denominations in England by emphasis on a common Protestantism which, he held, would satisfy most English denominations. To achieve this the Church of England would 'have to come down from all that is transcendental or mysterious in her pretensions'. In this Chalmers' doctrine in some sort resembles Arnold's proposals, but he fell short of Arnold's conception that a Christian establishment should serve a social purpose, for Chalmers clearly believed that the only purpose of a Christian establishment should be to teach the Christian religion. Still, the content of the lectures, and the fact that they should be given at all, is illustrative of the tensions of that moment. These are also reflected in the *Kingdom of Christ*. To Maurice the disestablishment of the Church would be catastrophic. Church and State should be inseparable, for they were complementary to each other – the Church had the function of giving moral direction, the State had that of carrying out executive and legislative action.[1]

The issue of popular education also revealed an important clash between Maurice and secular Liberalism. In principle many churchmen, including Maurice, believed that it was the right and duty of the Church to educate the children of England, while a number of Radicals, particularly Benthamite Radicals, were anxious to impose a universal system of education on the country. These educational enthusiasts had not much success with the first reformed Parliament, for all that was obtained in 1833 was the distribution of £20,000 to the National Society and to the British and Foreign Society to help in the building of school houses. But the issue did not die. In 1837 and 1838 Lord Brougham made moves towards the establishment of a State-controlled system of education and in 1839 the government took steps which seemed to point in that direction. These were resisted and a compromise system more satisfactory to the Church was introduced.

Maurice took part in this struggle. He wrote a pamphlet on the rights of the Church in national education, and he became involved in the agitation against the government's plans, an experience which for some reason gave him a distaste for the procedures of political agitation. Popular education is, of course, an important social question, but it does not seem as if Maurice's motives were primarily inspired by the challenge of the condition of England, at least initially. That was to come later. In 1848 a young associate of his, inspired by the excitement and high hopes generated by the revolution in Paris, wrote him a letter which brought squarely to his attention the nature of the social morality that had prevailed in France and England in the last twenty years or so, and the evil conditions that had resulted from them. Then indeed it became clear to him that if the Church occupied the position which he had claimed for it in its relations with government and society, it was his duty as a priest of the established Church to condemn both what was notoriously evil in the practice of society and what was wrong with the principles of universal competition

[1] Thomas Chalmers, D.D., LL.D., *Lectures on the Establishment and Extension of National Churches delivered in London from April 25th to May 12th 1838* (Glasgow, 1838).

which economists seemed to claim unavoidably dominated all the transactions of mankind. From these two convictions sprang the movement of Christian Socialists.

Maurice's views were idiosyncratic. He had not been originally a member of the Church and his view of the establishment was not something sanctioned by long usage and hereditary influences; he was not primarily a scholar, but seems to have reached his conclusions by reflecting on what seemed to him to be of primary spiritual importance rather than by a study of origins. For him therefore the threat to the traditional position of the historic Church may not have appeared as it did either to an hereditary churchman, or to an Oxford student; to such men the whole course of affairs was likely to seem full of menace; for many a disastrous train of events had started with the concession of Catholic emancipation in 1829.

A number of people felt that the admission of Roman Catholics to Parliament was a betrayal of the moral basis of the British constitution which till that date had been based on the identity of Church and State. This raised an important point; but the feeling was in itself illogical, since Protestant dissenters had been permitted to be members of the House of Commons since the seventeenth century. However, men's prejudices are not often logical and this action seemed to be the beginning of the destruction of the age-old relationships between Church and State, a process which the crisis of the Reform Act and its aftermath suggested might be pressed to the bitter end. But if that happened two questions would have to be faced. One of them would have seemed important to Maurice, the question of what would happen to the State if it lost the moral guidance and spiritual authority it had gained from the Church? The other might have impinged less on his consciousness: what would happen to the historical Church of England if it was parted from the State?

It was a question which had been answered with great ingenuity by Coleridge in a tract which he wrote in 1830 on *The Constitution of Church and State*. Coleridge recognized the moral significance of the union of Church and State, but in the historic Church which had been partner to the State he perceived two bodies. They might be made up of the same people, they might in present circumstances share the same organization and use the same endowments; but their functions were different and the sanction behind their authority was different, and therefore they could be separated. There was on the one hand the clerisy, the body of educated opinion upon which the moral guidance of the country depended, and on the other there was the Catholic Church, part of which was to be found in England, but which was peculiar to no nation, was subject to no nation and would be unaffected by anything the State might do to its national Church or clerisy. This was clearly a conception of the greatest value in the crisis which seemed to be developing. For if the State repudiated its connection with the Church there would still remain for churchmen the Catholic Church, and that it could not touch.

Significantly, this idea appealed to one whose primary interest was not in the secular functions of the clerisy, not in the political or social influence of the Church, but in the Church as the historic guardian of revealed truth and as the body charged with the administration of the sacraments. The connection between the thoughts of Coleridge and the development of the ideas of John Henry Newman is not quite clear. Certainly Newman said that he read Coleridge's work for the first time in 1835 and was surprised, to quote his own words, 'how much I thought mine is to be found there'. But Newman's ideas had been germinating for some time, and in some ways they were subtly and significantly different from those of Coleridge. However, Coleridge's ideas were well known and it seems possible that Newman had been influenced by them before 1835.[1]

What is clear is that Newman was profoundly affected by the situation in 1833. The tension had developed slowly; in 1830 and 1831 Newman does not seem to have been unduly disturbed. He was an anti-reformer and rejoiced that the bishops were playing so bold a part. He noted the arrival of the cholera and distributed papers to tell his parishioners what they should do if it reached Littlemore, but he seems to have

---

[1] Newman, *Letters* [op. cit., p. 50] Vol. II, p. 39n. For a comparison of the thought of Newman with that of Coleridge, see John Coulson, *Newman and the Common Tradition* (Oxford, 1970), particularly the appendix on 'How much of Coleridge had Newman read?', pp. 254–5.

been preoccupied mainly with a book on the Arians which he was writing. He seems to have spent the summer of 1832 completing his book, though it appears that he also had to deal with the need to destroy the bedclothes and effects of the one fatal case of cholera at Littlemore. In December he went on holiday to Italy and was in Rome when the news of the Act which abolished the Irish bishoprics reached him. This shocked him. However, he pressed on without his companions for a further tour in Sicily. There he fell dangerously ill, and while he lay at the door of death the full impact of the crisis seems to have come home to him, so much so that he says he was sustained in his illness by the thought that God would not allow him to die since it was clear that He had work for him to do in England. When he was well enough he struggled home, so angry with triumphant Liberalism that at Algiers he would not look at the tricolour on a French vessel, and in Paris he would not go out of doors, presumably because Paris had been desecrated by the July Revolution.[1]

When he reached Oxford he found a counter-attack already gathering force. There had been meetings to discuss what was to be done and on 14 July, the Sunday after his return, Keble preached his famous sermon on 'National Apostasy'. In the autumn the various activities which initiated the Oxford Movement got under way. Newman's chief contribution was, of course, to start the *Tracts*. The first of these, written by Newman but published anonymously, is sufficiently melodramatic. In it he says of the bishops, 'we could not wish them a more blessed termination of their course than the spoiling of their goods, and martyrdom.' However the line he takes is significant. He asks of the clergy: 'Should the Government and Country so far forget their God as to cast off the Church, to deprive it of its temporal honours and substance, *on what* will you rest the claim of respect which you will make on your flocks?' The answer was of course on the fact that they were priests of the Catholic Church. They should depend on the sacred gift which 'has been handed down to our present Bishops, who have appointed us as their assistants, and in some sort as their representatives'. It is an answer which is implicit in Coleridge's *Church and State*, but with this difference: New-

---

[1] Newman's *Apologia* (Oxford, 1913) pp. 135–6.

man seems to be exclusively interested in the purely theological side of the matter. The liberalism he feared was not a political but a theological conception; he defines it in his *Apologia* as 'the mistake of subjecting to human judgement those revealed doctrines which are in their nature beyond and independent of it', doctrines which must rest for their reception on the authority of the word of God received through the Church.[1] What was to be resisted in 1833 or 1834 was therefore not so much the disestablishment or disendowment of the Church as an attempt by the government to interfere with its formularies, or to impose unsuitable rulers upon it.

The sequel is well known. The social and political issues faded into insignificance; the theological problem grew gradually to be all-absorbing. It raised the question whether the Church of England was really part of the Catholic Church, and thus led to the crisis of 1845 and the moment when Newman left Littlemore, already a member of the Church of Rome.

Yet even Newman's history was not unaffected by the results of the challenge of the condition of England, and it certainly played its part in the minds of many of those who were disposed to follow him. The crisis of 1845 was precipitated by the condemnation of a book called *The Ideal of a Christian Church* published in 1844 by a fellow of Balliol named W. G. Ward. The book is a powerful indictment of the Church of England as Ward imagined it to be. Many of the counts that Ward makes are dogmatic and ecclesiastical, but he also accuses the Church of England for its failure in its social duties and he lays to its charge the evil social conditions which had come into existence in the country. By an irony of chance he chose as his source for information on this topic the evangelical work, *The Perils of the Nation*, whose author apparently derived much of her information from the pastoral experience of the clergymen of the Church of England.[2]

Ward's use of this particular issue is possibly adventitious. What probably is more significant is the effect which the

[1] ibid. p. 394.
[2] W. G. Ward, *The ideal of a Christian Church considered in comparison with existing practice containing a Defence of certain articles in the British critic in reply to remarks on them in Mr. Palmer's 'narrative'* (1844) pp. 27–30.

shadow of the condition of England had on those who were also attracted by the ways of thought that contributed to the Oxford Movement. An interesting example of the kind of literature that was influencing young people at this moment is reflected in the letters of a pupil of Ward's, Frederick Temple. Temple was the son of a distinguished soldier. He himself had known poverty; he must be one of the few archbishops of Canterbury who had at one time followed the plough. He came up to Balliol in 1839 and it is interesting to read in the letters to his sister and mother how he reacted to the things which were likely to influence a young man at Oxford at that time. He read Carlyle's *Chartism*, admired Newman's sermons, owed much to Wordsworth and read Coleridge and Keats, and no doubt responded to the teaching of Ward, who was kind to him. The result of all this was to create in him a deep dissatisfaction with the social practice of the Church of England and a belief that the Roman Catholic Church, through the devotion of its religious orders, was giving much better service to the poor.[1]

Temple's loyalty to the Church of England was too deeply rooted for him to be tempted to follow Newman and Ward; instead, he found the answer to his own problem in the surrender of his fellowship at Balliol to enter the embryonic education service, and he became in 1849 the head of a college for the training of workhouse schoolmasters. However, his dissatisfaction with what appeared to him to be the comfortable compromises of the Church of England and his admiration for the total commitment of the members of the religious orders of the Roman Catholic Church seems to typify what a good many young people were feeling at this point. Very often it took the form of a comparison between what were believed to be the habits of Church and society in nineteenth-century England with their vision of 'the middle ages' or 'the ages of faith'. The clearest example of this attitude is probably to be found in the illustrations to Pugin's *Contrasts*. It was a comparison of very doubtful historical validity, for the medieval England of which men dreamed had little to do with anything that had ever existed. But that is a point of little importance. What mattered was not the accuracy of the picture of the past which men used

---

[1] E. G. Sandford, ed., *Memoirs of Frederick Temple by Seven Friends* (2 vols., 1906) Vol. I, p. 70; Vol. II, pp. 422, 440, 456, 477.

as a touchstone, but the criticisms of contemporary society that the comparison evoked and the actions it inspired.[1]

For to not a few these ideas seemed to lead away from the shams, the soiled complacencies, the half beliefs of the England into which they had been born; and they followed where these ideas pointed. For some the road to truth led into the Roman Catholic Church, a journey which might well mean separation from friends, the renunciation of worldly ambitions and, possibly, penury in what were for them unavoidably alien surroundings. Others remained in the Church of England often at issue with their ecclesiastical superiors and many of their fellow clergy. Some became the ritualist clergy who worked in the slums, and confronted hostile mobs, partly of enraged Protestants and partly recruited by more sinister agencies. Others, both men and women, took part in the remarkable revival of religious orders in the English Church and faced the obloquy which monks, and in particular nuns, had to face in Protestant England, until the devotion shown by the Sisters of Mercy in nursing the cholera taught men their worth.[2]

Any survey of the scene in England between the First Reform Act and the middle of the nineteenth century will suggest how various and vigorous were the movements stirring within the Church of England. They did not make for peace in the Church. The evangelicals viewed with horror the behaviour of the ritualists, and the doctrine of the Liberals, and developed ugly habits of persecution and journalistic denunciation. Arnold sternly condemned Newman and his followers, and Newman seems to have believed that it would provide sufficient reason for the separation of Church and State were the government to make Arnold a bishop.[3] Maurice was hounded from his professorship at King's College on account of the laxness of his views on eternal punishment. The ritualists were the cause of prolonged controversy of a peculiar bitterness. Yet most of the members of these groups had certain points in common.

[1] On this, see Alice Chandler, *A Dream of Order. The Medieval Ideal in Nineteenth Century Literature* (1971).

[2] See A. M. Allchin, *The Silent Rebellion. Anglican Religious Communities 1845–1900* (1958).

[3] Newman, *Letters* [op. cit., p. 50] Vol. I, p. 450.

Most of them were impressed in one way or other by the challenge of the condition of England, and most of those who remained in the Church of England saw that their answer must be in terms of their duty as members of an established Church. That is, they saw that as members of a Church they had a responsibility not just for the elect but for the whole nation and, if they were parish priests, they knew that they had a responsibility for every man who lived in their parishes, even if he did not attend their churches or accept the validity of their ministrations. It was very largely in the parishes that the social conception of the establishment was to be worked out.

All this raises an important question. If churchmen still in mid century conceived that they had a special relationship with the nation, how after 1832 was the State, which wielded the power of the nation, going to act towards the Church? It was a question which could only be answered in terms of what happened in secular politics, and the critical period seems to be between 1835, when the reaction which might have renewed the union between Church and State had begun to take shape, and 1846, which was the end of Peel's ministry. What happened then might with profit be seen through the eyes of a number of different observers. It might, for instance, be seen through the eyes of Lord Ashley, who was a minister under Peel in 1835 but turned his back angrily on Peel in 1841 and throughout the years that followed. Or it might be seen through the eyes of the churchmen of the West Riding and Lancashire who hoped that Peel's government would mean factory reform and the reform of the New Poor Law, or those of an old-fashioned Tory like Sir Robert Inglis who hoped that it would supply a State subsidy for church extension. But it seems best to follow through the experience of a young man who during the years of opposition was an influential spokesman for the Church party, and then became an active minister in Peel's government.

W. E. Gladstone was the son of a strongly evangelical Liverpool merchant. He went to Eton and Oxford and while at Oxford adhered to his father's school of churchmanship. He was a deeply religious young man, and at one time wished to take orders. He was, however, diverted into politics. In 1833 he became a Tory member of Parliament and in 1834–5 achieved junior office. In politics he remained primarily interested in Church matters, and his own studies and friendships drew him into a close association with the Oxford Movement. Between 1837 and 1839 he performed an important service for the Church. These were years in which it seemed possible that a State-controlled, probably secular system of popular education might be imposed on the country. As a counter to this Gladstone, working with such friends as Thomas Dyke Acland and R. F. Wood, contrived to put new life into the National Society and developed among other things the scheme of supplying inspectors for schools and training colleges for teachers which were of the greatest value to the Church when the time for compromise came.[1]

The educational issue necessarily raised the question of the relation of the State to the Church, for if the Church occupied in the State the position which its friends believed it should occupy, then it was the duty of the Church to educate the children of the nation and of the State to help the Church in this task, and probably to help no other body. Moreover, apart from this, in these years the whole problem of Church and State was in the air, and so in 1838 Gladstone produced his first book, *The State in its relations with the Church*, which spelled out his principles. It is on the whole a more learned book than Maurice's *Kingdom of Christ*; indeed it is rather obviously the book of an able young man, just down from the university, who has read widely on a chosen subject. As a corollary it lacks, as Gladstone came to think in later life, some of that sense of reality which comes from experience and not from books. But the books he cited led Gladstone to ask the right question: of what nature is the moral authority of the State? Gladstone's answer was that to do what it does do, to make the claims it does make, the State must be conceived to be a moral personality with a knowledge of right and wrong which is analogous to that of an ordinary human being. For this reason the State must recognize the truths upon which the rules of right conduct are based. These truths are religious, therefore the State must accept a form of religion which will endorse them, and for this pur-

---

[1] H. J. Burgess [op. cit., p. 48] pp. 67–75, E. S. Purcell, *Life of Cardinal Manning* (2 vols., 1896) Vol. I, pp. 147–51.

pose it must accept and support an established Church which will maintain that version of the truth which the State has accepted.

Gladstone's views differ from those in Arnold's pamphlet, but it is important to recognize that in certain points they agree. Each saw that the State was an institution with purposes wider than the mere maintenance of law and order. Each saw that it must do some things not because they were common necessities but because they were morally right, and that consequently it must represent a conception with a deeper moral content than a mere union of convenience could provide. Each therefore saw that the State must possess a conscience to identify right from wrong. Since both were Christians, they believed that it was of the highest importance that the morality which guided the State should be Christian morality, and they tried to guarantee that this should be so by ensuring that an important component of the institutions of the State should be some sort of Christian establishment.

About the nature of that establishment they differed. But each scheme was subject to one of the two major objections that prevent any scheme which tries to solve this question by uniting a modern State with a Christian Church from working satisfactorily. On the one hand a Christian Church cannot be made a mere adjunct to the secular State and reshaped for its convenience with such rough surgery as Arnold wished to use. On the other hand a modern State will contain men of differing religious beliefs, or of no religious beliefs, and cannot be made the instrument of any one Church, or of any one version of Christianity.

Coleridge had tried to turn the flank of these difficulties by differentiating between the 'Catholic Church' and the 'established Church' or 'clerisy', so that the 'Catholic Church' and the 'clerisy' could be separated if the need of the State, or the integrity of the Church, demanded it. But, at least under nineteenth-century conditions, the separation would have been difficult and in any case the 'clerisy' remained an amorphous and unconvincing conception. Newman escaped these difficulties by joining a Church which was not established in the United Kingdom. Gladstone relied on what had become the classical Anglican doctrine of toleration. He accepted the sacredness of the right of personal decision on the part of those who dissented from the doctrines of the Church, but denied that this right carried with it the principle that all religious bodies had the right to claim complete religious equality. It was a doctrine that those who were to be merely tolerated had never believed to be satisfactory and, as the nineteenth century went forward and their strength increased, dissenters were not to grow the more satisfied with it.

Contrary to a prevailing impression, when his book appeared it had a reasonable success. Gladstone's friends, and they were neither few nor unintelligent, applauded it. Eminent ecclesiastics read it, and it must have appealed to a fairly wide public for it went quickly through four editions, the last a heavily revised one which appeared in 1841. It did not however please everyone. In 1839 Macaulay delivered a swingeing attack upon the second edition in the April number of the *Edinburgh Review*. This certainly did not kill Gladstone's book. It went on to two more editions, and then interest in it died. Its demise seems rather to have been the result of a change in the focus of discussion than of Macaulay's butchery. However, in due course the view developed that Macaulay's answer to Gladstone had been conclusive and final. It is an opinion which has on the whole been endorsed by those who have written Gladstone's life, which is the more unfortunate because this book and its fate seem to have had an important bearing on the central problem of Gladstone's career, at least as Gladstone saw it – the problem of how to relate the facts of politics to the will of God. As a result most people have contented themselves with reading Macaulay's rhetoric without taking trouble to find out what it was Gladstone was trying to say.

Even so Macaulay's arguments have not satisfied everyone. Leslie Stephen, for instance, saw the limitations of Macaulay's case and, more recently, Dr A. R. Vidler, in an important book, has placed Gladstone's views in their right perspective.[1] But even without Dr Vidler's assistance, it seems strange that Macaulay's criticism should have satisfied so many people for so long. Many of Macaulay's review articles were not in any

[1] Leslie Stephen, *Hours in a Library* (1st edn. 1876, 5th edn. 1909, 3 vols.) Vol. 2, pp. 331-3. A. R. Vidler, B.D., *The Orb and the Cross. A Normative Study in the Relations of Church and State with Reference to Gladstone's Early Writings* (1945).

real sense reviews of the book he was considering: they were
either general essays on subjects which the book suggested, or
polemical exercises. When intent on polemics he did not try
too hard to understand what his victim was trying to say; he
reconnoitred the position to see what points offered possibilities
for effective attack and then directed on to those points all his
formidable powers of bombardment and assault. In this case he
does not seem to have troubled himself much to find out what
problem it was that Gladstone was trying to discuss, or what
was the issue raised by the authorities which Gladstone had
carefully cited; though it might have been thought that at the
least the name and words of Burke would have given Macaulay
pause for thought. He attacked Gladstone effectively at his
weakest point, the issue of toleration, and he delivered a summary, and extemporized, on the opinion about the nature of
the State, which he triumphantly contrasted with the views
which he imputed to Gladstone.

All men, he said, were agreed on some of the objects of civil
government. They were agreed that civil government 'is designed to compel us to satisfy our wants, not by rapine but by
industry; that it is designed to compel us to settle our differences, not by the strong hand but by arbitration; that it is
designed to direct our whole force, as that of one man, against
any other society which may offer us injury'. Since these were
necessities which all must recognize there was no need to invoke
the authority of God, or the sanctions of a future life, to endorse the State's right to deal with them. Certainly men had
other needs which were of eternal significance. These made
necessary the propagation of religious truth; but such needs
were 'entirely distinct' from those common necessities on which
all men were agreed. On the subject of these eternal needs men
were indeed in profound disagreement: 'We must therefore
pause before we admit that the persons, be they who they may,
who were entrusted with power for the promotion of the former
object,' that is to secure these common necessities, 'ought
always to use that power for the promotion of the latter object', that is the promotion of the objects of eternal significance
for mankind.[1]

[1] Thomas Babington Lord Macaulay, *Critical and Historical Essays* (ed. in
5 vols., 1890) Vol. III, p. 281.

It is important to recognize that this view not only tended to preclude the State from the propagation of any form of religion, but also from the promotion of any object which went beyond the basic necessities of ordered life, and on which men might disagree. It is true that Macaulay said that the State ought to perform some functions which went beyond the mere protection of life and property, if it could do so without prejudice to the performance of its primary functions. But these were trivial functions – the purchase of works of art, the bestowal of patronage on learned men, the encouragement of geographical and astronomical discoveries.[1] He deplored any wide extension of the power of the State, and questioned Gladstone's conception that the duties of government were 'paternal; a doctrine that we shall not believe till he can show us some government which loves its subjects as a father loves a child, and which is as superior in intelligence to its subjects as a father to a child'. He therefore attacked Gladstone's conception of the general moral authority of the State, and said that if that conception was accepted he did not see why rulers should not assume all the functions which Plato had assigned to them. 'Why should not they take away the child from the mother, select the nurse, regulate the school, overlook the playground, fix the hours of labour and recreation?'[2] But there is no need to follow him when he is in that vein.

Gladstone's case was compromised by his wish to justify the duty of the State to promulgate the doctrine of the Church of England and by the difficulty of combining this principle with the need to extend complete toleration for any form of individual belief. Nevertheless it can be claimed that Gladstone saw the issue at stake, and that in this review Macaulay was pleased not to do so. Gladstone saw, as Arnold saw, as Maurice saw, as Coleridge and Burke had seen, as indeed Bentham had seen, that the State must have a wider moral authority than it could receive from the fact that it offered protection to life and property. In this article Macaulay dismissed such a possibility with ridicule and contempt. However, the theoretical implications of either point of view are not what is most important

[1] ibid., Vol. III, p. 338.
[2] ibid., Vol. III, p. 281.

here. What is important is that neither could be maintained consistently in the conditions that prevailed in mid nineteenth-century England.

Nemesis visited Gladstone first. In 1841 he produced the fourth edition of his book and in 1841, also, Peel became prime minister. He sent for Gladstone and offered him the post of vice-president of the Board of Trade. Gladstone was disappointed. He had rather absurdly hoped to gain office in the Cabinet, and he also believed that his interests lay in Church matters, not in trade. Peel, however, treated him with fatherly firmness. Gladstone was not permitted to refuse the office, and working under Peel's guidance he devoted his great powers to subjects which were, in fact, going to occupy much of the rest of his life. In due course he became president of the Board of Trade with a seat in the Cabinet, and he played an important part in the crucial fiscal revolution which began with Peel's reformed tariff in 1842 and ended in the repeal of the Corn Laws.

As a result Gladstone became a major figure in politics. But he had not done what he had set out to do. Many churchmen had by now become completely aware of the desperate need for the Church to extend its ministrations into those pagan areas which had slipped from its grasp. To do this it would be necessary to build churches and establish parishes, and many churchmen in the Conservative party had believed that the State would, and should, make a grant of money to help with this work, as it had done before 1830. This was a policy which appealed to Sir Robert Inglis, it was a policy which appealed to Lord Ashley, and in his book Gladstone had maintained that it was the duty of the State to supply such means as would enable the Church to do its work. But it was not a policy that commended itself to Sir Robert Peel. He did not believe that in the circumstances that had developed since the Reform Act it was politically desirable for the Church to go to the Exchequer for grants for the building of churches and the establishment of parishes. The policy he was determined to follow was the one he had initiated in 1835 by appointing the Ecclesiastical Commission to redeploy the Church's own finances to meet these needs. This policy he renewed with another act, passed in 1843, and he himself subscribed handsomely to the work. He was probably right in following this policy; he was a good friend to the Church and his sense of political reality was acute. But the fact remained that Gladstone was a prominent member of a Cabinet which was not doing what he had said it was the duty of the British government to do.

There was worse to come. Gladstone had not only said in his book that the government should give help to the established Church, but that it must not supply funds for any other Church, and he had given as his instance the grant made to the Irish Roman Catholic seminary at Maynooth. Of this he had said: 'In principle it is wholly vicious; and it can hardly fail to be a thorn in the side of these countries so long as it may continue.' In 1845, so far from abolishing the grant Peel determined to increase it as part of his policy for conciliating Ireland. Gladstone approved of Peel's policy, he saw the necessity for the increase of the grant; but he also felt that the contents of his book compelled him to retire from office. Peel was mystified and annoyed. He could not understand why a man should resign on account of a policy of which he approved, and he found it hard to understand Gladstone's letters, which were certainly made more difficult by those refinements of meaning to which, unfortunately, Gladstone was a lifelong addict. In fact, however, the reason for Gladstone's resignation is clear. It was a valedictory sacrifice on behalf of principles which he now knew could never be realized.[1]

Gladstone himself seems to have produced no new theory to replace the one that had broken in his hand. He did, however, see that it was desirable for the Church to withdraw from its old position. In 1863 he told the bishop of Oxford: 'The whole of my public life with respect to matters ecclesiastical, for the last twenty years or more, has been a continuous effort though a very weak one, to extricate her' (that is the Church) 'in some degree from entangled relations without shock or violence'.[2] That was no doubt in the circumstances the only sensible policy, but it had not been the policy of

[1] W. E. Gladstone, *The State in its Relations with the Church* (4th edn. revised and enlarged in two vols., 1841). The relevant passages in his book are Vol. I, p. 244; Vol. II, p. 300.

[2] John Morley, *The Life of William Ewart Gladstone* (3 vols., edn. 1903) Vol. II, p. 159.

the dynamic young churchman who in 1841 had been sent unwillingly to school among the ledgers of the Board of Trade.

It would, however, be wrong to think of what had happened only in terms of Gladstone's personal history. In later life Gladstone sometimes seemed to suggest that this collapse of principle was peculiar to himself. This is a misapprehension. Others had hoped that the government would produce funds for the 'propagation of the national creed', others had deplored the grant to Maynooth. They were mistaken in their assessment of political realities, but it was not a mistake confined to old-fashioned Protestants or out-of-date Tories. In 1843 Sir James Graham, the home secretary, had introduced a factory bill which contained clauses providing education for the factory children. Since these children were the responsibility of the State it had seemed natural to Graham to organize schools for them which would be largely under the control of the Church of England. In doing so he had not intended any denominational aggression, but he had completely misunderstood the situation. When the educational clauses were produced the fury of the dissenters rose to fever heat, and the bill had to be withdrawn and reintroduced in 1844 with those clauses modified. The fierceness of this agitation seems to have taught the wisest of the clergy that the Church could not hope to provide, with the help of the government, schools for all the children of England, and they began to feel their way towards a system which would use partially voluntarily supported denominational schools where it could, but supply those areas which the denominational schools did not cover with undenominational schools financed from the rates.

This was the policy embodied in Forster's education act in 1870 as it was first introduced, but the switch in policy seems to have started in 1843. In fact in a number of ways it seems to have become clear between 1841 and 1846 that though the Church of England was still established, though many of its ministers, particularly the parochial clergy, saw their duties as being those of ministers of an established Church, the union of Church and State was not what it had been before 1830. Thus was brought to an end a long tradition which stretched from Hooker to Gladstone, because it was no longer possible to act on Hooker's premise: 'With us one society is both the Church and Commonwealth.'[1]

If, however, political commonsense forbade the retention of Gladstone's theory, common humanity prevented the application of the view that Macaulay had put forward. The condition of England demanded a State which accepted much wider obligations than could be justified by the need to satisfy those minimal, unanimously accepted, requirements which Macaulay had enumerated. Macaulay himself accepted this. On 22 May 1846 he delivered an eloquent speech in favour of the Ten Hours Bill which restricted the hours of labour of factory children, in which he enforced the duty of the State to make regulations to protect 'public health and public morals'. He reiterated this principle the following year. In 1847 the government grant for education was increased. This raised anew the whole issue of the government's right to interfere with education. The government's action was attacked on a point of principle by the Congregational Union, and in the House of Commons the grant was opposed by a Radical called Duncombe. Duncombe was answered by Macaulay, then a minister of the crown. In a famous speech he roundly asserted the right, and duty, of the State to provide for the education of the people. He talked of the civilizing effects of education, and attacked a theory which he said came into existence in 1846, that the State was nothing more than 'a great hangman', that the statesman could only repress and that he must not think of forming the character of the population.[2] It would be interesting to reconstruct the mounting ridicule with which Macaulay would have greeted this argument had he found it in Gladstone's work less than ten years earlier.

If both Gladstone's and Macaulay's opinions were inapposite, it might have been thought that a working compromise could have been established whereby the State could have been endowed with sufficient moral authority to do what was necessary for the country without asking men to accept the privi-

---

[1] Hooker, *On the Laws of Ecclesiastical Polity*, Bk. VIII, Ch. I, para. 7 (*Works*, 2 vols., Oxford, 1865, Vol. II, p. 493).
[2] Lord Macaulay, *Miscellaneous Writing and Speeches* (edn. 1882) pp. 718–29 (speech on 22 May 1846), pp. 734–48 (speech on 18 April 1847).

leged position of the Church. Unfortunately the middle of the nineteenth century was not a period in which compromise was probable, if compromise means the rational combination of divergent opinions for practical ends. It was rather a period when contradictory opinions continued to survive in a political system which gave unusually ample opportunities for debate and was unusually well adapted for the obstruction of decisive action and the interruption of consistent policies. The prominent members of the Church of England may have realized that the Church could not return to that effective union with the State that had existed before 1830, yet they retained sufficiently large pretensions, and enjoyed sufficiently extensive privileges, to antagonize militant dissent. In educational matters many dissenters retained sufficiently rigid principles to make it impossible for them to collaborate with the government in the provision of schools. Many people could be convinced that a particular evil was so intolerable that legislation should be passed to control it and were even prepared to assent to some form of government agency to give that legislation effect. On the other hand many people, often the same people, adhered to something like the view of the functions of the State which Macaulay had advanced in his review of Gladstone's book. They talked about the virtues of the 'voluntary principle', or if some government authority had come into existence they harassed it lest it should inflict on the country the evils of 'centralization'. And all the time there were large numbers of people who had strong objections to any expenditure of public money.

The result was not that the evils which the condition of the country had produced were ignored, but that they were often ineffectively handled. This is not so much a period of complacency as of confusion. What was lacking was not a public conscience but sufficient clarity of mind, singleness of purpose and will power to do what was needed. The policy followed was too often uncertain in object, insufficient in scope and liable to be interrupted by inconclusive, if often violent, controversy and the vagaries of an undisciplined House of Commons.

The results of this situation can be read in the history of what were possibly the two most significant problems of social policy: how to safeguard public health in an overcrowded un-drained country in which disease was rampant and unspeak-able slums housed very large numbers of the people, and how to provide a general system of at least elementary education for all. At any point in this period these problems were very im-portant and very urgent, and what is more many people were at least intermittently aware of their importance and urgency, while a number of people were determined to do all that they could to find answers to them. Yet Parliament's treatment of these issues was hag-ridden by controversy and very often befogged by ignorance and prejudice; nor were ministers always in better case. Consequently the policy which was hammered out was insufficient, discontinuous and inconsistent. The lead which was given by those two great public servants Edwin Chadwick and Kay-Shuttleworth was not followed, and not till 1866 in the case of public health, and 1870 in the case of public education, did Parliament begin to impose com-mon standards on the whole country.

The result of this was that most of the important develop-ments of social policy in this period were, at least in part, the result of private enterprise and local initiative. The local initiative came from a variety of sources – the leading citizens in certain towns, professional bodies, local medical practi-tioners and charitable élites. But an important part was played by the parochial clergy of the Church of England. They did what they did partly under the influence of the moral climate of mid nineteenth-century England and in response to the ideas it engendered, but partly in continuance of practices which had originated before 1830 and were conceived in terms of the social pattern of the old regime. But whatever their motives, their activities are important in the context of English social history.

It is, therefore, to the activities of mid nineteenth-century parsons in their parishes that the next four chapters will be devoted.

4

The Mid Nineteenth-Century Parson

The Education of the People

One of the traditional duties of a parish priest was the instruction of the young in the elements of the faith. This could either be performed through catechetical instruction in the church, or in a school. The foundation of a school could be combined with what was a favourite object of charity from the middle ages onwards, the provision of free education for poor children. Both laity and clergy were active in this work, and as a result a number of free schools, or schools with free places, had come into existence, the number of which was greatly increased by the charity school movement in the reign of Queen Anne. In the sixteenth and seventeenth centuries, and probably later, a number of village schools also existed, possibly conducted in the church itself: over the porch at Melbourne in Cambridgeshire, in the chancel at Girton or Willingham in Cambridgeshire, in the Lady Chapel at Long Melford in Suffolk.

However, at any period before the development of the inquisitive newspaper press and the reforming spirit of the nineteenth century, old institutions could easily subside into inanition, and old emoluments find their way into private pockets as sinecure income. In due course a number of schools faded into nothing. Others, however, remained active, and it would be interesting to take a census of the education available in 1750 or 1760 in different parts of the country, particularly for poor boys and girls. Towards the end of the century with the revival of religion the educational ideals of churchmen also revived. The pioneer seems to have been Robert Raikes, a pious newspaper proprietor of Gloucester. With the aid of a local clergyman, Thomas Stock, he initiated the Sunday school movement; the first school was started in 1780 and after that the movement spread rapidly.

In the eighteenth century educational development was not always the work of the clergy, indeed the clergy hindered rather than helped Hannah More's activities; but in the first thirty years of the nineteenth century an increasing number of the clergy seem to have taken their educational duties seriously. In 1811 the National Society was founded largely under clerical auspices. The early history of William Barnes the Dorset poet shows how much a farmer's son could owe to education provided by local clergymen, these being in his case, T. H. Lane Fox of Sturminster, up to 1815, and then after 1815 J. H. Richman, rector of Holy Trinity and St Peter's at Dorchester. It became the ambition of a conscientious clergyman entering upon a cure to start, if not a day school, at least a Sunday school. In 1825, having become in 1824 curate of St Clements in Oxford, Newman managed to get a Sunday school started, which, since he could not get hold of a room, met in the church. In 1829 W. F. Hook became vicar of Holy Trinity in Coventry. Sunday schools already existed there, but when he arrived the children only numbered 120. By 1834 he had increased the number to 524 boys and 407 girls, and in 1830 he was already trying to establish an infant school, as well as a dispensary and a savings bank. H. S. Hawker, the remarkable vicar of Morwenstowe in Cornwall, arrived at his cure in 1834. He found that the children had to meet for school in a tumbledown cottage, and though he had also to face the heavy responsibility of building a vicarage, he built a school at his own expense in 1843.

These are chance examples of what was beginning to happen everywhere. Possibly after 1830 some of the impetus had gone out of the National Society; if so it was reinvigorated by Gladstone and his friends after 1838, and after 1839 there was more government money available. Even so the initiative still rested with the local clergy, and this fact raises an important consideration. Since they were providing an important public service there is a tendency to consider what was, or was not, done in terms of modern social policy and where the motives of those who were responsible cannot be explained in those terms, to substitute other motives which nowadays seem to be more intelligible, or to blame those involved for their obscurantism. This is, however, a failure to allow for the perspective of history. In order to understand their motives it is necessary to try to enter the minds of the clergy of more than a hundred years ago.

It is not too easy for a modern man to do this. Since the nineteenth century many people have forgotten what it was like to believe in Christianity, or, where the faith remains it has often shrunk into a formless and unsubstantial phantom at the back of the mind. It is not easy to recapture a state of mind in which it may be taken for granted that the acceptance or rejection of a particular belief would have decisive results for the happiness and good conduct of a man or woman in this life, and also in the after life. However, such assumptions would come naturally to a mid nineteenth-century parson and would unavoidably affect his view of the objects of the education which his school should provide. It was certainly realized that attendance at a day school, and possibly at a Sunday school, would provide secular advantages for a child; for it was clearly to his advantage in this life to learn to read, to write and to have some smattering of arithmetic. But it was natural for a clergyman to think that a child's most urgent need was to be fitted not so much for this life as for eternity. For this end it was more important than anything else that he should be taught the doctrines of the Church, and those rules of conduct which should bring a man peace at the last.

Seen in retrospect this outlook may have been unfortunate. The emphasis on religious teaching upset the balance of much education, the emphasis on the formularies of the Church made co-operation with Dissent difficult, and the belief that training in the knowledge and practice of religion might teach the poor to live better-regulated lives and abstain from such activities as rioting, rick-burning, poaching, or other forms of subversion that menaced the social order had morally dangerous possibilities. It was a consideration which might give an ugly twist to what men conceived to be the objects of religious education. It was particularly dangerous when education was so largely in the hands of men who believed that the hierarchy of society was necessary for social order and had been ordained by God; and that therefore it was a man's duty to obey and respect his betters.

How far teaching along these lines pervaded the teaching in church schools it would be difficult to say, but unfortunately it was certainly often present. Two things seem to be clear, however. It did not vitiate the advantage of much of the education that was given, and the desire to teach the poor to keep in their place was not the sole, or even the primary, motive of most of those who organized church education. To believe this one would have to disregard a mass of positive evidence about what men thought they were doing and to assume for the historian a right to reinterpret, and simplify, men's motives which is beyond what scholarship can allow. Nor is it credible that parsons would have done what they did do, making the sacrifices they did make, to teach the illiterate to read with the sole object of keeping the poor in check. Furthermore, such an attitude would be most unlikely at a time when many employers, particularly farmers, were ready to say that education rendered labour unmanageable. The best policy for those who wish to keep a class in subjection is to prevent literacy, not to encourage it.

> Since common folk who read and write and like their betters speak
> . . . want something more than pipes and beer and sermons twice a week.[1]

Nevertheless, however truly benevolent men's motives may be, they are likely to be cast in the mould provided by the common ideas of the day. For many people those ideas had been shaped by the unquestioned acceptance of an hierarchical society as a fact of life and that assumption shaped their view of what form popular education should take. They assumed that as the country was stratified into social classes so would the system of education be stratified. The pattern is clearly described in a pamphlet on university education by Whewell, when master of Trinity College, Cambridge.

> The education of the upper classes [he said] is termed *Liberal Education*, and the *Higher Education*; the education of the middle

[1] On the motives for promoting education, see Soloway [op. cit., p. 7] pp. 349–430.

classes will commonly be, in its highest parts, an imitation of the Higher Education, more or less incomplete; and the education of the people, when they are educated, will most generally be an Elementary Education; including little more than the first element of the Higher Education.[1]

It will be noticed that this is a statement not of value, nor of aspiration, but of fact. As a statement of fact it was in its way justified by its realism. In the circumstances of the day it was unlikely that anything more than an elementary education would be supplied for poor boys and girls. They would be fortunate if they got as much, and there was a case, a case which impressed even humane people, that it would make for unhappiness for a child to receive a more elaborate education than he would need in the station of life which he would certainly occupy. This pattern did not, however, preclude the possibility that an able boy might be able to climb from a lower to a higher level. Whewell's statement could hardly have meant that, for he himself was the son of a carpenter in Lancaster, who had taken advantage of the educational opportunities open to him to reach his present position.

Nevertheless the policy which this pattern implied was in reality harsh. It probably denied practicable opportunities of improvement to all but a small section of the population. What was more serious, it took for granted that men and women in lowly stations had no need for the intellectual and spiritual advantages which higher education might bring to anyone, whatever his function in life. It was precisely this assumption which F. D. Maurice and his friends would try to contradict by their foundation of working men's colleges, it also seems to have been in some way disregarded by some of the clergy who developed secondary education; but in the main the clergy seem to have accepted the common conception of a socially stratified system of education. They have as excuses for doing so not only that it was the common assumption but also that even that conception placed on their shoulders a burden which was more than they could carry, for, as they fully realized, the clergy of an established Church were in duty bound to serve each level of this hierarchy.

[1] William Whewell, *Of a Liberal Education in General* (2nd edn., 1850) pp. 1 and 2.

On the highest level, that of the liberal or higher education, possibly the most significant work of the clergy was at first at Oxford and Cambridge; fairly soon, however, they began to supplement this by building up the public school for the gentry, for clergymen's sons, for the would-be gentry and for the nobility. Much of the talent of the Church went into this. The list of clerical headmasters includes Thomas Arnold, Tait, Temple after his training college days, Prince Lee, Butler of Shrewsbury, Butler of Harrow, Benson and Thring. The emoluments of some of these posts were not inconsiderable, and the chance of preferment reasonable; the list I have given contains three archbishops of Canterbury, two bishops and one master of Trinity College, Cambridge. The duties were, however, undoubtedly important. Whewell followed his definition of higher education by defining its function 'as being the education of those who must direct the course of the community'.[1] In mid nineteenth-century conditions, at least, he was right. Perhaps the most significant results of the work which these men did can be seen most clearly not so much in the House of Commons and House of Lords, since the characteristics of those bodies seem to have been largely settled by older, and very varied, traditions, as in the future development of the later nineteenth-century civil service and universities.

The most serious difficulties which the clergy of the established Church had to confront were, probably, in relation to what Whewell called in his stratification, 'the education of the middle classes'. There were a variety of reasons for difficulty here. For one thing the people who might be called 'middle class' for educational purposes formed no coherent social group. They might be members of the professional classes, or even gentry, who could not afford, or did not wish, to pay for the 'higher education'. They might be commercial men or industrialists. They might be shopkeepers or shop assistants. They might be farmers, or clerks, or independent craftsmen, or members of what has been called the aristocracy of labour, who would then have been called 'artisans'. The educational needs of these groups were very various, and to many of them the facilities available were unsuitable. Where they were not torpid the old

[1] ibid., p. 2.

grammar schools were inclined to be confined to a rigid curriculum of Latin and Greek, and even in new schools schoolmasters were apt to trust to these well-tried specifics. It did not seem clear to everyone that this curriculum was the best possible for those who were to spend their lives in commerce, but it was not altogether clear what should be taught in its place. In particular cases other subjects were favoured, but no single form of curriculum could possibly be suitable for all the groups which might be considered to come within this bracket, and indeed the educational needs of some of the groups who were at the bottom of the bracket were not really distinguishable from people who were really working class.

In fact the problems presented by middle-class education were massive, various and complex, and there was no single or agreed solution to them. Suitable schools did not exist, and money must be found to build them. Nor was it clear that as far as the Church was concerned the demand existed. It was not clear that many of those who might be called middle class wanted much in the way of education for their children, and many of those who did were opposed to their children attending church schools, for this was the section of society in which religious Dissent and hostility to the Church of England was most prevalent.

However none of these difficulties prevented churchmen from attempting to gain control of the education of this stratum of society as far as was possible. Indeed the last point, the prevalence of Dissent in this class, acted as a spur rather than a deterrent, for if the Church was to be the Church of the whole nation it was obvious that it must try to recapture this lost territory. Consequently a series of attempts were made in the middle of the nineteenth century to develop middle-class education and to win the middle classes for the Church, which are remarkable for the enterprise of their authors, for the very large sums of money collected for the work and expended upon it, and for the optimism, or ignorance, which led men to address themselves to what was, as a whole, a hopeless task for the Church of England to undertake without assistance.

The first of these attempts was made by Gladstone and his friends when they revived the National Society in 1838 and 1839. Elaborate plans for middle-class education were made.

Country schools were to be expanded so as to offer opportunities for the 'higher branches of instruction', there were to be church commercial schools in the towns, and schools were to be attached to cathedrals. Meanwhile, apparently independently, attempts were being made to found church commercial schools in London and Winchester.

None of this had much staying power. The National Society was preoccupied with the overwhelming task of trying to provide primary education in as many parishes as required it, and its attention and funds were apt to be diverted to that work. In such circumstances it was not easy to find enough money, or probably sufficient local interest, to give the country a general system of secondary schools without the assistance of the State, or even to maintain particular schools. It is significant that what were probably the two most successful attempts in these early years to provide a church school for the middle classes were the personal work of parochial clergymen providing individual schools in their parishes. In 1842 Richard Dawes, rector of King's Samborne in Hampshire, developed a successful school for the children of tradesmen and farmers engrafted on to a national school which was primarily for labourers, and in 1846 Edward Monro, from 1842 to 1860 perpetual curate of Harrow Weald, started a very successful college for poor boys. It is also significant that this last venture was obviously not adequately financed, and disappeared after Monro moved on.

Nevertheless the dream persisted; indeed the man who was to make the most remarkable attempt to give it reality was about to come upon the stage. In 1846 Nathaniel Woodard became assistant curate at New Shoreham and began at once to start a school for his poorer neighbours. In 1848 he published a pamphlet entitled *A Plea for the Middle Classes*. This initiated a scheme for recapturing the middle classes by organizing a hierarchy of schools which should meet the needs of the different levels of the middle section of society. As finally conceived there were to be schools at three levels with their fees adjusted to the class which was going to use them. At the highest level there would be schools which were to be primarily for gentlemen of limited means, then came schools for tradesmen, farmers and the like and last there were schools for tradesmen in a smaller way of business, hucksters, and others who were naturally from a social and economic point of view associated with them. The schools were to some extent to support one another, that is the schools in the higher categories were to subsidize the schools in the lower, or at least to supply training for those who were to teach in them, and there were to be opportunities for able boys to move up from one category to another. It is an interesting comment on the social needs of the day that when the schools were established it was those at the lowest level that filled up most rapidly.[1]

Woodard does not seem to have been a man with great personal resources or with a naturally wide influence, and it says much for the generosity of church people and their sense of the urgency of this particular need, as well as for Woodard's own fund-raising and organizing abilities, that so much of his scheme was realized. As was to be expected, he was not able to create the general system which he had planned; but in the south of England he was able to found his public school at Lancing, the school at the second level at Hurstpierpont and the lowest at Ardingly. In the Midlands there was a school of the second category at Denstone and of the lowest at Ellesmere, and he broke into the West with a school at Taunton. Other schools were added, including schools for girls, and when he died in 1891 his system included 11 schools and had 1,350 pupils under instruction.[2] Between 1846 and 1891 the number of children who had been educated at one or other of his schools must have been great indeed, but he had not produced a scheme which provided a system of education for the whole middle class.

To judge from the number of men who wrote to Woodard offering him schools which were already going concerns a good many of the parish clergy in these years had also founded schools for the middle class. As a matter of principle Woodard did not normally accept such schools and, indeed, their weakness was normally that they depended on the personal energy of one incumbent; they did not normally have effective finances

[1] On Woodard's achievement and ideas and also on the whole question of Church middle-class education, see Brian Heeney, *Mission to the Middle Classes. The Woodard Schools 1848–91* (1969).
[2] ibid., p. 39.

E

or endowments and they were liable to fall into decay or disappear when the founder went away, grew old, or died. This was not always the case, however, as can be seen from the history of the schools founded by W. J. Butler, vicar of Wantage from 1847 to 1880, though he was partially helped by the sisterhood he had founded in Wantage.[1] The clergymen who offered their schools to Woodard must have been men who sympathized with his aims and were at the least not deterred by his churchmanship, which was markedly tractarian. There were other school founders who either rejected his churchmanship outright, or at least founded schools in a very different spirit from his. For instance Trent College was actually founded in direct competition with Denstone. An indefatigable promoter of schools, whose views on church education were completely different from those of Woodard, was that vigorous and cheerful man the Reverend William Rogers, significantly called 'hang theology Rogers'.[2] An even more remarkable man was another clergyman who also dreamed of a scheme for middle-class education which would serve the whole country, the now apparently largely forgotten J. L. Brereton.

Brereton was a Rugbeian, and at Oxford was the pupil of that leading broad churchman, A. P. Stanley. He held successively the cures of West Buckland and Little Massingham in Norfolk, and Bishop Phillpotts made him a prebendary of Exeter. In 1853 while at West Buckland he seems to have turned his attention to the problem of the education of the middle class and by 1858 had opened a Devon county school at West Buckland. He then went on to devise, apparently between 1863 and 1864, an elaborate educational system for the whole country. There were to be in each county third-grade schools in groups of parishes for small farmers, tradesmen and artisans and, second-grade schools for larger farmers and the like as at West Buckland. In groups of three or more counties there would be first-grade schools and at each university centre a county college.

The scheme was in fact too elaborate and too expensive. Brereton found it impossible to get enough schools started and those he did get started often failed because they were in-

[1] Kathleen Philip, *Victorian Wantage* (Wantage, 1968) pp. 86–9.
[2] R. H. Hadden, *Reminiscences of William Rogers* (1888) *passim*.

adequately financed. His positive achievement seems to have been no more than the West Buckland school, the planning of a first-grade school in Norfolk, and the establishment of one county college, Cavendish College at Cambridge, which lasted from 1876 to 1892. Other institutions which he planned seem to have collapsed, as did his association which had as its object the foundation of county schools for girls. But his example was followed by others. In 1865 two other county schools were founded, Framlingham in Suffolk and Cranleigh in Surrey. He also influenced the foundation of Barnard Castle school and Wellington school, Somerset.[1]

Brereton's proposal that there should be colleges in university towns shows that in his view some of those who were the recipients of 'middle-class education' should nonetheless have some access to that 'higher' or 'liberal' education which Whewell had stated as being the prerogative of the nobility and gentry. But the constitution of Oxford and Cambridge themselves forbade the conception that such an education should be a class monopoly, for at each university there was provision in the form of scholarships, exhibitions, sizarships, etc., to enable poor men to attend the university. It is true that from towards the end of the eighteenth century this had probably become more difficult for very poor men. The change in the status of the wealthier clergy, the increasing tendency of the gentry to send their sons to the university, and the general increase in the luxuries and complications of life had probably had the result of making residence at the universities at least potentially very expensive, with a very real danger of incurring debts. Certainly by the middle of the nineteenth century there were a good many complaints of the high cost of living at both Oxford and Cambridge, while it is possible that the opening of closed local scholarships had blocked a relatively easy way of access for poor men. But all this was accidental. It was deplored by many, and during the late forties and fifties a good deal of thought was given to the consideration of means by which some men could

[1] I received valuable information about Brereton from Mr S. R. de S. Honey of the Department of Education of the University of Durham. The best printed account is in Heeney [op. cit., p. 107], from which most of what appears in the text is derived. There is also an article in the *D.N.B.* by W. B. Owen.

live at the older universities at a cheaper rate, and in the sixties and seventies some important steps were taken to this end. In 1868 Oxford and in 1869 Cambridge permitted the admission of non-collegiate students. In 1870 Keble was opened at Oxford partly with the object of making it possible to lead a cheaper life there. In 1876 Cavendish College, and in 1882 Selwyn College, were opened at Cambridge partly with the same intention.

It would be wrong therefore to believe that though men often talked about a 'middle-class education' they necessarily had in mind a rigid caste system which denied access to higher education to all but the socially privileged. That was certainly not the view of many of those who promoted middle-class education. Woodard tried to develop a variety of schemes to enable poor students from his system to go to Oxford or Cambridge; indeed at one time he was considering buying land to enable him to found a college at Cambridge that should serve his purpose. It is also worth remembering that in the 1850s there were some clergymen who had an even more radical view of the distribution of the values of the 'higher' education.

In 1854 Maurice founded the Working Men's College in Red Lion Square in imitation of a people's college founded by an Independent minister at Sheffield. Maurice's object was to bring first of all working men, and then working women, into contact with those values for which it might be claimed the 'higher education' stood, and he managed to assemble a team of great intellectual distinction for the purpose. But his example was also copied, largely by clergy of the Church of England, in different parts of the country. For instance in 1855 a working man's college, before Cavendish College, was founded at Cambridge largely under the auspices of H. M. Butler, F. J. Hort the great New Testament scholar, Harvey Goodwin the vicar of St Mary's and others. In the following year one was opened at Oxford. In 1857 another was opened at Wolverhampton on the initiative of Dr W. A. Newman, the rector of Wolverhampton and the Rev. T. A. Campbell, headmaster of Wolverhampton grammar school. In 1862 one was founded at Leicester by D. S. Vaughan, vicar of St Martin's, Leicester.[1]

[1] For the working man's college at Cambridge, see T. D. Atkinson and J. W. Clarke, *Cambridge Described and Illustrated* (1897) pp. 221–2, and the

There seem to have been other colleges, but they are not very easy to trace. They apparently tended to be ephemeral institutions. Like so much else in this period they were dependent on the personal vigour of an individual and when that was removed, when for instance a particular vicar or rector died or removed to another parish, they tended to wilt and disappear. This happened at Cambridge where the college seems to have come to an end in 1865, after the original founders had been scattered. It happened the same year in Wolverhampton after Campbell's departure for New Zealand. It was probably only Vaughan's long and faithful service at St Martin's, Leicester and his continued interest in the college that has secured its survival as 'Vaughan College' to this day.

If, then, the thirty years after 1835 are taken as a whole they reveal a great many signs that not a few churchmen recognized the importance of a secondary education not strictly limited by the hierarchical pattern. There was also a good deal of personal initiative, and all things considered, some very remarkable achievements. These achievements are the more surprising when it is remembered that throughout this period it was not normally possible to get government grants for such work. To supply the kind of education needed for a secondary school it was necessary to charge the parents a weekly fee which, if modest, was larger than that required by a purely elementary school. Normally, if a school charged more than 9d a week it was not considered to be a school for the poor and therefore not eligible for grants; but if too large a fee was asked for in order more nearly to cover the expenses of the school, that school would not be available for many of the people it might be intended to serve. Richard Gregory, subsequently dean of St Paul's, but vicar of St Mary the Less Lambeth from 1853 to 1873, circumvented this difficulty by combining a secondary

---

lives of several of the participants, particularly Hort. My information about Wolverhampton was kindly supplied by Mr E. R. Taylor and Mr John Roper. For Leicester, see *The Vaughan Working Man's College, Leicester 1862–1912*, edited by the Rev. Edward Atkins (1912). There is much more to be learnt about this movement. There seem to have been colleges at Manchester, Salford, Ancoats, Sheffield, Halifax, Wolverhampton, Glasgow, Birkenhead, Ayr, Leicester, and Cambridge and Oxford. F. Maurice, *Life of F. D. Maurice* (2 vols., 1884) Vol. II, p. 377.

school with an elementary school and, by charging some parents a shilling a week and others very much less, he reached an average which was below the government's maximum, and so he was able to claim a grant. This practice was adopted elsewhere, but clearly it could not be, or was not, universally used. It was, in particular, not available to those who were unwilling to accept any form of government control.[1]

The margin would therefore have to come from private subscription. As the history of the Woodard schools goes to show, and that evidence could be reinforced from elsewhere, very large sums could be raised from this source, but as a source it necessarily had its limitations, and those limitations seem to enforce two other lessons which this period has to offer. The first was that the Church of England could not by itself cover the whole ground. Neither Gladstone and his friends, nor Woodard, nor Brereton, nor all these taken together and added to all the other schemes for church secondary education, all the ancient grammar schools and all the individual schools started by parsons in their parishes, could supply a tithe of the secondary education that the middle classes needed. And the second lesson was that any venture not backed by sound finance, that is not backed by a substantial and well-managed endowment, or a considerable and reliable income from fee payers and subscribers, was not likely long to survive when the impetus which had brought it into being died down, or the man who had started it went away.

A possible answer to these difficulties was to broaden the basis of the church system of education. Probably more than half the population of the country were dissenters from the Church. It might therefore greatly strengthen church schools if they admitted dissenters on terms equally satisfactory to both parties. This was not a possible policy for Woodard. Woodard's inspiration was tractarian. His aim had been frankly as much missionary as it was educational. He had set out to win the middle classes for the Church, and whatever else his schools taught they must teach the doctrine of the Church to all who attended them. He had never concealed his intentions, and from his own point of view they were perfectly reasonable. But it was otherwise with men like Rogers and Brereton.

[1] Heeney [op. cit., p. 107] pp. 168–9.

The contrast possibly corresponded to a profound difference in churchmanship. To the extent that a man believed that the truth of religion must be conveyed through the medium of dogma and authority, he would be the more likely to believe that it was important that public education should use its authority to convey that dogma. To the extent that he believed that the acceptance of these truths must be commended by reason, he might be sceptical about the value of the straight teaching of dogma and put more faith in a general education which would enable a boy or girl to use their reason, and by that means gain a knowledge of Christianity. Something like this argument seems to have appealed to Rogers. He became convinced that a good many church schools spent too much time on the teaching of religion and that much of what passed as religious teaching was of no value of any sort. He was therefore prepared to omit religious teaching from the school he founded at Marylebone. Possibly this way of thought affected Brereton, whose religious affinities seem to have been broad church, but whether this was so or not, he was certainly impressed by the proportion of dissenters to churchmen in the population and the need to make provision for them in any system of secondary education. He was therefore prepared to make provision for dissenters in his schools, and to take the secular unit, the county, and not the diocese as the unit for his administration.[1]

This broadening of the basis of the system does not seem in his case to have had much effect; at least, whatever may be the explanation, his work has had less staying power than that of the more exclusively denominational Woodard. It seems possible that one reason for this was the fact that he shrank from what might be the most fruitful result of a more liberal policy towards dissenters. This was not that dissenters might be attracted into church schools but that it might make it easier for the State, which by mid century had to treat all denominations equally, to take a part in first organizing, and then financing, secondary education. As did many people in the middle of the century, Brereton seems to have distrusted the idea of government-controlled education, yet in fact he inadvertently took part in a step which led by very devious

[1] Heeney [op. cit., p. 107], p. 163.

routes towards both a more effectively organized system and a system in which government action played a part.

Some time in the middle of the fifties Lord Ebrington, who had been Brereton's partner and patron in founding the school at West Buckland, seems to have been inspired by the activities of the Society of Arts in organizing examinations for mechanics institutes to think of the possibility of organizing a like examination for secondary schools, with a place in it for the Christian religion. He and Brereton put forward a proposal on the subject which in 1856 attracted the attention of a West countryman who was a close friend of Gladstone and had been involved in the attempt in 1838 and 1839 to plan middle-class education, Thomas Dyke Acland. A committee was formed to plan a West of England examination in which Acland seems to have been the most active member. In order to enlist an exterior authority to run such an examination this committee turned, not to the Society of Arts which would have been unsuitable but to the Education Committee of the Privy Council. Acland approached Lord Granville, then lord president of the council, Lingen, Temple's friend, who was secretary of that committee and, most importantly, Temple himself, who was at this point inspector of church training schools. Temple told Acland that the government would not take the matter up but that the University of Oxford might do so, and in 1858 first Oxford and then Cambridge accepted the responsibility of setting and correcting examinations which could be taken locally by school children.[1]

The full significance of this development may not be immediately apparent. Its importance is threefold. First, the network of local examinations and certificate examinations which developed from this point provided the ground plan for English secondary education, it set standards, prescribed subjects and held out objects to be worked for; second, this is the first occasion in the nineteenth century when the two ancient universities undertook important duties outside their walls.

[1] Arthur H. D. Acland, ed., *Memoirs and Letters of the Right Honourable Sir Thomas Dyke Acland* (London, printed for private circulation, 1902) pp. 178–88. See also John Roach, *Public Examinations in England 1850–1900* (Cambridge, 1971). I had not had the advantage of reading Professor Roach's book when I wrote this passage.

This was important for the nation, and it was important for Oxford and Cambridge, for it meant that they were changing from the two exceedingly strange, inward-looking, clerical republics that they had been in the first half of the nineteenth century into more normal institutions with a sense of general responsibility for national education. However, what is most important for present purposes is that it brought two remarkable men, Acland and Temple, together for the first time.

As with all Gladstone's immediate circle Acland's course of life had been profoundly changed by Peel's repeal of the Corn Laws in 1846. Like Gladstone Acland had followed Peel in 1846, and in 1847 this had cost him his seat in Parliament. Like Gladstone he went slowly across to the Liberals. In 1859 he stood for Parliament as a Liberal Conservative, and in 1865 he entered Parliament as a definite Liberal. He had kept up the interest in middle-class education that he had shown in 1838 and 1839, and during his absence from the House he had had an opportunity of seeing educational problems at first hand, for he was interested in the scientific improvement of agriculture as a substitute for protection and he recognized the difficulties which sprang from the farmers' lack of education. He became convinced that the problem of middle-class education was difficult enough and urgent enough to require a more drastic solution than would have appealed to the earnest young high churchmen who had gathered round Gladstone in 1838.

Temple's views had also probably changed a good deal from those of the rather naïve pupil whom Ward had taught at Balliol. He put his opinions on record twice: in a collection called *Oxford Essays* published in 1848, and in the answers he gave in 1860 to the Newcastle Commission on the education of the people. Three of the opinions which he developed show the shape of things to come. He did not believe that it would be possible to provide for an educational system which should adequately cover the country unless the schools were financed out of the rates. He wanted an enquiry into the use of those endowments which were, or should be, available for educational purposes, and he believed that the denominational control of education did not produce religious liberty, but rather control by the enthusiasts of a particular party in the Church.[1]

These opinions in fact mainly related to the problems of primary education, but he would reasonably soon have his chance to express his views on secondary education. During the 1860s instructed opinion in England began to feel uneasily aware of the deficiencies of the education available for the middle class, particularly of the lower middle class. Disquieting reports began to come to hand of the ways in which bad technical education was hampering the development of British industry. There were uncomfortable comparisons between the education available in England and what was regarded as normal in certain foreign countries. Matthew Arnold's writings began to make an impression, and in 1863 at the meeting of the National Association for the Promotion of the Social Sciences at Edinburgh Nassau Senior gave a rather startling address on the subject. He said: 'Of the manner in which the middle classes are educated, we know little, and seek to know little,' and proposed that the association should petition the crown to issue a commission on the subject.[2] In 1864, therefore, the Taunton Commission on middle-class education was appointed. Temple, Acland and Lord Lyttelton, who was married to the sister of Mrs Gladstone, were all members, and Temple seems to have written much of the report. Lyttelton was a devout high churchman, but at this juncture his opinions seem to have corresponded with those of Temple or Acland.[3]

The report states the position in uncompromising language.

> The most urgent educational need of the country is that of good schools of the third grade, that is, of those which shall carry education up to the age of 14 or 15. It is just here that the endowed schools appear most signally to fail, while nothing else takes their place. . . . The evidence is almost unanimous . . . that the artisans, the small shopkeepers, the smaller farmers are in many places without any convenient means of educating their children

[1] Sandford, *Temple* [op. cit., p. 85] Vol. I, pp. 120–8.
[2] *Transactions of the National Association for the Promotion of the Social Sciences – Edinburgh 1863* (1864) p. 56.
[3] For Temple's part in this report, see Sandford, *Temple* [op. cit., p. 85] Vol. I, pp. 133–44.

at all, and still more often have no security that what education
they do get is good.

It went on to describe what should be the three grades of this
education, and the importance of the education of women,
and it recommended the maintenance of endowments, 'so far
as they could be rendered really and adequately useful for the
great purposes for which they were intended'.[1]

The sting of the report lay in the last sentence. It was to
render these old educational endowments 'really and adequately useful' that the Endowed Schools Act was passed in
1869, the year after the report was published.[2] Under this act
commissioners were appointed whose task it was to remodel
endowed schools which were more than fifty years old, in
order that they should better suit the purposes of the middle
of the nineteenth century. To do this they had to get rid of the
many corruptions which had developed over the centuries, put
to better use obsolete or inappropriate charitable endowments,
and release the rules which bound many of the schools exclusively to the Church of England.

The chief commissioner was Lyttelton, who was an intimate
friend and connection of Gladstone; but if he had ever shared
the views which Gladstone had held about the Church of
England being the State's view of truth, he had come to see
that they were impracticable, and believed that the best
available system was a compulsory system of education with
free competition among the various religious bodies in a
variety of schools to be subsidized by the State. They were not,
however, to be wholly supported by the State, for he thought
that it was immoral and debilitating for people not to pay for the
education of their children if they could do so.[3]

With such views as these Lyttelton seems to have contrived
conscientiously to tread on as many toes as he reasonably
could. As he believed that 'indiscriminate gratuitous education'
was wrong, (an opinion which Temple seems to have shared at

[1] *Reports and Commissions 1867–8*, Vol. XVIII, pp. 78–88, 546–661. The
relevant passages can conveniently be found in *English Historical Docu-
ments*, gen. ed. D. C. Douglas, Vol. XII (1), *1833–74* (ed. G. M. Young
and W. D. Hancock, 1956) pp. 905–6, 908.
[2] 32 and 33 Vict., Ch. 56.
[3] Lord Lyttelton, *Thoughts on National Education* (1855).

this time, he set about reorganizing those ancient foundations that provided free education to the children of working men. In doing so he inevitably aroused the indignation of those who had benefited from such institutions.[1] Other old establishments were, perhaps inevitably, remodelled in such a way as to seem to violate the founders' wishes, which many still reverenced, while the partial secularization of many schools which had been the monopoly of the Church of England outraged churchmen, particularly high churchmen. As a result of this Lyttelton involved himself in a fairly sharp controversy with Woodard, of whose work he had once been a strong supporter, and in an even sharper one with Thring of Uppingham.[2]

Probably Lyttelton pressed matters too hard, and since he seems to have been a highly-strung, oversensitive man he was too apt to engage in controversy with those who disagreed with him. Therefore, largely it would seem for personal reasons, Disraeli's government in 1874 took the work out of his hands by abolishing the endowed school commissioners and putting it into the hands of the charity commissioners. In fact the extent of the secularization imposed on schools by virtue of this act was not drastic. In most cases the most important provision imposed on schools was a 'conscience clause', that is a rule that enabled a dissenter to withdraw his child from any religious instruction of which he disapproved, and the abolition of any rule that made it necessary for school-masters to be in orders. Both of these provisions were enjoined by the act itself (Clauses 15 and 18), and in spite of them co-operation proved to be possible between the endowed schools, the charity commissioners and those who wished to encourage the teaching of religion. Indeed in the last years of the century there was still room for the promotion of religious education; in particular much seems to have been done at that time for the religious education of girls. Yet for all this, in the Endowed Schools Act of 1869 an important turning point had been reached, and even in the partial reaction which followed after

[1] See Brian Simon, *Studies in the History of Education 1780–1870* (1960) pp. 318–36. For Temple's view on this, see Sandford, *Temple* [op. cit., p. 85] Vol. I, pp. 138–40.
[2] Heeney [op. cit., p. 107] pp. 91–4.

the change of government in 1874 there was no going back on
the principle that had been accepted.

In 1869 Parliament had accepted the fact that there was an
urgent need for a better system of secondary education which it
was the State's duty to supply. It had also accepted the corollary that if such a system was to be generally useful it must be
available for those who dissented from the teachings of the
established Church. This was simply a recognition of the plain
facts of the case; indeed it is interesting to note the large part
played in the acceptance of this principle by influential
churchmen such as Temple, Acland and Lyttelton. The position of Acland and Lyttelton seems to reflect the same process
as had caught up with their friend Gladstone between 1841 and
1845. Before 1841 a particular view of the Church had seemed
to Gladstone to carry with it a particular view of the principles
which resulted from the moral nature of the State. The condition of society had made those principles impracticable, and
policies had to be devised which were inconsistent with them.
Therefore Gladstone, Acland and Lyttelton alike had had to
accept policies which were in effect steps towards the realization
of the unavoidable conception of the secularized State drawing
its philosophy from the ambiguous conception of the agnostic
State.

It need hardly be said that the act of 1869 was only the
beginning of the new policy with regard to secondary schools.
The need of the country for a better system of secondary
education was not to be satisfied by the mere manipulation of
ancient endowments. Other expedients were adopted to provide
money for this work, and in 1894 another commission, the
Bryce Commission, was set up to look into the subject. This
further emphasized the country's pressing need for a satisfactory system of secondary education, and in 1902 a new
education act was passed by the Conservatives, who were,
ironically, also trying in the same act to salvage the church
elementary schools. This provided for secondary schools to be
financed out of public funds. Thus the twentieth century
initiated a system of secondary education supplied by the
secular State which, if independent schools are to be abolished,
might be able to secure for its philosophy, or lack of philosophy,
a monopoly which would have been out of the question

for the teaching of any body of doctrine in the nineteenth century.

That, however, will be a problem for the twentieth century. If in the middle of the nineteenth century the problems with which secondary or middle-class education confronted churchmen were difficult and in the last resort insoluble as far as the whole nation was concerned, the problem presented by the need to provide elementary education was much more extensive, menacing and urgent, and presented a much more immediate challenge to the parochial clergy. The problem was more extensive because, while according to nineteenth-century ways of thought it was possible to make a case that only a section of the community was in a position to make good use of a secondary education, it was difficult to deny that every sane boy or girl had a right to be taught such elementary accomplishments as learning to read and write. It was urgent because some educational grounding was necessarily the first step out of that barbarous illiteracy which prevailed in much of the country, an illiteracy which, it must be remembered, probably meant ignorance of those saving truths which in the view of clergy it behoved all men to know; an illiteracy which also perhaps made men and women more likely to misbehave.

In order to understand the question satisfactorily, however, it is I think necessary to recognize two points. First, there had always been a section of the poor who had been illiterate and probably barbarous, a fact which was probably accepted much more complacently before the nineteenth century. And second, from the beginning of the nineteenth century this primordial problem had reached unmanageable proportions as the result of an increase in population which had carried the number of people in England and Wales from about 9,000,000 in 1801 to 22,712,000 in 1871, a date which can be considered as being the end of the first nineteenth-century system of elementary education in England and Wales.

The point is important because though the increase in population took place in both town and country the movement of population from the countryside – from Wales, from the highlands of Scotland – resulted in great accumulations of human beings in the large cities, and it was the recognition after 1865 of the complete failure of the old system based on voluntary initiative to provide adequate facilities for the education of these great masses in the cities that led to the change in men's minds, particularly in the minds of leading dissenters. This change led to what can only be called the beginning of a revolution in 1870.

What I have called the first system of elementary education was based on the agreement which the government reached with the Church in 1840. The government made a grant towards the building of schools by two voluntary societies, the National Society, which was Church of England, and the British and Foreign School Society, which was undenominational. The grant was to be administered by a committee of the Privy Council whose secretary, during the first decade of the scheme, was that remarkable pioneer of English education Kay-Shuttleworth, and the schools that received grants were to be periodically inspected on behalf of the government. But the schools were to be built and largely maintained on the initiative of the two societies. Moreover, the inspectors of the schools belonging to the Church of England were to be appointed with the approval of the archbishops of Canterbury and York, and in 1843 agreement was reached to gain an appropriate approval for the inspectors who dealt with the schools of the British and Foreign Society.

Successive governments developed this scheme in various ways. It was enlarged to include other denominations on equal terms with the Church of England. The government grant was increased and made to cover other purposes than school building. In 1846 grants were made to schoolmasters for training pupil teachers and a system of scholarships to training colleges was instituted. From 1853 there were capitation grants for pupils who satisfied certain conditions, first for rural then for urban schools. The whole situation was reviewed by the Newcastle Commission, which reported on it in 1861 and at many points found it wanting, and an attempt was made to remedy its failure by a system of payment by results. Nevertheless the system should not be considered as at any time wholly a governmental system of education. During all this period the initiative in promoting the establishment of schools, and much of the finance which made it possible to run them, came from private subscriptions or, as seemed right in those days, from the parents of the children.

It is important to remember this for two reasons. First, to contemporaries this way of doing things seemed to be different from the authoritarian governmental organization of education which they saw in Prussia and France. This they felt was a system dependent on voluntary effort and payments for value received, and so was compatible with freedom and self-respect. Secondly, the arrangements of this system, although it gave opportunities to a number of denominations, enabled the Church of England to build and maintain by far the largest number of schools. The Newcastle Commission on the state of popular education reported in 1861 that of the schools which they had had under consideration the Church of England had established 19,549 weekday schools, 22,236 Sunday schools and 1,547 night schools. It was, according to the commissioners, educating 1,553,212 children in weekday schools and 2,388,397 in Sunday schools. It was therefore educating 76·2 per cent of the children being educated in the day schools and 45·8 per cent of the children in the Sunday schools of England, and had produced between nine-and ten-elevenths of the day schools in the country.[1] But none of this was the result of government favour, for the grant was offered on equal terms to a number of denominations.

The extent of this achievement is sometimes qualified in men's minds by the belief that, whether the grant was offered on equal terms or not, most of the money did in fact come from the government. This is not altogether correct, however. The figures giving the sources of money spent on national schools in 1870, that is for the year of Forster's bill – a year which might be considered the last year of the old dispensation – are: £42,734 from endowments, £329,846 from voluntary contributions, £351,928 from school pence (that is payment by the children's parents), £20,386 from other sources (these seem to be church collections, gifts, etc.), and £385,840 from government grants. In the same year the voluntary contributions on behalf of schools not connected with the Church of England (excluding the Roman Catholic schools,

[1] P.P. 1861, XXI, Pt. I, pp. 55 and 80.

the figures for which were given in a different return) were
£66,606.[1]

These figures should not however be considered by themselves. An educational system cannot be extemporized at the
beginning of the year for which the income is given. Its existence
depends on what may be called capital assets paid for in earlier
years – schools which are already going concerns, experienced,
and perhaps trained, schoolteachers, and school buildings.
Much of the money for all this must in this case have been
subscribed in earlier years, possibly when grants were smaller
or more restricted in their purposes, or even non-existent. It
would be difficult to work out with any certainty how much
had, in fact, been subscribed to build up this system, but in an
article which he published in 1875 in the *Church Quarterly Review*
Richard Gregory calculated that between 1811, when the
National Society was founded, and 1873, 'at the very smallest
estimate' 12 million pounds had been voluntarily subscribed
under its auspices for the building of schools, and 15 million
for their maintenance.[2] These figures have, however, been
worked from a series of inferences and must be considered as to
some extent hypothetical.

But even if Gregory's figures are left out of account, the fact
remains that the figures must have been considerable. And to
the sums which in any year were subscribed in such a way as to
earn government grants there were in addition those sums
spent on forms of education for which no grants or very inadequate grants were available; such activities, for instance,
as the various forms of secondary education which were developed at this time, or the night schools, which could play an
important part in teaching adults to read. There was also the
money needed to support schools whose promoters felt that
they could not conscientiously accept the conditions on which
the government money was given, as was the case with Archdeacon Denison when he was menaced with a 'conscience
clause'.

All this raises two related questions. Where did all this
money come from? And why did the dissenters, who were no

---

[1] P.P. 1876, LIX, pp. 108-9.
[2] *Church Quarterly Review*, Vol. I, (1876) 'The present state of the education
controversy', pp. 414-15.

less devoted to the interests of their congregations than the Anglicans, produce so much less money to earn grants and build and maintain schools?

To take the last question first. The normal answer is that the Church of England contained a larger number of rich men and women than did the various dissenting bodies, and dissenters had to pay their own ministers and build their own chapels, while the Church of England had inherited its churches and had an endowed clergy. No doubt there is something in this, but it cannot be enough to account for so great a difference. Against the sum dissenters paid to support their ministers and build chapels must be placed the considerable sums which members of the Church of England subscribed for the restoration and building of churches and for church extension.[1] In most large urban areas the inheritance of the Church of England did not extend nearly as far as its responsibilities; even now a very casual observation shows how many Anglican churches in urban environments were built in the nineteenth century. And as far as the comparative wealth of churchmen and dissenters is concerned it should be remembered that the industrial and commercial revolutions had been going on since before the beginning of the nineteenth century, and that there is much evidence that a good deal of the profits had accumulated in the hands of dissenters. If they had seen fit to do so it seems to be unquestionable that dissenters could have provided more money than they did to earn grants from the State to build schools.

But they did not see fit to do this, and this fact, together with a good many mid nineteenth-century pronouncements by dissenters and particularly by congregationalists, points to an issue of principle. To many dissenters independence from the State was a principle rooted in tradition and hallowed by long years of devotion in difficult times, and sometimes by martyrdom. The tradition which inspired many members of the Church of England was clean contrary to this. It was part of a man's duty to Church and king to co-operate with the Government by serving that part of the country for which he was responsible – the landowner his estate or his neighbour-

[1] For the sums subscribed for these purposes, see Kitson Clark, *The Making of Victorian England* (1962) pp. 169–70.

hood, the priest his parish. The provision of a school was part of
that duty, particularly obligatory for the parish priest.

That this conception was effective seems to be borne out by
what appear to be the answers to the first of the two questions
which were proposed: whence did the money come for this
educational effort? A certain amount came, of course, from the
munificence of church people in general. In addition to this a
number of landowners built and maintained, or partly maintained, schools on their estates, particularly it would seem in the
villages near their lodge gates. But a great deal of the money
which was used for the building and maintenance of elementary
schools came from or through the hands of the parochial
clergy. James Fraser, second bishop of Manchester, was a man
of wide experience. He was for much of his career an effective
parish incumbent in country parishes, and he collected evidence over a wide district, both for the Newcastle Commission
on popular education, which reported in 1861, and for the
commission on the employment of women and children in
agriculture which reported in 1868–70. He was also a man who
was prepared to express his mind frankly about what he
thought was wrong with social conditions. For the report on the
employment of women and children in agriculture Fraser
wrote:

> But for the zeal and activity of the clergy, and their large
> sacrifices, not only of money, but of labour and of time in three
> fourths of the rural parishes of England there would either be no
> school at all, or at best only the semblance of a school. Speaking
> broadly there is no other *class* of men in the kingdom who really
> take an intelligent and earnest interest in the subject. The
> farmers, possibly, may not oppose; the landowners, probably, may
> feel it their duty to subscribe; but the sustaining motive-power,
> springing from the desire to do the best they can for the spiritual
> and temporal interests of the children committed to their charge,
> without the presence of which any amount of money spent will do
> but little for a school, comes from the clergy.[1]

Fraser was, of course, speaking of his own order, but there
exists a good deal of evidence to support what he said. Perhaps
the largest collected body of such support can be found in the
reports of the other sub-commissioners for the Newcastle

[1] P.P. 1867–8, XVII, p. 79.

Commission,[1] but it also abounds in the records of parishes and in the biographies of individual clergymen. Even the enemies of the Church complain of the large number of parson-dominated schools in the countryside, though they do not seem always to give sufficient weight to the consideration that, probably in many villages, if there had been no parson there would have been no school.

In many villages it seems to have been part of the parson's duty to take the initiative in founding a school. He normally exercised a general supervision over it, quite probably visiting it every day; and quite possibly he, his wife and his daughters would teach, if not in the day school, then in the Sunday school. He was often landed with the duty of collecting money for it, and, when money was lacking, of finding money from his own pocket, even if it was not a very heavily loaded one, to make up the deficit. It is true that both landowners and employers often felt it their duty to provide for the education of the children of their tenants or work people. But they might not do so, and in any case there were many places in England where there were no resident landowners, no responsible employers, nor any substantial church people. In such cases an inescapable duty fell on the incumbent of the parish. Even when the school had been started with a satisfactory subscription from other people the subscriptions might after a time fall off, as is the way of subscriptions, or expenses might rise to more than had been budgeted for and the school might incur a debt. For this, apparently, the incumbent might be held to be, or at least often held himself to be, responsible. Small wonder that a number of the clergy got into financial difficulties as a result of their educational duties.[2]

It may seem strange that what was possibly the richest country in the world should be content to finance something that many countries were coming to see as a necessary service – the service of providing elementary education for those who needed it – so largely from the contributions of parsons who

[1] P.P. 1861, XXI, Pt. II, passim.
[2] Frank Smith, *The Life and Work of Sir James Kay-Shuttleworth* (1923) p. 166. For the debts incurred by a particular parson in founding schools, see 'Hang Theology' Rogers' account of his finances, Hadden, *Rogers* [op. cit., p. 108] passim.

often could ill afford them and the parents of children many of whom probably could afford them still less. But it must be remembered that in mid nineteenth-century England there were many people who believed that it was wrong for the State to spend money on behalf of people who could possibly pay for themselves, that such expenditure impeded rather than encouraged progress, that in fact education would have developed faster if the State had not intervened. In addition to those feelings there were the bitter religious divisions of the country and the belief of the dissenters that the State had no right to interfere in education. Indeed, with so many inhibitions at large it is arguable that the only way in which a system of popular education could have been developed was by an amplification of the old parochial ideals of the established Church by men who had not yet learnt to question them. If this is so, indeed in any case, the nation owes in this matter a very considerable debt to the clergy.

Nevertheless their efforts created a dangerously anomalous situation. For what *was* the educational system that came into existence in this way? Was it primarily a system of schools created by church people for the children of the Church to which, on account of its social usefulness, the State gave a subsidy? Or was it a system of State education in embryo, which ought progressively to be brought under lay control and reorganized in such a way as to meet the needs of those who dissented from the Church's doctrines as well as of those who were prepared to accept them?

Since there was no practicable alternative in mid century it was natural for a man like Kay-Shuttleworth, the first secretary of the Committee of the Privy Council on Education, a man dedicated to the task of equipping the country with a comprehensive system of popular education, to take the second view, and after 1846 the Committee of the Privy Council adopted the policy of trying to make such national schools as wished to receive government grants alter their constitutions so as to admit lay managers into the government of the school and to accept a 'conscience clause', whereby a dissenter could withdraw his child from religious instruction. In 1849 Kay-Shuttleworth was succeeded in his post by R. W. Lingen, a friend of Jowett and of Temple, and also at one time a fellow of Balliol. Lingen continued Kay-Shuttleworth's policy, but the policy was violently opposed by Archdeacon Denison, the brother of the bishop of Salisbury, who withdrew his own schools from the contaminating control of the Privy Council and managed for a time to prevent the National Society from co-operating with the Committee of the Privy Council in this matter.

The archdeacon was in many ways a truculent nuisance, if at times an amusing one. It is arguable that he harmed not only the development of national education but the cause of church education also. Nevertheless he had a case. A large part of the money which had made possible the foundation and maintenance of the schools of the National Society had come from the pockets of church people, and had been sub-scribed in order that the children should receive an education in the principles in which the subscribers believed. The objects of the National Society as expressed in its charter were 'the educating of the children of the Poor, without any exception, in the Doctrine and Discipline of the Established Church'. It is therefore not impossible to understand the feelings of men like Denison and for that matter of Keble, who attacked attempts to modify the management of the schools of the National Society, and also in some cases the teaching which they provided, in order to conciliate the feelings of dissenters.[1]

The educational controversies of the middle of the nineteenth century are so wearisome, and the social needs they seem to have masked appear in retrospect to have been so urgent, that historians of the twentieth century have found it difficult to be patient with them. They have treated the controversial-ists with some disdain as men so blinded by sectarian feeling that they wilfully impeded the development of what was obviously the most urgent need that confronted the country, the provision of an effective system of popular education. This is unfortunate, for behind the ill temper, the ill-judged delays, the tedious reiterations and unendurable verbosities of these quarrels there is hidden an important issue of principle, and it may be suggested that though this dreary babble of contending

[1] The best way to appreciating Denison's case is to read his own account of it, viz. G. A. Denison, *Notes of my Life* (1878) pp. 95–190.

voices has passed into silence it is still a live issue, that it has been evaded rather than resolved in modern Britain. Its implications are, in fact, most easy to discern in the practice of totalitarian dictatorships, be they fascist or communist; but it cannot be dismissed by invoking the rights of a majority, even in a liberal democracy. It is one of the issues that derive from the general problem concerning the source of the moral authority of the State, which the situation that followed the First Reform Bill proposed but could not settle. It is this. How far is it legitimate for the State, or any other body, to impose on the children in its charge a particular set of opinions in controversial matters?

Before 1830 English history had provided two possible but conflicting answers to that question. The first could spring from the old conception of the organic unity of Church and State. According to that conception the established Church was an essential part of the fundamental constitution of society. Since this was so its doctrine was part of the truth on which the organization of society was based. Therefore it was right that in the schools provided by the State the doctrines of the established Church should be taught. The nonconformists on the other hand had their historic answer. It was based on the absolute right of the individual to make up his own mind. They said that, except where urgent necessity made its intervention unavoidable, the State had no right to teach anything at all, and many of them went on saying this till late into the nineteenth century. This opinion was in fact given in 1861 by a sturdy minority among the Newcastle commissioners. 'They hold,' says the report, 'that in a country situated politically and socially as England is, Government has, ordinarily speaking, no educational duties except towards those whom destitution, vagrancy or crime casts upon its hands.'[1] This is, of course, an echo of what Edward Baines had said almost twenty years before.

The progress of affairs since 1830 had invalidated both of these answers. On the one hand it was no longer possible to base a policy on the union between Church and State, and on the other the Government had accepted the fact that it had undoubted educational duties. It had provided money to

[1] P.P. 1861, XXI, Pt. 1, p. 298.

finance first the building of schools and then the education that was conducted in them.

But, as was typical of the situation in England in this period of indecision, the position which had been achieved gave no clear answer to the problem of principle. Old conceptions had not been completely abandoned, a new theory had not been at all generally accepted. The system which had been developed was a hybrid – under it the State partially subsidized and partially controlled popular elementary education, but it was provided by the churches, who could teach their own doctrines in their own schools. This might possibly have been satisfactory if there had not lingered among church people the belief that the Church ought to educate the children of the country, and among the dissenters that no public authority should educate them. The result was not only that the Church provided too much and the dissenters too little of the country's educational system, but also that the Church tried to maintain a control over its schools which was natural but unsuitable if they were publicly financed.

As things worked out in many districts the Church of England school was the only school easily available. This might not matter so much in urban conditions, where there might still be some kind of choice, and where in truth the people do not always seem to have been as much troubled about the religious complexion of the schools to which they sent their children as their respective religious pastors thought they ought to be. It might, however, be a very serious matter in a small community where the separation of Church and State had never effectively taken place, where the shadow of the parson and of the social order for which he stood might lie heavily over the school, and where, conscience clause or no conscience clause, the teachers and indeed the other children might make things very unhappy for the small dissenter.[1]

But if the situation was unsatisfactory it was difficult to see a

---

[1] See W. L. Clay, ed., *Essays on Church Policy* (1868) pp. 211–12, and Margaret Penn, *Manchester Fourteen Miles* (Cambridge, 1948) pp. 120–1. The circumstances of the Manchester case are particularly interesting. The school was a Church of England school, the majority of the children being apparently Wesleyans of one sort or another, and the children ostracized the children of a very poor Irish Roman Catholic labourer.

way out. Churchmen were divided among themselves as to what was essential to the integrity of the Church's position, and those who saw the difficulties of the situation could not get the assent of their colleagues on the compromises and concessions which they believed to be necessary. In 1846 W. F. Hook, the great vicar of Leeds who knew at first hand what were the desperate educational needs of the manufacturing districts, produced a scheme for State-established rate-aided schools to take charge of secular subjects, leaving to the clergy of the Church and other ministers of religion the teaching of religion. He was bitterly attacked by his fellow churchmen and the scheme perished without trace. The violent dissenting onslaught on Sir James Graham's scheme for factory schools opened the eyes of many churchmen to the impossibility of the Church being able to educate all the poor children in the country as churchmen had dreamed that they could, and in Manchester in 1843, a church education society was formed whose secretary was Canon Charles Richson. They proposed a scheme for supplementing church schools with schools which were to be supported by the rates. This was remarkably similar to Forster's proposals of 1870; in the forties and fifties, however, this scheme was not found to be generally acceptable. Bishop Wilberforce, for instance, could not accept it. He was prepared to accept under proper safeguards the provisions about appointment of lay managers which the education office was trying to impose on church schools, but he was not prepared to accept the imposition of a conscience clause, though he wished the clergy to encourage the children of dissenters to come to their schools where they might accept as much of the education provided as their parents were prepared to allow.[1]

Archdeacon Denison fought both management clauses and conscience clause, but in his battle to prevent the Church of England accepting the thirty pieces of silver that the education department offered he found himself thwarted by his brother,

[1] S. E. Maltby, *Manchester and the Movements for National Elementary Education 1800–1870* (Manchester, 1918). Wilberforce, *A Charge to the Clergy of the Diocese of Oxford at his second visitation, November 1851* (1851) pp. 23–31; *A Charge delivered to the Diocese of Oxford at his seventh visitation, December 1866* (1867) pp. 29–30.

the bishop of Salisbury, and by Samuel Wilberforce, who put up Manning, still an eminent light of the Church of England, to move a wrecking amendment to a motion he was proposing at the annual meeting of the National Society in 1849. 'From that hour,' says Denison with passion, 'I date the ruin of "Church Education" in England at the hands of Churchmen.' But it had not ended Denison's power to deal with backsliders. In the past Gladstone had been a friend of Denison, but by 1853 Gladstone's political position had so changed that Denison suspected what his views on the education question might be, and opposed him when he was a candidate for the representation of the University of Oxford in Parliament. In 1853 he could only shake Gladstone, but he claimed to have done more than anyone else to drive Gladstone out of Oxford in 1865.[1]

Gladstone's expulsion from Oxford in 1865 and his reappearance in Lancashire as a candidate for election to Parliament 'unmuzzled' and prepared to address a much wider and more democratic audience is one of the signs that the mid nineteenth-century halt in politics, and with it the Church's immunity from effective attack, was drawing to an end. In two years' time there would be the Second Reform Bill followed by the election of 1868, which brought into Parliament a number of the Church's enemies and the renewal of attacks on the Church which had died away since the dangerous times of the First Reform Bill. In the interval the Church had not done much to conciliate the dissenters. So divided a Church with so many people clinging to fragments of its old position, was unlikely to be able to agree with its adversary. It can never be known whether a more conciliatory policy towards dissenters based on a more comprehensive view of the country's educational needs would have placed the Church in a better position when the time of reckoning came, for it had not been tried and affairs moved forward to the bitter crisis caused by the Education Bill of 1870.

The immediate occasion of the collapse of the first system of elementary education was not, however, only the result of attacks by the natural enemies of the system, it was also the result of the system's inherent defects. It has already been

[1] Denison, *Notes* [op. cit., p. 128] pp. 170 and 182–3.

suggested what some of these were. There was the over-preponderance of church schools, and the grievances of those dissenting parents for whose children only a church school was available. There was the fact that England, with the wealth of the industrial and commercial revolutions in her pockets, had equipped herself with a system of elementary education on the cheap. It is ironical to find members of Parliament expressing anxiety about the great sums which were being spent on education, when in fact the country ought to have been spending much more and could well have afforded to do so. As a result of this many of the school buildings seem to have been bad and the teachers underpaid, and too much of the system was subject to the whims of those who provided the funds made necessary by the government's economy.

Moreover the quality of the education given seems on the whole to have been poor. One possible reason for this is significant for present purposes. Since the initiative in the founding and maintenance of schools had so often come from the parsons, and the motive in founding schools was so largely religious, too much school time was often devoted to what passed as religious education. Unfortunately also it seems too often to have been rather poor religious education. There is a good deal of evidence to suggest that much of what passed as religious education consisted in training the children to rattle off by rote the answers to the church catechism, or the collects, or for that matter the kings of Judah and Israel. Nor is it clear that these exercises necessarily led to a very profound apprehension of spiritual truths. It would be interesting to try to understand the real conceptions of religion entertained by children whose training culminated in answering an examination paper in which a typical question was: 'Show from the Old Testament that God is long suffering.'[1] Or by the children of whom a clergyman reported in 1868: 'Ask a national school class, "How are you saved?" and they will shout in reply "By the blood of Jesus," ' and added, 'It never enters their heads for a moment that they do not understand what they say.'[2]

However, this is a matter about which confident generalization is likely to be deceptive. There exists evidence to the effect

[1] Hadden, *Rogers* [op. cit., p. 108] p. 208.
[2] W. L. Clay, *Essays in Church Policy* [op. cit., p. 130] p. 223.

that the religious education given in at least some church schools was better than the normal criticisms of it suggest. Moreover, to learn the collects and bible stories in the noble language of the prayer book and the Authorized version may have given a child a richer cultural background than he could have got from a bleaker or more utilitarian education, such as is described in *Hard Times*. However, whatever can be said on the other side there is one notable piece of evidence which seems to testify at least to the comparative failure of the founders of the church schools. The proportion of the number of adults who continued to attend church services to the numbers of children who had at one time or another attended church schools was disappointingly small.

It seems possible that this concentration on religious education had unfortunate results on the secular education sometimes given in church schools. That was certainly the opinion of William Rogers. He describes how on one occasion he visited a national school on behalf of the archbishop of Canterbury and found that the children were so 'dosed with the plagues, and types, and judges and kings' that their secular learning had disastrously suffered. They were, he said, great on geography, but it was the geography of Palestine.[1] There was, however, another more fundamental cause for the failure of the elementary education of this period, a cause typical both of the period and the system. There was no law to compel attendance at school. In those conditions such a law was out of the question; even if Parliament could have been induced to accept the principle – and the Newcastle Commission decided against it – it could not have been applied without hardship when so many of the schools were in the hands of one denomination. As a result of this the children too often attended spasmodically, and were liable to be withdrawn if at any time the chance of their being able to earn money for their families presented itself.

After 1860 these defects in the system were revealed in their full seriousness. In 1861 the Newcastle Commission scathingly exposed its educational failures; in fact it possibly exaggerated them. It also exposed the irregularity of the children's attendance at school, though it missed the most serious defect in the country's educational arrangements, that is the number of

[1] Hadden, *Rogers* [op. cit., p. 108] p. 201.

children who were going to no school at all, and indeed had no school to which they could possibly go. Those who advised the commission were apparently mistaken on this point, as apparently were most of those who were interested in education at that time. Possibly they concentrated too much of their attention on conditions in small towns and villages. When dealing with the question of the proportion of children in the population who received some sort of education the Newcastle Commission concluded that the situation was reasonably satisfactory. Said they: 'Looking, therefore, at mere numbers as indicating the state of popular education in England and Wales, the proportion of children receiving instruction to the whole population is, in our opinion, nearly as high as can be reasonably expected.' They calculated that in England and Wales it was 1 in 7·7, whereas in Prussia it was 1 in 6·27.[1] They apparently believed that in the distribution of school places the most serious outstanding problem was the provision of education in poor country districts, and they seem to have been mysteriously unaware of the desperate situation in the great towns.

This situation was revealed by a curious chance. In 1864 a society called the Manchester and Salford Educational Aid Society came into existence to subsidize the education of the very poor. In 1866, in order to calculate the extent of their task, they conducted by a process of sampling a survey of the educational situation in the Manchester district, and reached the startling estimate that 57 per cent of the children between 3 and 12 years of age in Manchester did not go to school at all.

This result apparently greatly surprised those who had made the enquiry. They seem to have attributed it to the fact that parents would not send their children to school rather than to what clearly greatly contributed to the situation, the fact that there were not enough schools to go round. However, these results received considerable publicity. They were reported to the Social Science Association which met in Manchester in 1866. There were further meetings of the Educational Aid Society and a conference in Manchester in 1868 on the subject. There were further enquiries in Liverpool, Birmingham and Leeds, which confirmed the results of the Manchester enquiry.

The situation was clearly very different from what had been

[1] P.P. 1861, XXI, Pt. I, p. 293 (see also pp. 78–88).

suggested by the estimates of the Newcastle Commission, and furnished an overwhelming case for drastic action. In 1867 and 1868 two leading Liberals, H. A. Bruce and W. E. Forster, proposed bills to remedy the situation. These came to nothing, but they enabled their promoters to give publicity to the results of the enquiries. In 1867 the Birmingham Educational Aid Society came into existence, to be followed by the founding in 1868 of the Education League, which brought Joseph Chamberlain into politics. In 1867, also, these revelations achieved their most noticeable result. At a meeting of the congregational union at Manchester Edward Baines, Samuel Morley, and apparently Edward Miall, acknowledged that their opinions were now changed on the attitude nonconformists should take up with regard to the government's interference in education. They now thought a national system of State education should be accepted.[1]

This was not only the reversal of a point of principle which had been reiterated six short years before; it was the reversal of the traditions of two stubbornly contested centuries of nonconformist history. It provided a new programme for political nonconformity, which no longer supported Baines' old principle that the State had no educational duties but rather the policy of the Educational League that it must provide a general system of elementary education which should be undenominational, compulsory and free. Meanwhile the political situation was developing fast, and developing in a way that made educational reforms probable. In 1867 the Second Reform Act was passed, and the promise, or threat, of democracy which it seemed to imply made men anxious to educate those who they thought were about to inherit power. In 1868 there was a general election at which, as has been said, a number of militant dissenters were elected. Gladstone, freed politically if not altogether intellectually from the loyalties of his youth, became prime minister. W. E. Forster became vice-president of the Committee of the Privy Council on Education, and in 1869

[1] I owe my knowledge of the enquiry of the Manchester Educational Aid Society and of the events to which it led to the researches of Mr Henry Roper, now a student at Trinity College, Cambridge, who I hope will in due course produce a book on the policy of the Education Office in the later part of the nineteenth century.

Forster passed through Parliament the Endowed Schools Act, and in 1870, after a bitter struggle with his old dissenting friends, his act to provide a general system of elementary education.

Forster's 1870 Education Act is a turning point in English history, but some of its most revolutionary effects were not intended by him. He was faced as he saw it by an extremely serious situation. The country was educating, more or less imperfectly, about 1,500,000 children in the schools subsidized by the government; but he calculated that only two-fifths of the children of the working classes between the ages of six and ten, and only one-third of those between the ages of ten and twelve, were on the registers of these government schools. He was therefore inspired by the laudable intention of trying to provide a school for every child in the appropriate age groups. He was not prepared to abolish, or starve out, the denominational schools, but he intended to fill in the gaps with undenominational schools subsidized from the rates.[1] It was a task which proved to require considerable courage, a quality never lacking in Forster, for this policy was not that favoured by the nonconformist-inspired Education League. They wanted the complete elimination of the church schools, and they bitterly attacked Forster's measure, pursuing him personally with a venom which is fortunately rare in British politics.

But the act, as introduced, differed in some respects from Forster's initial intention. In its initial form it had permitted local authorities to make grants to denominational schools. That provision was cut out during its passage through Parliament, and the period of grace during which new denominational schools could receive building grants was reduced to six months. This left the denominational schools, which were necessarily partly supported by private subscription, in unequal competition with the board schools called into existence by the act, which were wholly supported by public funds or the rates. After 1880 when the curriculum became more elaborate the position of the denominational schools became increasingly difficult, and in due course an ever larger sector of English education passed completely into public control.

Moreover, if one of the League's requirements was never

[1] See T. Wemys Reid, *Life of the Right Hon. W. E. Forster* (2 vols., 1888) Vol. I, pp. 463-4; and Hansard 3rd Series, CXCXIX, 440-6.

fully complied with – for many of the church schools survived, and indeed still survive – the other two were soon satisfied, or nearly satisfied. In 1870 Forster himself would have wished to have gone further than the Cabinet allowed him to do in making education compulsory, and two acts of 1876 and 1880 did so, while in 1891 steps were taken to make education free for most of the children in the elementary schools.

Even till the end of the century the system was confused by the claims and difficulties of the leaders of the Church of England. In these years the forces of democracy and of Dissent were no doubt stronger than they had been before 1867, but they were not masters of the State; indeed the accidents of politics prevented them from realizing their full strength, and the political control of the country lay in the hands of the friends of the Church, a situation which led to the bitter political controversy over the Education Act of 1902. But however complicated and confused the educational system might remain the general logic of events from 1833 till the end of the century seems clear. In 1833 and the years that followed an important social need, the need to provide education for the people, had become apparent. On the whole the country had not been prepared to entrust the State with sufficient power to provide for it, and a system had been devised which had left much of the initiative and much of the financial responsibility in the hands of the Churches. Very great efforts had been made to achieve a satisfactory system, but they were palpably insufficient to provide for the educational needs of the country. There was only one authority which could do this, and that was the secular State.

The road to collectivism had been long and many people had travelled it reluctantly, but given the circumstances of nineteenth-century England and its needs, there was no other road, and if this was so it seems very unfortunate that as far as popular education was concerned it was not travelled at a greater rate. If England had contrived to speed up the process a serious lag in its educational development need not have occurred. But perhaps to desire that is to wish for a different England than existed, or could exist, in the middle of the nineteenth century.

To say this is not to discount the value of what had been done, nor the personal devotion of those who did it. If England before 1867 was not prepared to equip herself with a satisfactory system of popular education, then an unsatisfactory system of popular education was better than nothing, and the country owed a deep debt to those who provided it. Of these probably the most important was Kay-Shuttleworth, whose services must never be forgotten. It would probably be right also to name certain statesmen, of whom perhaps Lord John Russell and Lord Lansdowne played the most important parts, but it is necessary to recognize that without the enterprise, work and sacrifice of the parochial clergy of the established Church very little education would have been provided while this system persisted.

However, to understand the activities of the clergy of the mid century it is necessary to consider them in the light of the values of their day, not of ours. To do this it is important to take account of two differences between the way in which they for the most part thought and the way men and women are likely to think nowadays.

The first is a difference which I tried to suggest at the beginning of this chapter. To nearly all clergymen, and indeed to most laymen, the dogmas of religion would seem more important than they would seem to most people today; and they would seem to be important in a different way. It would seem to be all-important for a boy or girl to be correctly taught what they should believe. This would probably affect their conduct in this world, and almost certainly affect their destiny after death. This was a consideration which was responsible for much stupid teaching, much stultifying controversy and much fanaticism. It is difficult nowadays to recover the ways in which men thought and felt on points like these, and yet perhaps the educational controversies over this point may have this amount of significance for us. All educational systems must inculcate a morality, even if it is only what purports to be a permissive morality. All moralities are founded upon dogma, even if it is only what purports to be the dogma of agnosticism. It will always be a matter of importance who shall choose the dogma taught in the schools – Church, State, parent or teacher.

The other point to remember is, of course, the fact that

F

much of this work was done by men who still accepted the values of the old order of society. The shape of the educational system, as men then conceived it, was at least in part dictated by the old hierarchy of classes. Much of the activity in providing schools was in obedience to duties proscribed by the philosophy of that hierarchy, and it is to be feared that the lessons of contentment and obedience were too often taught in church schools as an inherent part of the morality by which men and women should direct their lives.

Much of this must seem to us regrettable. Even so it is still necessary to consider the men and women of the past in the terms of the values which they inherited, not of those which we would have wished them to anticipate. Moreover it is necessary to look to the results of their actions. Even defective values can lead men to perform, perhaps at considerable cost to themselves, services which are, at that moment, of the greatest value to those who benefit from them.

The results may, however, be rather different from what was expected. It is impossible to forecast, or control, the effect education may have on a man or woman. There is no reason to believe that it will make him contented, or grateful, or that he will certainly accept the values of the system which has provided it. On the contrary it may open his eyes to the inadequacy of those values or to the inequalities of a system which may seem to have yielded so little to him so grudgingly. It would be interesting to know to what extent the way was prepared for the agricultural trade unionism of the last thirty years of the nineteenth century by the education which mid nineteenth-century parsons had been active in providing. Certainly Joseph Arch records the fact that he owed a great deal to his own village school, which was a church school, though, characteristically, he claims that he owed what he did to the independence of the schoolmaster, and pours contempt on the other church schools in his neighbourhood.[1]

This, however, relates more to the problems of the third phase. In the next chapters it will be desirable to turn to the more definitely secular services of the clergy in the middle of the century.

[1] Joseph Arch, *The Story of his Life* (1898) pp. 25 and 26.

5

The Mid Nineteenth-
Century Parson

The Governmental Order

If before 1830 the parish priest occupied a place in three
hierarchies – the spiritual, the governmental and the social –
mid nineteenth-century conditions would pose an important
problem. The unique importance of the parson's spiritual
functions were going to be emphasized as, in general, they had
not been emphasized in the eighteenth and early nineteenth
centuries. The evangelical vicar or rector would recognize his
terrifying responsibility for the eternal welfare of the inhabitants of a parish many of whom were, as is the case with most
human communities, unredeemed sinners. Those who had been
inspired by the Oxford Movement would know themselves to
be before anything else priests of the eternal and universal
Catholic Church. And the ordinary parson, responding conscientiously, if a trifle confusedly, to the spiritual compulsions
of the period would realize that he was something other than a
dedicated country gentleman. What effect then would these
spiritual perceptions have on the parson's conception of his
secular duties? Would the clergy begin to reject their secular
responsibilities as being incompatible with their spiritual
functions? Or would a renewed social conscience widen their
conception of their secular duty and intensify it? Or would
things go on much as before?

Of one thing there can be no doubt. There would be no
sudden, extensive change all over the country. Men, and
particularly parsons, often cling tenaciously to ideas that have
on any reasonable calculation become anachronistic. Moreover

if after 1832, or even after 1850, the clergy had given up all secular duties it would not have been at all clear how the gap could be filled. In many districts people had come to rely on the parson performing certain secular services – Connop Thirlwall found that in Kirby Underdale in Yorkshire they came to the parson when they wanted a letter written – and in many places it was not clear to whom the parish, or the country, would turn if the parsons were not available.[1]

There was a danger here. It was possible that the clergy might be forced into unsuitable duties because custom sanctioned them or public necessity demanded them. It was a possibility which, it may be held, was realized in some of the things the clergy did. But it is important to recognize the fact that in mid century the acceptance by the parochial clergy of heavy secular responsibilities was by no means solely in response to custom or unavoidable need. It was not the result of fading memories obstinately retained by ageing men, nor the recognition of tiresome duties which an irrelevant past had left as its legacy. It was the conscious acceptance of what seemed to be perfectly appropriate duties, the result of a living tradition handed on from one age to the next, reinvigorated by the new spirit in the Church and therefore not contracting but expanding as the century went forward.

This fact can be best recognized in the language of those who were to be the leaders of the Church. In the period which immediately followed the Reform Act Blomfield was bishop of London and probably at that time the ablest bishop on the Bench. Before 1830 Blomfield had expressed doubts as to whether the numerous secular duties in which many of the clergy had involved themselves were really compatible with the proper performance of their spiritual functions; apparently he was particularly doubtful about their acting as magistrates. However, after 1832 he showed clearly that he believed that some of the secular services which they were apparently performing were not only defensible but commendable, indeed necessary, for the moral health of England. In 1834 he spoke about the clergy in terms which could have been put into the mouth of Sir Thomas Bertram twenty years before.

[1] For Connop Thirlwall, see *Trench* [op. cit., p. 60] Vol. I, p. 188.

Surely [said he] it is not possible to estimate at too high a rate the moral influence which is exerted by a well educated and pious man, stationed in the midst of a poor, unenlightened, population, labouring solely for their good . . ., inquiring with tenderness and delicacy into their wants and woes, and devising methods for their relief; assisting, superintending, perhaps conducting, the education of their children; contriving and facilitating methods of economy and humble independence.

Take their endowments from the clergy and, he said, 'You will shut up, in many a village and hamlet of our land not only the parsonage, but the school, and the dispensary; the local centre and shrine of knowledge, and charity, and sympathy, and order.'[1]

Such were the activities which in 1834 Blomfield believed occupied the time of those of the parochial clergy who were doing their duty. They are an inseparable amalgam of the moral and spiritual and the secular, and Blomfield clearly valued the secular element in the mixture. In fact looking back in 1854 on what had happened in the twenty years that had passed since 1834, he believed that they had played a considerable part in bringing greater social unity and a happier spirit to the troubled and divided England of the second quarter of the century, 'and', he said,

although I may be thought not to be an impartial judge in such a case, I cannot hesitate to declare my conviction, that the clergy have been the chief instruments in bettering the condition of the poor in this country; not merely by the assiduous inculcation of Christian principle in their churches and schools; not merely by devoting their time, and a more than proportionate measure of their worldly means, to the works of education; but by their attention to the temporal wants of their parishioners; by their activity and judgment in carrying into effect the sanitary improvements suggested by the humanity of true philanthropists, and sanctioned by the wisdom of a Christian legislature. The annals of the Cholera will attest the debt of gratitude which the country owes to its clergy; as well as to many lay members of the Church, not more eminent for their rank and intellectual acquirements, than for their unwearied exertions in the cause of charity.[2]

[1] Charles Blomfield, *The Uses of a Standing Ministry and an Established Church. Two sermons preached at the consecration of Churches* (1834) pp. 37 and 40.
[2] Charles Blomfield, *A Charge delivered to the Clergy of the Diocese of London, at the Visitation in November 1854* (1854) p. 5.

His ideal for the parochial clergy was therefore that they should perform a judicious mixture of spiritual and secular functions. For instance, in this charge he recommended house to house visitation not only for spiritual objects but also for the purpose of detecting and removing the sources of malignant disease. He declared that every parish should have not only its daily Sunday and infant schools but also its dispensary, its district visiting society, its lending library and its provident fund.

Blomfield was of course a man who had emerged only partially transmuted by the passage of time from the old regime, and to confirm that these really were to be the ideals of a later generation it may be as well to turn to one who, more than anyone else, is considered to be the prototype of a Victorian bishop, that is to Samuel Wilberforce who became bishop of Oxford in 1845 and of Winchester from 1869 to 1873. When he became bishop of Oxford Wilberforce received from Prince Albert, whose chaplain he had been, a directive which showed clearly what the prince thought were the functions of the clergy in secular matters.

> A Bishop ought to abstain completely from mixing himself up with the politics of the day, and beyond giving a general support to the Queen's government, and occasionally voting for it, should take no part in the discussion of State affairs (for instance Corn Laws, Game Laws, Trade or Financial questions); but he should come forward whenever the interests of humanity are at stake, and give boldly and manfully his advice to the House and country (I mean questions like Negro emancipation, education of the people, improvement of the health of towns, measures for the recreation of the poor, against cruelty to animals, for regulating factory labour, etc. etc.).[1]

These instructions must have been congenial to Wilberforce for they are echoed in his charge at his primary visitation as bishop of Oxford in 1848. 'And first,' he said,

> let me speak on some public matters which I think must interest us all. For though the clergy should never so lower down their high calling as to become political rather than spiritual men, yet in the true and Christian sense of the word, the highest interests of

[1] T. Martin, *The Life of His Royal Highness the Prince Consort* (5 vols., Vol. II, 1876) p. 133.

the πολῖτεία are their special charge. It appertains to their office, as instructors and guides of thought and opinion, that they should closely watch all measures which tend to promote the general welfare, and above all, the morals of the people. The tendency, in many quarters, to multiply such efforts is one of the most favourable symptoms of the present time; and you may greatly aid such good works by being ready to give them, in your several spheres, your support and co-operation. I allude, and I can only allude, to such measures as those for protecting women from the execrable arts of the pander; for limiting the hours on which houses for the sale of fermented or spirituous liquors can be opened on the Sunday; for maintaining by protective enactments, for shopkeepers and others, the rest of the Lord's day; for preventing the brutalizing sports which inflict torture on animals, and degrade those addicted to them; for correcting the grievous abuses by which so many charitable trusts are diverted from their lawful purposes; for improving our system of prison discipline, and the moral treatment of our convicts; and for promoting in various ways, by sanitary measures and by improvements in the poor laws, the welfare and comforts of the labouring population.[1]

The secular ideal is therefore an explicit one, and if the words of Blomfield, Wilberforce and the prince are taken together it covers many of the urgent social needs of mid Victorian England. And this did not remain simply an abstract ideal. As will be seen, many of the parochial clergy tried with varying success to satisfy these, and other, social needs. With these efforts, however, were mixed other activities, which might to a twentieth-century observer seem to have less desirable tendencies. For there is an awkward question to be asked. The ideal as it has been described so far is one that is suitable for a responsible person in an influential position in the old social hierarchy, but what was to be the future of the clergy's functions in the hierarchy of government?

The most significant position which parochial clergymen had occupied in that hierarchy was that of justice of the peace. Blomfield had come to disapprove of clergymen acting as justices, and probably after 1835 an increasing number of the clergy came to share his opinion, but clearly many clergymen did not do so, for a large number of clergymen, in at least the

[1] Samuel Wilberforce, *A Charge delivered to the Clergy of the Diocese of Oxford at his primary Visitation* (1848) pp. 12–14.

first three-quarters of the century, continued to sit on the bench.

According to a return made in the year 1831–2 there were in the English counties 1,154 clerical magistrates as against 3,372 lay magistrates and in the Welsh counties 166 clerical magistrates to 437 lay magistrates. In the English boroughs there were 86 clerical magistrates to 1,212 lay magistrates and in the Welsh boroughs 11 clerical magistrates to 52 lay magistrates.[1] This of course represents the situation under the old regime. But the old regime did not come to an abrupt end with the passing of the Reform Act of 1832. Many of these clergymen continued to act as magistrates for a long time after that, as various returns in later years were to show, and other clergymen were added to them. As late as 1873 after the scandal of the Chipping Norton case, with which I will deal in a later chapter, a return showed that at that date 1,187 clergymen with a cure of souls, or performing some clerical duty, were magistrates, of whom at least 253 had been appointed between 1853 and 1863, and at least 220 between 1863 and 1873.[2] After 1873 the practice seems to have fallen off, though even in 1873 a bill to disqualify clergymen with a cure of souls from becoming magistrates failed to pass the House of Commons, in which at that time there was a Liberal majority.

Therefore during the first three-quarters of the century various governments were prepared to appoint clergymen as magistrates, and many clergymen were willing to become magistrates. The usual defence for such appointments was that the clergy would understand the conditions under which their parishioners lived and impart to the administration of justice a leaven of mercy and sympathy which it might otherwise have lacked. They may have done this, though it would be very difficult to establish whether they did so or not. In the past at least there had been the contrary theory that they were the most severe magistrates. However, it seems most probable that in reality they were not appointed on account of their humanity, but rather for the duller reason that they were the obvious

[1] P.P. 1831–2, XXXV, pp. 231–72. There seem to be some problems about this return, and it might be possible to get a result from it which was slightly different from my result. For another estimate, see S. and B. Webb, *Local Government – the Parish and the County* (1906) p. 383, n. 1.

[2] P.P. 1873, LIV, p. 57.

people to take on the job, and probably, at least before 1840, in some areas the only suitable people to be found. Certainly in the earlier years of the period there seems to have been an insufficiency in some parts of the country of persons of substance, intelligence, literacy and assiduity in public business to do this work in place of the clergy. Certainly in Oxfordshire before 1840 the bulk of the work at quarter sessions seems to have been done by clerical magistrates.[1]

The results of this situation were probably serious. However sympathetic individual clergymen might be, work as a magistrate would inevitably affect the clergy's relations with their flocks. If a large part of the burden of maintaining secular order rested on their shoulders, then in a time of disorder they might have to assume a position of unfortunate prominence in repressing riot and punishing rioters, as seems to have happened in 1830. What was even more serious during the middle years of the century when the countryside was not threatened by major disorders, was the fact that they had to enforce the laws protecting the preservation of game. Even in the 1820s the game laws had sickened Blomfield, and in the 1840s they had excited young Temple's deep detestation. But apparently, at least in Oxfordshire, some of the clerical magistrates with the best records in other matters were extremely severe on poachers.[2]

In judging this it is only fair to consider the views on poaching of not unreasonable men in the class that furnished magistrates. Poaching for many people was one of the activities which disfigured a largely uncivilized countryside. It could be put alongside the cruel sports of which Wilberforce spoke in his charge – bull baiting, badger drawing, cock fighting, dog fighting – and also other unpleasant things such as the really bestial drunkenness, which was endemic all over the country, the lingering belief in witchcraft, which could sometimes have very ugly consequences, and the cruelties which were at times practised on women and children and helpless idiots. None of this, however, alters the fact that the game laws as they existed in England in the middle of the century were both oppressive in their provisions, and harsh in their operation, and that they

[1] Diana McClatchey, *Oxfordshire Clergy 1777–1869* (Oxford, 1960) p. 191.
[2] ibid., pp. 195–6.

had as their object the defence of indefensible class privilege, facts which it was perfectly possible for a contemporary clergyman to recognize if his mind and conscience were not blinded by his position in the county hierarchy.[1]

It would, however, be hazardous to go on from this conclusion to generalize about the effect which this, or any other of the activities of the clergy, had on their relationship with their parishioners. The picture must be a very extensive and complicated one. Of much of it little is known, and it is not legitimate to fill in the gaps by *a priori* methods. What evidence does exist seems to suggest that there were a great variety of attitudes and, certainly, some of the attitudes recorded do not seem to be consistent with the pattern which modern historians tend to impose generally on the whole English countryside. All that can be said with certainty is that the fact that so many of the clergy were prepared to serve as magistrates indicates a view of their position and way of thinking about their work which was likely to affect profoundly the way in which they approached the social problems that confronted them. Their thoughts on such matters were, however, likely to be even more decisively influenced by their experience of another government activity in which most clergymen would probably be involved at some time in one way or another, that is the administration of the Poor Law.

The Poor Law, and the problems to which it gave rise in the first half of the nineteenth century, have a peculiar importance in the formation of social policy for two reasons. First, there is the obvious fact that the causes and results of poverty, and its extent and severity, together with the ways in which it may be relieved or diminished, provide at any time the most fundamental social problems; and secondly, as far as the nineteenth century was concerned, the issues to which the administration of the Poor Law gave rise had, in the late eighteenth or early nineteenth century, occasioned a controversy which was relevant to every contemporary social problem.

[1] For a condemnation by a contemporary clergyman of the game laws, see the report of the Rev. John Clay, chaplain of Preston Gaol, to Lord Stanley, 2 February 1855: W. L. Clay, *The Prison Chaplain: a Memoir of the Rev. John Clay B.D.* (1861) pp. 563–9. See also Charles Kingsley's novel *Yeast*.

It was a long controversy. It can be said to have started about 1795 with the years of dearth and high prices with which the eighteenth century ended. To meet the problems caused by the resultant distress various poor law authorities had adopted certain expedients. They had granted to labourers allowances in money or kind in proportion to the number of children they had to support. They had given allowances to make a labourer's wage up to a living wage. They had tried to spread the employment in a parish so that it could sustain as many people as possible. They had created employment, normally on the roads, for those who could not obtain employment elsewhere. In the first years of the nineteenth century there developed a sharp reaction against all these innovations. It was said that the mismanagement of the poor crippled those who had to pay the rates and did not really benefit those whom it was intended to benefit, for to subsidize wages from the rates merely kept wages down, since employers obviously paid as little as they could so that as much of the payment as possible should fall on the parish. The provision of money for labour-providing schemes meant the taxation of productive activities for activities which were essentially artificial and unproductive, and that in the long run could do no one any good. Meanwhile, the end result of all these activities was to increase rates to astronomical heights in order to support labourers who were being encouraged to believe that they had a right to be supported by others, and who produced babies in reckless profusion in the secure knowledge that they could get allowances for them.

These strictures dominated the controversy from a little after 1800 till 1834, when the Poor Law Amendment Act was passed to put an end to those practices which were held to be the source of trouble. After this the centre of the storm changed with the development of a violent attack on the cruelties of the new law. But before 1834 the controversy had extended itself beyond the practical problems raised by the working of a particular law to the general issues of the causes of poverty and the proper treatment of poverty, and had drawn into its vortex two important social philosophers, T. R. Malthus and Jeremy Bentham.

Malthus produced the theory that poverty was caused by

the, to him ineluctible, fact that the natural increase of population always tended to outrun the supply of food. For this reason the Poor Law was suspect. It was possible that it encouraged early marriage and the reckless procreation of children, for whom there was no natural endowment in the world as it was then constituted. As a matter of fact Malthus does not seem to have been quite decisive in his opinions on this matter, but the thought that he inspired tended that way. In any case, at best the Poor Law diverted attention from what seemed to Malthus the best hope for improving the condition of the working class, which was the encouragement of late marriage and self-control. Malthus's, influence seems to have been at its greatest in the early years of the nineteenth century. After 1819 his direct influence seems to have faded; those who would normally have been his disciples were coming to believe that industrial development would balance the results of the increase of population, so that Malthus remained in the field mainly as a symbol, and as a target for abuse, on the part of those who probably knew little more of his work than a few objectionable passages. In those roles, however, he continued to play a considerable part in the formation of opinion.

Bentham's contribution was greater and more permanent. In 1797 he produced an elaborate plan for the management of the poor, and from time to time he reverted to the subject, making fantastic elaborations to the detailed organization of large colonies in which he planned to house the indigent poor, their work being farmed out to contractors, the chief contractor being Jeremy Bentham. None of this was likely to come to anything; it was little more than a rather ugly fairy tale, though whether it was only that to Bentham is problematical. However, apart from that, Bentham made two contributions to the subject which were of lasting importance. He devised the principle of *less eligibility*, which was that relief to an able-bodied adult should be only sufficient to provide him with a way of life which would be 'less eligible' than that enjoyed by anyone who was earning his living without assistance. It was a principle embodied in the thought and practice of most poor law reformers, but Bentham gave clear expression to it. There was, however, this difference between Bentham's thought and that of most of the others who contributed to the subject. They tended to see the problem in moral terms. It was moral failure which made men and women rely on relief; to make it difficult for them to do so was to encourage moral independence. Such ideas do not seem to have appealed to Bentham. He was merely concerned with social engineering. He simply believed that if a man found that a life dependent on relief was going to be more disagreeable than it would be if he depended on his own efforts, he would try to support himself. In fact it is unlikely that this difference in the two points of view would lead to any noticeable difference in the enforcement of the principle.

Bentham's other lasting contribution was his conception that a national poor law policy should be imposed by central government on clearly thought out, rational principles which should override the ancient institutions habits and ideas, these being in his view responsible for the failures of the old system. This ideal was realized in the New Poor Law of 1834. This act was devised by Edwin Chadwick, and there is some controversy about the extent to which Chadwick derived his ideas from Bentham, but it seems without question that this conception of an all-embracing framework enforcing a policy from the centre was based on Bentham's philosophy.[1]

As has been said, the principles which were to be imposed, the principles of encouraging self-help and discouraging reliance on the rates, were common to a good many people. They seemed to have been supported not only by sound argument but by the experiments of men who had gained control of the administration of the Poor Law in their own neighbourhoods. It is significant for the purposes of this book that most of those who were responsible for these experiments were parochial clergymen. There was J. T. Becher, vicar general of Southwell, Robert Lowe, rector of Bingham in Nottinghamshire, the father of Robert Lowe the Victorian statesman, C. D. Brereton, rector of Little Massingham in Norfolk, the father of the Brereton who became an ambitious promoter of secondary schools, and others whose opinions and actions are duly noted in the royal commission of enquiry which the Whig

---

[1] J. R. Poynter, *Society and Pauperism, English Ideas on Poor Relief, 1793–1834* (1969). On Bentham and Malthus, pp. 106–85; on Bentham and the New Poor Law, pp. 323–9.

government appointed to enquire into the operation of the Poor Laws.[1]

That commission was appointed in 1832 and reported in 1834. Blomfield and J. B. Sumner, then bishop of Chester, were both members, but its report was largely written by Chadwick and Nassau Senior.[2] It squarely placed the blame for what was wrong and for much of the distress in the country on the past mismanagement of the Poor Law. In fact this was deceptive. Indeed it seems clear that this was the conclusion that the writers of the report had expected to find and that the evidence was to some extent selected and interpreted in such a way as to establish their preconceptions. A more recent analysis of the evidence has made a strong case that in fact the old poor law abuses had, at least in the twenty years or so before 1832, not much to answer for, and that the probable cause of distress was chronic unemployment and substandard wages which are, it is said, typical conditions in areas specializing in the production of wheat and lacking alternatives in industry.[3] In fact, taking this and other evidence into account, the fundamental factor in the situation seems to have been that the purely agricultural areas of England, Ireland, Scotland and Wales were, in the early nineteenth century, possibly as the result of a considerable rise in population in the eighteenth century, carrying a far larger number of people than they could support in decent conditions on the forms of employment available. In certain areas this condition may have been aggravated by the loss of resources owing to enclosures, though it seems to be by no means clear to what extent this affected the situation, and in which areas at what periods. But neither the results of over-population, nor of enclosures, were likely to be remedied by the reform of the Poor Law. Indeed the results of over-population seem to have dominated those English counties which were

[1] J. D. Marshall, *Econ. Hist. Review*, 2nd series, XIII (1961) pp. 382–96: 'The Nottinghamshire Reformers and their contribution to the New Poor Laws.' See also P.P. 1834, XXIX, particularly appendix A, pt. I, pp. 169–240.

[2] S. E. Finer, *The Life and Times of Sir Edwin Chadwick* (1952) pp. 69–93.

[3] Mark Blaug, *Journal of Economic History* (New York) Vol. XXIII (1963) pp. 151–84: 'The Myth of the Old Poor Law and the Making of the New'; Vol. XXIV (1964) pp. 229–45: 'The Poor Law Report Re-examined.'

remote from the employment given by industry for the first three-quarters of the century. But in 1834 the report of the commission asserted that it had been the mismanagement of the Poor Law that had been the cause of trouble. Its conclusions were accepted, and the act was straightway passed to enable the old poor law authorities to be remoulded and placed under the healthy discipline of an authority which should make sure that the old abuses should be brought to an end.

Since it did all these things the Poor Law Amendment Act of 1834 provided one of the most important turning points in the history of English institutions. It is also in its own right a very remarkable act. There can be few acts on the statute book which have been designed to grant to a subordinate body such extensive and unlimited powers of delegated legislation as this act did. The intention of the act was to replace the historic parishes, which in the main had been the units by which the Poor Law had been administered, by unions governed by elected boards of guardians. The principles on which these unions were to work were to be prescribed by a body of three commissioners, who were to bring them into existence, organize the building of workhouses, etc., prescribe rules on which they were to administer relief and control the servants they were to use.

The act also laid down guide-lines for these rules. These were to get rid of such practices as giving relief outside the workhouse to the able-bodied or their families, while they were in whole or part-time employment or unless the circumstances were exceptional.[1] But how this was to be achieved, when it was to be achieved and what was to be the treatment of such of the destitute as were not able-bodied adults, were matters which were very much left to the commissioners, subject only to the rather remote and uncertain control of the home secretary and Parliament. For this reason the way in which the act was to work depended to an unusual extent on the policy followed by the commissioners. Chadwick was not made a commissioner, but he was appointed secretary with the promise of promotion, which was not fulfilled. Thereafter the policy followed differed in some ways from the original intention of its author, and those involved in working it became involved in bitter feuds, which

[1] 4 and 5 Wm IV, c. 76, s. 52.

came to the surface over the Andover scandal in 1846. Meanwhile the act itself and the policy it was supposed to embody were subject to vehement attack from outside. This started while the act was being passed and became more violent and wild as the provisions of the act were extended into the manufacturing North in the years from 1836 onwards, which were unfortunately also years of deep depression in commerce and industry and of widespread and harsh distress and misery.

Richard Oastler, the factory reformer, turned his movement into a violent agitation against the New Poor Law and the attack became an important component in the Chartist agitation. A number of Tory politicians took the matter up, partly because they sincerely believed that the object of the act was the cruel destruction of ancient rights at the instigation of Liberal political economists, and partly because they were in opposition and this was a very good way of attacking the government. Novelists such as Disraeli and Dickens painted harsh pictures of the men responsible for the operation of the Poor Law and what it meant for the poor who were subjected to it, and John Walter, the proprietor of *The Times*, gave his reporters every chance to publish any reports which seemed to demonstrate the cruelties which the law inflicted.

It is a little difficult to penetrate through the dense smoke left behind by all this heavy drum fire to the facts. There can be little doubt that a number of the workhouse scandals were real examples of cruelty and maladministration. There can also be little doubt that the rule denying relief to the able-bodied except in the workhouse could be a very hard one, especially to a man or woman who was the victim of temporary unemployment, or when it meant the splitting up of a family, or the consignment of anyone to a house which was cruelly and meanly administered, and where all types of the destitute were herded together in common misery. On the other hand, many of the assertions of those who attacked the Poor Law were patently unreliable; indeed, many of the statements of fact which they made seem to have been disproved, and if the reports of the poor law commissioners are examined they seem to contain the accounts of a number of effectively and humanely run unions. It is a little difficult entirely to discount all these favourable reports, and where there has been close research into the administration of the New Poor Law in particular districts it appears that in fact, in those districts at least, the new law could be administered with considerable humanity and understanding.[1]

The agitation in the North is not perhaps very satisfactory evidence for the harshness of the law's operation in industrial conditions, since the most violent riots seem to have taken place to prevent its being introduced, not after it had been introduced. Moreover, there was never a general prohibition of outdoor relief. In the quarter ending Lady Day 1844, 231,000 people in England and Wales were relieved in workhouses and 1,247,000 outside them. In the corresponding quarter in 1848, 306,000 were relieved in workhouses and 1,877,000 outside them, the numbers of the destitute having been increased by the immigration of the Irish fleeing from the potato famine. Nor was it possible at any period in the century to stop the practice of paying allowances to people who were also earning money from wages or some sort of trade, or giving relief outside the workhouse.[2]

The whole matter requires further detailed research, which will put on one side the confident general statements which propagandists have made and historians have too readily accepted on the subject, and will deal with what happened union by union as far as it is possible to find this out. But even without such research it seems possible to venture the not very surprising opinion that the humanity or harshness of the New Poor Law varied greatly from place to place. It is true that the general policy of denying outdoor relief was on the face of it a harsh one, but it must be remembered that it was only to be applied to able-bodied adults, and that even where they were concerned exceptions could be made and, as has been seen, were made. It is also true that the commissioners did on occasion try to pursue that policy of pinchbeck economy which

---

[1] David Roberts, *Historical Journal*, Vol. VI (1963) pp. 97–107: 'How Cruel was the Victorian Poor Law?' (but see Ursula Henriques, *Historical Journal*, Vol. XI (1968) pp. 365–71). Norman McCord, *International Review of Social History*, Vol. XIV (1969) Pt. I, pp. 90–108 (for the application of the New Poor Law in the Tyneside area).

[2] J. H. Clapham [op. cit., p. 18] Vol. I, pp. 578–83. M. E. Rose, *Econ. Hist. Review* (2nd series) Vol. 19 (1966) pp. 607–20: 'The Allowance System under the New Poor Law.'

Victorians too often confounded with good administration. But in reality, for all their legal powers the commissioners' real powers of continuous control over the administration of any one particular union must have been, in those days of local independence and poor communications, limited, and the effectiveness of their control cannot have been improved by the feuds in the office, which extended to the relationships between the commissioners and the assistant commissioners who were supposed to keep in touch with what was going on in the country. In fact it seems very probable that events often depended very largely on the character of the important people on the spot, particularly on the behaviour of the chairmen of the boards of guardians. Where the chairman and his fellow guardians were active and responsible a union might be effectively and humanely administered. If, however, they were negligent or callous, and in particular if the management of the union fell into the hands of people whose own economic margin was small and whose primary interest was to keep down the rates, then the administration might become extremely callous and harsh. This seems to have been the more likely because apparently the kind of people who were available in the eighteenth and early nineteenth century for such posts as masters of workhouses, relieving officers, wardens in prisons, etc., seem for some reason often to have been brutal and unsatisfactory characters who without adequate oversight would certainly abuse their opportunities.

All this is of importance for present purposes because in one way or another a great many of the parochial clergy had much to do with poor law administration. Under the system that had prevailed before 1834 a clergyman might, if he was a magistrate, help to lay down rules for the management of the poor with the other magistrates in quarter sessions. He might order relief and serve as the authority to whom appeal could be made on poor law matters if some sort of quarrel arose. He could also act as chairman of the vestry meeting in his parish, and, indeed, if he was a masterful man, could gain complete control of the administration of the Poor Law there. This had been done by the clerical reformers of the Poor Law, whose work led towards the reform of the law in 1834. However, it is clear from the evidence received by the royal commission of 1832 to 1834 that there were large areas of the country where the clergy did not in general attend the vestry or interfere in the administration of the Poor Law. No doubt in a number of cases this was because the clergyman was negligent or an absentee, but apparently in some cases they did not attend because they were not wanted and feared they might be insulted if they came. There were also some cases where a clergyman apparently felt that to be an active member of a body whose duty it might be to refuse relief might place him in an awkward or unsuitable relationship with his parishioners, especially since it was his duty to urge in his sermons the virtue of charity.[1]

This scruple does not seem to have troubled the more robust of the clerical poor law reformers but it nevertheless points to another function which a parochial clergyman might perform. He might act not so much as an administrator of the Poor Law, but as a critic of the way in which it was administered. His experience of the way in which his parishioners had been treated placed him in a position to press charges of cruelty or neglect which those who had suffered from them were unable to do. There is an example of this before 1834 from Somerset. John Skinner was rector of Camerton between 1800 and 1839. His diary between 1822 and 1832 has been published. In it there are several complaints about the bad influence and harshness of the old Poor Law, and about the callousness and negligence of the overseer of the poor in his parish, one Hicks, whom Skinner calls 'a truly brutified English farmer of the modern school'.[2]

As has been said, the reform of 1834 was in part carried through both as a result of clerical experience and also with the approval of clerical opinion. Before 1832 the clerical poor law reformers had led the way, in 1832–4 Blomfield and Sumner had served on the commission of enquiry and it seems clear that, whatever qualms Blomfield had about the way in which the law worked out after 1834, he remained an ally of Chadwick's and supported his schemes. It was not therefore likely that a profession which had been so active in poor law affairs

[1] P.P. 1834, XXVIII, Appendix A, Pt. I, pp. 172, 483; XXIX, Appendix A, Pt. II, p. 51A.
[2] Howard Toombs and the Rev. Arthur N. Bax, M.A., eds., *Journal of a Somerset Rector, John Skinner A.M. Antiquary 1772–1839, Parochial Affairs of the Parish of Camerton 1822–32* (1930) pp. 27, 119, 198, 269.

before 1834 would cease to be so afterwards. There were, in fact, various ways in which under the new law a clergyman could still take a hand. If he were a magistrate he could take advantage of the provision of the act that a justice of the peace could act as an *ex-officio* member of the board of guardians acting for the parish in which he resided supposing he was on the commission of the peace for that county.[1] If he was not a magistrate, or was a magistrate for another county, he could get himself elected to the board of guardians and possibly become chairman. Even after 1834 a clergyman might act as a visitor to a Gilbert Act Incorporation, and it is clear that some clergymen did. He might act officially, or unofficially, as chaplain to a workhouse in his neighbourhood, or he might simply interest himself in the working of the Poor Law as it affected his parishioners.

It is evident that some clergymen took advantage of all these opportunities and it would be of some importance to know how many did so and in particular how many were involved in the actual administration of the law, and what they thought of it. These questions present difficulties, however. It seems clear from the early reports of the commissioners that it could be a clerical guardian, often a clerical magistrate, who brought the new law into working order after 1834.[2] The personal records of a number of clergymen show that they were active members of their local boards of guardians. For instance, John Ballard, vicar of Cropredy in Oxfordshire, apparently acted as chairman to the Banbury Board of Guardians for the four years before 1840.[3] That remarkable man Richard Durnford, who held the living at Middleton in Lancashire from 1831 to 1870, though he refused to be a magistrate was 'for years' on the local board of guardians, which he found most disagreeable.[4] The Rev. E. B. Ellman, for sixty years rector of Berwick in Sussex, was for more than forty years before 1888 a member of the West Firle

---

[1] 4 and 5 Wm IV, c. 76, s. 38.
[2] e.g. see P.P. 1836, XXIX, Pt. I, pp. 490–501. To the clergymen mentioned there can be added the Rev. E. S. Thurlow, first chairman of the Houghton-le-Spring union (communicated by Mr Roy Barker of the University of Newcastle upon Tyne).
[3] McClatchey [op. cit., p. 147] p. 219.
[4] W. R. W. Stephens, *A Memoir of Richard Durnford* (1899) p. 98.

Board of Guardians of which he became first vice-chairman and then for at least thirty-five years chairman. He has left on record some of his views on the operation of the Poor Law.[1] William Stubbs, the great constitutional historian and subsequently bishop of Oxford, was vicar of Navestock in Essex from 1850 to 1866 and apparently throughout that time an active member of the local board of guardians.[2] Another Oxford historian, J. R. Green, while incumbent of St Philip's, Stepney between 1866 and 1869, became an *ex-officio* member of the local board of guardians and, as will be seen, wrote on poor law subjects.[3] Brooke Lambert, first curate then incumbent of St Jude's, Whitechapel, and an important contributor to the problem of pauperism, became a member of the Whitechapel Board of Guardians.[4] Brooke Lambert became an important early member of the Charity Organization Society, as did the Rev. L. R. Phelps, who in 1914 became provost of Oriel but apparently for many years before that was chairman and controlling figure of the Oxford Board of Guardians.[5]

No doubt a more extensive and systematic search would yield other names, though this kind of evidence seems to provide limited results; unfortunately this is not the kind of subject which always interests a clerical biographer, and probably the kind of clergymen most active in this matter are unlikely to have biographies. The number of clerical guardians can be eked out a little by controversies and scandals. These produce the Rev. Edward Sobell as chairman of the Marylebone Board of Guardians in 1843 and the Rev. C. Dodson, chairman of the Andover Board of Guardians in 1845,[6] but the best evidence of the commitment of a large number of the clergy to the administration of the Poor Law is in the Parliamentary

---

[1] Rev. Edward Boys Ellman, *Recollections of a Sussex Parson* (1912) pp. 98, 203–6, 287–8.

[2] W. H. Hutton, *Letters of William Stubbs, Bishop of Oxford 1825–1901* (1904) p. 53.

[3] Leslie Stephen, ed., *Letters of John Richard Green* (1901) p. 56.

[4] Rev. Ronald Bayne, ed., *Sermons and Lectures by the late Rev. Brooke Lambert, M.A., D.C.L. (Vicar of Greenwich)*, with a memoir by J. E. G. DeMontmorency, B.A., Ll.B. (1871).

[5] C. L. Mowat, *The Charity Organization Society 1869–1913, its ideas and work* (1961) pp. 133, 159–60.

[6] P.P. 1843, XLV, pp. 256–7; P.P. 1846, V, Pt. I, p. 178.

Papers generally. They may give some idea of the proportion of laity to clergy engaged in the administration of the law as, for instance, in 1844 when before a select committee on medical poor relief 6 clerical witnesses appeared as opposed to 31 lay witnesses, or in 1847 when before a committee on the law of settlement 11 clerical witnesses appeared as opposed to 34 lay witnesses, the lay witnesses not all being involved in the administration of the law.[1]

All this, I am afraid, leaves a very unsatisfactory conclusion. The available evidence does not suggest satisfactorily how many of the clergy were involved in the administration of the law, or how many of the parochial clergy had nothing to do with it, or the proportion of clerical guardians to lay guardians, and whether this proportion differed, as is probable, in different parts of the country. All this must be learnt, if it can be learnt, by more extensive research. All that can be concluded here is that a large number of clergymen were involved in the adminis-tration of the Poor Law, and there is a strong *prima facie* case that this service was likely to have an important bearing on their conceptions of social policy. Even so it is important to be very careful. Men gave their services to the Poor Law with different objects in mind and practised different standards of humanity and conscientiousness. It is worth comparing Dodson, chairman of the Andover union, and Brooke Lambert. If the parliamentary enquiry is any guide Dodson had been guilty of culpable negligence in permitting a brutal master of the workhouse to abuse his position and starve and maltreat the paupers, and if the report of *The Times* correspondent has any validity he had been the conscious agent of an attempt to enforce the policy of the New Poor Law at its harshest, had dominated the guardians and reduced a fellow clergyman, who had his doubts about the Poor Law, to being his accomplice.[2] Brooke Lambert, on the other hand, set out to mitigate the operation of the Poor Law in favour of those who were subject to it, as far as that was desirable, to prevent nepotism and to learn what he could about the condition of the poor.[3] The men

---

[1] P.P. 1844, IX and 1847, XI.
[2] P.P. 1846, V, Pt. I, pp. 178–247 and Pt. II, pp. 213–20. *The Times*, 15 September 1845, p. 8, col. 2.
[3] Brooke Lambert, *Pauperism* (1871) pp. vi–xviii, 57–70.

are so wide apart that perhaps the comparison is meaningless. Even so one can compare Dodson with a number of contemporary clerical chairmen whose unions were, to judge from the reports, very much more humanely and efficiently run than that at Andover.

So even those of the clergy who were engaged in the administration of the Poor Law differed widely from one another, and there were of course a large number of clergymen who had nothing to do with it. Indeed after 1834 there continued to be clergymen who disapproved altogether of the way in which the administration of the Poor Law affected their parishioners. For instance, in 1837 a number of the clergy in Hampshire and West Sussex complained of the harshness of the administration of the Poor Law in the unions in which their parishes were situated and the inadequacy of the food in the workhouse.[1] Or to go much later into the century, in 1861 a number of clergy in the East End of London complained that the administration of poor relief had broken down in the relevant unions in the emergency of a very severe frost which had occasioned widespread suffering.[2] Or in 1863 J. H. Blunt, curate of Newbottle and Herrington in County Durham, complained that the relieving officer of the Houghton-le-Spring union had grossly neglected a mentally sick pauper. The relieving officer was called before the board of guardians and forced to express his regret, and in 1864 was dismissed for inefficiency and misconduct.[3] These are cases thrown up by chance, but they should be enough to disturb any nascent generalization that the parochial clergy were committed to the Poor Law however hardly it bore upon the poor, or for that matter that they were ever of one mind on the subject. To emphasize the last point it should be said that the chairman of one of the unions about which complaint was made in the London case was the Rev. Thomas Parry, chairman of the Walthamstow Board of Guardians.

Nevertheless the fact that many of the clergy were prepared to become guardians seems to reveal something about their conception of their role. The fact that they were prepared to

[1] P.P. 1837, XVII, Pt. I, pp. 19, 272, 285, 326, 586.
[2] P.P. 1861, IX, pp. 128–43, 144.
[3] Communicated by Mr Roy Barker [see p. 158, n. 2].

become guardians, and still more the fact that they were ready to become magistrates, meant that the masterful assumptions of the old order had not wholly passed from the minds of the clergy. Whatever they thought of themselves as priests they were still prepared to accept heavy responsibilities which were not only secular but also executive and governmental. Sometimes these responsibilities led to actions which were oppressive and inspired by class interest; often enough they were useful, indeed at times they supplied services which in that period only the parish clergyman was likely to perform. It was not, therefore, unreasonable for a clergyman to feel that many of these services most obviously came within the duties of his office. Nevertheless they were essentially rather magisterial than pastoral. They could be combined with pastoral work, but they introduced an element into the relationship of an English Church parson and his parishioners which was very likely to affect the way in which they saw one another.

The poor parishioner might, and no doubt in many cases did, accept the parson as a natural superior with traditional rights of superintendence, perhaps to be criticized and often secretly to be laughed at, but accepted as part of the unchangeable order of things; or he might feel deep inward resentment, which would develop into open attack as the century went forward and the area of political consciousness increased. But in few cases, even when the relationship was coloured by genuine feelings of affection and respect, was it likely to be the simple relationship of a Christian man or woman to his spiritual pastor. And, though the parson might fully realize that his primary duties were spiritual, it was likely that he would instinctively assume rights of secular direction and control which had little to do with his spiritual office. Furthermore, the way in which he performed his spiritual functions, his treatment of individuals, the social policy which he commended, would probably also be influenced by any work that he did in the administration of the Poor Law.

It is important not to exaggerate here. The principles on which the Poor Law was conducted were in fact principles which at that time were accepted by many people who had nothing to do with its administration. Talk about the necessity for encouraging self-respect and manly independence was the natural language of the day, and many excellent people in all walks of life and on all sides in politics were convinced of the importance of preventing an able-bodied adult from depending on others for his subsistence. There was no need to sit on a board of guardians in order to learn that language or imbibe that principle. Nevertheless, any prolonged service in the administration of any system of relief or public assistance at any date naturally impresses on those involved the need to be on guard lest the unscrupulous should take unworthy advantage of what is offered; and in the mid nineteenth century the crucial importance of that duty was likely to be strongly enforced by experience of the working of a system at whose inception the principle of 'less eligibility' had been so clearly enunciated.

Again it is important not to exaggerate. The principle of 'less eligibility' calls up a picture of dreary workhouse wards, of meals of watery gruel, of brutal workhouse masters and callous woman superintendents, and of human beings treated without any regard for human dignity. No doubt the facts too often corresponded to that picture, but it seems probable that they did not always do so, and the vividness of that picture should not be allowed to obscure the real humanity of many of those who operated the Poor Law, even if after some sort they accepted the principle. Still less should it be used as the justification for an undiscriminating attack on those who had inspired and devised the New Poor Law. It is important to remember that the poor law reformers had only intended the principle to be applied to able-bodied adults who could earn their own living if they wanted to do so. It had not been their intention to apply the principle to victims of sudden misfortune or to those who were in some way incapacitated owing to causes beyond their control.

Bentham, for instance, who had first, in so many words, formulated the principle of 'less eligibility', wished also to bring into existence a number of 'collateral aids' to help the independent labourer to remain independent.[1] Chadwick, who possibly more than anyone else explicitly introduced the principle into the New Poor Law, wished to have classified workhouses to secure that the treatment of the aged, the youthful and the sick could be distinguished from that accorded to the

[1] J. R. Poynter [op. cit., p. 151] pp. 122–7.

able-bodied.[1] These proposals came to nothing, but Chadwick spent the most important part of his official life attacking the most pervasive of the causes of poverty and disease. Blomfield, who had served on the commission and whose report led to the adoption of the New Poor Law, according to his biographer changed his mind when he saw how it worked out. Having believed that it would bring the labouring classes 'to depend on their own honest exertions for the supply of their wants', the author believed that he came to the conclusion that in fact it led to 'the severance of parochial relief to the poor and needy, the sick and the aged, from the influence of Christian charity and spiritual supervision, by handing it over to the heartless rule of political economy and bureaucratic formality'.[2] It would be interesting to know what lies behind this statement. It was certainly not a breach of Blomfield's alliance with Chadwick. There are a good many instances which show that he continued to support Chadwick and his policy. In 1839 he proposed, at Chadwick's instigation, the appointment of a critical select committee of the House of Lords on public health. It looks as if an amendment which he proposed to the Public Health Act of 1848 was also one which Chadwick desired, and he continued to commend the cause of public health to his clergy. Nor is it probable that Blomfield at any time supported the policy of indiscriminate charity. In 1843, working with Gladstone, Sir Robert Inglis and others, he founded 'The Metropolitan Visiting and Relief Association', the object of which was to secure a careful investigation into the circumstances of those who were to be helped in order to make sure that the unworthy did not participate.[3] It seems possible, therefore, that what Blomfield reacted against was not the principle of the Poor Law as originally defined, but the administration of that law once Chadwick's influence had been eliminated.

Certainly the Poor Law as it came to be administered was probably very different from Chadwick's original conception.

[1] S. E. Finer [op. cit., p. 152] p. 85.
[2] Biber, *Blomfield* [op. cit., p. 51] pp. 209, 211.
[3] J. C. Pringle, *Social Work of the London Churches being some account of the Metropolitan Visiting and Relief Association 1843–1937* (Oxford, 1937).

There was less discrimination between different types of poverty, those relieved were often thrust into one common workhouse, and there was no real attempt to trace the causes of poverty. In order, however, to measure the Poor Law as it may have appeared to clerical reformers and administrators both before and after 1834 it is important to consider a point which it is possible that Chadwick himself had consciously left out of his calculations.

Before the reform of the Poor Law several of the clergy, some of the poor law reformers, had adopted expedients to save men from relying on the Poor Law. They had promoted schemes of allotments, the produce of which would enable a labourer to supplement his wages without the parish adopting the vicious expedient of making up insufficient wages out of the rates. They had also promoted savings banks and friendly societies to enable a man to provide against the accidents of life, and in some cases they had tried to promote emigration. Chadwick seems to have been so sure that the real need was a reform of the Poor Law itself that he seems to have taken no interest in these expedients. But to a parochial clergyman they might be important. However, the next chapter must attempt to deal with them, for they come within a parson's social duties rather than his official ones, in so far as these can be separated.

6

The Mid Nineteenth-
Century Parson

The Social Order (1)

When considering the social obligations of a parish priest there is one point which in the early nineteenth century it is easy to forget, but which is, even for that date, important to remember. However secular his cast of mind, however much his activities among his parishioners resembled those of a landowner among his tenants, or a rich man among his neighbours, his position was essentially different from theirs. He was a man in a known position in a recognized hierarchy, which carried with it recognized duties. If he was present, and not completely negligent, a minimum of ministerial duty would be assumed. He would probably be expected to visit the sick, particularly the dying. He would be expected to relieve those who were in extreme want, either from the alms contributed at the communion service, or from parish charities, or from his own pocket, if it had anything in it. In cases of urgency he would be expected to give relief in kind – probably soup to the hungry, which seems to have been a normal nineteenth-century method of relief. He might be expected to provide help, probably baby clothes, on the birth of a child. His parishioners would look to him to fulfil these duties, and would criticize the way he did them, even perhaps the quality of his soup, as in the case of an unfortunate incumbent whose soup was thought to contain maggots because his cook had put rice into it.

Of course if the rector or vicar was an absentee they would look in vain, and if the absence was prolonged they might forget the possibility that anyone might occupy any such position; they might apparently even forget where the parish church had been. But when he did reside and was not torpid or wholly secularized, there were recognized forms which his actions in secular matters might take, and which helped to form part of the tradition of parochial life in mid nineteenth-century England. On the basis of that tradition were based some of the great pastorates of the nineteenth century and, what is more important for present purposes, that tradition seems to have suggested certain secular activities which seem to be common enough among mid nineteenth-century parish priests as to present something like a common social policy on the part of the clergy of the Church of England.

That statement is one that can only be made with considerable reservations. For one thing, until there has been much more research it cannot be known how common any of these activities were, and, apart from that, anything that we would consider an adequate social policy was out of the question. Any action taken was likely to be no more than a mitigation of the grievous evils suffered by the poor, even in the case of that section of the poor over whose condition in all probability the clergy could exercise most influence, the hard-pressed, ill-used agricultural labourers. Nevertheless these activities form part of the picture. They ought not to be left out of it, as they very often are. At the least they supply evidence of intention, and of some form of social thought that transcended the narrow bounds of class interest and went beyond what was purely negative in the principles of the New Poor Law. Moreover, it seems probable that any relief action did in fact mitigate the lot of men and women for whom few other people were prepared to do much, or indeed anything at all.

However, when placing these activities in their historic perspective, there is one important point to bear in mind. It would be very natural to attribute much of the growing social sensibility of mid nineteenth-century England to the influence of the Oxford Movement. Certainly the Oxford Movement promoted a new and enlightened attitude towards social reform (see pp. 84–6). But in fact many of the secular practices which are typical of parochial practice in the middle of the century began well before 1830. We have already mentioned the work of such enlightened ministers as Lane Fox at Sturminster

Newton, Hook at Holy Trinity, Coventry and Leeds parish church, John Keble at Hursley, Hawker at Morwenstowe; and there were many others.

This fact must be taken into account in any systematic study of the behaviour of the Anglican clergy in the first thirty years of the century. Its immediate significance here is that the general ground plan in point of time of the development of the social attitudes of the clergy may be rather different from what might be expected. If these practices constitute anything of a social policy it was one at least partly conceived in the early years of the nineteenth century, and though in the middle of the century it was no doubt much more extensively applied, and possibly applied with greater social sensitivity, it was not essentially different from what had been conceived before the Reform Act. It was therefore likely to be richly coloured by the thought and values of the old order.

This is true of what could be, possibly, the most important of the social activities of a parish priest. One way of trying to alleviate poverty without pauperizing the recipient, which found favour in the eyes of many of the clergy, was the provision of allotments and cottage gardens. An allotment seems normally to have been a piece of ground varying in size from a rood – that is a quarter of an acre – to an acre or more, for which a labourer might pay rent, though not necessarily an economic one. A garden would probably be a smaller patch, possibly one or half a rood, which would quite probably go with a man's cottage and adjoin it. In either case if the land was reasonably good these patches could be effectively used to supplement a labouring household's food supply, particularly if there were space enough to keep a pig, or better still two pigs. The provision of allotments and gardens even attracted many of those who had wanted to stiffen the administration of the Poor Law. There were obvious reasons for this. The produce they yielded might keep a man off the rates and help towards the comfort of his family. The work on the land enabled a man to supply himself by his own efforts and incidentally kept him out of the public house, while, unless the allotment was so large as to occupy most of his time, it gave him some independence but did not keep him out of the labour market.

Indeed there were those for whom the idea of allotments supplied a wider and more richly gilded vision. There was a dream which haunted with a curious persistency almost throughout the nineteenth century the minds of all sorts of benevolent people drawn from a very remarkable assortment of groups – the followers of Owen, the romantic Tories, the Chartists, the Christian Socialists and the late nineteenth-century Radicals. It was the dream of solving the social problems of the country by converting a large section of the poor into smallholders living moral and happy lives upon the products of spade husbandry.[1] The dream, of course, was far-fetched, but as a practical policy of possibly limited application the provision of allotments had undoubted social value, and in fact allotments had actually been provided for labourers from very early in the century; and they had been provided by the clergy.

For instance, in 1843 a select committee on the subject was appointed by the House of Commons, and one of their witnesses was a garrulous and apparently rather self-satisfied old gentleman, the Reverend Stephen Demainbray, rector of Broad Somerford in Wiltshire. He claimed to have started the provision of allotments in his parish when it was enclosed in 1806. He had apparently secured that half an acre of land was attached to the cottages in the waste, and, with the help of the lord of the manor, to other cottages in the parish and, also as a result of the enclosure, to the cottages in the village itself. The land was held free of rates, was vested in the rector and the church wardens to prevent its being built upon, and the grant was renewed yearly to ensure proper cultivation. To this land the rector had added a portion of his glebe which had not proved to be profitable and which had been returned to his hands by a succession of tenants. This he now let out in smallholdings which were eagerly taken up and in the end yielded him a better rent than his previous tenants had given. By 1843 such holdings accommodated every family in the village, and Demainbray was exceedingly well pleased with himself, with his parishioners, and with his results. From that time rent had never been in arrears, no one had ever had to be turned out for bad husbandry. The villagers were contented, there had been

[1] See W. H. G. Armytage, *Heavens Below. Utopian Experiments in England 1560–1860* (1961).

no agrarian troubles in Somerford and, rather mysteriously, the granting of allotments seemed to have induced more people to go to church. His example, so he said, had been followed by the other parishes in that part of Wiltshire, and there had been no disturbances in that area also. A mob had advanced into it, but could gain no adherents since the labourers where this system prevailed had a stake in the country.[1]

It might take a little research to determine how far, and how effectively, this idyllic system had really prevailed in the neighbourhood of Somerford. What is certain is that relatively early in the century other clergymen had adopted the policy of providing land for labourers. For instance, by 1834 H. T. Becher of Southwell, the poor law reformer, had been perpetual curate of Thurgarton, which he held with other livings, since the beginning of the century. When the commission on the Poor Laws came to look into conditions in Nottinghamshire between 1832 and 1834 they found that every labourer in Thurgarton had a garden and, according to merit, was allotted enough grazing for a cow. This would seem to have been Becher's work. He followed the same policy elsewhere. He had managed to reduce the rates in Southwell by careful administration without the help of allotments, but in the preceding two years he had divided 8 acres, which had been devised for charitable purposes, into gardens which could be rented by the poor inhabitants of the township of Easthorpe which was apparently part of Southwell.[2] It was reported to the commission enquiring into the Poor Law that by 1834 the practice of letting small plots of land to labourers 'has become almost universal in Northamptonshire, the clergyman of the parish being in general the person who has set the thing on foot'.[3] There were also two notable sets of allotments provided by bishops: those provided by the bishop of Bath and Wells at Wells, and those provided by the bishop of London at Ealing. The bishop of Bath and Wells was George Henry Law who, according to his obituary in the *Gentleman's Magazine*, had long become convinced of the value of the provision of allotments for labourers.[4] The bishop of

[1] P.P. 1843, VII, pp. 219–21.
[2] P.P. 1834, XXIX, p. 108 (a).
[3] P.P. 1834, XXVIII, Pt. I, Appendix A, p. 410.
[4] P.P. 1834, XXXVII, p. 439. *Gentleman's Magazine*, 1845, Vol. II, p. 529.

London was of course Blomfield. His allotments at Ealing had only existed since 1832, but he had tried his hand at the policy before that when he was rector of Great Chesterford.[1]

Before 1834, therefore, the policy of creating allotments and gardens for labourers seems to have been fairly widely adopted by the clergy, having been at least in some cases initiated early in the century. It would be very interesting to know how widely it spread after the New Poor Law had been imposed; whether in fact it produced the benefits and created the social contentment so often claimed for it; and, in particular, how far it in any way replaced what was lost to cottagers and labourers through enclosures, or was, as in Somerford, supplemented by what was allocated to smallholders at the time of enclosure. All that can be said here is that between 1830 and 1850 there is evidence of considerable activity. Various organizations came into existence to provide allotments for working men. In 1830 the bishop of Bath and Wells seems to have founded a 'Labourer's Friend' society for this purpose. In due course it became moribund, as did the bishop, and in 1844 the society was taken over by a group in which Sidney Godolphin Osborne and Lord Ashley were prominent. They changed its name to the 'Society for Improving the Condition of the Labouring Classes', and began to interest themselves in working-class housing, but its old title was never quite forgotten, and it never lost its interest in allotments. A good many other schemes to provide allotments, either promoted by societies or by individuals, seem also to have been started in this period and most of them seem to have relied pretty extensively on the co-operation of the clergy, either as chairmen for local committees, or as the actual administrators whose task it was to allocate the allotments in a parish. And where there was a public subscription the clergy seem to have made up a large proportion of the subscribers.[2]

As far as the Church of England was concerned the most flamboyant scheme in the middle of the century was that proposed by a man called John Minter Morgan. This was a scheme

---

[1] Clapham [op. cit., p. 18] Vol. I, p. 472; P.P. 1843, VII, p. 247.

[2] P.P. 1843, VII, pp. 303 and 309, evidence of James Orange of the Northern and Midland District Labourer's Friend Society; p. 342, evidence of G. Bolts, and pp. 316 and 318, for the evidence of W. Miles. See D. O. Wagner, *The Church of England and Social Reform since 1854* (New York, 1930) pp. 146–7.

G

to establish self-supporting villages under the superintendence
of the Church, which closely resembles the utopian plans of
Owen or the Chartists for the creation of home colonies. Those
who proposed it were patently utopian idealists; in addition to
Morgan there was the Rev. Joseph Brown, the chaplain to the
poor law schools at Norwood, and the Rev. S. Larkin, rector of
Burton near Lincoln, an enthusiast for co-operation and association on Christian principles. However, the scheme gained a
surprising number of, one would have said, level-headed supporters both clerical and lay, among whom were Edward
Stanley, the bishop of Norwich, and W. F. Cowper, a nephew
of Lord Melbourne and a reasonably prominent Whig
politician.[1]

A community was started in Wales, and as was to be expected
came to nothing; after Morgan's death in 1855 most of the
support it had won was transferred to the promotion of the
colony of Christchurch in New Zealand, a colony with, as will
be seen, a strong Church of England flavour. The interest of the
scheme lies in the fact that it suggests that a good many of the
clergy were anxious to find even a drastic cure for the social
problems of the day and were prepared to dream dreams which
one would not have thought would have found easy entry into
clerical, still less episcopal, bedrooms.

The practical schemes promoted in particular parishes were,
of course, of far more value than this fiasco. But all these
schemes, whether practical or not, suggest certain problems
which urgently require more extensive research. What per-
centage of the country clergy promoted such schemes? And
once a scheme was promoted, how permanent was it likely to
be? There would seem to be one *prima facie* difficulty in the way
of a parish incumbent imposing a permanent scheme on his
parish. Supposing, as was certainly done in a variety of cases,
he cut up his glebe into allotments, how could he be sure that
his successors would maintain the arrangement? After all, the
glebe was not his to give away. This is the difficulty which,
fairly late in the century, W. Tuckwell found in the Warwickshire village of Stockton. On the other hand, Archdeacon John
Allen at Prees in Shropshire, also an enthusiast for smallholdings, said: 'A cottager on the glebe holds his land in the

[1] Armytage [op. cit., p. 169] pp. 209–23.

ninth generation under successive vicars of this place'.[1] But that aside, since many farmers were hostile to labourers' allotments, was it possible for them to destroy a scheme once it had been established?

This hostility on the part of the farmers raises another question which is best exemplified by the history of a village in Suffolk. One of the most attractive figures among the clergy of the early and mid nineteenth century was J. S. Henslow, professor of botany in the University of Cambridge. His most notable claim to fame is no doubt the fact that his friendship, encouragement and tuition converted Charles Darwin from being a rather unlikely ordinand, first into the 'man who walks with Henslow' and then into an accomplished naturalist, and that it was Henslow who despatched Darwin on his voyage in H.M.S. *Beagle*, from which he brought back the ideas that in turn altered many of our conceptions of the world. Apart from that, however, Henslow was a distinguished scientist in his own right, and, what is more germane for present purposes, became a devoted parish priest. In 1837 he was presented to the valuable crown living of Hitcham in Suffolk. At first he tried to work the living while residing at Cambridge, as he had worked another living, but in 1839 he decided that he could not fulfil his duties at Hitcham in that way. He therefore gave up his life at Cambridge, only returning at intervals to lecture as professor, and spent the rest of his life in almost continual residence at Hitcham.

The situation which Henslow faced at Hitcham was the same as that faced by a good many incoming incumbents in the thirties and forties. There was a neglected church, no school to speak of, a rough and uncivilized labouring population, miserable housing conditions and much rural unemployment. The story of how he tackled these problems is interesting because it reveals the tensions which could exist in a Suffolk village and the difficulties that these could produce for its pastor.

[1] W. Tuckwell, *Reminiscences of a Radical Parson* (1905) pp. 128–46. R. M. Grier, *John Allen Archdeacon* (1889) pp. 243–6. The problem of long leases does not seem to have impeded schemes for cutting up the glebe, or part of it, into allotments; it is not mentioned in *Glebe Allotments and Co-operative Small Farming* (1880) by C. W. Stubbs (Stubbs was at that date vicar of Granborough, Buckinghamshire, and was subsequently bishop of Truro. He was an enthusiast for allotments. His own scheme at Granborough was managed by a 'village parliament'.).

In the years after his arrival at Hitcham there were violent divisions in the Suffolk countryside. There was bitter popular discontent among the labourers, which broke out in 1844 in widespread midnight incendiarism, and there was among the farmers a hard, ignorant, prejudiced spirit, which made them resent and suspect anything which was done for their workers. It was this spirit which led Henslow to write in 1850 that:

> All schemes, educational, recreational, or however tending to elevate (the labourer) in the social scale, are positively distasteful to some of the employers of labour, whom, nevertheless we are bound to recognize as worthy men, not wilfully opposed to the comforts of those beneath them.[1]

Whether he found it easy to retain the last emollient conviction with regard to the farmers in his own village may be open to doubt. His fight to civilize Hitcham was both long and hard. He built a school and paid for a teacher at his own cost, for he could get little help from his parishioners. He tried to introduce ploughing matches which the farmers disrupted by making fair competition impossible. He attempted to put his science at the disposal of the farmers with at first but a slow response, and he introduced allotments. He apparently did this last with two objects. He wanted to supply a remedy for rural unemployment or under-employment, which he apparently believed was responsible for very many of the evils of the countryside, and he was also in favour of the labourers being allowed some more direct interest in the soil than they at that time possessed, for, said he, 'Wherever the labourers are so completely prostrate at the feet of their masters, as they are in some of our villages, we shall look in vain for that wholesome independence of spirit which was so notoriously the attribute of our free peasantry in times not very long by.' The farmers replied with some violence, and at the vestry meeting in March 1852 they tried to make a pledge among themselves that they would 'refuse all employment and show no favour to any day-labourer who should hold an allotment'.[2]

By the time he died Henslow seems to have won this battle, but perhaps the significant fact about it is that according to his

[1] Rev. Leonard Jenyns, *Memoir of the Rev. John Stevens Henslow* (1862) p. 73.
[2] ibid., pp. 88–92.

biographer Jenyns, also a distinguished naturalist and also a country clergyman, his experience was by no means unique. Jenyns says:

> Perhaps every clergyman who has attempted to establish the allotment system in his parish, has met with opposition, more or less, at first. I myself experienced it when introducing it in my own parish in Cambridgeshire many years back. In my case some said the men would give their masters short time and easy work, in order to reserve themselves for working on their own account at the end of the day.

Jenyns' own fight had apparently been an easy one; it was clearly not always so. Nor was the victory always on one side, and perhaps the battle was not always fought; for as Jenyns said when looking back on Henslow's own battle:

> It is not every clergyman that will boldly stand up against a body of farmers, who have long had their own way in everything, and who look upon the parson as one set to attend to the souls of his people, but as having no business to meddle in the general affairs of the parish.[1]

Allotments were probably of some value in promoting the comfort and independence of the agricultural labourer, but they were at best palliatives. The best hope for any permanent improvement for the countryman was no doubt to encourage a considerable number of them to take themselves and their families away from the overcrowded English countryside, and to go where life would offer them better chances. This would not only benefit those who went, it would benefit those who stayed, for it would reduce that redundancy of labour which in a good many counties kept down agricultural wages and left the labourer very much at the mercy of his employer. It is significant that it was the promotion of migration which produced in a Devonshire village one of the most severe conflicts of the century between a parish priest and his parishioners (see pp. 178–9).

This happened between 1866 and 1872, but as in so many other matters the need for emigration overseas, or migration from the English countryside to other areas in England where there was a greater demand for labour, had been recognized earlier in the century, and in this, as in other matters, Becher of

[1] ibid., pp. 75 and 92.

Southwell was a notable pioneer. In 1819 a sum of about £5,000 was collected in Nottinghamshire to assist emigration and was paid into the hands of Becher and the clerk of the peace. They sent out between 200 and 300 people to be settled in South Africa in and about Bathurst town and Grahamstown. Some returned, but most remained and expressed themselves contented with their new life.[1]

Though this may have been a desirable policy, it was probably not a very easy one to promote. Men and women, however broken and unhappy, were naturally loath to leave the countryside which they had known all their lives, and when they reached their new country they often found conditions there uncongenial and unpromising, and came back if they could do so. In fact there seems to have been less readiness on the part of the English countryman to move any considerable distance from his home than there was on the part of the Irishman or the highlander from Scotland or Wales, perhaps because, though conditions were very bad in parts of England, they were not as desperate as they were elsewhere. Certainly Becher discovered that not all of the money that had been collected in 1819 could be used, and though it was thought that by 1834 working-class opinion had changed on the topic, in fact in other sections of the report of the commission on the Poor Laws there seem to be a good many complaints about the difficulties of getting people to go, and stay, overseas.

In the circumstances, it would not seem reasonable to expect the individual parish clergyman to do much in this matter, even if he recognized the social necessity of this particular policy. There was, however, at least one important example of planned emigration in which a large number of the clergy played an important part. This was the settlement of the Canterbury district in the South Island of New Zealand. The man who projected this scheme was J. R. Godley, the son of an Irish landowner. In 1847, at the time of the Irish famine, he produced a scheme for the organized emigration of Irish families under the leadership of Roman Catholic priests. Unfortunately this scheme was blocked by the prejudices of the day, and so Godley turned to the promotion of a scheme organized under the auspices of the Church of England. Here he had better luck. His

[1] P.P. 1834, XXIX, 108 (a).

scheme seems to have made a powerful appeal to churchmen. It is true that to a large extent it owed its conception to that very unecclesiastical personage, Gibbon Wakefield, with whom Godley was in close touch. But Wakefield wisely kept in the background and the project rapidly gained supporters of such ecclesiastical weight and significance as might guarantee the respectability of any project.

Indeed the list of the fifty or so original members of the Canterbury Association might easily, with a few additions, serve as a list of the natural leaders in matters relating to social policy of the mid nineteenth-century English Church. The archbishop of Canterbury, J. B. Sumner, was president. From the bench of bishops there were Blomfield of London, C. R. Sumner of Winchester, Phillpotts of Exeter, Connop Thirlwall of St David's and Samuel Wilberforce of Oxford. Among the other clergy were Gleig, the chaplain general of the forces, the dean of Canterbury, Archdeacon Wilberforce the brother of the bishop of Oxford, J. C. Hare, Maurice's brother-in-law, Hook of Leeds and Chenevix Trench. Among the laity there were the inevitable Lord Ashley, Lord John Manners of the Young England group and C. B. Adderley, another idealistic Tory. Gladstone did not allow his name to appear, but he gave his assistance and was amply represented by Lord Lyttleton, who in fact after Godley was probably the man who did most to make the project a success.[1]

Other significant names could be cited, and the favourable reaction to the project illustrates the interest of churchmen in the type of social problem which colonization either in Britain or overseas might relieve. Yet possibly, as is the case with Minter Morgan's scheme, a general scheme which a man might support simply by giving a subscription or attending a meeting does not really tell as much about the social morality of the clergy as the services which a parson must perform in person in his parish.

Nor for that matter did any mid nineteenth-century emigration cure the ills of the counties of England. Though there was fairly extensive emigration in the middle of the century to the United States, to Canada, to Australia, New Zealand and elsewhere – sometimes as a result of personal initiative, sometimes

[1] C. E. Carrington, *John Robert Godley of Canterbury* (Cambridge, 1950) particularly pp. 65–8 and 224–30.

assisted officially or privately – it was not enough to relieve those areas of England where the countryside was over-populated. It has been calculated that in general, if the period between 1851 and 1881 is taken, such migration as there had been did little more than cancel the natural increases in the most completely agricultural areas.[1] Indeed in a number of regions the population was about the same in the sixties and seventies as it had been at the reform of the Poor Law in 1834, and, at least in many cases, the conditions on which life was offered to the agricultural labourer were not much better, if they were better at all. On the last point it is difficult to generalize.

Conditions varied greatly in different parts of the country. Where there was the possibility of forms of employment other than agricultural, or the possibility of relatively easy migration to an industrial district, conditions were a good deal better than they were in purely agricultural districts. Even in the latter areas conditions seem to have varied from village to village. Apparently an energetic landowner, an effective parson, generous farmers or good local traditions could do much for the labourers. Conditions may have been generally better in the North than the South, and, perhaps, in closed rather than in open villages. But there were many places where they remained very bad; where wages remained intolerably low and the perquisites which helped elsewhere to eke out wages were lacking or negligible; where the housing was disgraceful; where the treatment of labourers was invariably harsh; where allotments and potato patches were hard to get and highly rented, while the farmers objected to labourers keeping pigs and poultry in case they should steal food for them.

It was conditions such as these that stirred Edward Girdlestone into activity between 1862 and 1872. Between 1828 and 1852 Girdlestone had served a parish at Dean in South Lancashire, first as curate then as vicar. Then, after an interval in Bristol and Gloucestershire, he was in 1862 instituted into the living of Halberton in North Devon. He was horrified at the conditions which he found there, at the wages, the houses, the hours worked, the way the farmers treated their men; all of which was in harsh contrast to the conditions he was used to in

[1] J. H. Clapham [op. cit., p. 18] Vol. II, p. 252.

Lancashire. He tried to mend matters by private remonstrance, and when this availed nothing he rebuked the farmers from the pulpit. This caused an uproar but no change, and so Girdlestone wrote a letter to *The Times* giving a clear account of conditions at Halberton. In mid nineteenth-century England, as was to be demonstrated a few years later – again in relation to agrarian conditions (see pp. 245–50) – a letter to *The Times* could be a very potent instrument. He received in answer a good many letters of sympathy, and gifts of money which he used to help labourers, together with their families, to leave Halberton and its neighbourhood for situations which he found for them in other parts of England where housing and wages were better.

As might be expected this increased the violence of the attacks upon him. He was obscenely abused in his vestry meeting, and an unsuccessful attempt was made to secure for the parishioners the appointment of the vicar's warden. There were disturbances in his church, after which several of the local farmers left it, and tried to go to the Wesleyan chapel, where the minister apparently frankly told them what he thought of them, however. Girdlestone's family were slighted in public, and he received no countenance from the local gentry or clergy. For example, when one of the men he was helping to leave Halberton was sued by the employer he was leaving for the breach of an obviously factitious contract not only was the case given against the man, but when the case was over the chairman violently abused Girdlestone in open court for what he was doing. Girdlestone persisted, however, and between 1866 and 1872, when he left Halberton, he had managed to move into better circumstances between four and five hundred men and their families. As a direct result of his efforts there seems to have been a noticeable change for the better in the conditions which prevailed in that neighbourhood.[1]

It was natural that Girdlestone should take every opportunity he could to bring the state of affairs that had been revealed to him at Halberton before the public, and one of the opportunities he used was the submission of a paper to the economics section of the British Association at its meeting at Norwich in August 1868. At the end of this he produced a series of extremely

[1] F. G. Heath, *British Rural Life and Labour* (1911) pp. 227–45 and 295–7.

interesting suggestions as to what might be done to protect the agricultural labourer. The fifth of these was that 'Agricultural Labourers' Unions of a strictly protective character, and well guarded against intimidation to either employers or fellow workmen might be formed with advantage.'[1] The same idea seems to have appealed to other clergymen at this time. For instance, towards the end of 1870 an Agricultural Labourers' Union was formed at Leintwardine in Herefordshire with the encouragement of a favourably disposed vicar, the Rev. Edward Jonathan Green. It spread rapidly into six counties and gained, so it is reported, 'about thirty thousand members', though that number is difficult to accept. It dispatched surplus labour from the agricultural counties into Yorkshire, Lancashire and Staffordshire. The secretary was a dissenter, but its president was the Rev. D. Rodney Murray, rector of Brampton Bryan, a village to the west of Leintwardine in north Herefordshire. Twenty of its vice-presidents were clergymen of the Church of England.[2]

This does not mean that a large number of the country clergy had gone over to the policy of militant trade unionism on behalf of the agricultural labourer. This was still the mid century phase of the nineteenth century, when even those middle-class writers who, like Dickens, felt most strongly the case for labour, instinctively shrank from what seemed to them the dangers of trade unionism and the disaster of a strike.[3] The same limitation of view appears in the declared aim of the Herefordshire Union which was *'emigration, migration but no strikes'*, and it can be realized in the care with which Girdlestone wrapped up his proposal for the formation of agricultural labourers' unions. And if men who were plainly very anxious to do something for the agricultural labourer were reluctant to support militant trade unionism, what was likely to be the attitude of those who were timid, or bewildered, or instinctively hostile to any working-

---

[1] *Report of the Proceedings of the 38th Meeting of the British Association for the Advancement of Science*, held at Norwich in August 1868: *Notes and Abstracts*, pp. 165–6.

[2] Wagner [op. cit., p. 171] p. 153. E. Selley, *Village Trade Unions in Two Centuries* (1919) pp. 36–7.

[3] Patrick Brantlinger, 'The Case against Trade Unions in Early Victorian Fiction', *Victorian Studies* (Indiana University) Vol. XIII, No. 1 (September 1969), pp. 37–52.

class movement, particularly when it seemed to be the weapon of politically-minded Dissent?

After all, a parish clergyman of the Church of England was a man occupying a place in an established order of society. Such hierarchies transmit to those whose lives they govern their inherited loyalties and inhibitions; they are apt to prescribe limits to a man's thoughts, the more effectively perhaps when they are unconscious. More than this, a social hierarchy has its own way of exerting pressure on those who are suspected of using their position in it to threaten its security. A subversive parson who supported a militant policy, or even too dangerously radical a policy, might discover this. W. Tuckwell, who has already been mentioned, held the Warwickshire living of Stockton from 1878 to 1893. Profoundly moved by the conditions he found in his village he became a Radical, and he has left on record the penalties which county society could exact from a Radical parson – the social ostracism, the cutting of his wife and daughters at dances and parties, the emptying of his church, the drying up of subscriptions which might be necessary for the continuance of his work and the welfare of his people.[1]

It would be hard to say how effective and how general was this sanction. It is not satisfactory to take one man's description and one man's experience as a general account of what was implicit in a large number of social relationships which must have presented a very great variety of different human characters and situations. On the other hand it sounds possible, it is what one might have expected. One thing seems clear. If this sanction did exist there seem to have been a large number of clergymen whose personal record suggests they were not conscious of it. If their views were restricted, it would seem from what they wrote and said that the inhibitions lay in their own minds, and did not spring from fear of the consequences. Indeed the record of the agricultural strikes between 1872 and 1874 shows that there were at least some clergymen who were prepared confidently to express opinions which it might have been thought these sanctions forbade. That record also suggests that the most serious danger to a country clergyman's independence was not the views of the gentry, who were often remote and not directly interested in labour conditions, but as Girdlestone had

[1] Tuckwell [op. cit., p. 173] pp. 26–9.

already experienced, the anger of the farmers, with whom an incumbent was unavoidably closely associated.

The troubles between 1872 and 1874 were, however, at the beginning of a new phase of history; the feelings which boiled over then seem to have been largely kept under the surface during the long confident Victorian afternoon, and not to have been suspected by many of those who believed that the social policy which satisfied them would also seem adequate to the labouring population. Between 1850 and 1872 the rectors and vicars of England seem on the whole to have felt sure of their position, proud of their progress from an unregenerate past, and to have looked to the future with confidence. Many of them seem to have been aware that much needed to be done to improve the condition of the working class; indeed, as will be seen, some were beginning to realize that it would have to be done by confiding increased powers to the State. But they appear to have believed that this could be done without compromising their own position.

This is in fact the period of the high rectory culture of Victorian England, when strenuous piety could often be combined with reasonable comfort. Most of the clergy resided in their livings and attended to their duties, the economic position of many of them was satisfactory, parish life was often vigorous, and in many parishes things were being done which are possibly a better guide to the social policy of the clergy than are allotments, for they are characteristic of the life in most manageable parishes, which, as far as I can see, was not the case with schemes for allotments, still less schemes for encouraging migration.

In his life of Henslow, which was published in 1872, Jenyns wrote:

> It is unnecessary to speak of other institutions Professor Henslow originated in the village, such as the Wife's Society, coal and clothing clubs, Medical Club, Loan and Blanket Fund etc., none of which existed in the place when he first came to it. These are now so common in all well regulated parishes that they call for no particular remark here.[1]

---

[1] Jenyns [op. cit., p. 174] p. 124.

There is much evidence to support this last statement, and to the list which Jenyns gives could be added, at least in some cases, the provision of libraries or reading rooms, the direction of self-improvement societies and, in many parishes, the organizing of those mysterious, but apparently popular, entertainments called 'penny readings'.

The provision of such facilities was part of the parson's duty. But the actual running of the more domestic side of these fell naturally into the hands of his wife and daughters. For this reason possibly the most vivid account of many of the daily activities of a parson's family can be found in the work of two women novelists who had an intimate knowledge of the realities of mid nineteenth-century parochial life, Miss Charlotte M. Yonge and Mrs Ewing.

Some of these institutions perhaps need a little explanation. In a clothing club the women seem to have paid into the hands of some treasurer, normally the parson's wife or daughter, 'a weekly subscription of from one penny to sixpence to which one penny weekly is added out of the fund subscribed by the benevolent persons of the parish'. At the end of the year the depositors received tickets representing the moneys owing to them which could be presented to a draper. However, the list of objects to be purchased was first checked as a precaution against 'the money being expended on light, useless finery'. Boot clubs and coal clubs were no doubt managed in the same way. A blanket club was apparently rather different. A blanket was lent from November to June to any poor woman who liked to apply for one. She paid 6d a year for two years, and 4d a year for the four years following. At the end of six years the blanket became hers.[1] Savings clubs and medical clubs served obvious purposes, as did, of course, the friendly societies.

Some parochial activities were more simply co-operative. In a number of parishes some essential goods were purchased in bulk so that they could be sold at wholesale prices to the poorer parishioners, and at Stoneleigh in Warwickshire the Hon. and Rev. J. W. Leigh had a complete co-operative store. It was started in 1867 and he believed that it was one of the first village stores of that nature in England. Leigh was a wealthy man

[1] F. G. Heath [op. cit., p. 179] p. 291. Charlotte M. Yonge, *Scenes and Characters* (1889 – first published 1847) pp. 155–6.

occupying the family living near his family estate, and it was suggested at the time that he had taken advantage of his opportunities to make unusually lavish provision for his parish. Leigh himself denied that this was so. He said that the store was itself financially sound and was run by a committee of working men over whom he did no more than preside. Certainly the co-operative principle was accepted elsewhere. The Rev. R. C. Christie had a co-operative store at Castle Combe in Wiltshire, and the West of England Labourers' Improvement Association, that is the association which was instituted at Leintwardine, seems to have aspired to run a co-operative farm such as apparently existed at Assington in Suffolk.[1]

Leigh had a reading room and an institute at Stoneleigh and Christie a lending library at Castle Combe. Indeed lending libraries, of sorts, seem to have been reasonably common. It would be very interesting to know what books they contained, and who borrowed from them. Institutes were possibly most likely to be found in urban parishes. Certainly they seem in some cases to have been founded in imitation of the mechanics' institutes and as an alternative to them, for at first the mechanics' institutes were suspected of secularist and radical tendencies.[2] Institutes seem to have been places where the lectures and readings, for which people of all classes and beliefs in the nineteenth century seem to have had a curious relish, could be given. Some of their work must have resembled what was done in adult schools and working mens' colleges of which mention has been made. Both looked forward to university extension.

The various saving schemes seem to have varied from arrangements by which sixpences were collected week by week, marked up in an exercise book and put in a safe place to elaborate banking and friendly society operations. At one end of the scale there are the operations of such people as the parson's daughter of whom Mrs Ewing has left us an attractive picture,

[1] J. W. Leigh, *Other Days* (1921) pp. 86–7, 122–3. P.P. 1868/69, XIII, pp. 462 and 475; *Guardian*, 11 September 1872, pp. 1156 (col. 3), 1157 (col. 1); letter from Baldwyn Leighton.

[2] Viscount Ingestre, ed., *Meliora. Better Times to Come; being the contribution of men touching the present state and prospects of society* (1852), see pp. 24–50: W. F. Hook on 'Institutions for Adult Education'.

sitting and making up her reckoning with the help of eight bags each clearly labelled in marking ink 'Savings Bank', 'Clothing Club', 'Library', 'Magazines and Hymn Books', with three other bags for her own private income and expenditure. At the other end of the scale there were parsons who founded savings banks or acted as local receivers for them, or became experts in the complicated problems of friendly society finance, a notable example of this being the Hon. and Rev. Samuel Best, rector of Abbotts Ann in Hampshire.[1]

There was as it happened a significant competition between different friendly societies. A number of them were run under the auspices of the Church either by devoted laymen, or by the clergy themselves. But there were others. In the early years of the century some of these had also come under suspicion, because of their rituals and oaths and pretensions to secrecy, but in due course these suspicions seem to have evaporated and, in some parishes at least, the friendly societies on occasion came in procession to the parish church with their banners and music.[2] Nevertheless there remained a potential rivalry between the friendly societies which were run by the clergy and those which were not, and there seems to be evidence that many people preferred those which were not. There may be various reasons for this. The weekly payments for the church societies would have tended to be higher if, as seems probable, their finances were better conducted; the church societies were also less likely to spend their sums on feasting, and there is evidence that the keepers of public houses encouraged their clients to join those societies which were more likely to bring them custom. However, in addition to these reasons there appears to have been one of greater significance. Many poor people seem to have preferred those societies which were freer from the supervision of the clergy and gentry; for instance, the choice of a friendly society was an important turning point in the life of Joseph

[1] J. H. Ewing, *Daddy Darwin's Dovecote* (1881) pp. 68 ff. McClatchey [op. cit., p. 147] pp. 218–19. P.P. 1868/9, XIII, p. 121. Wagner [op. cit., p. 171] pp. 117–19; for Best, see the Hon. and Rev. S. Best, *Parochial Ministrations* (1839); P.P. 1874, XXIII, Pt. I, pp. 22, 83, 84, 86, 87, 89–91.

[2] e.g. B. J. Armstrong, *A Norfolk Diary. Passages from the Diary of the Rev. Benjamin John Armstrong M.A.*, edited by his grandson Herbert B. J. Armstrong (1949) p. 51.

Ashby of Tysoe.[1] Most of the clergy's services were given in good faith, with conscientious or benevolent intentions, but they were often conceived within the terms of and in the spirit of the old order. Their schemes were sometimes administered with condescension and there could be an element of charity about them: the funds often came from an inherited parish charity, and were partly supplied by the parson or benevolent persons in the neighbourhood. Moreover they might be administered on humiliating conditions, such as the censorship on the purchase of 'unsuitable finery' by members of a clothing club, or benefits given only to those who regularly attended church, or showed suitable respect for their betters.[2]

All this gave opportunities which a tyrannical or impercipient rector or vicar, or rector's or vicar's wife, might abuse, as in the often repeated case when the parson in Arch's village apparently cut the allowance of soup and coal to Arch's family because his mother was not sufficiently humble.[3] It would not be easy to say how far this kind of thing extended, or how consistently it was resented. The diaries, the letters, the memories of a great many of the clergy and their wives suggest that their personal relations with their parishioners were not poisoned by this kind of thing; but no man's account of his own situation, be he parson or labourer, tells all the facts, or is completely reliable. It is certainly not legitimate to infer from what is believed to have been a man's economic situation what his unrecorded feelings must have been; but in a case like this it is difficult to know to what positive evidence it is satisfactory to turn.

A few things can perhaps be said with assurance. These institutions – medical clubs, clothing and savings clubs, etc. – were in full activity in a very large number of parishes in mid nineteenth-century England. They were clearly being used by a number of poor people, and were clearly of great use to them. The fact that there were those who preferred friendly societies

---

[1] M. K. Ashby, *Joseph Ashby of Tysoe 1859–1919, a Study of English Village Life* (Cambridge, 1961) pp. 68–72.

[2] e.g. P.P. 1868/9, XIII, p. 454, evidence of Kempson, vicar of Claverdon in Warwickshire; P.P. 1874, XXIII, see particularly report of Hon. E. Lyulph Stanley in Pt. II, pp. 193–437.

[3] Arch [op. cit., p. 140] pp. 20–2, 53–4.

which were not dominated by the clergy does not seriously modify this statement. It is clear that there were many people who did not share this feeling, for the friendly societies run by the clergy also flourished; and in any case it seems clear from the report of the committee of 1874 that many of the poorest people involved, particularly the agricultural labourers, were below the economic level at which the membership of any ordinary friendly society was possible. The social and economic situation was always changing, and it seems probable, indeed the record suggests this, that what might be taken as a matter of course by many members of one generation would be resented by their sons, as can be seen in the contrast between the attitudes of Arch with those of his father and Ashby with those of his mother.

In fact, as was the case with so much that existed in mid nineteenth-century England, this pattern of parochial activity was something that had survived from an earlier period and was increasingly out of place in the last quarter of the nineteenth century. For instance, as has been said, there was a parliamentary enquiry into the working of the New Poor Law in South Hampshire in 1837. In the course of it a curate attached to the parish of West Meon described the institutions which existed there. 'There is', he said,

> a clothing club in which there are 50 poor people, and in addition to 5s that they subscribe, 5s is added. Archdeacon Bailey has a clothing club of his own, of 20 members. There is a clothing club in the school of 30 members. Men's Provident Society, 15 members; the men pay per week, sixpence, and have added by the rector, three pence to each shilling; that is laid out for them at Christmas in fuel and clothing. There is a sick agricultural club, with 90 members in it; there is a Trades' Union Friendly Society with 36 members in it; and I myself have started a fuel club, at which I sell coals and faggots at half price.

The number of the population in the parish was 750 of whom 99 were agricultural labourers and 9 were labourers who were not agricultural, so that very few of the villagers can have been outside these organizations.[1]

With the exception of the fuel club these clubs and societies

[1] P.P. 1837, XVII, Pt. I, p. 541 ff.

at West Meon seem to have been in existence before the New Poor Law of 1834 was imposed, but it is not clear when exactly they came into existence; indeed it seems probable that the curate who gave the evidence, and who had been in the parish for five years, did not know. At any rate whatever the exact date at which they began it cannot be questioned that here is a parish which was unusually lavishly equipped with the institutions which might have been thought to be typical of a mid Victorian parish, but which in this case had come into existence certainly before Victoria had come to the throne, and probably before the First Reform Act.

But the matter can be carried further back still. Much of what was done in the nineteenth century seems to have precedents in late eighteenth-century charity, in, for instance, the work which Mrs Trimmer started at Brentford in 1786, or Hannah More at Cheddar in 1788, or in the remarkable activities of Mrs Priscilla Wakefield of Tottenham, who developed schemes to help poor people accumulate reserves to meet what were going to be for them considerable items of necessary expenditure, such as the payment of apprenticeship fees or the purchase of suitable clothes for going into service. She also initiated in 1804 the Tottenham Benefit Bank which was open to everyone and in which small sums up from a shilling could be deposited. But these ladies were only part of a larger movement. In the last years of the eighteenth century there seems to have been a good deal of charitable activity, the general spirit of which may be reflected in Mrs Trimmer's book the *Oeconomy of Charity*. The ultimate object was to encourage thrift and self-help and to prevent the alms of the charitable from being wasted on those who would do nothing for themselves or spent what was given to them in profligacy and drink. For this purpose schemes were developed and institutions called into being which would make it easier for the poor to save and help themselves.[1]

---

[1] S. Trimmer, *The Oeconomy of Charity or an address to ladies adapted to the present state of charitable institutions in England*, 2 vols. (1801). For the relevant activities of Hannah More, see M. G. Jones, *Hannah More* (Cambridge, 1952) pp. 152, 155–8, 207. For Mrs Wakefield and the other charitable schemes of this period, see H. Oliver Horne, *A History of Savings Banks* (Oxford, 1947) passim.

These institutions appear to be the models of the typical institutions of a Victorian parish but, when they were first developed, they did not necessarily have anything to do with the clergy. They were quite likely to be the work of men and women who were not church people – Mrs Wakefield, for instance, was a member of the Society of Friends – and indeed, particularly in the eighteenth century, the local clergy might be unlikely to help at all. When Hannah More started operations at Cheddar thirteen of the parishes in the neighbourhood were without even a resident curate and the incumbent of another living was drunk six days a week. But not all eighteenth-century parishes were like that. Leading churchmen took an important part in some of the projects of this period, and they in their turn suggested improvements that other clergymen might make and things they might do in their own parishes. For instance, in 1796 a society for 'bettering the condition of the poor' was founded. The leading figure was a layman, a barrister called Bernard, who produced a series of reports on such matters as friendly societies, village shops for supplying necessaries at cheap prices, workshops for the unemployed, model workhouses and educational reforms. However, the president was the bishop of Durham, Shute Barrington, and he suggested that the clergy in his diocese should do something for the aged. Two incumbents took the matter in hand, Burgess of Winston and Gilpin of Bishop Auckland. They started old people's clubs which were so organized as also to encourage saving. This seems to have inspired the Rev. Joseph Smith of Wendover in Buckingham. In 1799 he started a 'Sunday bank' to enable the poorer members of his congregation to buy warm garments, or fuel or other comforts in the winter. His example was copied, notably at Hertford by the Rev. Thomas Lloyd in 1808. Lloyd also founded a real savings bank at Hertford in 1816.

The movement for the foundation of organized savings banks began in Scotland on the initiative of a minister of the Church of Scotland, and in England no doubt owed much to the example of Mrs Wakefield, but it was soon taken up by the clergy of the Church of England and it has, in fact, been claimed that the first savings bank in England was founded, probably in 1807 or soon afterwards, by the Rev. Charles Thorp, incumbent of Ryton in County Durham. This bank was said to be 'of great benefit to the numerous bodies of forgemen, colliers and other industrious workmen in this and neighbouring villages'. These banks, indeed, had a decided philanthropic, or at least social ameliorative, intention; their object was to enable poor people to preserve such money as they could put by in order to prepare for old age or to insure against disease or misfortune. It was clearly this aspect that attracted a good many of the clergy. For instance, in 1811 a Liverpool society for 'Bettering the condition of the Poor' developed a 'Mechanics', Servants' and Labourers' Fund'. This was transformed in 1815 under the masterful guidance of Archdeacon Jonathan Green into a savings bank, but until his death in 1855 it also retained its charitable objectives. It even maintained a library which depositors could join on the payment of a shilling a quarter. But clergymen did not only found banks, they also acted as agents for them, collecting deposits locally which was no doubt of direct service to their parishioners. In 1816 the Devon and Exeter Bank started business and developed a fairly extensive system of local agents who were, it is said, 'principally clergymen'.[1]

In fact in the last years of the eighteenth century and the first quarter of the nineteenth the institutions, such as clubs for providing necessities, facilities for saving and schemes for providing allotments and gardens, were beginning to make an appearance, and were to provide the staples for the social policy of the mid nineteenth-century clergy. The reform of the Poor Laws and the acceptance of poor law principles made no difference to this development. All these activities were based on the principle of encouraging and facilitating self-help, and they formed the positive side of the policy of poor law reform. This is probably best exemplified by the ideas and activities of the leading poor law reformer, the Rev. J. T. Becher. Even his famous pamphlet *The Antipauper System*, which might appear from its title to be most bleakly negative in object, does, in fact, contain a number of positive and humane suggestions; for Becher's ideas apparently included parish cottages for the aged and widows and possibly for indigent men with large families, small gardens for the industrious, employment for the able-bodied, medical care for the poor and a number of other facilities. As has been said, to some of this policy he gave practical

[1] Horne [op. cit., p. 188] pp. 58–70.

effect. He was party to the building of two workhouses, one at
Thurgarton and one at Southwell, and reformed the working of
the Poor Law at Southwell. He seems to have secured that every
labourer at Thurgarton had a garden and where possible
facilities for keeping a cow. He tried to relieve the pressure on
population by helping men to emigrate. In 1818 he founded a
savings bank, and he founded an important friendly society and
established principles on which much friendly society administration came to be based.[1]

Unfortunately it was the negative side of poor law reform, the
principle of less eligibility and the reform of abuses, which
was emphasized both in the report of the 1832–4 commission
on the poor, and in the administration of the 1834 act. This
would probably not have been so marked if Chadwick had
been able to control the administration of the act as he had
intended to control it, and in any case the parochial clergy
continued to develop the institutions which embodied the positive side of their policy until Jenyns could say in 1873 of the
clubs and societies which Henslow inaugurated at Hitcham that
no well-regulated parish was without them.

As a policy it naturally had its defects, but it must be remembered that at least at its inception, whatever its defects it
certainly represented a step forward in humanity. When
Hannah More started work at Cheddar she found a population
which had been in every way scandalously neglected and for
whose education and improvement no one else cared at all.
The same situation is observable in the history of the reform of
many parishes in the nineteenth century, and it seems legitimate
always to put alongside any criticism of these activities this
question: Who else was likely in sober reality to do what these
institutions did for those who benefited from them? That does
not, of course, cancel the fact that what was done had, from
the beginning, certain unfortunate characteristics. These

[1] J. D. Marshall, *Econ. Hist. Review*, 2nd series, XIII (1961) pp. 382–96:
'The Nottinghamshire Reformers and the Contribution to the New Poor
Law'. J. T. Becher, *The Antipauper system exemplifying the positive and practical
good realized by the relievers and the relieved under the frugal beneficial and lawful
administration of the Poor Laws prevailing at Southwell and in the neighbouring
district* (1828). J. T. Becher, *The Constitution of friendly societies upon legal and
scientific principles exemplified by the rules and table of calculations of the Friendly
Institution at Southwell* (2nd edn., 1824).

institutions had their origins in a stiffly and self-consciously hierarchical society. Both Hannah More and Mrs Trimmer continually emphasize how important for the poor are the duties of obedience and subordination to their betters, and it is clear that the administration of these institutions never completely freed itself from the ways of thought which such a social system engendered.

Closely connected with that condition was the fact that when these schemes were developed and administered by the clergy they were inevitably associated with the officers of a body to which there was always some covert, some open, hostility. There was always some popular opposition to the Church. It is re-flected in much that Cobbett writes about parsons, and in much that was done and said in the popular disorders of the thirties. It was of course strongly represented in the various forms of nonconformity and it was to come out strongly in much of the trade unionism and radicalism of the seventies and eighties. For this reason, if for no other, even if these institutions had embodied a social policy which the men of the future would find satisfactory it would not have been operated through the agency of the parochial clergy.

But the social policy these schemes embodied was not found to be satisfactory. As with all policies based on the principle of self-help, those who developed and commended these institu-tions seem always to have tended to exaggerate the extent to which poor people could help themselves. Friendly societies, savings banks, sick clubs and the like institutions were all very well, but it seems unlikely that for instance an ill-paid agri-cultural labourer, married and with children, would be able through these agencies to provide himself with sufficient cover to protect him when confronted with the accidents of life and the certainty of old age; and, of course, if the urban population is brought into the picture there were very large numbers of people who were out of reach of any of these facilities. The necessary facilities could only be supplied by the coercive powers, the universal responsibility and almost limitless resources of the secular State.

However, a policy based on defective principles and obsoles-cent social values may yet supply ideas and precedents which are of use in preparing the way for the future. The conception of a system based on self-help admits the employment of two ideas which could be of use in social conditions very different from those that prevailed in mid nineteenth-century England. One was the idea of co-operation and the other the idea of insurance. The idea of co-operation was of great moral importance in the nineteenth century, and had many idealistic interpretations; in the twentieth century it was to be reduced to one very specialized application. The idea of insurance was to be carried over from nineteenth-century individualism to become the keystone of much twentieth-century social policy.

Only, again this must be said, if it were going to develop in this way it would need the reinforcement of the coercive powers of the State. One of the difficulties of voluntary insurance was that young men who were not yet married but had reached full earning power did not insure but waited till they were older and had a wife and children, by which time they were less attractive actuarial propositions. If a scheme of insurance was really to provide satisfactory cover for sickness, unemployment and old age it must be universal; everyone must be compelled to join from the moment they started earning, and employers must be compelled to pay their share while the man or woman to be insured was working for them; and, even so, if the scheme was to succeed it would probably be necessary for the State to subsidize it heavily.

Towards the end of the nineteenth century there was at least one clergyman who realized something of this, one Canon Blackley. Blackley was a curate at St Peter's, Southwark, during the cholera epidemic of 1854. While tending the sick he caught the disease and, though he was fortunate enough to survive, he had to spend the next thirty years of his life in country parishes. It must have been during this period that he developed the ideas about insurance that he described in 1878 in an article in the November number of *The Nineteenth Century*. Blackley's scheme was that everybody between seventeen and twenty-one should be required to pay, in instalments, £10 into a national fund, so that he might receive eight shillings a week in sickness, and four shillings a week as a pension at the age of seventy. The scheme was wholly contributory, except in so far that Blackley calculated that the wealthier contributors would not take up the money owed to them and so would leave more available for the poorer contributors, who would do so. He calculated that at the level of prices which then maintained, the pension would be enough to keep an elderly man off the rates, that is from dependence on the enforced contributions of his neighbours, and from the misery and degradation that could exist in the workhouse.

The scheme excited a good deal of interest. Blackley repeated the substance of his article in *The Contemporary Review* and reproduced his ideas in a good many addresses and discussions up and down the country. It was discussed at the Church Congress at Leicester in 1880 and again at Reading in 1883, and, though on the first occasion some of the clergy seem to have been apprehensive about the element of compulsion in it and preferred the schemes they were used to or thought that an agricultural labourer would believe that for him the only satis-factory form of insurance was an allotment, it received very general support on both occasions. Between 1880 and 1886 a large number of boards of guardians seem to have taken an interest in the matter, and an association was formed to educate the public on the question of national insurance.[1]

In contrast to Bismarck's Germany no scheme was imple-mented in Britain in the nineteenth century. Parliament seems to have been deterred by the opposition of the friendly societies, Joseph Chamberlain probably confused the issue by taking up the idea of old age pensions, and then not proceeding with it; and in fact a scheme much more elaborate than Blackley's was needed that would make much greater inroads on the National Exchequer. The matter therefore had to wait till Lloyd George's acts of 1908 and 1911 were passed. But looking back from that vantage point it seems clear that that development was in-evitable, to use a word which no doubt historians should eschew. In this matter the pattern is the same as it was in education, as it was also in public health. The State, equipped with compul-sory powers, imposing universal standards and endowed with the resources yielded by taxation, inevitably took into its hands ideas which men in the nineteenth century had conceived, but

[1] M. J. J. Blackley, *Thrift and National Insurance as a Security against Pauperism with a memoir of the late Rev. Canon Blackley and a reprint of his Essay* (1906); *Report of the Church Congress, Leicester 1880* (1881) (Discussion on Pauper-ism) pp. 53–81; *Report of the Church Congress, Reading 1883* (1883) pp. 237–259.

which voluntary efforts could never fully realize. It was a process fraught with important consequences for the clergy who had a natural place in a voluntary system but, after 1832, none in a system which was run by the now secular State. It will therefore overshadow what I have to say about the last phase of nineteenth-century history with which I wish to deal.

However, before that phase can be discussed it is necessary to consider how one particular series of social problems affected the clergy, for they are of peculiar significance. They are the problems connected with health and disease.

7

The Mid Nineteenth-
Century Parson:
The Social Order (2)

If the provision of allotments, clothing clubs and savings clubs
were typical nineteenth-century preoccupations, there was one
clerical duty that had a far longer past, but which was to make
heavy and searching demands on the nineteenth-century
clergyman.

Visiting the sick, particularly those who are likely to die, is
one of the oldest, the most universal, the least avoidable, of a
priest's duties. It was recognized as an obligation even at a
period when many of the clergy were notoriously worldly. Jane
Austen's novel *Persuasion* was apparently written between 1811
and 1816. In the third chapter there is a silly discussion about
the effect of a man's work on his appearance, designed to flatter
Sir Walter Elliott who had never done any work. In the course
of this discussion one Mrs Clay, who was setting her cap at Sir
Walter, says: 'Even the clergyman, you know, is obliged to go
into infected rooms, and expose his health and his looks to all
the injury of a poisonous atmosphere.' It would be hard to
say how generally this obligation was observed between 1811
and 1816, but the diary of John Skinner shows how seriously
a conscientious priest of that period could take this duty, and
the readiness with which his parishioners sent for him when
someone was at the point of death seems to illustrate what his
parishioners expected of him.[1] Where it is recorded, the behaviour of many of the clergy who were confronted by the

[1] *John Skinner. Journal of a Somerset Rector*, edited by H. Coombs and A. N.
Box (1930).

cholera of 1831 and 1832 seems to show that at that date there were parochial clergy, several of whom had been ordained at least ten years before, who were prepared to do their duty in very difficult, and what no doubt seemed to them highly dangerous, circumstances. It may not be legitimate to use these individual cases to make a general assessment, but at the least there is enough in the record to show that the tradition had not been abandoned or forgotten.

Where the sick are concerned it is not easy to separate the cure of souls from the cure of bodies. It was natural to credit the parson as the one learned man among ignorant folk with a knowledge of medicine, and, if he was at all active, it was natural that he should use such skills as he had for the benefit of his parishioners. For instance, as the result of an act of 1808 Sydney Smith was forced, most unwillingly, to reside in his, apparently significantly named, living of Foston-le-Clay in Yorkshire. While there he exercised his medical skill for the benefit of his poorer neighbours. He seems to have made some 'ludicrous mistakes', but such skill as he had stood him in good stead in 1816 when there was a great shortage of decent food, which seems to have been experienced by his family as well, owing to the failure of the harvest, and also to an outbreak in his village of a fever of a 'very dangerous and infectious kind'. Sydney Smith went from cottage to cottage with food and medicine. His task seems to have been an increasingly difficult one. When the toll of death mounted it was not easy to persuade the villagers to go into the infected cottages to nurse the sick, or carry out the dead to the grave. He shamed them into doing so by proposing to carry them there himself.[1]

This was in the first quarter of the nineteenth century when conditions in country places were probably normally pretty primitive. At a later period it seems probable that matters would be organized in such a way that the duty of the physical treatment of the sick was less likely to fall on the parson personally. However, even in the later nineteenth century the parish clergy and their wives seem to have been expected to give medical advice and help, and where necessary simple medicine.[2]

[1] *A Memoir of the Reverend Sydney Smith by his daughter Lady Holland with a selection from his letters.* (2 vols., 1855) Vol. I, pp. 117, 160 and 171.
[2] McClatchey [op. cit., p. 147] p. 166.

Indeed there were cases where they might have to do more. In the middle of the century E. B. Ellman was vicar of Wartling in Sussex. It was a neglected village, hostile to its clergyman and badly served by the parish doctor of whom the best that the villagers could say was that 'he did not torment poor people but left them to die'. Ellman's knowledge of drugs and medicine thus came in useful, and enabled him to win his way into cottages that would otherwise have been closed to him. The task was at times a heavy one; soon after he arrived an epidemic of measles of 'a bad type' struck the village and for two or three weeks the average number of cases he visited was over eighty, adults as well as children.[1]

Possibly by the forties and fifties the situation in Wartling was exceptional, for in the preceding hundred years there had begun an important development which it is not too much to say would revolutionize the conditions of English life, and for that matter life in all countries. Medical skill was being consolidated and professionalized and would in due course become more scientific and, what was even more important, it was becoming much more generally available both to rich and poor. The process can be seen in England in the progressive foundation both of hospitals and of dispensaries where poor people could receive treatment. Between 1720 and 1800 11 hospitals were founded in London, and between 1800 and 1840 another 14. Between 1769 and 1800 13 dispensaries were founded in London and by 1840 there were a further 10. Before 1720 there were apparently only 2 hospitals in our sense of the word in the provinces, by 1760 there were 16, by 1800 there were 38 and by 1860, 114. Before 1800 13 dispensaries were opened in the provinces and apparently 67 between 1800 and 1840.

During the eighteenth century an increasing number of medical men started practice, and as time went forward they were to an increasing extent, in a real sense, professionally trained. It has been calculated that the proportion of medical men to the population in 1782 was not very different from what it was in 1911. Meanwhile in the last thirty or so years of the eighteenth century the progress of medical training was developing rapidly in London, and in the first thirty years of the nineteenth century the great provincial medical schools grew

[1] Ellman, *Recollections* [op. cit., p. 159] p. 167.

up. And perhaps most important of all, a number of men trained in the medical schools of Edinburgh and Glasgow came to practise in England, where they very greatly increased the general level of professional competence in the country.[1]

These developments not only unavoidably affected social practice all over the country, they also initiated a revolution in social policy. They did this the more certainly because a number of leading doctors in the late eighteenth and early nineteenth centuries began the systematic study of such things as the incidence of disease and the factors affecting the physical condition of large sections of the people. The pioneers in this work were men like J. C. Lettsom of London, James Currie of Liverpool, Thomas Percival and John Ferriar of Manchester, Haygarth of Chester, Alison of Edinburgh and Thackrah of Leeds. These studies formed the basis of what is called the 'sanitary principle', the recognition, that is, of the important part played by the factors which make for good health, or encourage disease, in the life of a people, and of the social advantages which might be gained by an attack on the conditions which cause disease. This medical tradition was happily reinforced by a political doctrine which was able to turn it into a viable social programme, for Bentham's conception of systematic government based on effective central control and armed with statistics provided precisely the instrument which a policy based on the 'sanitary principle' required, and the two traditions joined forces. The Unitarian doctor and minister Southwood Smith – trained in the Edinburgh medical school which also produced Dr Alison, an important exponent of the sanitary principle in Scotland, and Kay-Shuttleworth, who was to play an important part in English administration – came to London in 1820 and became a close associate of Bentham, and it was another of Bentham's associates, Edwin Chadwick, who initiated the policy of public health by commissioning Southwood Smith and Kay-Shuttleworth and another doctor, Arnott, to enquire into the conditions which caused disease in the East End of London.

All this had important results for the clergy. In the eighteenth

[1] G. T. Griffith, *Population Problems of the Age of Malthus* (Cambridge, 1926) pp. 217–26. Charles Newman, M.D., F.R.C.P., *The Evolution of Medical Education in the Nineteenth Century* (1957).

century many of them had been closely associated with the foundation of hospitals. It is true that in this they seem often to have acted rather as benevolent local notabilities, not much different from the merchants, lawyers and other laymen with whom they were associated in this work, than as men with special pastoral responsibilities. This, however, was not always so. It is clear that it was a realization of the needs of his flock that led Isaac Maddox, bishop of Worcester from 1743 to 1759, to found the Royal Infirmary, Worcester, and the same seems to be true of the clergy with whom he was associated.[1] As the sense of parochial responsibility became more general in the nineteenth century this motive clearly became more dominant; indeed a history of hospitals in the nineteenth century in so far as it reveals the motives of the clergy who co-operated in the work, may help towards a study of the development of the sense of pastoral duty on the part of the nineteenth-century clergy.

It may also prove enlightening in other ways. The foundation of hospitals was only part of a large movement, the development of more professional and, in the end, more scientific, medicine. This was a factor of which the clergy would have to take account in their parochial work and which must affect their views on social policy. Possibly a study of the activities of those of the clergy who were associated with hospitals may throw some light on what the relationship of the clergy and this new factor was likely to be. Indeed both issues can be studied in the history of the Radcliffe Infirmary at Oxford. In the eighteenth and early nineteenth centuries the Radcliffe Infirmary was largely governed by clergymen. The lists of managers, treasurers and other officers and the committee of management are full of them. This was to be expected in the kind of community that early nineteenth-century Oxford was. The bursars and heads of houses who were active in this business were the local magnates and often no doubt men whose condition as priests was to a large extent fortuitous. If they had parochial responsibilities they were probably not unduly troubled by them. However, it is clear that as the nineteenth century went forward clergymen of a very different sort were

[1] W. H. McMenemey, *History of Worcester Royal Infirmary* (1947) pp. 10-70.

being attracted into hospital work. For instance, there were a number of clerical house visitors whose task it was to watch over the good order and discipline of the hospital and to receive any complaints the patients might make, and the list includes John Keble, J. H. Newman, E. B. Pusey and A. P. Stanley, later dean of Westminster.[1] At the same time it becomes clear that in the nineteenth century parochial preoccupations were affecting the relations with the hospital of many of the clergy who had dealings with the Radcliffe, for they seem to have spent much of their time negotiating to get their parishioners beds in the hospital, or trying to look after their interests when they were there.[2]

However, the most interesting of the clergymen connected with the Radcliffe does not draw his significance from his parochial assiduity. He was in many ways an old-fashioned man, a pluralist, and his services were administrative and general rather than parochial. Perhaps his achievement can be described as the work of a magnate rather than a priest; nevertheless his activities point to factors of which parish priests would have to take account. The clergyman in question is Vaughan Thomas, the incumbent of two livings in the Oxford and one in the Gloucester diocese. Between 1836 and 1856 Vaughan Thomas performed the heavy task of revising the rules and organization of the Radcliffe Infirmary. He also organized the Radcliffe lunatic asylum as a place where lunatics were humanely treated. In the cholera epidemic of 1831 he was chairman of the Oxford Board of Health. At the time of the cholera outbreak of 1854 he issued a series of papers giving advice on how to avoid infection. They seem to have been both intelligent and full of kindly understanding and to have shown a real care for his people. It is interesting to contrast this fact with the fact that as a magistrate he seems to have been unusually hard on poachers.[3]

As a pluralist, and also a justice of the peace punishing poachers, no doubt Vaughan Thomas looks back to the unreformed magisterial past of the English clergy rather than forward to its pastoral and parochial future, and it may be held

[1] A. G. Gibson, *The Radcliffe Infirmary* (Oxford, 1926) pp. 74-6.
[2] McClatchey [op. cit., p. 147] pp. 169-74.
[3] ibid., pp. 166, 173, 175-6, 196.

that his main significance is that he survived so long. Even so, his activities also show how the magisterial traditions of the English clergy were to shape their pastoral and parochial work in the middle of the century. Vaughan Thomas's medical pre-occupations found their counterparts in the kind of thing that many of the most spiritually-minded of the clergy believed came within the sphere of their responsibilities. In fact simply because their parochial tradition had so largely been moulded by men who saw their duty in terms of secular government, secular responsibilities and secular needs, the English clergy could not evade the fact that the incidence of disease and the physical conditions in which their congregations lived were relevant to their pastoral work and that the development of medical science placed inescapable responsibilities upon them.

Unfortunately it is not easy to study the way in which the progressive development of medical skill and its diffusion through the country affected what actually happened in nineteenth-century parishes. This is largely because there does not seem to be any satisfactory history of medical practice in the nineteenth century, and particularly of medical practice in country districts. It would be useful, for instance, to learn what medical skill was likely to be available in a particular district at a given date. It is therefore not easy to answer some questions which may be of considerable importance in envisaging and understanding what was taking place. For instance in 1834 Blomfield said that if the clergy were deprived of their revenue in many villages the 'dispensary' would be shut up, and in 1854 he expressed a wish that there should be a 'dispensary' in every village. But what kind of institution had he in mind? Was it a place where treatment and medicine were free, or one where they were normally restricted to those who had paid a subscription? In some parishes the clergy seem to have created quite elaborate medical centres; did Blomfield mean such institutions, or did he mean simply a store for the distribution of medicines – of which there is likely to be no record?[1] Unless that point is cleared up it is not easy to guess how generally his wishes were obeyed, or how reasonable they were. Above all, what was the relation of the operation of

[1] e.g. ibid., pp. 93–5, 168, 176.

such 'dispensaries' to the work of the local doctors? Was it supplementary or was it a substitute?

The operation of the medical clubs and sick clubs, which were very frequently part of the organization of a parish in the middle of the century, also raises some interesting problems. For instance, it was said that the attraction of a medical club was that it enabled a poor man to choose his medical attendant instead of resorting to the doctor appointed by the board of guardians.[1] But what choice was there likely to be in this matter in a mid nineteenth-century village, and what was the nature of the medical skill which was likely to be available? As a matter of fact some of the evidence seems to suggest that at least the *choice* was often surprisingly large.

For those who were really poor there would of course be no choice. They would have to submit themselves to treatment by the doctor chosen by the guardians, which clearly raises the question: what treatment would they be likely to receive at his hands? In many cases no doubt it would be unsatisfactory; in many cases, particularly when the board was dominated by small farmers or small tradesmen whose primary object was to keep down the rates, the appointment went to the medical man who would come for least money, and they were apt to follow up such an appointment by a ruthless endeavour to keep down their chosen doctor's medical expenses at whatever cost to his patients. At times the local clergy made bitter complaint at the way such a doctor behaved to their parishioners.[2] But such an attitude was by no means uniform; there were other clergymen who seem to have been perfectly satisfied with the system. It is true that such clergymen seem normally to have been chairmen, or at least members, of a board of guardians and their attitude may have been no more than the result of official complacency. On the other hand, it is possible that when the guardians were under the responsible control of more substantial people, better appointments might

[1] P.P. 1868/69, XIII, p. 454 (evidence of the Rev. E. Kempson).
[2] e.g. P.P. 1844, IX, pp. 529–35 (the complaint of the Rev. W. J. Coppard, incumbent of Plympton St Mary in Devonshire, of the local poor law doctor). The best account of the treatment of a workhouse doctor by a board of guardians run by small tradesmen is that by Joseph Rogers, *Reminiscences of a Workhouse Medical Officer with a preface by Thorold Rogers* (1889).

H

be made and more humane service given. Probably it would be wrong to generalize. There is a smell of complacency about some of the evidence, but some of it suggests that under enlightened direction the service could be both effective and humane, as for instance in the Leighton Buzzard union under the chairmanship of the Rev. W. B. Wroth.[1]

It is a pity not to know the answers to these questions. If more were known it would help to reveal much that is important about the realities of social life in town and country in mid nineteenth-century England. Greater knowledge on these points would, for instance, throw light on a very important problem: What was the result at any given date of the development of medical skill in terms of prevalent social conditions? It would also assist a realistic understanding of what, for instance, the administration of the Poor Law actually meant to the human beings who came into contact with it in different parts of the country. It would also reveal much about the behaviour and attitudes of the clergy.

However, where so much is doubtful one point is clear. That is the significance for all nineteenth-century practice, for all nineteenth-century social policy, indeed, for all nineteenth-century life, of the continual presence of virulent, and in many cases probably fatal, infectious disease. Infectious diseases were among the potent factors that determined events in nineteenth-century England. Their ravages sometimes climbed to a peak, and they were never absent. Between 1831 and 1866 there were the intermittent visitations of cholera. Less spectacular, but probably more deadly, was the continual presence of various forms of 'fever'. They were called variously 'typhus', 'typhoid', 'enteric' or sometimes just 'low fever', but these names were loosely used and it is not always clear what was meant. Men had also to fear more clearly identifiable diseases. Scarlet fever, for instance, was in the middle of the century a killing disease. It was not till towards the end of the century that smallpox was effectively brought under control by vaccination; diphtheria, which seems to have been a new disease in the middle of the century, was never brought under control. Tuberculosis was everywhere. In fact no picture of Victorian England has any relation to accuracy unless it takes account of

[1] P.P. 1844, IX, pp. 552–6.

the fact that in any Victorian community fatal infectious disease was lurking somewhere, and that any year might produce an epidemic which spared neither class, generation or sex, and left a broad swathe of bitter domestic tragedies in its train.

This placed a heavy burden on a parish priest. It was his duty to visit the sick, and an outbreak of infectious disease made that duty, not only extremely exacting and distressing but dangerous as well, although the danger may not have been as great as he thought it was. Cholera was water-borne, real typhus was louse-borne, and so long as a man did not drink or sleep in a stricken house he was probably safe. But men could not know these facts in the middle of the century, and when they saw with what speed a disease could work through those who were exposed to infection, and the deaths they died, it was natural that they should fear. Even so robust a character as W. F. Hook confessed that his experiences during the cholera epidemic at Leeds in 1849 had made him a terrible coward. To punish himself he took on the task of visiting all the cholera patients himself. There was, however, nothing a clergyman could do to protect himself. The duty was unavoidable, such precautions as might be taken were nugatory, and the only thing to do was to cheer oneself with the belief that it was the timid and shrinking who were most likely to be attacked.[1]

There were, however, duties besides visiting the sick a parish clergyman might be expected to do when confronted by an epidemic. When an epidemic was anticipated he might lay in stocks of drugs. He might distribute lime for the cleansing of insanitary corners, he might distribute papers giving practical advice, such as those Vaughan Thomas drew up. He might have to play a leading part on a board of health which would be formed to fight the disease and he might have to make arrangements for the burial of the dead. It is true that in 1831, and indeed later, many of the clergy believed that the cholera was a punishment inflicted on the nation by an angry God and that their primary duty was to call men to self-examination, repentance and penance; but the practical side of the tradition they had inherited was strong, and that belief does not seem to have prevented them, even in 1831, from taking more mundane

[1] Stephens, *W. F. Hook* [op. cit., p. 63] Vol. II, pp. 261–2. See also Rev. Canon Bateman (Senex), *Clerical Reminiscences* (3rd edn., 1882) pp. 120–1.

action and giving more mundane advice, as when, in 1832, Newman distributed papers, almost certainly containing practical advice, in case the cholera should visit Littlemore.

As it happened the cholera only visited Littlemore lightly. There was only one death. It struck much more heavily in Oxford itself, particularly in the parish of St Ebbe's where the evangelical W. W. Champneys was curate and had to bear the full brunt of it. If it had not been so Newman would not, as he fully realized, have been able to leave his parish and go on his famous holiday to Italy and Sicily. It is tempting to suggest that this might have altered the intellectual history of the nineteenth century, but it seems that even when he was intent on mundane responsibilities Newman's mind returned to the issues which made the argument of his life. For instance, when he discovered to his great annoyance that the people had not burnt the bed furniture of the one cholera victim, as they had been instructed to do, but had buried it and then dug it up again, presumably to use again, he said: 'is not this the very spirit of Whiggery – opposition for its own sake, striving against the truth, because it happens to be commanded us; as if wisdom were less wise because it is powerful?'[1] Nevertheless, Newman was fortunate. To recognize the full weight that the summer of 1832 could place on a man in charge of a parish it is as well to read the sombre, sometimes macabre, account written by William Leigh, of the outbreak of cholera at Bilston in Staffordshire between Walsall and Wolverhampton. Leigh was the incumbent of Bilston, and he had to act, not only as far as he could as a parish priest but also as chairman of the local board of health, convener of many important meetings responsible for the organization of medical help and, when they ran short, provider of coffins.[2]

It is understandable, then, that the sanitary principle should have been of particular significance to clergymen. To men who had seen at close quarters the devastation which disease could

[1] Newman, *Letters and Correspondence* [op. cit., p. 50] Vol. I, p. 269.
[2] The Rev. W. Leigh, A.M., Worcester College, Oxford, and incumbent of Bilston, *An authentic narrative of the melancholy occurrences at Bilston, in the county of Stafford, during the awful visitation in that town by cholera, in the months of August and September 1832* (Wolverhampton, 1833). The substance is reproduced in Norman R. Longmate, *King Cholera* (1966) pp. 107–15.

work, and who lived very near to its threat themselves, the fact that in the forties Edwin Chadwick had pointed both to the cause of disease, and to ways in which it might be prevented, naturally seemed not only a matter of high political importance but of great moral significance as well. Such, for instance, was the view of Charles Kingsley. In his parish at Eversley, in Hampshire, 'low fever' was apparently endemic, a fact which Kingsley, probably correctly, attributed to the bad conditions permitted by the landlord. In the summer of 1849 there was a peculiarly virulent outbreak and Kingsley's ministrations to the sick were so exacting that in the end his own health broke down and he was ordered away for a rest. On his recovery he went to London and visited Bermondsey, where he was horrified at what he saw. This threw him into rather febrile activity. He and his friends laid plans for cleaning up 'Jacob's Island' in the East End; he wanted to appeal to any number of higher powers to get them to act; he considered forming a sanitary league.

None of this came to very much. Kingsley was a highly-strung, delicate, impetuous man, more effective as a propagandist than an executant, and in this case what he wrote was more important than what he did. When in 1849 cholera threatened the country he preached three sermons to his parish on the subject, with the title 'Who causes Pestilence?' In 1854 he published them with a preface, and in 1857 he followed this up with a novel (*Two Years Ago*), which deals drastically with the same subject and is a book of some power.

His tract of 1854 is peculiarly interesting for in it he suggests three reasons which might prevent clergymen from taking up the cause of sanitary reform, as they ought to do. First, they might believe that they were only concerned with what could be clearly docketed as 'spiritual' and that anything else was not their province, an attitude which Kingsley called, as he called a good many of the things he disliked, 'manichaean'. Second, they might shrink from the possibility that the conclusions of sanitary science might interfere with preconceived religious ideas since pestilence and disease are punishments from God; and, lastly, there might be clergymen who were afraid to press the policies which sanitary science demanded in case they should threaten to disturb the vested interests of influential and wealthy members of their congregations, and so excite their displeasure and dry up their subscriptions.[1]

It is not easy to find out how far in fact any of these impediments did prevent clergymen of the Church of England from taking up sanitary reform. No doubt there were clergymen who were so firmly convinced that their functions were exclusively spiritual that they conscientiously, or conveniently, eschewed anything that might be called secular. No doubt, also, there were clergymen whose views on the operation of the moral forces that control society and history were so confident and rigid that they did not wish even to consider the possibility that disease might have material causes as well. And there may well have been clergymen who were too timid, too lazy, too stupid, too callous or too impercipient, to do anything positive. But such clergymen are not easy to find, and without doubt there were a number of clergymen other than Charles Kingsley who eagerly advocated the cause of sanitary reform, and many who did yeoman service for it as well.

Among the bishops, Blomfield constantly emphasized the importance of public health in his charges. Among the senior clergy there was, for instance, Canon Richson of the Manchester Collegiate Church, a man already notable in relation to elementary education. On 30 April 1854 Richson preached an important sermon at Manchester in favour of sanitary reform, which he subsequently published as a tract. It is, indeed, a curious production significant of the variety of authorities which could make claims on the mid nineteenth-century mind. In it he took the precepts of the board of health in London and supported them by reference to the precepts of the law of Moses in Exodus and Leviticus, which as he pointed out had the authority of a divinely appointed exemplar. When he published the sermon, to drive the lesson home and to gain the endorsement, not only of Moses but of contemporary science, he arranged that Dr Sutherland, the great authority on sanitary science, the man whom Florence Nightingale called 'the man without a soul', should add confirmatory notes. But Richson did not confine himself to propaganda. In 1853, with a few

---

[1] *Charles Kingsley: his letters and memories of his life edited by his wife* (1877) Vol. I, pp. 206–7, 215–18, 414–17. Una Pope-Hennessy, *Canon Charles Kingsley: a Biography* (1948) pp. 61, 90–2.

friends he founded the Manchester and Salford Sanitary Association, which did important work for public health during the rest of the century.[1]

Or there was Charles Girdlestone, the brother of Edward. It does not seem extravagant to suggest that the revealing experience in his life was when, in 1832, he faced the cholera as incumbent of Sedgely in Staffordshire. He certainly became an enthusiastic sanitary reformer. In 1843-4 he became an early supporter of the Metropolitan Association for Improving the Dwellings of the Industrious Classes, and in 1845 he published twelve 'Letters on the Unhealthy condition of the Lower Class of Dwellings', which were apparently of value. He presumably found confirmation of his opinions when, in 1849, he had to handle another severe outbreak of cholera as rector of Winford in Staffordshire.[2] Or there are cases when the arrival of an active priest, and his recognition of the prevailing state of affairs, led to the cleaning up of a town, as for instance when the drainage of Wantage was effectively renewed after the appointment of W. J. Butler as vicar in 1847, or when Edward Elton forcibly took Wheatley, a much neglected village in Oxfordshire, in hand, after he had become vicar in 1851.[3] Indeed the fact that an attack on the material causes of disease necessarily played an important part in the spiritual cure of souls became for many Anglicans an accepted doctrine. It is reflected in the work of those two quintessentially Anglican novelists, Mrs Ewing and Miss Yonge.[4] This does not mean that

[1] The Rev. Charles Richson, *The Observance of the Sanitary Laws divinely appointed, in the Old Testament Scripture, sufficient to ward off preventible diseases from Christians as well as Israelites. A sermon preached in the Cathedral Manchester on Sunday morning April 30th*, with notes by John Sutherland M.D. of the General Board of Health, London (1854). I owe my knowledge of the Manchester and Salford Society to the researches in the Manchester Central Library kindly undertaken on my behalf by Miss Sheila Lemoine.
[2] See the article on Charles Girdlestone in the *D.N.B.* by W. A. Greenhill.
[3] Kathleen Philip [op. cit., p. 108] p. 43; McClatchey [op. cit., p. 147] pp. 93-5.
[4] For Mrs Ewing, see *Jan of the Windmill*, first published in 1872-3 under the title of *The Miller's Thumb*, and appearing later in *Sunflowers and a Rushlight*, first published in 1882. (This was communicated to me by my sister Mrs Chitty.) For Miss Yonge, see Alethea Hayter, *History Today*, Vol. XIX, No. 12 (December 1969) pp. 840-7: 'The Sanitary Idea and a Victorian Novelist.'

parsons met with no opposition when they took up sanitary reform. The third possibility that Kingsley had envisaged, that is that such reforms might excite the displeasure of influential members of a man's congregation or community, was very much of a reality. As Archdeacon Fearon, archdeacon of Leicester, said in his charge of 1865:

> Sanitary improvements come very naturally within a clergy-man's province. In fact he frequently finds himself compelled to labour for their introduction, perhaps amidst vehement opposition, in order that he may clear away the obstacles which hinder and defeat his own spiritual work among his people.[1]

The fact was that any inhabited area, whether it was the section of a great city, a middle-sized town or a village, was likely to contain a good many natural enemies of sanitary reform. There were the owners of house property, possibly insanitary property, who did not want to be disturbed, or the owners of land who did not want sewers or water mains to pass through their ground, or the owners of mounds of ripening filth which they hoped to sell as manure. To these must be added those who saw no harm in the old stenches, indeed found in them a friendly and reassuring quality, and the large number of people whose primary object in all public activities was a passionate desire to prevent any expenditure which might come on the rates. By no means all of these potential opponents were very rich or very powerful, but they were often numerous and vehement and very jealous of their own rights, and they were also apt to fill vestry meetings and get themselves elected to select vestries, to boards of guardians, or even boards of health, normally with the single-minded object of keeping down local expenditure and preventing anything being done.

There are a number of examples of the clergy coming into conflict with this type of opposition. During the cholera year of 1854 B. J. Armstrong, the vicar of East Dereham in Norfolk, held a vestry meeting to put forward a scheme for supplying the town with water and thoroughly draining it. According to Armstrong the project was turned down by the farmers outside the town who felt the scheme would bring no advantage to

[1] Henry Fearon, archdeacon of Leicester and rector of Loughborough, *Charge 1865* (1865) p. 22.

them, and the smallholders in the town 'because unwilling to spend a shilling on anything'.[1] In 1865 the Hon. and Rev. E. V. Bligh, having been faced with an outbreak of what he called 'typhus' in his parish at Birling in Kent, tried to get the East Malling board of guardians, of which he was a member, to appoint an inspector of nuisances. He was successfully resisted by similar opponents, supported it is sad to say by a loquacious clergyman; however, with the aid of a third clergyman, the rector of Snodland, he rallied to the assault and carried his point next year. The rector of Snodland apparently extended the attack to the state of the cottages in his parish and the landlords who were responsible for them.[2] Or there is the story of Fearon as he told it to a meeting of the Church Congress in 1874:

> When I first went to live at Loughborough [he said] where I now reside, I found it in great want of water and with no sanitary arrangements. I and my brother clergymen stirred in the matter, but the principal inhabitants gave us the cold shoulder, on account of the additional rates that would be required. It consequently took ten years before we got the town drained, and twenty years before we got water, though it was close to us on the neighbouring hills.

He was, in fact, instituted in 1848, and the date of the Loughborough water-works is 1868.[3]

At the same meeting of the Church Congress the presiding bishop, the bishop of Chichester, told a similar story. He was Richard Durnford who had been rector of Middleton in Lancashire from 1833 to 1870. It was apparently, according to his biographer, a place where there were 'few resident gentry and no resident squire', and he was forced to take a leading part in its secular affairs. As has been said, he refused to become a magistrate but served for years on the board of guardians. For the same reason he had to take a lead in sani-

[1] B. J. Armstrong [op. cit., p. 185] p. 24.
[2] Esmé Wingfield-Stratford, *This was a Man. The Biography of the Honourable Edward Vesey Bligh, Diplomat–Parson–Squire* (Letchworth, 1949) pp. 191–4 and 198.
[3] *Church Congress (Brighton) 1874*, p. 495. I gained my knowledge of the confirmatory facts from Dr D. M. Thompson of Fitzwilliam College.

tary matters. In 1861, when people in the town wished to promote a local act to set up commissioners to control such matters as roads, gas and drainage, he saw it through into law and acted as chairman of the commissioners from 1861 till he left Middleton in 1870. But what happened had best be described in his own words.

> The place in which for many years I lived in Lancashire was almost wholly undrained. In certain districts typhus periodically appeared, low fever was seldom absent, deaths too frequent from these causes, and the work of the clergy in consequence most perilous. The beginning of effectual drainage was made by a Board of which I was a constant member, consisting mainly of small traders and working men, elected annually by the parish-ioners. The owners of property were almost to a man hostile, and our difficulties in enforcing an imperfect law were considerable. In fact, we were driven to the Queen's Bench, and Middleton had the honour of obtaining a decision which rules the law on this subject. We were triumphant, and the result was beyond our expectations.

He told the clergy that since then the law had been strengthened and that in such cases they should summon an inspector, which it was now the duty of every district to appoint.[1]

These examples are unfortunately only the result of selection by chance. It would be very desirable for the whole question to be reviewed so that the forces working locally for and against sanitary reform could be examined systematically over the whole country. This should help to provide an accurate picture not only of what proportion of the clergy played a part in this work but also of what part was played by the medical profession, by groups like the Unitarians and other members of what may be called the philanthropic élite.[2] But as they stand they suggest two points which are relevant for present purposes. The first is suggested by the speech of the bishop of Chichester. He spoke of the imperfections of the law under which at first he had worked, and advised the clergy to make use of a law

---

[1] Stephens, *Durnford* [op. cit., p. 158] pp. 68–110. *Church Congress (Brighton) 1874*, pp. 499–500.
[2] On the philanthropic élites, see G. Kitson Clark, *An Expanding Society: Britain 1830–1900* (Melbourne and Cambridge, 1967) p. 134.

which had since been passed making the appointment of inspectors of nuisances compulsory. This was presumably the act of 1866 of which Sir John Simon, the medical officer of the Privy Council, said drily: 'The grammar of common legislation acquired the novel virtue of the imperative mood.' It was time that it should do so. Simon's report on the general state of the country in 1865 shows clearly in how many places the battle against the forces of dirt and obstruction had been lost, or had not been fought at all, and how terrible were the consequences of these failures.

The act of 1866 by no means brought immediate victory everywhere, that much is clear from the evidence given by the clergy between 1867 and 1870 to the royal commission on the employment of children, young persons in agriculture. For instance, in the evidence reported in 1868–9 the Rev. G. R. Portal of Albury, a member of the Guildford Union, is represented as saying that the act of 1866 was not enforced and the guardians were indifferent about nuisances, and the Rev. E. Kempson of Claverdon in Warwickshire as saying that nobody liked to complain of a nuisance.[1] Both no doubt spoke from bitter experience. But 1866 was only a beginning; it was the first of a series of acts leading to the great consolidating act of 1875, on which the powerful apparatus that now exists of securing public health and fighting disease was to be erected. In fact the moral of the whole period before 1866 seems to be the old moral which is written plain through all this history. The old system of individual responsibility and local initiative, in which the clergy had an important part to play, had failed. It had made a far more notable and a far more valuable effort than is ever credited to it, but it lacked the force and the uniformity of standard which the needs of the country demanded, and its place had to be taken by more powerful local authorities, working under the effective control of a powerful centralized State – a system in which the role of the parochial clergy would progressively become less significant. It is the same moral as is apparent in the history of savings clubs and insurance and old age pensions, and also in the history of education.

[1] P.P. 1868/69, XIII, Pt. 2, pp. 443, 454.

The second point which this history demonstrates is equally significant in relation to the ideas, and the limitations of perception, which were common in this middle period, and it is equally important. The common assumption on which most thought on social policy was based in this period was that in dealing with poverty the only healthy policies were those that encouraged self-help on the part of the poor. Thought on these lines tended towards the acceptance of another assumption, that poverty was often the result of the moral failure of the individual to help himself. The assumption does not seem to have been normally accepted with the absoluteness and ruthlessness which is sometimes credited to most of those who were impressed by it. It was normal to accept the fact that an individual might be plunged into poverty by circumstances beyond his control. This reservation, however, clearly raises a most critical question. Obviously the extent to which the basic assumption of the need to encourage self-help and the possibility of relying on it was valid would depend on what circumstances were accepted as coming in the category of the unavoidable and what power over an individual's behaviour was credited to them.

Obviously also, this was an issue which was necessarily raised by the social significance of disease. Not only were the onset and the course of disease matters which were unlikely to be affected by the personal efforts of the sufferer, but a study of the causes of disease drew attention to living conditions in which it was extremely unlikely that an individual would be able to help himself. The tenement houses and hovels, the courts and alleys, where fever always lurked and cholera struck its hardest, were also places where decency was impossible and profligacy and drunkenness venial. Those who were interested in public health, particularly those whose duty it was to visit such places, could not help but recognize this fact. It was a recognition which did not necessarily lead men to abandon their earlier assumptions, but it enforced on them convictions about the effect of environment which were held in unstable equilibrium with those assumptions. There is an interesting example of this in a volume of essays by different hands called *Meliora. Better Times to Come*, published in 1852, to which reference has already been made. In that book Charles Girdle-

stone produced an essay on 'Rich and Poor', in which he re-
peats the old assumption. He says that the difference between
the rich and the poor derives ultimately from their personal
qualities; that if they were reduced to an equality they would,
in a short time, draw apart again, and he adds the aphorism:
'Abject want is almost always the result of grievous error, or of
gross misconduct.' But Charles Girdlestone was also an active
parish priest with drastic experience of the results of disease
and he was an enthusiastic sanitary reformer, a cause the importance of which he extols in this article. Therefore he adds
this qualification to his primary assertion:

> The bare walls of a bleak garret, the damp floor of a dark
> cellar, the crowded room in the narrow alley or lane, washed out,
> if ever, with foetid water and ventilated, if at all, with foul air,
> these have much more to do than has been heretofore supposed
> with those habits of idleness and intemperance which lead
> naturally to abject poverty, and which are prevailing forms of
> immorality. These are homes in which the virtues taught in
> Christian schools and Churches can scarcely fail to droop and
> wither.[1]

Such views were not uncommon in these years, and the
logical conclusion to be derived from them was to attack the
conditions which prevented poor people from helping themselves. This was indeed an additional reason for the clergy to
see sanitary reform as a moral issue. Apart from the fact that
here was patently an attack on conditions that caused human
suffering and misery, here was also an attack on conditions
that were morally distorting to their victims. It was, however,
no good trying to provide drains and a pure water supply
unless something was done to provide reasonable housing as
well, and this presented a difficult, almost an insoluble, problem. To improve housing on a large scale is not only always
a formidable physical task requiring massive expenditure, but
it can be severely complicated by the fact that bad housing may
be the symptom of bad social and economic conditions, which
may not be corrected by making housing conditions physically
better but which may cancel the results of any improvement.
It is, for instance, no good providing good houses for people

---

[1] Viscount Ingestre, *Meliora* [op. cit., p. 184] pp. 18 and 23.

whose earning capacity, in existing conditions, is not sufficient to maintain them. Nevertheless, clearly the improvement of housing conditions was all-important if the conditions of the working class were to be improved also, so an attempt was made to attack this problem.

The most obvious target was London where conditions were most notorious. The first organization to be formed for this purpose was apparently the 'Association for Improving the Dwellings of the Industrious Classes'. The moving spirit in this body was one Charles Gatliff, and it was this body which apparently attracted Charles Girdlestone. It was a body which, like other mid nineteenth-century housing societies, combined two aims: the provision of better housing for the working classes and the return of a dividend at a moderate rate to those who had provided the capital. It was followed into the field by other associations, or personal schemes, for providing model dwellings for the poor. There was the Society for Improving the Condition of the Working Classes, the lineal descendant of the bishop of Bath and Wells' Labourer's Friend Society. In this society Lord Shaftesbury became the leading figure and Prince Albert a reasonably active president who himself planned artisans' cottages; and there were the schemes for building working-class houses promoted variously by Miss Burdett-Coutts, Sydney Waterlow and George Peabody. In the provinces Titus Salt built a factory community at Saltaire near Bradford and Edward Akroyd a model village near Halifax. In London again Octavia Hill developed her plan for the renovation of old houses whose occupants were placed under the benevolent direction of trained rent collectors.

The schemes of Octavia Hill are closely connected with the charitable activities of the Church of England, but she herself is an example of the way the various streams of intelligent philanthropy tended in the nineteenth century to flow together, for she was the granddaughter of Southwood Smith. In 1852 she started work at a ladies' guild, a co-operative association promoted by Maurice and the Christian Socialists of which her mother became manager. In 1856 she became secretary to the classes for women at the Working Men's College in Great Ormond Street, also a creation of Maurice. Her work interested her in the problem of housing, and in 1864 and 1865 with the help of Ruskin she acquired control of three dilapidated houses in Marylebone. The houses were to be left in her management, both as the collector of rents and as the guide and director of the families who lived in them. The scheme proved successful. More houses were bought, more women were recruited and trained as rent collectors and advisers. In 1884 she was given what was probably her most important task. There had been attacks on the management of their London property by the ecclesiastical commissioners. They were in fact malicious and ill instructed, but they meant that the commissioners had to be careful in what they did, and in 1884 they called in Octavia Hill to advise about the development of some of their other properties as well. As a result of all this, her activities developed very considerably, the houses she controlled and the number of her rent collectors both increasing greatly in number. These rent collectors were to be important in the development of nineteenth-century social policy.[1]

During the middle period of the century, therefore, there came into existence a good many institutions which had as their object the improvement of the housing of the poor, and as far as their capacity went much good work was done. But in due course it became quite clear that it did not go far enough. As the third quarter of the century drew to its end, men began to realize that they had only touched the edges of the problem. There were various reasons for this. The most obvious was of course that the resources available either by gift or investment could not possibly suffice for what needed to be done, and the number actually rehoused was infinitesimal compared with the number who needed rehousing, and indeed also with the rate at which the population was increasing each year.[2] But in addition to this much of what was done could not reach the most serious elements in the problem. Many housing schemes were apt to concentrate on respectable tenants in steady jobs, whose need was obviously not the greatest. Octavia Hill and her ladies were accustomed to dealing with rougher types,

---

[1] For these housing schemes, see David Owen, *English Philanthropy 1660–1960* (Cambridge, Mass., 1964) pp. 371–93. G. F. A. Best, *Temporal Pillars* (Cambridge, 1964) pp. 480–98.

[2] See the estimate of R. A. Cross in 1875, *Hansard*, 3rd series, Vol. 222, col. 99.

but amongst them there seem to have been some who would not or could not accept her discipline, and beyond the reach of all these schemes were those for whom no decent houses were available, or those whose poverty was such, or whose livelihood was so unreliable, that it was not possible for them to establish a home at all. To deal with some of these problems it was necessary to use the credit of public bodies, either local authorities or the central State, and it was also necessary to take legal power to handle effectively the owners of slum property, or of the land on which slums were built.

What has been said so far necessarily refers to urban housing, on which public attention was increasingly concentrated. This was of course an important matter for city incumbents, but for the men in charge of urban parishes probably the responsibility was not so immediate and personal as were the problems of rural housing for a country parson. These problems were also very serious. The revelations in the letters to *The Times* of Sidney Godolphin Osborne in the 1840s, or the terrible words which Charles Kingsley put into his song on 'The Poacher's Widow' suggest, as does much other evidence, what the cottages in a smiling countryside could be like once you got inside. Earth floors often running with water, leaking roofs and walls, windows blocked with sacking, the whole family packed into one sleeping room, no privy or other convenience – these conditions made for a life which lacked the amenities which a well-kept animal might expect to enjoy. As always in the country the situation differed widely from district to district and from place to place, according to the level of prosperity and probably the materials traditionally available for building. It had a variety of causes. The primary one in most districts was, of course, poverty – poor wages and over-population. But in many districts there was also the working of the Poor Law before the Union Chargeability Act of 1865. Before that act a parish was only responsible for the relief of those who had a 'settlement' in it. The result was a tendency on the part of the owners of land to pull down cottages in which poor people might live and produce children, or to prevent the building of cottages, with the result that labourers were forced to crowd into an adjoining village where there was no such control.

There was one other factor which helped to complicate

matters. Some of the practices to which men in the nineteenth century violently objected seem to have been traditional practice; this was particularly the case with the habit of a whole family of all sexes and ages sleeping in one room. As a result of this housing reform was necessary even where there did not exist the severe poverty and over-population which prevailed in the worst counties. This seems to have been the case in J. C. Atkinson's parish in Cleveland in Yorkshire, and in parts of Northumberland.[1] Where this was the main source of trouble, housing reform was probably a simpler affair than in counties where the real need was for whole-scale revision of wages, and a general migration of the labouring population to a more favoured area.

Where a clergyman found that housing was bad, in most cases his appropriate action was to appeal to the landowner. This was what Atkinson seems to have done with apparently good effect in his parish, and it is what Archdeacon Fearon advised the clergy to do later in the century in the charge which I have already cited. After talking about housing deficiencies he said,

in cases where from want of sufficient house accommodation the requirements of health cannot be answered, and the sentiments of self-respect and decorum must be continually violated, there can be no doubt that a representation from the clergyman to a landlord, or the owner of a house, would come with great weight.

Then he went on to praise 'those landlords (and they are numerous now) who are providing suitable houses for their labourers throughout their whole estates'.[2]

No doubt the improving landlord provided the best hope for housing reform in the English nineteenth-century countryside, and in certain great estates there had been for some time a good tradition in this matter. Good cottages for labourers were built on the estates of the Duke of Bedford, the Duke of Northumberland, the Earl Spencer and the Duke of Rutland

[1] J. C. Atkinson, *Forty Years in a Moorland Parish* (2nd edn., 1891) pp. 18–27. James Caird, *English Agriculture in 1851. With a New Introduction by G. E. Mingay* (2nd edn., 1968) p. 389.
[2] Fearon, *Charge 1865* [op. cit., p. 210] p. 23.

and others of the really big landowners.[1] On the other hand, in his preface to the 4th edition of *Yeast* written in 1859 Charles Kingsley, while claiming a general improvement in the agricultural labourer's condition since the book was first published, said:

> Cottage improvement, and sanitary reform, throughout the country districts, are going on at a fearfully slow rate. Here and there high-hearted landlords like the Duke of Bedford are doing their duty like men; but in general the apathy of the educated classes is most disgraceful.

It is perhaps relevant to remember that at Eversley Kingsley seems to have been confronted by bad cottages and a landlord who was reluctant to do much,[2] and it is possible that, at least by the time Fearon delivered his charge, there had been a more general improvement than Kingsley suggests. Even so the conscience of a landowner or, perhaps more importantly, the activity of his agent, might at best be uncertain instruments for social development. In any case there were many cottages over which landowners had relinquished, or never had, control. Many cottages were let with a farm to house the labourers who worked on the farm, a practice to which, judging by the evidence they presented to the report on women and children in agriculture, many of the clergy objected, as putting the labourer much too much under the control of the farmer. Moreover many of the worst cottages had been built by the labourers themselves or by very small contractors, on small parcels of ground, over which no substantial landlord had any control at all.

Consequently any improvement in the cottages in large areas of the English countryside in mid century must have been extremely limited. The picture can be seen reasonably clearly in the evidence given by many of the clergy between 1868 and 1870 to the agricultural commission. As it happens Godolphin Osborne reported in his evidence that there had been a great improvement in housing.[3] It must, however, be guessed that

---

[1] For Bedford, Spencer and Northumberland, see Caird [op. cit., p. 219] pp. 389, 433.

[2] Pope-Hennessy [op. cit., p. 208] p. 127.

[3] P.P. 1868/69, XIII, Pt. 2, p. 238.

that improvement was local, for his statement is contradicted by much of the evidence given by other people, and it seems not unfair to sum up the matter generally in the words of one who was always one of the most outspoken of the clergy. James Fraser, referring to the areas which he had investigated as assistant commissioner, wrote: 'The majority of the cottages that exist in rural parishes are deficient in almost every requisite that should constitute a home for a Christian family in a civilized community.'[1]

These are terrible words, but unfortunately there is much evidence to support them. They reveal a situation which was probably not to be remedied until the countryside was effectively emptied, a process which did not begin in earnest till several years after they were written.

Here without doubt were circumstances which were beyond the control of those who suffered from them. If a poor man could not by his own efforts procure a home in which he could live a self-respecting life, either in town or country; if he could not by his own efforts avoid the cholera, typhus, low fever or what you will – the evil things which were begotten and pullulated in the alleys or hamlets where he had to live; if, as was becoming clear in the sixties, he was likely to have no chance of educating his children unless the public power intervened to help provide a school for him; if his wife and his child and incidentally himself needed the protection of the State in the factory or shop where they worked, then it might have been thought the time had come to change the fundamental philosophy on which men based their thoughts. It might have been thought that the time had come to drop the old illusions about the extent to which poor people could be expected to extricate themselves by their own efforts from the evils that encompassed them, to jettison the belief that each intervention of the government was at best a necessary evil, and to accept cheerfully the doctrine that if the mass of men and women were to gain self-fulfilment the State must first intervene to correct the terms on which life was offered to the poorest citizens.

Some men were beginning to think in these terms, but many

[1] P.P. 1867–8, XVII, Pt. I, p. 95.

people seem to have clung to what they could retain of the old doctrine. They accepted the fact that it might be necessary in particular matters for the law to arm local or central government with power to interfere with the free play of such social and economic forces as might be too powerful for their victims, but they gave great weight to the principle that in the last resort a man must live by his own efforts and that anxious care must be taken not to remove that responsibility from him; and it is impossible to understand the nineteenth century unless it is realized that this way of thinking, even in the 1860s, commended itself to people who were not inhumane or ignorant.

For instance, between 1863 and 1869 the Oxford historian J. R. Green worked as a clergyman in various slum parishes in London. Probably the most terrible part of his work was when he was at St Philip's, Stepney, and faced the cholera outbreak of 1866. Adequate local organization to cope with the outbreak seems to have been non-existent or to have broken down, and the neighbours were terrified and refused to help, so that Green had himself to face the task of carrying the dying, or dead, out of the tenements where they lay. Green was not physically a very powerful man, but often the only people who had sufficient courage or generosity to give him a hand were what his biographer calls, rather primly, 'the lowest women of the town'. The cholera was a passing affliction, but severe distress was endemic in the parishes in which he served. Green took a deep interest in the matter, yet he seems to have come to the conclusion that a major cause of poverty was a lax administration of the Poor Laws and the granting of indiscriminate charity. Indeed he wrote articles in the *Saturday Review* emphasizing the importance of a steady application of the labour test and a limitation of almsgiving to exceptional cases.[1]

Or to take a still later example. In 1883 a good deal of public attention had been drawn to the deplorable state of the slums in the great cities, and in December *The Nineteenth Century* published a number of articles on the subject by eminent people who might be expected to know about it. One was by Octavia Hill and one by Lord Shaftesbury, and each insisted on the

[1] Leslie Stephen, *Letters of John Richard Green* [op. cit., p. 159] pp. 55–6.

importance of self-help, each feared the results of State benevolence. It seemed to Octavia Hill dreadful to think that in a moment of excitement 'we may have schemes actually proposed which would be in effect to restore the old Poor Law system; to enable the improvident to throw the burden of his support upon the provident', and she talked of 'the disastrous policy of attempting to supply by the aid of the community a necessity of life (such as lodging is) for the working classes'.[1] On his part Shaftesbury said:

> If the State is to be summoned not only to provide houses for the labouring classes but also to supply such dwellings at nominal rents, it will, while doing something on behalf of their physical condition, utterly destroy their moral energies. . . . The State is bound, in a case such as this, to give every facility by law and enabling statutes; but the work itself should be founded, and proceed, on voluntary effort, for which there is in the country an adequate amount of wealth, zeal and intelligence.[2]

Yet Shaftesbury was the man who had been more responsible than anyone else for the State's interference to protect women and children in industry, who had been Chadwick's close ally and colleague in the days of the board of health and had hated with all the vehemence of an over-taut nature the forces which had impeded their work; and who had, incidentally, tried for forty years to handle this particular problem of housing by voluntary effort, and had palpably failed. His attitude may seem strange. However, looked at from the vantage point of the twentieth century the attitude of a good many of his contemporaries will no doubt seem both strange and indefensible. It only becomes intelligible when it is approached so to speak from the other side, when it is recognized as being the attitude of men and women who had reached this point having lived in the atmosphere of the middle years of the nineteenth century, and possibly having started their course, as had Shaftesbury, even before the Poor Law was first reformed. Then it may be recognized as a point of view natural to those who had reached maturity before 1870.

Nevertheless, after 1880 such attitudes would become in-

---

[1] *The Nineteenth Century*, Vol. XIV, No. LXXXII (December 1883) p. 925.
[2] ibid., p. 935.

creasingly untenable. The fear of State action would have to be abandoned. Politicians and philosophers would have drastically to modify their view that the State should only interfere to tackle certain specified evils, while other evils such as unemployment, or the overwhelming power of the owners of capital or land, were left untouched, even if that modification would require some hard and uncomfortable thought about fundamentals. And if the clergy were to continue to play a significant part in what was to follow, their ways of thought would also have to be modified; and they would also have to accommodate themselves, if they could, to the new forces, political, economic and moral, which were to dominate the era that was about to start.

PHASE III

Democracy and Collectivism, 1865 – 85

8

Parliamentary Reform, Social Change and Collectivism

The third phase of English history in the nineteenth century may be held to start in 1865. This is an arbitrary date, for the conditions which typified the third phase were the result of a continuous social development, and, except for convenience, it is wrong to suggest any precise point at which it can be held to begin. However, 1865 was the year of a general election and the death of Palmerston, and from that point political events moved forward steadily, and probably inexorably, to the second reform of the electorate in 1867. The Second Reform Act was defective both in its redistribution of seats and in its extension of the franchise; it left much of their old power in the hands of the proprietary classes, and it was necessary to follow it up with the Third Reform Act of 1884. Nevertheless the passage of the act of 1867 not only signalized the final acceptance of the principle of democracy, it also enfranchised a large number of working-class voters. The new voters were often concentrated in particular constituencies. To bring them to the poll new methods were necessary, and in Birmingham a form of constituency organization was developed which seemed to place it under the control of the electors. This was copied by other towns. The towns organized on the Birmingham model were in due course brought together by Joseph Chamberlain, the leading spirit in Birmingham, to form in 1877 the National Liberal Federation, and this under his dynamic leadership seemed to portend a new era in politics.

The Reform Act of 1867 was not, however, the only act that marked the beginning of this new phase. There were also the acts which dealt with trade unions and industrial relations, the Trade Union Act of 1871 which was modified by an amending act of 1876, the Conspiracy and Property Act of 1875 which replaced the obnoxious Criminal Law Amendment Act of 1871, and the act of 1875 which replaced the old unequal law of master and servant. These acts were not only important because they placed trade unions and trade union activities upon a satisfactory legal basis and gave the workman better protection in his relations with his employer, but also because they marked the surrender of what many people had throughout the second phase believed to be an incontrovertible principle, the principle that it was impossible to raise wages above the rate 'naturally' fixed by 'the laws of supply and demand', and that consequently those trade unions which tried to raise the rate of wages were obnoxious institutions and could only do harm to employer and workmen. Now trade unions had to be recognized as acceptable institutions, which might even benefit their members by raising their wages.

At about the same time a more serious breach was being made in the curtain wall of Victorian principle. It had long been the proud boast of Englishmen that in the English polity as little as possible was left to the supervision and compulsion of the State, particularly of the central authorities of the State, and that as many as possible of the needs of society were supplied by voluntary effort, or at least by the free action of local authorities reflecting the wishes of the neighbourhood affected. From the beginning of this phase a number of acts increased the powers of the government at the expense of the independence of individuals, and of the autonomy of local opinion. The most obvious examples are those dealing with public health and public education. Between 1866 and 1875 a number of acts were passed imposing a common standard in sanitary matters on all districts, and in 1870 the Elementary Education Act secured that there should be a board school supported by the rates in every place where the education supplied by a denominational school was insufficient, or where one was required by those who lived there. This was followed by acts making elementary education generally free and generally compulsory. These acts were by no means the only acts passed at this time which expanded, or consolidated, the powers of government. There was Bruce's Licensing Act of

1872 controlling the scale of drink, the laws of 1874 and 1878 consolidating the labour code, and other more technical acts. The powers of the State were increasing and would certainly continue to increase, so that political theorists often choose this moment to mark the change from the 'period of *laissez-faire*' to the period of 'collectivism'.

In order, however, to understand the conditions that were to prevail in the third phase it is important to realize that these acts are not only significant on account of what they did but also as evidence of the massive social changes that were going forward in the country. The wealth in the country had not only greatly increased but much of it was widely diffused through society, some of it even reached a section of the working class. As a result there were now large classes whose importance and self-confidence had increased, and who were no longer prepared to tolerate a system in which their political significance was little and their wishes and interests apparently lightly considered. One result of this was the quickening of the movement towards parliamentary reform. After the act of 1867 was passed the same force can be seen in the formation of the various constituency organizations, which imitated the Birmingham caucus, for these organizations appealed to local men who had not been able to achieve satisfactory positions under the old system. And the trade union legislation, together with the change of principle that accompanied it, show that an important section of the working classes had advanced to a position which made it impossible to disregard their view of what they needed.

Not all the collectivist measures, however, fit easily into this pattern. Some of the measures which were passed at this time were, certainly at least in part, reactions to the demands of the contemporary social situation. The Elementary Education Act was a response to a fairly general demand for a comprehensive educational system, as it was also a recognition of the need to educate classes who, so it seemed, were likely to have an increasing share in the government of the country. Bruce's Licensing Act was in part a response to the increased power of the temperance agitation in the country, which was strongest among the middle class. The democratic Liberalism, which such men as Chamberlain and Mundella sponsored, had strong collectivist tendencies. It was consciously designed to improve the lot of the poor, and to appeal to them. There had, indeed, been an earnest of what was intended to follow in Chamberlain's activities in Birmingham between 1873 and 1875. It is, however, relevant to remember that much of what was done in these years in Birmingham had in fact been done at an earlier date in other cities, for many of the collectivist measures of the beginning of the third phase had, in fact, no special reference to the social conditions and demands of that moment. Some of these measures were the response to technical needs that had been revealed in one way or another at different points in the century; the Alkali Acts, for instance, acts controlling the fumes emitted by industrial processes, originated in a parliamentary enquiry in 1862. Much of the policy which followed had roots stretching back to an earlier phase of the nineteenth century, much in fact originated in the undeniably collectivist ideas of Chadwick and Bentham, which were partially adopted in the years which immediately followed the First Reform Act.[1]

But there was a thread which stretched further back still. In 1866 and 1870 collectivist measures were adopted for a reason which had appeared in other contexts in the eighteenth and early nineteenth centuries. As has been described in an earlier chapter (see pp. 19–20), in the eighteenth century the ordinary system of justices of the peace, who conducted voluntary and unpaid work alongside the parish constables and the local watch, could not provide an adequate force to maintain reasonable order and safety in London. Consequently they were gradually replaced by stipendiary magistrates and a professional police force. A little later it became clear that neither magistrates nor local authorities could do what was wanted in early nineteenth-century Ireland. Consequently the government developed that remarkable system of centrally-controlled police, government-sponsored economic schemes, and State education and medical services, which originated in the work of Robert Peel as chief secretary. In exactly the same way, at this later date the devastating reports of Sir John

---

[1] On the development of the powers of the State in the nineteenth century, see G. Kitson Clark, *An Expanding Society* [op. cit., p. 212) pp. 126–82.

Simon, issued annually during his term as medical officer from 1858 to 1865, showed clearly the disastrous failure of the attempt to handle the sanitary problems of the country by entrusting them to the free initiative of local authorities. Consequently in 1866 the policy of compulsion from the centre had to be developed. In the same way the educational enquiries of 1866 demonstrated clearly that the voluntary system had left more than half the children, at least in the great cities, without education. It was thus necessary to pass the Education Act of 1870. In fact it had been amply demonstrated that, whatever the social stresses or the dominant political philosophy at any given moment, if the British nation wished for effective public services then it must put aside its prejudices and call in the power of the State to see that the work was done properly over the whole country.

These changes in the structure of English institutions and English society necessarily affected the situation of English churchmen.

As it happened, what promised to have the most serious results for the Church came to very little. The politically-minded dissenters were apparently very successful at the elections which followed the Second Reform Act, and they persuaded themselves that the new Parliament would start the process of disestablishing and disendowing the Church of England. They were mistaken. The Church in Ireland was disestablished and partially disendowed, and the outstanding grievances of the dissenters were removed. The dissenters were able to modify Forster's Education Act, but not to eliminate the church schools as they desired. Their strength in the House was not sufficient to enable them to make a start on the disestablishment of the Church of England, and motions to that end were defeated by large majorities. The Liberals were defeated at the general election of 1874, but by 1880 the National Liberal Federation, which was largely dissenting, was better organized than the dissenters had been in 1868. However, from 1880 to 1885 the House of Commons was still dominated by Gladstone who was against disestablishment, and politicians became preoccupied with other matters. In 1886 the Liberals were split over Home Rule, and after 1886, with one short interval, the Conservatives were in office till 1906. There was still heat in the ashes, which was fanned into flame by the Education Act of 1902, and after 1906 the dissenters secured the disestablishment and partial disendowment of the Church in Wales. But after 1906 sectarian passion became increasingly irrelevant in politics, and so it was that the Church of England ended a long period of controversy and peril with its historic position superficially intact.

Compared with these dangers the development of collectivism might seem to present a less serious challenge to the Church. The objects of the collectivist measures were often such as many churchmen would welcome, indeed they were often objects which churchmen had been trying to achieve with insufficient resources. Leading ecclesiastics had recognized the failure of the old system and the need to do better. In 1868 Robert Gregory, at that time a canon of St Paul's, where he was afterwards dean, preached a sermon on the 'past and present ways of dealing with the poorer classes'. He contrasted the old system of personal relationships and personal duties with the corporate responsibilities which should have replaced them now that they had become impossible in an overcrowded impersonal Britain. He recognized the failure of the old system, but emphasized the inadequacy of what was being done at that moment, particularly for the aged, the sick, the inadequate and the unemployed. 'The Community,' said he, 'may have accepted the responsibility for these unfortunates, but as yet, beyond the much grudged and harshly dispensed relief afforded by the Union workhouses and subscribing its money when its sympathies are touched, it does little or nothing,' and he summed up the matter in a phrase which does not unfairly epitomize the situation at the time: 'The burden is thrown from the individual on to the Community and the Community has never realized the change.'[1]

Other churchmen made the same diagnosis and, as will be seen, there were in these years churchmen who looked to a period of increased social activity on the part of the State, with the Church acting in co-operation as a close and congenial ally. But things were not going to work out like that. The

---

[1] *Sermons on the Poorer Classes of London preached before the University of Oxford* (Oxford and London, 1969) pp. 55–6.

secular State would act not so much as an ally of the Church but as a substitute for it, taking over many of the functions of the Church, but not its creed. There were many reasons for this. One was the fact that as the agent of a community in which there was a multiplicity of beliefs the State must seem to be agnostic, but during these years another reason emerged which was increasingly important. As the programme of social reform developed it became increasingly professional, using methods which required the employment of trained experts, for which an untrained priest and parochial volunteers would be unsuited. Nor would the objects of social policy be those defined by the simple insights of Christian charity; they would be the results of systematic thought by men who had considered matters from an exclusively secular point of view. Moreover, as the State developed its policy it would develop its own institutions and would no longer rely on the parochial organization of the Church of England.

These tendencies were enhanced by a change which at the beginning of the third phase took place in the ways of thought of several men who earlier in the century might have become leading churchmen, but who became in these years advocates and architects of the new secular State. Since the eighteenth century there had always been a number of very intelligent men in Britain who were atheists and agnostics, and between 1860 and 1880 agnosticism spread rapidly among the more highly educated groups in the country; in particular it penetrated into a group which till this point in the century had been relatively unaffected by it, the leading figures at Oxford and Cambridge. In Cambridge such men as Leslie Stephen, Henry Sidgwick and Alfred Marshall ceased to be in any real sense Christians, and the same is true of such men as T. H. Green, R. L. Nettleship and probably Arnold Toynbee at Oxford.[1]

The personal histories of these men naturally differ, but they seem often to have some points in common. After half a century's feverish religious activity and propaganda many educated men had come to view with distaste and mistrust the dominant forms of Christianity as they had been presented

[1] See the article by Lord Keynes on Alfred Marshall in the *D.N.B. 1922–30* (Oxford, 1937) p. 562.

to them. They were unimpressed by the arguments by which the claims of the various brands of Christianity were normally endorsed. They were affronted by endless controversies in which intolerance and obscurantism seemed to be contending with obscurantism and intolerance. They were repelled by the unappetizing doctrines which Christians were apt, with noise and passion, to claim were essential parts of their creed – doctrines such as a belief in the eternal punishment of sinners, or in the inerrancy of the bible, or in a repugnantly forensic explanation of the atonement. To many such men the repudiation of such doctrines did not seem to be the same as the repudiation of what was real and valuable in Christianity. In fact all that a number of them wanted was to throw overboard a lot of nasty rubbish which, so they felt, had never had any business to be where it was. Thus unencumbered they would be able to cut through the accretions, get rid of what claimed to be 'miraculous', and reach the simple spiritual and philanthropic creed, which was no doubt what had really been taught by Jesus of Nazareth. Indeed those who had been brought up in that tradition believed that they might even retain something of the old conception of an established Church and of its mission to the nation.

But to understand this state of mind and the conclusions to which it tended, perhaps it is best to consider the views of two men who were in their different ways very influential in the critical period. One was J. R. Seeley, subsequently regius professor of modern history at Cambridge, who in 1865 published a popular humanizing study of Christ called *Ecce Homo*. The other was T. H. Green, the leading figure of an important group at Balliol College, and between about 1870 and his death the most influential teacher of philosophy at Oxford.

Each came from a religious background. Seeley's father was R. B. Seeley, a well-known evangelical publisher. Green was a Rugbeian, the son of a country clergyman and the nephew of D. J. Vaughan, vicar of St Martin's, Leicester. In each case the Christianity with which they had been in closest contact had been permeated with a well-developed sense of social mission. R. B. Seeley had published the two evangelical commentaries on the social conditions of the forties, the *Perils of the Nation* and *Remedies for the Perils of the Nation*, and he had himself written a eulogistic life of Michael Sadler, the factory reformer. All three books described the evils that afflicted nineteenth-century society and contrasted the Christian answers with those of the political economists. Green had been prominent at Rugby, and seems to have inherited that active and inconvenient conscience which had been Arnold's legacy to his school. But probably the most important influence with Green was that of his uncle D. J. Vaughan, who was a faithful disciple of F. D. Maurice, a convinced Christian Socialist and an interesting thinker about social problems on his own account.[1]

Each rejected Christianity as it had been transmitted to him. Seeley wrote: 'We are to remember that nothing has been subjected to such multiform and grotesque perversion as Christianity. Certainly the direct love of Christ as it was felt by his first followers is a rare thing among modern Christians.'[2] Green told his hearers that they were not to 'assume, as hasty and passionate theologians would do, that God reveals himself in some other form than reason, or that he suddenly set up the Christian Church as a miraculous institution owing nothing to the other influences of the world'.[3] In each case this rejection was combined with a passionate advocacy of what was held to be Christian morality; indeed the fervour and to some extent the doctrine of Green's lay sermons would not have been out of place if he had followed his uncle and been ordained.

In each case there was in this advocacy much emphasis on social duty. The chapter on Christian morality in *Ecce Homo* is entitled 'Enthusiasm of Humanity', and in another publication Seeley wrote that the province of religion was 'much more national and political, much less personal than is commonly supposed'.[4] Green was a committed Radical reformer, active both in local politics and in furthering the cause of

---

[1] On J. R. Seeley, see the essay by R. T. Shannon on 'John Robert Seeley and the Idea of a National Church', in *Ideas and Institutions of Victorian Britain*, ed. R. Robson (1967) pp. 236–67. On T. H. Green, see Melvin Richter, *The Politics of Conscience. T. H. Green and his Age* (Letchworth, 1964), and *Works of Thomas Hill Green*, ed. R. L. Nettleship (3 vols., 1888).

[2] *Ecce Homo: a Survey of the Life and Work of Jesus Christ* (3rd edn., 1866) p. 170.

[3] *Works* [op. cit.] Vol. III, p. 239, from the address on the 'Witness of God'.

[4] Quoted in R. T. Shannon [op. cit., p. 235] p. 242.

I

popular education; he strongly approved of the steps towards collectivism taken by the Liberal government between 1868 and 1874.[1] And in each case their social morality seems to be a projection from the old conception of Church and State. Seeley said that 'State and Church belong together, and the link between them is nationality'.[2] Though he admired John Bright, Green would not support the Liberal demand for the disestablishment of the Church of England, and one of the arguments he gives against disestablishment is that it 'would make the clergyman of the future a mere priest or a mere preacher, instead of the leader in useful social work and in the administration of such public business as is not directly administered by the State, as he now often is'.[3] In fact he wished to continue what he thought to be valuable in the parochial tradition of the Church of England, with which he was of course familiar through his home and through his uncle, with whom for much of his life he lived on intimate terms.

Indeed the step from the old union between Church and State to a community embodying the kind of morality he desired must have seemed to Green to be a short one. He seems to have believed that it could be taken without disestablishing or disendowing the Church, and even retaining some sort of episcopal organization, if congregations were granted 'control over the appointment of the clergy and over the formulas used in worship', and if no declarations of opinion were required at ordination.[4] Nevertheless it might be a more decisive step than he realized. The established Church had been compromised by its close association with the old secular order of society, but its theory, and, potentially, its practice and morality, had been focused on an authority that transcended the needs, and remained outside the scope of the will, of the community; and by the end of the seventeenth century men in Britain had learnt that the nature of that authority guaranteed to men and women the right of dissent. Green also believed in such an authority, but its nature in his philosophy was ambiguous and obscure, and

---

[1] See his lecture on 'Liberal Legislation and Freedom of Contract' (delivered 1880), *Works* [op. cit., p. 235] Vol. III, pp. 365–6.
[2] Quoted by Shannon (loc. cit.) p. 242.
[3] *Works* [op. cit., p. 235] Vol. III, pp. cxxii–iii.
[4] ibid., Vol. III, p. cxxiii.

its hold on human loyalty and obedience likely to be uncertain. If it faded it might be replaced by a simple belief in the paramount sovereignty of human needs as defined by the majority of a nation, and so there might develop a system in which men would be expected to achieve no higher, and permitted to pursue no other, ends than those which the community willed. For the right to dissent surely implies the recognition of a value that transcends the will of the community.

In the twentieth century the abandonment of the dualism that accepts both the authority of the State and the authority of a value that remains beyond the needs and will of the State leads to the totalitarian State. In the nineteenth century it might lead to the acceptance of the philosophy of Hegel, or to its counterpart in human affairs, the authoritarian organization of men's lives such as was normal in a State like Prussia. It is interesting to recognize a tendency in this direction both in Green and Seeley. Green moved in the direction of Hegel's philosophy, but he was too much of an individualist, and also too nearly a Christian, to go far. Though he defined political freedom as meaning 'the power on the part of the citizens as a body to make the most and best of themselves' and 'to contribute equally to a common good', nevertheless to him 'Hegel's account of freedom as realized in the State does not seem to correspond to the facts of society as it is, or even as, under the unalterable conditions of human nature, it ever could be'.[1] His pupil, Bernard Bosanquet, seems to have gone further. But the most interesting development can be seen in Seeley. He became convinced that the morality of the future would be mediated through the agency of the State, and he made it his supreme task as a professional historian to write *The Life and Times of Stein*, as the architect of the modern Prussian State. The light in which he viewed this work is demonstrated by a curious story. On one occasion Seeley was asked whether he intended to bring out another life of Christ. 'The answer, most unexpectedly, was to the effect that he had fulfilled this intention already. On being pressed for an explanation he said that he meant his Life of Stein.'[2]

[1] ibid., Vol. II, p. 324.
[2] Quoted by Shannon [op. cit., p. 235] p. 248. Dr Shannon's article contains an important discussion of this whole point.

The tendency of neither Green's nor Seeley's thought was likely to find exact fulfilment in what was to come. Hegelian philosophy is not congenial to Englishmen – it never got beyond the walls of university lecture rooms, and even there it was fairly soon displaced by a more congenial system – and there have been very few people in this country who have wanted to re-create the Prussian State. Nor would the State of the future be brought into being by philosophers and historians. Its architects would be civil servants and politicians, and as a result its development would be empirical, piecemeal and not directed by any philosophy at all. Nevertheless its end might not be altogether different from that to which the thought of both Green and Seeley pointed.

However, the act for parliamentary reform and the collectivist measures are only two of the three groups of acts which were cited as defining the beginning of the third phase of English history. The third group comprised the acts legitimizing the trade unions. Clearly these acts were likely to cause a good deal of stress and strain on society in general and on the behaviour and activities of churchmen. In considering this question, the material must be divided in two. On the one hand there are the problems of the countryside, where the Church on the whole supported the traditional order of society; on the other there are the problems of urban society towards which churchmen could take a more independent line.

9

The Problems of the Countryside

The third phase saw the culmination of the process by which Britain became predominantly a nation of town-dwellers in which the townsman's interests – good wages, cheap food and a flourishing export trade – took pride of place and a decreasing minority could be said to live in rural conditions. At the same time the old hierarchy which for so long had dominated the counties began gradually to disintegrate. The mid-Victorian agricultural prosperity came to an end, and those of the nobility and gentry who depended on agricultural rents were in difficulties. These difficulties were shared by those of the clergy who depended on tithe or the renting of their glebes, and the long period of increasing clerical poverty began. Meanwhile rural radicalism had raised its head more effectively than ever before, first in the form of trade unionism and then in competing for seats in the House of Commons.

However, many of these changes were slow and in many cases they were not effective in the first years of the third phase. The Reform Act of 1867 did not enfranchise the agricultural labourers, and the landowners' monopoly of power seems to have continued till about 1880. The decline in agricultural prosperity did not begin effectively till after 1874, the first serious blow being the series of bad harvests which ended in that of the terrible year of 1879. The decline was, at least at first, primarily confined to those parts of the country which were dependent on the cultivation of corn, and even so it did not communicate its effects to many of the clergy at once, since tithe was taken through a tithe rent charge calculated on a seven-year average.[1] Therefore, at least superficially, in the

---

[1] The fall in the yield of the tithe rent charge can be followed in the figures produced in successive volumes of *Whitaker's Almanac*.

first years of the third phase the old system seemed to be intact and secure.

Certain signs of danger, however, were soon to appear. The Liberalism of Joseph Chamberlain gave new force to the old radical attack on the landowners and the Church, and when in 1872 trade unionism appeared in the countryside it was strongly supported by Chamberlain and his friends and received very friendly publicity in the Liberal press, which was particularly critical of the behaviour of the clergy of the established Church. This fact has to some extent disguised the significance of what was happening. The claims of labour after all challenged more than the position of the rural landowner and farmer and country clergyman; it challenged the industrialist, the capitalist and the fund holder as well. During the years of trouble in the countryside there was also trouble in industry, which was not so well publicized. One of the actions which caused most clamour against the clergy was the enforcement of the Criminal Law Amendment Act passed a short time before by a Liberal government, which, so it would seem, was being more ruthlessly enforced by lay magistrates in the towns. Moreover, the capitalist, the industrialist, the landowner, the farmer, and where necessary the country clergyman, had alike to unlearn the teaching of the economists that the rate of wages was inexorably settled by the laws of supply and demand and could not be affected by the actions of trade unions. They had to accept the fact that the trade unions were a legitimate element in the life of the country, that they could do good to their members, that their actions ought to be protected or at least not hampered by law, even if they included picketing premises where a strike had been declared, and that trade union leaders and organizers were responsible members of society and not mere 'trouble makers' battening on their workmates.

The acceptance of these principles required a revolution in most middle-class and upper-class minds, whether their owners lived in country or town. The story of this revolution can be followed in the development of public policy from its starting point in the extremely shrewd presentation of the trade union case to the royal commission that was appointed in 1867, through the Trade Union Act of 1871 to the legislation of 1875 and 1876. But it can also be followed in the development of opinion. The process can be watched in successive articles in *The Edinburgh Review*. In 1868 *The Edinburgh Review* was talking about the 'lawless tyranny of the Trade Unions'. In 1869, after the report of the royal commission, it was prepared to admit the legitimacy of trade unions, but it hoped that if they did come into the open this would enable the working man to 'cast off the narrow and stupid dogmas which interested agitators and crafty drones have imposed upon him'. It spoke severely of such practices as picketing, and came down hard on a book by W. T. Thornton which actually questioned the orthodox doctrine that the rate of wages was settled by the process of supply and demand. If wages were so settled obviously trade union action could not affect their amount, nevertheless in 1878 *The Edinburgh Review* was prepared to say that though trade unions had done both good and evil, they had done good by raising wages.

Other examples could doubtless be given from the serious journals, but perhaps by way of complement it might be well to take one from a more frivolous setting. In *Punch* of 20 April 1872, that is shortly after Joseph Arch had initiated his trade union movement among the agricultural labourers, there appeared a cartoon entitled 'Land or Labour or "How to settle it" '. It portrays four figures. Three are in conversation, an emaciated and sullen-looking labourer, a fattish farmer and a landlord with the points of a coronet in his hat. With his back to them is a fourth man, with a roll of paper bearing the word 'agency' projecting from his pocket, pasting on the wall a notice about a strike. The landlord, 'Lord Broadacres', is represented as saying, 'Come farmer, I think we may manage to mend matters for our friend Hodge without the help of that Professional Meddler,' and the Professional Meddler is made to look very odious indeed – obese, brutish and callous. Two years afterwards, in 1874, the farmers organized a lockout to bring down wages again and bishop Fraser of Manchester wrote a severe letter to *The Times* attacking them, and on 18 April 1874 there appeared another cartoon in *Punch* entitled, 'A new Archbishop'. In it Joseph Arch, given his right name this time, is shaking the bishop's hand before a body of cheering rustics and saying, 'Ah! my Lord, I never expected to find your Lordship on our side.' The rustics are strikingly different from the ill-used and sour figure of 'Hodge' in the first cartoon, but the most notable contrast is between the pictures of the 'Professional Meddler' and that of 'Joseph Arch'. The 'meddler' is a Caliban whose interference is likely to be interested and disastrous, the picture of Joseph Arch is the friendly portrait of a real man with whom every right-minded person must sympathize. Yet they are in reality portrayals of the same man, performing the same function, and only two years have elapsed between the publication of the two cartoons.[1]

While such a revolution in opinion was going on an obvious advantage would be enjoyed by those who could remain uncommitted till they had accommodated their minds to it. Those who had at some point during the course of the change been called upon to take action might easily find that they were attacked for acting on opinions which a short time before would have been generally held, even by some of those who attacked them. This was in some sort the fate of the Liberal government which held office between 1868 and 1874. It fell to them to take the first steps to legitimize the trade unions, and, under considerable pressure, they passed the act which ensured that trade unions were no longer unlawful associations because they acted in 'restraint of trade', and that therefore their funds were protected by law. But the Liberals still believed in the heinousness of such practices as picketing. They therefore also passed the Criminal Law Amendment Act which imposed potentially heavy penalties on those guilty of such offences as 'molestation', 'obstruction', 'intimidation', 'persistently following' any person, or 'watching and besetting' the premises where he was, or the approaches to them.

Given the state of opinion at that moment it was perhaps natural that some such act should be passed; even so this was an unusually bad one. The offences referred to were ill-defined and comprehensive and could be stretched to cover actions which were at worst trivial, and possibly on any count completely innocent. Moreover the act was to be enforced by courts of summary jurisdiction without an appeal to a court with a jury; it could therefore be made the instrument of class oppression, as indeed it was. As a result it caused much resentment and was

---

[1] *Punch*, Vol. LXII, 20 April 1872, and Vol. LXVI, 18 April 1874.

an obvious target for Conservative attack in the general election of 1874. When the Conservatives came into office Assheton Cross, the home secretary, appointed a commission to enquire into the working of the act which strangely enough only recommended the provision of an appeal to quarter sessions with a jury. However, the clamour against the act continued, and in 1875 Cross repealed it altogether. This was all part of the more equitable treatment of the trade unions, for which Disraeli's Government is celebrated, and which has been attributed to some sort of Tory mystique, a distant echo from *Sybil* or *Coningsby* or 'Young England'. Perhaps it was, but it is interesting to speculate what might have happened if the Conservative Government had come first and the Liberals had been able to profit by the mistakes of their opponents.

The same kind of trap closed in these years on many of the country clergy and produced a situation which did the Church more harm than all Miall's attacks in the House of Commons.

The occasion was the situation produced by the movement among agricultural labourers which Joseph Arch began in 1872. It is not altogether easy to see the background of that movement clearly. In the first half of the century there had been bitter feeling among the poor of the countryside against the classes above them in the economic scale. This had been responsible, or partly responsible, for the disturbance in the country at the time of the Reform Bill, and, to judge by the incidence of incendiarism, continued well on into the forties, though it is not always easy to differentiate between the violence which was in effect a wild gesture against the harsh inequalities of rural society and the violence, often at the expense of people of the same class as the aggressor, which was the natural result of the uncontrolled barbarism of a countryside which had never been completely civilized and was always inadequately policed. One thing however seems clear; there was a continuous tradition of rural independence and opposition to the powers that controlled the countryside, particularly where there was a tradition of rural nonconformity. There is, however, a marked contrast between the violence often prevalent in the first half of the century and the sober, intelligent and orderly trade unionism of the seventies.

No doubt this was because the labourers in the seventies were the products of a more generally civilized society. Many factors had combined to produce this. The forces of law had become more effective, particularly with the development of the rural police forces. In some cases there were rather better wages and conditions. A certain amount had been done by improving landlords and much more by the country clergy, who had secured that there should be a school in nearly every village and tried to serve places and populations which had hitherto been completely neglected. However, another civilizing agent had possibly achieved more than any of these: popular evangelism, the movement which derived from the Methodist revival, particularly Primitive Methodism. It was the opinion of Thorold Rogers that Primitive Methodism had done more with limited means for labourers in the countryside than any other religious agency. It was also his opinion that without the organization which Primitive Methodism gave to the scattered, depressed and suspicious body of agricultural labourers there would have been no movement among them in the seventies.[1] In this case also the forces of democracy were working through a religious agency, but leading towards an important secular organization.

The agricultural labourers had every right and every need to take active measures to improve their lot. Even in the seventies, after a long period of national prosperity, their wages were still too often miserable, their housing too often appalling. They were frequently treated very harshly by those who employed them, and they suffered from a sense of degradation, of being the despised serfs of society. It was a feeling which seems to have been made more unbearable by the behaviour towards them of the farmers, and too often of the gentry, and also it is to be feared at times by the behaviour of the parson or his wife. This naturally rankled the more as men grew articulate, educated and civilized. No doubt it helped to fill the chapels of the Primitive Methodists, and presented the agitation with such leaders as Joseph Arch and Joseph Ashby.

The immediate cause of the development of the movement in the seventies among the agricultural labourers was no doubt

[1] James E. Thorold Rogers, M.P., *Six Centuries of Work and Wages* (2 vols., 1884) Vol. II, p. 516.

the general development of trade unions in the late sixties and seventies in the industrial districts, which was naturally copied in the country districts. The story of what happened is well known. On 7 February 1872 three men called on Joseph Arch, who was an independent labourer and in a small way a contractor, and a preacher in the Primitive Methodist Church. They asked him to address a meeting at Wellesbourne in Warwickshire that evening. From that meeting was formed the Warwickshire Agricultural Labourers' Trade Union, and from that time Arch carried his cause over a large part of the country. In May a National Union was formed which by 1873–4 claimed 100,000 members and branches in every English county except Cumberland, Westmorland, Yorkshire, Lancashire, Cheshire and Cornwall. There were strikes everywhere, but in 1874 the movement received a check. The farmers organized a lockout and many of the advances in wages which had been won by the strikes of 1872 and 1873 were lost.

From the beginning Radicals and Liberals took an interest in the movement. Auberon Herbert, G. Dixon and Jesse Collins, all of whom were associated with Chamberlain in Birmingham, took part in it. Early in the proceedings the *Daily News*, at that moment the leading Radical newspaper, sent down to Warwickshire Archibald Forbes, their star war correspondent, who had outdone G. W. E. Russell in his reports on the Franco-Prussian war. Other national newspapers followed suit. *The Times* opened its pages to reports on the movement; indeed the standard history of the farmers' lockout in 1874 was written by *The Times* correspondent, F. Clifford. R. H. Hutton, the editor of the *Spectator*, acting, as in 1864 when he had supported Newman against Kingsley, as the candid friend of the Church of England, discussed and deplored what he believed to be the failure of the country clergy to sympathize with the labourers, drawing his material largely from the savagely polemical *Chronicle* of the National Labourers' Union. *The Guardian*, probably the best of the church newspapers, took a judicial middle-of-the-road attitude. Other church newspapers, and some specifically conservative newspapers, took sides against the strikers, but on the whole the most influential and intelligent sections of the British press supported them.

It was as well that they did. The labourers' needs were great and their position inherently weak. It seems probable that Arch's campaign would have failed to get far if Forbes of the *Daily News* had not given it publicity when he did.[1] This slant, however, makes it necessary to treat much of the evidence which is usually accepted about the attitude of the opponents of the strike with some caution. As happened in other episodes in history where all the obvious sources lean in one direction, the case made by one side has passed straight into the historical record without critical examination, and, at least in one case, without any attempt to check what was considered to be an important quotation.

Probably the main sufferers from this imbalance have been the country clergy. Many of the clergy who lived in the area affected could not avoid being involved in the strikes. In a significant number of cases the labourers appealed to the parson in their parish for support. In some cases the clergy were drawn into the councils of the farmers and landowners. Many felt it necessary to make some pronouncement on what was happening in their village. At least two clerical magistrates had to try offences deriving from the strike. There were therefore plenty of opportunities for clerical mismanagement, hesitation and error, and the evidence which has reached the history books has normally been derived from the anti-clerical leaders of the strike, such as Joseph Arch, and the meaning they put upon it has been readily accepted.

This is obviously unsatisfactory. Clearly the accuracy of what is imputed to particular clergymen must be tested. There must be some consideration of its relation to the actions and attitudes of the other clergy who may have been involved in the strike and also to the attitudes of the very large body of the clergy who were not involved, and it must be compared with the general body of contemporary lay opinion. To do this properly would be a heavy task, perhaps an impossible one, but until it has at the least been attempted it is clear that no generalization about the attitude of the clergy can be accepted. In some cases an attempt has been made to set against the case, which the opponents of the clergy make, individual incidents which seem to tell a different story. But a general assessment

---

[1] Joseph Arch [op. cit., p. 140] pp. 83–4.

has not been made, and in all accounts two incidents, involving three clergymen, which were used at the time with great propaganda effect, have been allowed a completely disproportionate influence over the conclusions and generalizations which have been accepted.[1]

This is certainly unacceptable. However, since these two incidents have coloured so much of the discussion it may be as well to consider them before considering anything else.

The first took place in 1872. On Friday, 2 August, at a dinner of the Gloucestershire Agricultural Society, C. J. Ellicott as bishop of Gloucester replied to the toast of the bishop and clergy of the diocese. He spoke of the agitation among the agricultural labourers and most of what he said simply repeated the kind of things which were being said in a good many speeches, lay as well as clerical, at that moment. He deplored the attempt to set class against class, but said that it had little success in Gloucestershire, because the labourers knew that their employers were ready to respond to any request for an increase in wages based on proven need. He attacked those who 'came from afar' to seek out the disaffected and organize 'iniquitous combinations'. He said that it was possible that the labourer might receive too little in money, but pointed out how much they received in allowances, and ended with a stirring peroration about the identity of interests between farmer and labourer.

There is much that could be criticized here, but nothing that would have been worthy of much notice if it had not been for what he said of those who 'came from afar'. To quote from the report in *The Times* of 6 August 1872,

> He denounced them as strongly as any man could denounce any un-English proceeding, and it was not for him, a man of peace, to say anything stronger than that he hoped all his friends would keep the peace, and remember their Bishop advised them that if the village horse-pond stood invitingly near, not by any means to put these men into it. He had given this advice, and he hoped it would be followed; perhaps it would be hard, but they must resist the temptation.[2]

These words caused immediate and protracted trouble. They

[1] Probably the best general attempt to form a balanced judgement is to be found in D. O. Wagner [op. cit., p. 171] pp. 142–73.

[2] *The Times*, 6 August 1872, p. 11, col. 4.

were immediately taken as meaning that the bishop had recommended throwing the union organizers into the horse-pond,
and they were bitterly denounced at union meetings as evidence
of the violent and persecuting spirit of the established Church.
It is this interpretation that has passed into the history books,
and the passage that is habitually quoted is not what was
reported in *The Times* four days after the speech was delivered
but what Arch, writing his autobiography some time afterwards,
thought he remembered, and Arch's interpretation of the
bishop's intention in saying what he did is always accepted.[1]

The abuse of which he was the target brought to Ellicott
some sense of what he had done. He seems to have become
ashamed of his speech, the notoriety of which he accounted for
by saying that 'a certain number of humorous words readily
attracted a certain amount of attention, because nobody just
now had anything else to turn their attention to'.[2] What was
more to the point, his conscience seems to have been touched.
He became less sure that all was always as it should be in the lot
of the agricultural labourer even in Gloucestershire, and he
arranged for a conference in his palace between a member of
Parliament, a justice of the peace, several labourers, and Mr
Yates, the Gloucestershire secretary of the National Union. He
told Estcourt, the member of Parliament, that he did this
because, though he still disapproved of trade unions, 'I yet
also feel . . . that our labourers may from time to time, by their
very isolated position, suffer hardships at the hands of unjust
employers, and that, too, without redress'. He felt that the only
way to correct this was by the creation of an enlightened public
opinion whose influence should be brought to bear on individual cases. To his mind, this could only be achieved by
organizing sober conferences between employers and employed,
or by ensuring that wages were subjected to the oversight of
high-minded country gentlemen. At the conference he put
forward his own solution to the problems of the agricultural
labourers which included more allotments, improvements in
rural housing, and, if there were to be increases in wages,

---

[1] Arch [op. cit., p. 140] p. 121. 'If I remember right he said with reference to
me, "There is an old saying, 'Don't nail their ears to the pump, and don't
duck them in the horse-pond.'"'

[2] *Spectator*, 28 September 1872, p. 1223.

precautions against drunkenness. But in his review of the work of the diocese during the year he still told his clergy that he had no words but of severity and rebuke for those who broke the peace of the countryside.[1]

This incident fills a considerable space in most of the accounts of the strike, but it is impossible to believe that it has the significance, or the importance, that has always been accorded to it. The offending words were no doubt silly and provocative, but at least as reported in *The Times* they are less than an incitement to violence; and they are after all words spoken lightly in an after-dinner speech, of which Ellicott had the good taste afterwards to be ashamed. Of course a more sensible man would not have been guilty of them, but it did not need this evidence to establish the fact that Ellicott, though a good biblical scholar and in many ways a good-hearted man, was not sensible. When Disraeli wanted to make him archbishop of Canterbury Dean Wellesley had described him as 'an amiable, insignificant man, talking constantly and irrelevantly, with some book learning', and on one occasion Lord Granville was apparently driven to say of him, 'Is he *really* such a fool as he seems to be?'[2] It is true that in his more responsible moments Ellicott still set his face against trade unions and those who organized them, but such opposition was common to many of his contemporaries who did not try to find an alternative protection for labour as Ellicott tried to do.

The other incident is of more real importance. On 12 May 1873 there was a local strike at Ascott in Oxfordshire on the farm of a man called Hambridge. Hambridge called in two men from a neighbouring village to replace the strikers. As these men approached Hambridge's farm they were met by a crowd of 20 to 30 women who wanted to prevent them taking on the work and so breaking the strike. Some of the women carried sticks, but if there was any violence it was very mild; indeed at one point they tried to deflect the strike breakers by

---

[1] *The Times*, 28 September 1872, p. 11, col. 5. Ellicott, *An Address to the Clergy and Laity of Gloucester and Bristol* (Gloucester, 1873). On Ellicott, see also Wagner [op. cit., p. 171] pp. 159–60; D. Bowen, *The Idea of the Victorian Church* (Montreal, 1968) pp. 244–5, 247–8.

[2] *Letters of Queen Victoria, second series* (2 vols., 1926) Vol. I, p. 545. P. T. Marsh, *The Victorian Church in Decline: Archbishop Tait and the Church of England* (1969) p. 28.

offering them beer. When a policeman appeared the crowd melted away. However, an offence had undoubtedly been committed under the Criminal Law Amendment Act, and Hambridge prosecuted seventeen of the women. The case was heard at Chipping Norton before two magistrates who were both clergymen, Thomas Harris, an ex-fellow of Magdalen College, Oxford who had been a magistrate since 1852, and W. D. Carter, an ex-fellow of New College who had been a magistrate since 1855. Carter was obviously disturbed by the prospect of sending all these women, some of them carrying babies, to Oxford gaol and more than once he begged Hambridge not to press the case. However, Hambridge would not withdraw his charge, and, after having been out of the court for an unusually long period, the magistrates convicted 16 of the women and sentenced 7 of them to 10 days' imprisonment with hard labour, and 9 to 7 days' imprisonment with hard labour.

The hard labour in this case, with which Arch in his account makes play, was in fact only washing and ironing from which the women with babies were exempted. Still, 16 working women had been sent to prison for a negligible offence, and there was naturally an immediate outcry. C. Holloway, the chairman of the Oxfordshire district branch of the Labourers' Union, wrote *The Times* a letter describing the case, which was published on 23 May under the heading 'Impossible'.[1] *The Times* sent down to Oxfordshire a special correspondent, and other papers took up the matter. Questions were asked in Parliament, Bruce the home secretary was instructed to discover the facts, and in due course the lord chancellor, Lord Selborne, through the lord lieutenant of Oxford, the Duke of Marlborough, required the two magistrates to explain their actions.[2]

Bruce believed that an offence had been committed and that a conviction was inevitable, but that the punishment was excessive, particularly since one of the magistrates had tried to persuade the prosecutor to stop the case. He gave it as his opinion that the magistrates could have imposed a fine, or bound the defendants over to come up for judgement as had been done at Woodstock in 1871. It looks as if there was some mis-

[1] *The Times*, 23 May 1873, p. 5, col. 5.
[2] *Hansard* (3rd series) CCXVI (May to 7 July 1873) pp. 429 and 548.

understanding here. The magistrates stated that it was not usual to delay sentence unless the accused pleaded guilty, or there were very cogent alleviating circumstances, and that the only punishment prescribed in the act was imprisonment with or without hard labour. Arch also says that one of the journalists from London in the court stated that the Criminal Law Amendment Act did not allow the option of a fine.[1] Even if these doubts were unreal, it is possible that they may have confused Carter's mind. In his rather tearful account to the Duke of Marlborough, Carter seems to show that he believed there was no alternative to imprisonment, and therefore, since he could not induce Hambridge to drop the prosecution and since an offence had undeniably been committed, since the law had to be vindicated and Hambridge's rights protected and since his colleague was unshaken, he did in the end assent to the sentences.[2] Probably it was his unhappy hesitation that made for the long delay before the magistrates reached their decision.

The agitation caused by this case was directed primarily against clerical magistrates in general. A return of the number of clerical magistrates was called for, and a bill was promoted to prevent the appointment as magistrates of any cleric with a cure of souls. It was dropped, but it seems probable that from this time the practice of appointing them fell into desuetude. But it may be questioned whether this case reveals any attitude peculiar to clergymen; or at least whether lay magistrates might not have acted in the same way if they had been confronted with Hambridge's prosecution of the 17 women. There is a certain amount of evidence which bears on this. As has been said, a royal commission was appointed in 1874 to examine the working of the Criminal Law Amendment Act. It reported that between 1871 and 1873 there had been 135 convictions under the act in England and Wales, 12 in Scotland, 17 in Ireland, and between 1873 and 1874, 39 in England and Wales, 9 in Scotland, 12 in Ireland. They analysed 54 cases on information given by the clerks to the justices. Unfortunately the names of the magistrates are not always given, but it seems clear that the great majority of the magistrates involved were laymen.

The cases come from both industrial and agricultural dis-

---

[1] P.P. 1873, LIV, p. 29. Arch [op. cit., p. 140] p. 141.
[2] P.P. 1873, LIV, p. 22.

tricts, and a number of them are obviously the results of the same kind of agricultural strike as the Chipping Norton case. It is a little difficult to judge from the abbreviated reports how trivial the offences were, but a number of them seem simply to turn on words spoken without physical violence of any sort. Indeed Lord and Lady Passfield report a case in 1871 where seven women were sent to prison merely for saying 'Bah' to one blackleg.[1] The Chipping Norton case seems to stand out from the others in the number of defendants and the fact that they were women. But on the whole, compared with the other cases the sentences inflicted in the Chipping Norton case seem to have been among the lightest. In the other cases the sentences seem to vary from 6 days to 3 months with hard labour, but it is true that where some of the longer sentences were inflicted there seems to have been more violence than in the Chipping Norton case.[2]

The moral of the return seems to be that what is at issue here has little to do with the propensities of clerical magistrates as such; it is, rather, the opportunities for class oppression offered by the Criminal Law Amendment Act, and the fact that the employing classes, whether industrialists or farmers, were prepared to use them to the hilt. To the pressure of that class interest two clerical magistrates at Chipping Norton unfortunately yielded, one of them very reluctantly, as clearly a large number of lay magistrates yielded elsewhere. The nature of the pressure in the Chipping Norton case can be seen not only in the pertinacity of Hambridge in prosecuting the seventeen women, but also in the long list of local farmers which the magistrates cited in their report as endorsing the value of the decision, and also in a letter to *The Times* in which a large number of the local farmers reiterated their support for Hambridge.[3]

There is little more to say about this case, but it would be interesting to know more about the two clergymen involved,

<hr>

[1] S. and B. Webb, *The History of Trade Unionism* (revised edition extended to 1920) p. 284.

[2] P.P. 1875, XXX, pp. 28 and 43–80. See also letter from Frederick Harrison on the savagery of sentences under the Criminal Law Amendment Act, *The Times*, 2 June 1873, p. 8, col. 3.

[3] P.P. 1873, LIV, pp. 24–7; *The Times*, 2 June 1873, p. 8, col. 4.

particularly perhaps about the personality and motives of Harris, whose resolve to convict seems to have overborne the unhappy Carter. It does not seem possible to recover much, but there is one fact which may be relevant. Harris' life stretched back to an earlier generation. He took his bachelor's degree in Oxford in 1833, and was senior proctor there in 1845–6. Since 1849 he had been installed in the comfortable living to which his college had presented him. Forty years of social and intellectual progress had passed since he had taken his degree in an Oxford still shuddering from the threat of the first Reform Act and the agitations which had preceded it. Perhaps they had passed him by.

It is obviously unsatisfactory to infer too much about the state of opinion of the clergy of the Church of England from the unconsidered words of one silly bishop and the action of two elderly clerical magistrates. It is indeed pertinent to remember that very many of the clergy were not directly involved in these agricultural strikes at all. By now the bulk of the population of England lived in towns. Though in all probability a larger proportion of the Anglican clergy than the distribution of the population would warrant still lived in country conditions, the number of purely urban clergy must by now have been great, and though no doubt many of them were interested in these issues they were not directly committed to this particular controversy. Nor was by any means the whole of rural England affected. Arch's union had not spread into all counties, and there were clearly fairly large areas in England where the conditions which had caused the strikes did not exist, or where Arch's propaganda had not penetrated. For instance, at the meeting of the Church Congress in 1873 Archdeacon Hamilton reported that there was no trouble in Northumberland and the same thing seems to have been true of other districts remote from the corn-growing midland and southern counties, which seem to have been most often the centre of activity.

There also seems to have been no noticeable trouble in some parishes which were not very far away from the areas affected. Francis Kilvert's diary runs through 1872 and 1873. He travelled about a good deal, mixing freely and happily with all classes, and at least when he was in Wiltshire it might have been thought he was near some of the centres of trouble. He certainly attended the meeting of the Church Congress at Oxford in 1873 at which the problem of labour was discussed.[1] Yet he shows no awareness of the challenge which the clergy of the Church of England were facing, and apparently felt no tension between himself and the villagers he met. In this he was clearly not singular, and in order to form a correct picture of these years it is probably right to envisage a number of parishes, even in the Midlands and southern England, in which life went on as before and the relations of parson and people were undisturbed.

There is a fair amount of evidence about the attitudes of the clergy who did become involved, but it is unfortunately fragmentary and incomplete. It is never ample enough to make it possible to give a comprehensive judgement. It is only possible to say that certain opinions existed, and any general estimate of how many of the clergy inclined to any particular attitude must be based on a guess, or the impressions of contemporaries. As far as their particular opinions go it seems possible, however, to divide the clergy into three groups, those who supported the union and saw the justice of the strikes, those who supported the farmers, and those who were undecided or believed that the clergy ought to be neutral.

The first group contained some outstanding personalities. There was the Hon. and Rev. J. W. Leigh, vicar of Stoneleigh, and pioneer in village co-operation. When the movement started he went to see Joseph Arch and he supported him at his various meetings.[2] There was, as might be expected, Edward Girdlestone, who supported the movement until its anti-clerical character made it impossible for him to go on doing so. James Fraser, bishop of Manchester, speaking at the Church Congress in Leeds in 1872, made a robust appeal on behalf of the labourers' right to combine and praised Joseph Arch, and in 1874 wrote a vigorous letter to *The Times* denouncing the farmers' lockout, starting with the widely remembered phrase, 'Are the farmers of England going mad?'[3] Some clergymen who held, or had held, parishes in London, and who indeed had had no pastoral experience of rural conditions but were deeply

---

[1] *Kilvert's Diary*, edited by W. Plomer (2 vols., reissued 1969) Vol. II, p. 381.
[2] Leigh, *Other Days* [op. cit., p. 184] pp. 120–5.
[3] *Church Congress, Leeds 1872* (Leeds, 1872) p. 363. *The Times*, 2 April 1874, p. 7, col. 2.

interested in the Church's relation to trade unions, supported the Labourers' Union on general grounds. These were Brooke Lambert, who had now moved from Whitechapel to Tamworth, Harry Jones, rector of St George's in the East, and H. Llewellyn Davies, rector of Christ Church, Marylebone. Of these the most influential part was played by Llewellyn Davies. He was a friend and disciple of Maurice, an ex-fellow of Trinity College, Cambridge, and a man of considerable intellectual distinction. His great value in this, as in other matters, was that he was a courteous, level-headed controversialist of considerable power, who did a very useful service in establishing the case that it was the duty of the clergy to support the Labourers' Union.[1]

These more theoretical pleas for the union were supported by men who had parochial experience of the labourers' condition, or of working with the union. For instance, a man calling himself 'Leicestershire Incumbent' wrote to *The Guardian* to say that Davies was not singular in his views, that it was the duty of the clergy to sympathize with the labourer's legal efforts to help himself, that in common with others of his clerical brethren he had long deplored in silence what he was compelled to know but could not alter.[2] Others commended the members of the union and denied that their leaders were agitators. A 'Cambridgeshire vicar' writing in the *Spectator* in October 1873 said he had had 'the happiest results' from supporting the Labourers' Union.[3] Harry Burgess, vicar of Whittlesey, also in Cambridgeshire, contributed to the funds of the union, presided at the annual dinner of his local branch and preached four times a year on topics they suggested.[4] The Rev. C. E. Roberts was agent of the Littleport branch of the union.[5] The discussion in the Church Congress in 1873 also revealed others who supported trade unions in their parishes. H. Blagg Smyth of Houghton Regis in Bedfordshire said that the union

[1] e.g. his article in *The Guardian* (14 August 1872, p. 1041), 'On labourers' combinations from the clerical point of view', or his speech at the Church Congress at Bath, 1873, p. 29.
[2] *The Guardian*, 28 August 1872, p. 1088; 4 September 1872, p. 1127; Wagner [op. cit., p. 171] p. 164.
[3] *Spectator*, 11 October 1873, p. 1272.
[4] *The Times*, 15 April 1874, p. 12, col. 2; Wagner, op. cit.
[5] *The Times*, 15 April 1874, p. 12, col. 3; Wagner, op. cit.

men in his parish were excellent men of the highest character, and constant attendants at the Sunday schools, and described how they came to him at the beginning of the agricultural strike to ask for his support. R. M. Grier, vicar of Rugely, said he spoke as a strong Conservative and looked on trade unions as symptoms of a most unhealthy state of things, but if under present circumstances they were right the Church ought to support them. He added that he had some experience of the leaders of the Amalgamated Miners' Union in his parish and denied that they went about setting class against class. He had lent them the use of his schoolroom for their meetings and when the school was not available they met in the vicarage.[1]

Other supporters of the Agricultural Union emerge in the course of the various discussions that took place during these days, and Anglican parsons can be identified as sitting on the platform at Arch's meetings or presiding over them, though such actions may mean something less than actual support of the union. In contrast to these men there were certainly some clergymen who were frankly on the other side. For instance, it was Archdeacon C. W. Holbeche, rector of Banbury, who proposed the operative motion at a landowners' meeting in Oxfordshire in April 1872 and he was supported, possibly significantly, by C. D. Francis, the incumbent of Tysoe.[2] There is also a distinct note of definite hostility in some Tory and clerical newspapers. But evidence of open hostility, or of a resolve openly to side with the farmers against the unions, though no doubt it exists, is not easy to find. There is much more evidence, not so much of opposition to the labourers' claims, as of bewilderment, hesitation and timidity, and a reluctance to take sides.

This is not surprising; bewilderment and timidity are natural emotions for men who have been overtaken by a new and difficult situation, and the problem many of the clergy had to face in 1872 and 1873 was both difficult and new to them. According to J. W. Leigh a movement among the labourers astonished the squires and farmers, and there is no reason to believe that the parsons were any better prepared.[3] They were

---

[1] *Church Congress, Bath 1873* (Leeds, n.d.) pp. 23–44.
[2] *The Guardian*, 3 April 1872, p. 438.
[3] Leigh, *Other Days* [op. cit., p. 184] p. 120.

used to acting as the patrons of the labourers, but not to the labourers acting independently. In such circumstances no doubt it was tempting to suggest that what the labourers were doing was not in their 'best interests', particularly when there seemed to be reason to believe that this really was so. For there seemed to be a real reason to doubt whether strikes and unions would help the labourers. Many of the clergy seem to have shared the current beliefs about the way in which the rates of wages were settled. For instance, the South Warwickshire clerical meeting in April 1872 produced a manifesto in which the members recognized the right of the labourers to combine, but deplored strikes and lockouts as justifiable but useless, since the rate of wages must in the end be settled by the natural law of supply and demand.[1] This belief, whatever it meant, was commonly held to be true of all wages. However, agricultural wages presented peculiar difficulties, since in addition to his money wages an agricultural labourer might receive allowances and perquisites in kind. There was therefore some uncertainty as to the real value of any one labourer's earnings, and a distinct possibility that if wages were settled by strict trade union negotiation these allowances would be cut off.[2]

The evidence which the clergy gave to the commission on the employment of women and children in agriculture shows that many of them were perfectly familiar with the hardship of the labourers' lot and wanted to improve it, but they were tempted to believe that there were more certain ways of doing this than by encouraging strike action. Even a man who was prepared to support the union and the strike, such as Blagg Smyth, was inclined to believe that a permanent improvement in the condition of the labourer would be best assured by the old plan of distributing allotments.[3] Many people apparently believed that much could be done by a concerted attempt to improve rural housing. But whatever was to be done it clearly seemed to many of the clergy that the best way to achieve these ends was by appealing to the landowners and farmers rather than by trying to force their hands. Consequently, in April 1872

[1] See *The Guardian*, 24 April 1872, p. 550. Wagner [op. cit., p. 171] pp. 165, 168. *Spectator*, 7 September 1872, p. 1127.
[2] See the letter of Lord Lyttleton, *Spectator*, 7 September 1872, p. 1138.
[3] Hugh Blagg Smyth, *Church Congress, 1873* [*V.S.*, p. 255–6] p. 39.

the Rev. D. R. Murray, rector of Brampton Bryan, issued in the name of the Herefordshire Union an appeal to landowners and tenants, couched in curiously humble terms, to bring the wages of all able-bodied men in their employment up to 15s a week, with the addition of better cottages, allotments and money to assist emigration.[1]

Of course behind all this there lurked class feeling. No doubt, as Girdlestone recorded, many of the clergy instinctively identified themselves with the landowners and farmers and the old hierarchy. In not a few cases their own income probably seemed to be at stake, or their own sense of dignity, but fear and timidity seem to have been more powerful emotions. It is probable that many of them were afraid to offend the landowners and gentry; it is quite clear that many of them were afraid to offend the farmers, who were often much closer neighbours to the country clergy, and on whose co-operation they depended for so much that was done in their parishes.

The farmers were much more directly involved in agricultural strikes than the remoter owners of the land, and there is much evidence that there were limits to what the farmers would stand. When the 'Cambridgeshire vicar' declared that he had obtained 'excellent results' from co-operation with the Labourers' Union he was immediately challenged by other clergymen on the ground that this was simply not possible in all parishes. As one man said of farmers: 'although they will bear to be told, about the low wages, hovel cottages and poor fare of their men they will not – unless in exceptional cases like that mentioned by your "Cambridgeshire vicar" – tolerate the wholesale, whole-hog advocacy of the labourers' side, by a clergyman who should be the friend of all'.[2] In fact the limits of the farmers' toleration might be a great deal less than this suggests. In the *Spectator* of the year before there is a letter from a parson whose congregation had been deserted by many leading farmers because he spoke of the dangers to

---

[1] *The Guardian*, 11 September 1872, pp. 1156–7. Wagner [op. cit., p. 171] p. 153.

[2] 'A country parson', *Spectator*, 27 September 1873, p. 1212; S. B. James, *Spectator*, 25 October 1873, p. 1336.

pregnant women of working in the fields, something he knew from pastoral experience.[1]

Uncertainty about the issues, or fear of the consequences, tended to make many of the country clergy feel that they ought not to take sides over the agricultural strike, that they ought to remain neutral; perhaps try to mediate, certainly preach peace. It was an attitude which Joseph Arch viewed with contempt, as he did most of the things the clergy did or said. His attitude can well be understood. When two parties are so unequally placed as were the agricultural labourers and the farmers, when the need on one side is so great and on the other side the disposition to satisfy it is so little, neutrality, mediation, the preaching of peace must seem to be a fraud and a mockery, a display of virtue masking either self-interest or cowardice, or most probably both self-interest and cowardice. Nevertheless the attitude of the clergy is intelligible also. After all, the problem of agricultural wages, of what the labourers received and what the farmers could pay, was a technical one. On the last analysis the doctrine that the rate of wages was in all circumstances inexorably settled by the laws of supply and demand was a piece of educated superstition the meaning of which had not been thought through; but it looked scientific and conclusive, and was accepted without question by many people who might be expected to know more economics than the country clergy. In such circumstances it was perhaps natural for a clergyman to feel that it was not his duty to pronounce on such matters, but that it was his duty to prevent strife being encouraged in his parish, or class being set against class. It is, indeed, significant that *The Guardian*, which was a level-headed, moderate, church paper, and which itself expressed the opinion that the labourers' claims were not excessive and ought to be satisfied, nevertheless believed that the clergy ought to be neutral.[2]

There is, therefore, evidence for the existence among the clergy for a variety of attitudes towards the Agricultural Labourers' Union and the agricultural strikes – open sympathy for the labourers, open partisanship for the farmers, and

---

[1] *Spectator*, 23 November 1872, p. 1489.
[2] *The Guardian*, 17 April 1872, p. 505; 5 June 1872, p. 737; 26 June 1872, p. 825.

various grades of hesitation or declarations of the duty of neutrality. Unfortunately the evidence is too fortuitous and fragmentary to form a satisfactory basis for generalizations about the prevalent attitudes of all the clergy involved, nor is it possible to do more than guess what proportion of them inclined to any particular point of view. There was one occasion when men with different opinions on this subject confronted one another – the discussion on the Church's attitude to strikes and trade unions at the Church Congress at Bath in October 1873. As far as that discussion went it was apparently marked by a notable absence of expressions of hostility to the Labourers' Union or direct partisanship for their opponents. This is particularly true if no account is taken of the speeches made by laymen, though it is also true that among the speeches made by the clergy there are expressions of sympathy for the farmers. The issue seems to lie somewhere between those who believed that the clergy ought to be neutral and those who believed that they ought to support the union.

The discussion was opened by the bishop of Oxford, a staunch Liberal, who put the case for neutrality. He was supported by other speakers. There were, however, powerful speeches on the other side. Llewellyn Davies and Edward Girdlestone made the speeches which might have been expected of them. Blagg Smyth and Grier spoke of their co-operation with trade unions. Archdeacon Earle spoke of the responsibility of landowners whose prosperity had not reached the labourers, and W. H. Jones, vicar of Mottram in Longendale in north-east Cheshire, roundly attacked the bishop of Oxford, declaring that if the clergy had not sufficient knowledge to pronounce on these matters they ought to have had that knowledge, and that if they had not been invited to intervene they ought not to have waited for the invitation. The policy of neutrality was not that which Christ observed towards the Pharisees.[1]

If the speakers at the Church Congress had been a representative sample it might almost seem that those who supported the union were, if not a majority, at least a very large minority, of the clergy affected; but it seems clear that it was not a representative sample. The general impressions of a good many

[1] *Church Congress, Bath 1873* [op. cit., p. 257] pp. 23–8.

observers suggest that the majority of those of the clergy who were challenged by the strike were hesitant, or explicitly neutral, and that they disappointed such of the labourers as appealed to them. The effect of this was cumulative. It threw the movement even more effectively into the hands of the enemies of the Church, who made much of the hesitations, or occasional hostility, of the clergy. From the beginning there had been a strong anti-clerical element among the leaders of the union, of whom Joseph Arch himself is an obvious example. From very early on, from the moment when the *Daily News* sent Forbes to report on events in Warwickshire or the Birmingham Radicals extended their patronage to the movement, they had been joined by men who saw it as part of a crusade against the landed aristocracy and the Church. When clergymen refused to support the union or there were expressions of hostility to it the power of these elements must have increased. Unsatisfactory interviews with reluctant or partially hostile clergymen were scornfully reported in the *Chronicle* of the Labourers' Union, to be relayed to a wider public by the *Spectator*, active in its office of candid friend of the Church. Bishop Ellicott's foolish words were reported *ad nauseam*, and the relations between the Church and the union came to be described in terms which have passed into history.

This again had a cumulative effect. As the *Chronicle* of the Labourers' Union became more vituperative, as it became increasingly clear that the Radical enemies of the Church were playing an important part in the movement, the clergy tended to become hostile and to see the movement as an attack on the establishment by its old enemies, and they naturally objected to the harsh abuse of which they were the target. It seemed therefore to become increasingly questionable whether clergymen should give such a movement their countenance, and clergymen were blamed for taking the chair at Arch's meetings. In November 1872 W. H. Lyttleton, the brother of Gladstone's Lord Lyttleton, who was at this time rector of Hagley in Worcestershire, drew attention to the way things were going. He said that all clergymen, landlords and gentlemen who sympathized with the labourers ought to say so. 'There is,' he said,

a tone of bitterness growing up in some quarters, which is natural, but much to be regretted. Surely we ought to have the manliness and good temper to stand a little strength of language in men whose grievances have been (and still are in some places, as, for instance, in Dorsetshire – see the letters just published in the *Spectator*) very great, and even terrible?[1]

It was, however, probably not possible to prevent the rift widening. In December 1872 there was a large meeting at Exeter Hall at which the Radicals who supported the labourers were very much in evidence. *The Guardian* noted with regret that it appeared to be dominated by such men as Charles Bradlaugh, Charles Dilke and Samuel Morley, and the *Spectator* felt some shame that it was left to Cardinal Manning to press the moral issue and that 'not a single minister of either the national or the nonconformist churches' was there to take up the cause. In this the *Spectator* was not in fact being quite fair, and Llewellyn Davies wrote to correct the impression. Girdlestone, he said, had been asked to speak but could not come, but there were several of the London clergy on the platform, including probably Davies himself.[2] However, the time would come when even Girdlestone announced he could no longer support the union, since it was devoting its energies to attacks on the clergy and on the connection between Church and State. It is not easy to say when he made the final break since the date and reference normally given for his statement is palpably wrong; but in an article which he published in 1873 in the September number of *Macmillan's Magazine*, he expressed his fears about the way things might go.[3]

In his article in *Macmillan's Magazine*, Girdlestone spoke of the good which the union might do, but he also said that there were political agitators who were anxious to divert it from the object of benefiting the agricultural labourer to suit

[1] W. H. Lyttleton, *The Guardian*, 27 November 1872, p. 1491.
[2] *The Guardian*, 18 December 1872, p. 1569; *Spectator*, 14 December 1872, p. 1578, and 21 December 1872, p. 1627.
[3] Girdlestone's statement breaking with the union is always referred back to E. Selley [op. cit., p. 171] p. 88, e.g. Wagner [op. cit., p. 180] p. 171. Selley gives as his reference, *Spectator*, 6 September 1873. But there is no such statement in that number of the *Spectator*, nor can I find such a statement anywhere in the *Spectator* for 1873 or 1874. The statement as given is unlikely to have been made as early as September 1873 since its purport is not compatible with Girdlestone's article in *Macmillan's Magazine*, nor with his speech at the Church Congress in October 1873.

their own ends. They might use it for an attack on the land laws
and they might use it to try to secure the disestablishment and
disendowment of the Church of England. In Girdlestone's view
this would not be to the advantage of the agricultural labourer.
It was quite true, he said, that the clergy had not done all they
should have done to help the labourer to improve his position;
that almost all of them had stood aloof from this movement,
that some had opposed it, that many had instinctively sided
with the landowners and farmers. But, he added,

> It is equally true that, were it not for the kindness of the clergy
> in the rural districts; for the sacrifices which they have made to
> build and endow schools; for the many meals which they have
> sent from the parsonage to the cottage, when the breadwinner is
> ill, the wife confined, the children poorly fed; the many comforts
> which they have denied to themselves and their families in order
> to clothe and feed the naked and hungry among their flock; not to
> mention their prayers by the sick-bed, and their loving words of
> comfort to the widow and fatherless in their sorrow, the conditions
> of the agricultural labourer would have been very much worse
> than it is.

And he spoke of the loss which the labourer might suffer if the
villages were left without resident clergymen.[1]

This was the same argument Blomfield had used forty years
before, and, taking into account what clergymen had learnt to
do in those forty years and were doing in their parishes at that
moment it was better justified in 1873 than it had been in 1833.
But it had less relevance for the future. It was only relevant to
a social order the days of which were numbered in 1873. In due
course a social pattern would develop in which the services of
the country parson were to be less needed by his parishioners
and possibly less acceptable to them, and in which he would
not have the resources to offer them on the scale on which he
had been used to give them.

The National Agricultural Union was not in fact to be an
operative agent in this change. Its own days of effectiveness were
very short. It reached its highest point in 1873. In 1874 the
farmers organized that lockout against which the bishop of

[1] Rev. Edward Girdlestone, article on 'The National Agricultural Labourers'
Union', *Macmillan's Magazine*, Vol. XXVIII (May 1873 to October 1873)
pp. 436–46.

Manchester protested so vigorously. He protested in vain. As has been said, the lockout was successful in robbing the labourers of much of what they had gained in 1872–3. 1874 was followed by two developments which struck lethal blows at agricultural trade unionism: the severe agricultural depression in those corn-growing counties where the union had been most active and the increased mechanization of agriculture which meant that much agricultural labour became redundant. The best chance of self-improvement for an agricultural labourer was still, in fact, migration from an overcrowded countryside.

Agricultural radicalism fared a little better than the agricultural trade unions. It was adopted as a cause by Chamberlain and Jesse Collins and in 1884 they managed to get the Third Reform Act passed which enfranchised the agricultural labourer and put an end to a number of small constituencies which the nobility and gentry had dominated. The results were seen in the general election of 1885 at which Chamberlain preached land reform, and the enfranchised labourers under the cover of the ballot brought Liberals in for a good many country constituencies, Arch himself being elected for north-west Norfolk. But the hopes of 1885 were forfeited by Gladstone in 1886. The Liberals split over Home Rule, Arch and Jesse Collins taking different sides. There was a general election in 1886 which the Conservatives won, and Arch lost his seat. There was it is true a Liberal revival in 1892 which brought Arch back into Parliament, but it was largely ephemeral and much less was accomplished than the social revolution of which men had had hopes.

A change was indeed taking place in country society, but it was taking place over a wider area and at a deeper level than could be affected by the ephemeral shock of agricultural trade unionism or the flux and reflux of party politics. The depression of agriculture and the resultant decline in the income of the parochial clergy were probably a more effective solvent of the traditional pattern of the countryside than either trade unionism or Radicalism. The decline in a clergyman's income would be likely to affect his activities in a number of ways. He could no longer afford the help of a curate whom he needed if he was to work the parish properly; he would probably reduce his contributions to the various institutions which had been a feature of the high rectory culture; above all, he could probably no longer afford to sufficiently finance the local school, thus bringing nearer the day when the school was handed over to a school board. It was in fact the beginning of the long painful decline of the country clergy from the prestige, power and wealth which many of the clergy in the middle of the nineteenth century had enjoyed to the shabbier circumstances of the harsher way of life, which was all that was available to their successors.[1]

Even if the decline in clerical incomes had not taken place it seems probable that the old system would not have survived intact, and indeed ought not to have survived. The rural population of England owed much to the old parochial tradition – much more than is often realized. It had frequently been a civilizing factor in conditions which were often noticeably harsh and uncivilized. But it was founded on the principle of inequality. This was true even when the parson worked hard and sacrificed himself for his people. It was a principle which was based on traditions that ran back to an indiscernible antiquity, though as far as the clergy were concerned their effects had been enhanced by events in the eighteenth and early nineteenth centuries. But on the last analysis it was indefensible; it was right that it should disappear. There had probably been for many centuries in the countryside an opposition to the social order in which it was embodied, an opposition which was most consistently represented in the history of rural Dissent. As the nineteenth century went forward it was natural that this opposition should grow in strength. It might be suggested that the trade unionism and rural Radicalism of the 1870s and 1880s are symptoms that this opposition had achieved a position in society which made it impossible to disregard their views, particularly since there had also been a general change of values in the whole country. In fact an era was beginning in which the old hierarchy would no longer be tolerated.

Social traditions tend to die hard and slowly, particularly in country places. At the beginning of the last quarter of the

1 There are three very percipient and sympathetic studies of the problems of the clergy at the end of the 1870s in Richard Jefferies, *Hodge and his Masters* (2 vols., 1880) Vol. I, Ch. XIV, pp. 317–34: 'The Parson's Wife'; Ch. XV, pp. 335–59: 'A Modern Country Curate'; Vol. II, pp. 246–58: 'Modern Clergy'.

nineteenth century, though it had been challenged, the old tradition was still vigorous and operative. Much of it would survive into the new century. Many parsons would struggle to continue to do their duty on the old terms with dwindling resources. Many villagers would accord to them something of the old respect and also, even more markedly, expect the same services from them. These survivals would, however, be the ghosts of what had been. This is the end of a long and important chapter in English history.

10

The Problems of the Town

The article of faith about the factors which controlled the rate of wages was only one of the superstitions which the conditions of the third phase was to challenge. There was the even more obstructive and dangerous overestimate of what the able-bodied adult could be expected to do for himself, and the corresponding underestimate of what the community ought to do for him. This was a superstition encouraged by the teaching of the economists, by the views of Bentham on the causes of pauperism and the proper cure for it, by the principles of the New Poor Law of 1834 and by what appeared to be the results of departures from those principles since 1834. Until it was dissipated it was unlikely that a fully satisfactory social policy would be developed, for it led to a disregard of those factors which were able to prevent the able-bodied adult from helping himself – such factors as unemployment, underemployment, the power of the capitalist employer and of the ground landlord. It also encouraged the belief that it was easy to discriminate between those who deserved full relief and those who deserved as little as possible because they could, if they had wanted to, have helped themselves.

At the beginning of the third phase these superstitions had deep roots in middle-class and upper-class minds. They could only be eradicated by more intimate and more accurate knowledge of the factors which controlled the lives of the poor, and even then a revolution in economic doctrine would probably be needed before that knowledge could be rightly interpreted. In the sprawling late nineteenth-century cities and towns, in which those who were better off lived in fashionable streets and suburbs cordoned off from the homes of the poor, such knowledge was not readily available, and it was for this reason that the testimony of ministers of religion was important. At the end of

K

the century Charles Booth made a street survey of London which showed how many ministers from all churches were at work in all parts of the great city.[1] Many of these men were in contact with urban society at its most desolate. It was, of course, their object to reclaim those pagan areas which Christianity had lost; in this they were not always noticeably successful, but if they were unable to Christianize the dark places of England at least they might be qualified to tell their fellow Christians what life in those places was like.

The various denominations made contact with urban problems in different ways. From the point of view of the Church of England the important factor was the network of parishes which at least in theory covered every part of every town. In many cases the influx of population had rendered that organization meaningless, but by the beginning of the third phase a determined attempt had been made to reconstruct it. In most districts there were churches; sometimes they were ancient parish churches with crowded churchyards whose greasy soil excited sinister speculations; or there were the results of church extension, sometimes thriving, sometimes desolate monuments to disappointed hopes. The clergy who served these churches seem to have differed widely from one another in churchmanship, assiduity and intelligence – and in hopefulness, for these were posts which were very likely to lead a man to surrender to relatively inert despair. However, among the clergy with urban parishes, particularly in London, were some of the ablest priests of the Church of England whose lead in social policy might be of the greatest importance.

Nevertheless, even the ablest and most sympathetic of these men continually encountered in their work two factors which encouraged them to exaggerate the need to rely on self-help in the relief of poverty and destitution, and the danger of doing anything else; for one suggested that many of the poor were in fact themselves responsible for their condition, and could amend it given proper discipline, and the other that it was necessary to be on one's guard when trying to do anything for them. The first of these was drunkenness and the second mendicity.

Addiction to strong drink was probably one of the most

---

[1] Charles Booth, *Life and Labour of the People in London. Third Series: Influences*, Vols. I and VII (1902).

normal immediate reasons for destitution and misery in nineteenth-century Britain. Its prevalence had many and complex causes – unfortunate traditions, the fact that strong drink was cheap and easily obtainable, the miserable terms on which life was offered to so many people. Indeed, the conditions under which they lived explained, and went very far to excuse, the habit of heavy drinking in a large section of the working class. So much was at least intermittently recognized by many of the clergy; but when a man was constantly confronted in his work by the personal disasters which resulted from the habit of drinking it was obviously difficult for him to discount the personal responsibility of the drunkard.

The result of such experiences was often a passionate personal commitment to the causes either of temperance, or of total abstinence. Probably the Protestant dissenters were most generally and fanatically committed to total abstinence, but there were also Church of England temperance societies and a number of eminent churchmen became total abstainers. From a recognition of the evils which were the direct result of heavy drinking the step was short to a belief that the original cause of most social evils was in fact drink itself. In 1862, at the Church Congress at Oxford, the Rev. H. J. Ellison said that a parochial clergyman who had laboured among the working class

> can go far to say: 'If it were not for this drink poverty and rags would come to an end; union workhouses and pauper lunatic asylums would lose two thirds of their inmates; the education question, the working man's dwelling question would settle themselves.'

This was too much for many of Ellison's contemporaries, and a brother clergyman pointed out that other impediments to right conduct were poor education, ill-constructed houses with evil or non-existent drainage, and unhealthy work. Nevertheless the state of every slum, the calendar of offences at every assize, the ruin in most parishes of human lives continued to emphasize the ways in which drink destroyed men and women.[1]

If the evils caused by drink might suggest to a working

---

[1] *Church Congress, 1862* (Oxford, 1862) p. 230. The Rev. E. S. Lowndes, Curate of Cleobury Mortimer, two sermons on *Total Abstinence not Christian Temperance* (1865). See also Brian Harrison, *Drink and the Victorians. The Temperance Question in England 1815–1872* (1971).

clergyman that many of the poor were responsible for their condition, the prevalence of mendicity would suggest, rightly, that many claims for relief were factitious. Victorian charity was profuse and much of it ill-regulated. Much could be gained by direct appeal to the compassionate. There were many loosely-controlled charities, and when a well-advertised cause of distress came to public notice a public subscription would be opened, such as a Mansion House fund, and a momentary flood of badly-administered charitable money released. Much of this would be diverted from those who needed it to those who made it their life's work to get it. Money given in the street or at the door was gathered in by professional beggars. The writing of begging letters had apparently become a profitable industry. Since the parochial clergy were expected to administer charitable funds, the more obstreperous beggars were on occasion prepared to offer violence to a clergyman who was not satisfied that their claims were legitimate and withheld a dole which they had come to regard as a right.

As a result of this the parochial clergy were liable to be continually pestered by claims for charity, many of them highly questionable. It is probable that the urban clergy were more troubled by this than the rural clergy, and that the worst sufferers were the London clergy. It is, indeed, worth remembering that all of those London clergymen who would help to develop social doctrine – Brooke Lambert, H. R. Haweiss, J. R. Green, J. Llewellyn Davies and Samuel Barnett – had good reason to be aware of the evils of mendicity. In fact in his early days as vicar of St Jude's, Whitechapel, Barnett was actually besieged by men violently demanding doles and had to have a door cut into the church through which he could escape and summon the police.[1]

The obvious answer to this was to make a searching enquiry into the circumstances of all those who applied for help, as was done by the Metropolitan Visiting and Relief Association which Blomfield, Gladstone and others founded in 1843. This organization seems to have continued to work on its chosen lines for the rest of the century, but it must have covered only a relatively small part of the field, and in 1860 there was a re-

[1] Henrietta O. Barnett, *Canon Barnett: His Life, Work and Friends* (2 vols., 1918) Vol. I, p. 84.

newal of interest in the whole subject. There were two reasons for this. It was believed that there were causes for unusually widespread distress in London that year which it was necessary to relieve, and it was also believed that owing to an increasingly lax administration of the Poor Law the number of paupers was rising to an alarming extent. Subsequent calculations have suggested that this may not have been altogether true; to judge by contemporary evidence it seems possible that those who held this opinion had been too much impressed by individual instances of what appeared to be negligent administration in particular unions. However, as a result of all this another body came into existence in London called the 'Society for the Relief of Distress', which recruited a number of voluntary almoners and assigned to them specified districts. This was followed in Liverpool in 1863 by the amalgamation by William Rathbone of three relief agencies into a Central Relief Society, and in Edinburgh in 1867 by the formation of a society for improving the condition of the poor.

The enquiry into the causes of poverty in individual cases naturally led to the study of individual cases in order to identify the causes of poverty. A number of people turned their minds to this. Between 1866 and 1870 Brooke Lambert as vicar of St Mark's, Whitechapel, conducted a census of a portion of his parish, making careful enquiries into the earnings of the people involved in relation to the cost of living, and Edward Denison, to whom I must return, who had served as one of the almoners for the relief of distress, went to live in the East End to study the life of the poor at close quarters. But the most important development was the creation in 1869 from an older society called the London Association for the Prevention of Pauperism and Crime of a new society, the Society for Organizing Charitable Relief and Repressing Mendicity, better known perhaps as the Charity Organization Society, under which title it achieved fame, if not always affection.

The Charity Organization Society was founded with the highest hopes and the best auguries. Its objects were important – to prevent the overlapping of different forms of charity, to determine the relationship between charity and the Poor Law, to investigate individual cases, to prevent fraud, and to secure that any aid should be of lasting value to those who were helped.

And it did good work. It exposed some very ripe frauds and it promoted some important reforms, particularly in the administration of hospitals. Unfortunately it remained very heavily charged with the old spirit. Many of its members seem to have felt confidently assured that they could discriminate between legitimate causes for poverty and those that were unfounded, and, in certain districts at least, the society's investigators developed a sharp, suspicious method of enquiry which seemed better suited for the counsel for a prosecution than for a friend in need. Consequently several of those who had been most enthusiastic at its birth began to doubt whether it satisfied their ideals.[1]

In spite of this the Charity Organization Society represents an important development in social policy. The intentions with which it had been founded were neither negative nor inhumane. It had not been intended to reduce the amount of relief given but to regulate it, and the work it conducted required more devoted personal service and closer contact with those who received it than was required of those who merely sent in a subscription, or handed out a sentimentally extracted half-crown. And as a result of its methods the Charity Organization Society promoted a technique of case study which was to be of the greatest use to the social reformer, and in due course would serve ideals which were not to be restricted by the old conceptions of the deserving and the undeserving poor.

To understand the significance of this stage in the development of social policy it is possibly desirable to turn to a book written by a man who was one of its pioneers, William Rathbone, a wealthy Unitarian Liverpool merchant. Rathbone had intended to call his book *Method Versus Muddle in Charitable Work*, but unfortunately a 'literary friend' persuaded him to give it a more ponderous title.[2] He based his argument on the often repeated statement about the disintegration of society in the later nineteenth century and the disappearance of the old sense of personal responsibility and friendship that had existed when society was smaller and men of different classes lived

[1] D. Owen, *English Philanthropy 1660–1960* (Cambridge, Mass., 1964) pp. 213–46.
[2] *Social Duties considered with reference to the organization of effort in works of Benevolence and Public Utility by a man of Business* (Cambridge, 1867).

nearer to each other. However, he claimed that 'there is among the rich much desultory and indolent good will towards the poor; much sentimental and inoperative sympathy with them'. This, he held, if properly stimulated by a sense of positive and imperative obligation and guided to a safe and effectual mode of action might be instrumental in effecting much good that was at present undone. As it was it did little good, and some harm.

His remedy was the reorganization of charity by men with business habits and orderly minds. This would not only lead to the work being more effectively done, but would close up the gaps which existed in the present system, and he gave as an example the lack of any provision for people who were discharged from hospitals as convalescent, or with an incurable disease. In imposing system on charity he did not mean to eliminate voluntary individual service. He certainly believed that large-scale causes of suffering required large-scale organizations and institutions to deal with them; indeed he felt that the necessities of the labouring class in a large city could not be handled in any other way. But he also believed that there was much that could be done by individual personal service, not rendered in a superior or patronizing way but humbly as an imperative duty which one human being owed to another, and of course intelligently with a view to the lasting benefit of those who were served.

Rathbone's ideals were enlightened and full of promise, and his actions endorsed them. He promoted the Central Relief Society, and after the death of his first wife in 1859, he persuaded the nurse who had attended her to take a turn at nursing the poor, and from that point developed a system of district nursing which enabled the poor to be treated in their homes by trained nurses. He also managed to introduce trained nurses and a lady superintendent into a poor law infirmary at Liverpool, which was the beginning of a revolution in the treatment of the sick poor. Nor was Rathbone alone at this time in the development of intelligent social work; others like him were active in different parts of the country, and a variety of factors combined to teach them how to introduce system and science into what they did. The Crimean War had created trained nurses and liberated the energies of Florence Nightingale.

The distress in Lancashire caused by the cotton famine at the time of the American Civil War had given valuable experience in the organization of relief. Much was being learnt from the working of local societies like the Manchester and Salford Sanitary Association which Canon Richson had founded, or the Yorkshire Ladies Council of Education which was formed in 1866. There were also the conferences of the Social Science Association, and there were national societies to press particular issues, like the Infant Life Protection Society founded in 1870.

The activities which developed from this newly gained knowledge and experience were in fact stages in the development of the collectivist State. It is true that many of the men and women involved probably retained a firm belief in the general doctrines of *laissez-faire*. It is also true that in many cases they were inspired by the principles and attitudes of an hierarchical society, for this work was often the product of the sense of the duty which men, or more often women, of the upper middle class or of the aristocracy owed to the class at the bottom of the social scale. But systematic philanthropy was necessarily a step away from a system based on the ordinary personal service, which anyone can render, towards the creation of a scientifically organized State whose services could only be staffed by professionals. Rathbone certainly laid much stress on the importance of voluntary personal service by individual men and women, but he could not have wished to rely on the service of individuals guided only by their uninstructed good nature, for the activities of such might have made hay of the system which he desired to establish. To work within the terms of a system is to accept the germs of professionalism, and the people employed by the Charity Organization Society to examine and advise on the cases to be relieved were in their way professionals; so were the lady rent collectors employed by Octavia Hill. The employment of trained nurses, such as Rathbone introduced to Liverpool, is clearly a further step forward into professionalism in the social services.

The development of charitable societies organized on more professional lines necessarily led in time to greater State participation. The support of a professional service and the provision of its facilities were often far beyond the resources of any private society, and if the work proved itself of use to the community, some public authority would have to take over if the work was to be effectively continued. This happened in a large number of cases, though at what date it happened depended on circumstances. For instance, Rathbone's poor law nurses passed into the hands of the poor law authorities almost at once, while many of the most important hospitals remained independent till the middle of the twentieth century. The intervening period is full of the history of activities of important services initiated by private persons and taken over in the end by the public power. The history of infant and child welfare provides an example of what happened in different departments of social policy.

This process inevitably tended to take social service out of the hands of those whose vocation was primarily religious. The more scientific and systematic social work became the less effectively could it be done by a minister of religion and devoted members of his congregation simply because he was a minister of religion and they were members of his congregation, and the wider the sphere of action the more certainly was the work beyond the resources of any religious denomination. Rathbone realized something of this tendency. He believed that all responsibility for the relief of destitution should be taken from ministers of religion, which would have the advantage of freeing them to perform their proper functions. At that time many ministers of religion refused to accept this verdict and they clung to their charitable work. But the general tendency was not to be deflected. Any future development would be away from a community in which much social service was voluntary, and an exercise in Christian duty and Christian responsibility, towards a State served and to a large extent directed by professionals who were not necessarily exponents of any form of orthodox Christianity, and embodying the authority of democratic power which was at best neutral in religious matters.

In the early years of the third phase, however, that development had not got very far. The powers and activities of the secular State were limited, the authority of democracy not yet complete, and most of the articulate section of the nation retained at least a nominal allegiance to some form of Christianity. It was therefore natural that in this period much of the initiative in social matters should still come from ministers of religion, though as was to be expected, by no means all of those responsible for this moral leadership were ministers of the Church of England. There was J. H. Thom, the Unitarian minister in Liverpool who inspired the activities of Rathbone, in so far as that warm-hearted man required inspiration; there was R. W. Dale of Birmingham, who supplied the impetus for the movement which threw up Chamberlain; or Henry Solly, the pioneer of, among other things, working men's clubs. Rather later in the century Cardinal Manning became a leading figure in social matters and so did General Booth of the Salvation Army. However, at this moment possibly the most interesting line of development starts, significantly, in an Anglican parish and derives directly from the parochial tradition of the English Church.

The parish was that of St Mary's, Bryanston Square, in the Marylebone district in London, and between 1866 and 1882 its vicar was W. A. Fremantle, later dean of Ripon. Fremantle was a man of impeccably Conservative origins, but, probably at Balliol under Jowett, he had imbibed certain Liberal principles, which were possibly not in line with his family tradition. He applied these in his views of the way in which a parish should be run, for not only did he maintain the old ideal that the incumbent of a parish of the established Church was responsible for everyone living within its geographical limits whatever their personal beliefs, but he also believed that the laity ought to be given a share in the running of the parish by establishing elected parish councils. He had been a member of a group which had promoted a bill to establish parish councils, but this had miscarried, and when he reached Marylebone he was determined to put his ideas into action and to try to turn his whole parish into one Christian community fused as far as that was possible into one family. To do this he successfully organized an elective council on which he encouraged leading dissenters to take an active part. In fact the secretary of the committee which dealt with poor relief was Mr Leon, a Jewish parishioner.

The relief of distress was one of the main tasks of the organization Fremantle had set up. The committee that dealt with it worked in close alliance with the Charity Organization Society, when that body came into existence. It consulted the society on all cases that came before it, though it did not consider itself to be bound by the society's decisions. Fremantle's district, however, came to be one of the most effective within the society's sphere of influence. It was in fact the only one in which the activities of the society, of the local workers and of the poor law authorities were all effectively integrated into one system.[1]

This might have been no more than a reasonably interesting instance of the way in which an urban parish of the established Church could at this date be developed into a body comprising all denominations and performing what might be thought to be secular functions, but, as Fremantle himself recognized, it gained a peculiar importance from the remarkable characters who happened to get caught up in it. One of his parishioners was Octavia Hill. Fremantle pressed her to take over the management of poor relief in one section of the parish, working under his supervision. She did the work so well that he soon put her in charge of another section, and in due course the special success of the whole district seems to have resulted from the fact that she was able to act as a link between the parish, the Charity Organization Society and the local board of guardians.[2] Part of the success of the system she developed depended on the introduction into the parish of a number of lady district visitors, rather on the analogy of her lady rent collectors, whose task it was to enquire into the cases requiring help. One of these, Miss H. O. Howland, a very pretty girl of nineteen, was courted, and, rather to her own surprise, won in marriage by one of Fremantle's curates, Samuel Barnett.

Before appointing him Fremantle had made sure that Barnett 'agreed with me in considering each person in the parish as a member of the Church of England and as a fellow-worker in the carrying out of the high ideal for which the Church exists'.[3] It was a high ideal that clearly demanded personal sacrifice. So after his marriage in 1873 Barnett got himself appointed to the parish of St Jude, Whitechapel. This was a derelict parish

[1] W. H. Draper, Master of the Temple, ed., *Recollections of Dean Fremantle chiefly by himself* (1921). C. Mowat, *Charity Organization Society* [op. cit. p. 59] p. 23.

[2] Edmund Maurice, ed., *Life of Octavia Hill as told in her Letters* (1913) pp. 253–62.

[3] Henrietta Barnett [op. cit., p. 270] Vol. I, p. 25.

in a slum area, reputedly one of the worst parishes in London. It was, therefore, Barnett's intention to try to put this parochial ideal into effect in much more difficult conditions than the parish in Marylebone, which was only partly a slum area.

There are affectionate accounts of Barnett by his wife, by Lady Passfield and by others who valued him. He was an ugly little man, with a high forehead, rather coarse features and a straggling beard. He was habitually dressed in ill-fitting black clothes which had been made for him by out-of-work tailors. His top hat never fitted him because it had always been bought by post, and he always wore black cotton gloves two or three sizes too large for him. With all this he must have been a man of great charm, humble, sensitive and humorous, and it was no doubt these qualities that enabled him and his very remarkable wife to do the noticeable things they did in that terrible parish. However, in this context that achievement is of less importance than the contacts they made with men and women who were going to shape the social thought of the future.

One of the most interesting of these came to them through Octavia Hill. In 1875 she sent down to them as a rent collector Kate Potter, the daughter of a wealthy man of business who was a member of a well-known Lancashire family. She in her turn brought in her train a sister. Beatrice Potter was beautiful, dissatisfied and highly intelligent. Like so many of the intelligent people in that generation she was anxiously searching for a religion and a purpose, and in fact the Barnetts' influence seems to have been one of the factors which helped her to focus her energies on that career in which, as Mrs Sidney Webb, she and her husband did so much to shape socialist thought in England. It was also through a connection of hers, Charles Booth, whose wife was her cousin, that Barnett was able to suggest a project which was also to have a profound effect on the social policy of the State. Charles Booth was a wealthy man with a deep interest in social problems and it was Barnett who suggested to him that he should undertake his remarkable *Survey of the Life and Labour of the People of London*, which gave a new accuracy to the knowledge which statesmen and social scientists possessed about the incidence of poverty; though it is true that Booth's primary purpose was to test the accuracy of the assertions of

Hyndman the social democrat, which he had started by dis-
believing.[1]

In each of these cases Barnett and his wife had some influence
in furthering activities which were ultimately to have a profound effect on what became completely secular social policy.
But by far the most important and significant of their contacts
were their friends in Oxford. Oxford was Barnett's old university and in 1875 they visited Oxford partly to enjoy Eights
Week, partly, at least on Henrietta's side, on the chance that
they might fulfil a hope which she says she often expressed in
her youth, when confronted by the conditions in Whitechapel.
'If men,' she had said, 'cultivated young thinking men, could
only know of those things, they would be altered'; for according
to her report the people who at that time were directly involved in the affairs of the East End tended to be either clergymen or elderly women. As it happened the 'cultivated young
thinking men' whom they met on that occasion were members
of a predominantly Balliol group which included men like
Arnold Toynbee, Alfred Milner and R. L. Nettleship; the
original connection was apparently the fact that Arnold Toynbee's sister had been at school with Henrietta Barnett, but in
fact no group could have been more apt for her purpose.[2]

For at that moment the most important centre of youth and
thought at Oxford was probably Balliol. This was the result of
the activities of Benjamin Jowett, first as tutor and then after
1870 as master, when T. H. Green took over the functions of
tutor. Jowett had not only secured that as a place of education
Balliol was outstanding, he had also managed to collect within
its walls a remarkable body of young men, many of whom
were among 'the cultivated young thinking men' whom the
Barnetts met. Of T. H. Green I have already spoken (see pp.
234–8). Nettleship had been the favourite pupil of Thring, the
great headmaster of Uppingham. He became a fellow of Balliol
and edited Green's works. His friend Scott Holland, who subsequently migrated to Christchurch, became a canon of St Paul's
and helped to found the Christian Social Union. Alfred Milner
became Lord Milner; his friend Arnold Toynbee, the most

[1] T. S. Simey and M. B. Simey, *Charles Booth, Social Scientist* (1960) pp. 64
and 69–70.
[2] Henrietta Barnett [op. cit., p. 270] Vol. I, pp. 302–4.

attractive of them all, was probably at least as important as Green in the history of opinion. He was the son of a distinguished, very idealistic, ear surgeon who killed himself while experimenting with anaesthetics in order to mitigate the pain of operations on the ear. In 1873 Arnold Toynbee came up to Oxford as an undergraduate in Pembroke College, but he was trepanned by Jowett into Balliol which he entered as an undergraduate in 1875. In 1878 he became tutor in economics there.

As a group these men had much in common. They shared a deep, almost conscience-stricken, interest in the social condition of the country. These moods normally build up slowly and there seems to have been in most cases an influence moving them in that direction before they reached Balliol. With Green it was probably his uncle, with Nettleship Thring, with Scott Holland possibly Cory Johnson when he was at Eton, with Toynbee probably his father, in spite of the fact that his father died when he was sixteen. But at Balliol the mood was brought into focus by the teaching of Green, who was older than the others, and invigorated by the visits to Oxford of Ruskin as Slade professor between 1870 and 1879. The mixture of artistic, moral and social ideals which was characteristic of Ruskin's thought at this time was rather strangely symbolized by the building of the Hinksey road. On this work Alfred Milner and Arnold Toynbee laboured, indeed Toynbee rose to the rank of 'foreman' with the privilege of breakfasting with Ruskin.[1]

And, as was probable with highly educated men of that generation, they all, with the exception of Scott Holland, found it necessary to turn away from the Christian religion as they had received it. To judge by his letters to Scott Holland Nettleship only did this after a period of acute distress, but it may be doubted whether Arnold Toynbee was fully conscious of what he was doing. He had always been very much interested in religion and in his own way he remained so, but he developed a way of thought which was in fact typical of that moment in time. After Toynbee's tragically early death his friend Alfred Milner said of him, 'Incredulous of miracle and indifferent to dogma, he was yet intensely conscious of the all-pervading presence of the Divine.'[2]

[1] E. T. Cook, *The Life of John Ruskin* (2 vols., 1911) Vol. II, pp. 190, 191.
[2] A. Milner, *Arnold Toynbee: a Reminiscence* (1895) p. 36.

Whatever their basic beliefs these were clearly exactly the kind of cultivated young thinking men for whom Henrietta Barnett had longed. There was evidence that the minds of other young men in Oxford and Cambridge were moving in the same direction and Samuel Barnett was able to hammer his message home on successive visits to Oxford. In return several of the men whom the Barnetts got to know came to visit them in Whitechapel. Arnold Toynbee seems to have come more often than others, indeed for several vacations he took lodgings in the Commercial Road so that he could see for himself what life in the East End was like. He was too delicate a man to stand that life for long, but he had gained a perception of the real meaning of poverty to instruct his teaching in economic theory and economic history.

Unfortunately the time granted to Toynbee was very short. He died early in March 1883. Barnett took steps to ensure that the link should not be broken. In 1884 on his motion, Toynbee Hall was founded as a memorial to be a settlement in White-chapel where men of the educated classes, of all denominations or of none, should live their own lives, but live them in constant contact with the realities of life in the East End and with the problems to which those realities gave rise.

This was not a new idea. In 1864 Thring of Uppingham had been anxious to find a way in which rich boys should learn to help poor boys and in 1869 he started what must have been the first school mission. In 1869, also, he encouraged Nettleship, already at Balliol, to base the foundation of his thought and knowledge on the realities to be learnt by visiting the poor, and two years earlier another Oxford man, Edward Denison, had made the experiment of trying to learn about the conditions under which the poor lived by living among them.[1]

Denison, who had been born in 1840, was the son of the bishop of Salisbury and nephew to the truculent Archdeacon Denison. He may well have inherited his social conscience from his father, who in the cholera outbreak of 1849 insisted on visiting, as bishop, every house in Salisbury where the disease had

---

[1] G. R. Parkin, *Edward Thring, Headmaster of Uppingham. School, Life, Diary and Letters* (2 vols., 1898) Vol. I, pp. 283, 310, 312. Sir Baldwyn Leighton, Bart., ed., *Letters and other Writings of the late Edward Denison, M.P. for Newark* (People's edition, 1875).

broken out. Edward Denison the younger was educated at Eton and Christchurch, and after travelling abroad he settled down to study law. While he was doing this he became an almoner for the Society for the Relief of Distress in the Stepney district. This experience taught him how unsatisfactory were the results of giving relief 'by doles' and the need for more knowledge. To gain this he moved in 1867 to Philpot Street off the Mile End Road. There he remained for eight months, teaching in a school he had built and endowed, giving classes to adults and learning what he could. In all this he seems to have been followed by one Edmund Hollond, a Cambridge man, also destined for a legal career, who became a leading figure in the Charity Organization Society and was incidentally the man who persuaded the bishop of London to present Samuel Barnett to St Jude's, Whitechapel.

It was while Denison was living in the East End that the idea of a settlement was first sketched out. According to Brooke Lambert, about this time Ruskin summoned Denison, possibly Hollond, J. R. Green who was then serving St Philip's Stepney and himself, the vicar of St Mark's, Whitechapel, to discuss whether something could not be done for the poor. Denison and Green hit on the idea of a group of university men living as Denison was doing, that is pursuing their own professions but living in an East End district, where they could study its problems, improve its culture and serve on local boards, to do which they would have to become ratepayers in the appropriate locality. According to Lambert this scheme would have been an innovation since 'Those were days when the work in East London was almost wholly religious, in the common acceptance of the term. There was not then the same outlet for the philanthropy of men, who, whatever their religious views, may choose the field of non-religious work' – he was writing in 1884.[1]

In 1867 the matter went no further. Denison's sojourn in the East End was short, and so was his life. In 1868 he travelled to France, and then Edinburgh, to study different systems of poor relief. At the general election of 1868 he contested Newark as a Liberal. He won the seat, but was already in the grip of a fatal disease. He had almost at once to give up his seat and in 1869 he left for Australia, partly to prospect the lines of emi-

[1] In *Contemporary Review*, Vol. XLVI (September 1884) p. 377.

gration and partly in the hopes of regaining his health by a long sea voyage. The voyage was fatal, and in January 1870 he died at Melbourne within a fortnight of landing.

In 1884, however, with the foundation of Toynbee Hall the idea became a reality. It spread rapidly. Just before the First World War a German scholar, Dr Werner Picht, wrote a book on the English Settlement Movement in which he listed 39 settlements which had been started in England between 1884 and 1914, 27 of them in London. There were also 5 in Scotland, 1 in Wales and 1 in Belfast, and this calculation seems to leave out of account a number of college and school missions which were founded in the same period. Many of these settlements started their existence under the auspices of some religious denomination, most often the Church of England, but several of them were frankly secular from the beginning, and many of the activities of the religious settlements and clubs were the same as the activities of the secular ones. Indeed it is noticeable that the Ratcliffe Settlement in the Commercial Road, which had started under the aegis of the Church of England, made it-self independent in 1907 'in order not to be affected by the existing prejudice against the Church'.

Many of the settlements had among their objects not only the provision of such services as the running of clubs for boys and girls or old people, free legal advice and various cultural and medical facilities, but also the study of social problems. Such study was of course most likely to bear fruit in legislation or policy if future legislators and administrators, civil servants or politicians, were for a time members of a settlement; and it is in this matter that the record of Toynbee Hall is outstanding. A very remarkable number of people who would later be influential were at one time connected with it, and in some cases it started a man on a career of social service which would in the end have an important influence on the development of public policy. This would seem to be true of Hubert Llewellyn Smith who, as a civil servant, was the real architect of some of the most important social legislation before 1914; it was also largely true of William Beveridge who was also important before 1914, but whose main claim to fame is the plan of social in-surance which was adopted after the Second World War. C. R. Attlee, who became leader of the Labour party and prime minister, was for a time secretary of Toynbee Hall; but his career started in connection with the Haileybury School Mission where he lived for a time. He is, however, a good example of a man whose career received its first direction through the experiences gained in the settlement system.[1]

This history, starting in Marylebone and ending in Toynbee Hall and the social legislation of the twentieth century, seems therefore to plot the road which was traversed in much of the development of social thought in the last period of the nineteenth century. It begins with a religious impulse and the adaptation of a religious tradition, in this case the parochial tradition of the Church of England. It soon becomes necessarily undenominational, and then the directly religious element in it fades, and it ends in the hands of secular, and professional, social scientists, administrators and politicians, supported by the legislation of a secular State.

This was a decisive change; but besides the secularization and professionalizing of the conception of social service there was another important development going on, and there is another turning point to plot from this history. It is more a change of attitude which seems to come between Edward Denison and Arnold Toynbee. Denison was in his way and for his day an enlightened man. He welcomed the advent of the power of labour which he saw in the reports of the meeting of the first international in 1866.[2] He defended trade unions. He thought that they had done much for the working man, though he doubted whether they had put more money into his pocket.[3] He did not shrink from the extension of the power of the State, but believed that if Britain needed a stronger executive it must be under effective democratic control.[4] In spite of the direction of his last desperate journey he saw that it was impossible to solve the problem of poverty by shovelling out paupers in

---

[1] Dr Werner Picht, *Toynbee Hall and the English Settlement Movement* (revised edition translated from the German by William A. Cowell, 1914) pp. 92–102 and 209–45 (development of the settlement and the details of other settlements) and p. 31 for important members of Tonybee Hall.

[2] Leighton, *Letters of Denison* [op. cit., p. 281] pp. 28–9.

[3] ibid., pp. 124–6.

[4] ibid., pp. 25–6.

indiscriminate emigration overseas, which was the facile remedy that appealed to a large number of those who were comfortably off.[1] Yet, in spite of this, his thought seems to move within the limits that restricted so many of his contemporaries. There is the over-emphasis on the dangers of pauperism, on the effect of ill-considered monetary doles, on the need for a stricter administration of the Poor Law, on the importance of co-ordinating charitable effort, in fact an emphasis on the policies that led to the Charity Organization Society.

There is no ground for personal criticism here. Denison's preoccupations were shared by most of those who were at that moment intelligently and humanely interested in the problems of the London poor – by Fremantle, by Brooke Lambert, by J. R. Green, by Samuel Barnett and, reluctantly, by Henrietta Barnett. It is true that in due course Samuel Barnett was revolted by the attitude of the Charity Organization Society and that Henrietta Barnett had a dream, which she regarded as a message, that she was one of the undeserving poor; and they both adopted larger views. But they had both assented to the policy of the Charity Organization Society for a longish period, and there is no knowing how Denison's views would have developed if he had been granted more time.

Even as it was, Denison's views on the central problems of the Poor Law were within their limits percipient and intelligent. As he saw it the poor law authorities in the East End had, in order to save money, satisfied themselves by giving the destitute inadequate monetary doles instead of supporting them in the workhouse. As these doles were little more than a mockery, private benevolence had been called in to do what it should never have had to do, and had brought with it all the disastrous results of ill-regulated charity. What was needed was a better regulated administration of the Poor Law. Relief should be adapted to the condition of those who applied for it. There should be discrimination between the treatment of the temporary destitution of highly skilled artisans and the relief of those whose distress was chronic. Special provision should be made for the sick and impotent, and the union officers should have the delicate task of relieving the aged and hopelessly infirm in their own homes. Sharp and certain punishment should

[1] ibid., pp. 19 and 149.

be imposed on the beggar and the vagrant. Much of this is a return to the Poor Law of 1834 as it was intended to be, but at one point he saw further than the first poor law reformers. He realized that they never considered sufficiently seriously how they should find work for the destitute.[1]

All this was intelligent and humane as far as it went, but unfortunately it did not go far enough. Denison was anxious to better the condition of the poor, he wished to improve their education and housing, but he does not seem to have realized how hardly the structure of society and the working of the economic system pressed upon them. Consequently he exaggerated what could be done for them, or rather what they could do for themselves, without effecting changes in that structure or that system. He seems to have placed exaggerated hopes on the results of a greater mobility of labour. He greatly exaggerated the amount that a young unmarried labourer could save to protect himself against the accidents of later life. He probably exaggerated the extent to which personal failure was the cause of pauperism, and he certainly exaggerated the probable results of a reform of the Poor Law as an effective cure for the problem of poverty.[2]

The cause of his blindness would seem to lie in the fact that, in spite of his intelligence and his patent sincerity and honesty, in spite of his commendable desire to see things for himself, he yet saw the problems of poverty from the outside. He saw them instinctively from a secure position in an accepted social hierarchy with a defensible economic system. His way of looking at things seems to be reflected in a comment which he made and repeated on the cause of the plight of those people in the district he was studying: 'I imagine that the evil condition of the population is rather owing to the total absence of residents of a better class – to the dead level of labour which prevails over that wide region, than to anything else.'[3] No doubt this was in its way true. An educated class with some leisure, a little removed from the dire struggle for existence, was badly needed in the East End to watch over the behaviour of the officers of the Poor Law, to keep the sanitary authorities up to the mark

[1] ibid., pp. 83 and 146–8.
[2] ibid., pp. 20, 61–83, 85.
[3] ibid., pp. 17, 63, etc.

and to give intelligent thought to all the problems involved. What the statement lacks is a realization of those aspects residents of a better class might fail to see because they were of a better class. It is worth while comparing this statement with the often-quoted last words of Arnold Toynbee spoken at the end of a lecture he gave in January in 1883, partly about, partly to, some workmen in his audience, who had 'shouted for revolution':

> What I do feel is, that they are justified, in a way, in looking with dislike and suspicion on those who are better-to-do. We – the middle classes, I mean, not merely the very rich – we have neglected you; instead of justice we have offered you charity, and instead of sympathy we have offered you hard and unreal advice; but I think we are changing.[1]

The words were spoken at the end of the last of two lectures which had as their object the criticism of Henry George's book, *Progress and Poverty*, which at that moment had great vogue. It was for Toynbee a moment of great exhaustion. He had been too weak to deliver part of what he had intended to say in his last lecture, and he had less than two months more of life left to him. Yet the lectures are not gloomy or pessimistic. The last sentence was neither casual nor uncertain in its meaning. It was to Toynbee a fact pregnant with importance and hope that the middle class was 'changing' in this context, and the lectures are full of a programme which all classes could accomplish together – the taxation of land values so far as that was practicable, a remodelled House of Lords, county boards, better sanitary education and so on and so forth. As a programme it looks nowadays both moderate and jejune, but together with what else he had to say it spells out a change of attitude which is all important.

In fact middle-class speakers had before this said things quite as severe about their own class and were prepared to support much more advanced programmes. This was true of some of the clergy. As far back as 1869 Thomas Hancock, preaching to a middle-class congregation, had said: 'The spirit of the Son of Man speaking to the Church through the artisans and the

---

[1] *'Progress and Poverty': a criticism of Mr. Henry George being two lectures delivered in St. Andrew's Hall Newman Street, London by the late Arnold Toynbee MA Senior Bursar and Tutor of Balliol College Oxford* (1883) p. 53.

labourers of our time asks for justice, for rights. We ask Him to be content with alms and charities.'[1] In 1881 Charles Marson arrived at St Jude's, Whitechapel, 'surfeited with all the middle-class patterings while the poor rot just because we are not brave enough to quarrel with usury, anarchy, competition, swindling, banking, etc.'[2] Meanwhile in 1870 Stewart Headlam had started his tempestuous clerical career and in 1877 he initiated with 40 members his Guild of St Matthew, which in 1884 held an open-air demonstration in Trafalgar Square at which all churchmen were urged to support measures which would among other things restore to the people the value they gave to the land and bring about a better distribution of the wealth created by labour.[3]

Arnold Toynbee's declaration was more significant than the statements and proposals of these men partly because he was more influential and representative. Though perhaps few of the ordinary upper-class people would have said what he said, yet, as far as the upper and middle classes were concerned, his whole position was nearer the high road along which very many men and women of good will were going to advance. But what he said is also significant because in saying it he had the know-ledge and percipience to recognize those historical forces that had provided the circumstances which made the hopes that he had expressed in his speech practicable ones.

One of those forces was naturally the development of democracy. It was the principle of democracy which would lead to the co-operation of the middle class with the working class. Toynbee saw in democracy a unifying principle, which though it might force individuals to abandon special advantages would compensate them by re-uniting them to the main body of the community. Certainly the victory of democracy over oligarchy was necessary for the realization of his programme, but his programme had also become practicable because a critical stage had been reached in another conflict of forces, which he describes in the first of his lectures.

It was the conflict between what he calls 'the socialists' – a term which he is surely using loosely here, and the 'econo-

[1] T. Hancock, *Christ and the People* (1875) p. 17.
[2] Maurice B. Reckitt, ed., *For Christ and People* (1968) p. 94.
[3] F. G. Bettany, *Stewart Headlam: a biography* (1926) pp. 79–96.

mists'. He believed that this was a conflict which dated back to the industrial revolution. It was, he said, then that the great 'socialist' writers appeared. But

> the same epoch, which gave birth to the socialists, gave also birth to their enemies the economists. These writers – Malthus, James Mill, David Ricardo – men of intellect and upright character, framed an explanation of the misery they saw before them which denied hope to the human race.

They did this by affirming the existence of economic laws which inexorably controlled the human condition and destiny, without regard for human wishes and values. Those who pleaded for humanity, Thomas Arnold, the Christian Socialists and above all Carlyle protested bitterly against the policies which this conception dictated. The first dawning conception of the claims of humanity by an economist came in J. S. Mill's *Principles* published in 1848, but by 1883 the battle was won.

> At last it is now apparent to all the world, that the long and bitter controversy between economists and human beings has ended in the conversion of the economists. The economist now dares to say that the end of his practical science is not wealth, but man; and further, he owns that his intellectual theories have also undergone a vast change. He has learnt to recognize that the laws which he supposed were universal are often only partial and provisional.[1]

It is not altogether easy to make all the details of this conflict as Toynbee describes it in this lecture fit in with what would appear to be the relevant facts of history. Nevertheless in general he was certainly right. There was, certainly, this bitter conflict between those who claimed to speak for political economy and those who claimed to speak for humanity. It is also true that it had reached a critical point with the beginning of the third phase of nineteenth-century history and the retreat from *laissez-faire*. To that conflict I will devote my next chapter.

[1] Toynbee, *Progress and Poverty* [op. cit., p. 287] pp. 6–7.

II

The Dismal Science
and its Enemies

Without doubt the controversy between those who spoke in the name of political economy, and those who claimed to speak for humanity lies at the centre of the history of social and public policy in nineteenth-century Britain; but it is not always easy to define the issues involved or to identify the contestants. This is partly because the policy of the economists is often summed up in the comprehensive phrase '*laissez-faire*', which presumably implies a policy in which government interference was reduced to its barest essentials, but in fact this wish to limit government activity was often promoted by historic traditions which had nothing to do with economic thought. But confusion is also caused by the fact that it is not always clear which economists taught the doctrines that are thought to be opposed to the claims of humanity.

Certainly 'the political economists' as a group played an important part in the intellectual, indeed in the emotional, life of nineteenth-century Britain. There were two views of their nature. To many they were the best minds in the country whose teaching it was folly to question and disastrous to disobey. There were others for whom 'the economists' formed part of the demonology of the time; they were men who were responsible for a dark orthodoxy which made intolerable claims to infallibility, forbade the exercise of all humane and Christian feeling and inexorably enshrined the pursuit of wealth as the only desirable, indeed the only possible objective for corporate human endeavour. It is possible to sympathise with the impulse behind the feeling on both sides, but not always to be sure whether those who were venerated, or repudiated, did actually say, or mean, what was credited to them.

In fact it is clear that sometimes they did not do so. There is, for instance, a marked contrast between the harsh doctrine which was conceived to be imposed by those who have a right to be called the classical economists, and any reasonable interpretation of the implication of their own words. Of all the classical economists the most consistently attacked and vilified was Thomas Malthus on account of his fear of over-population. But any impartial study of his life and writings shows clearly that both the objects and content of his teaching were normally, and for that matter still are, consistently misrepresented. Lord Robbins has demonstrated that much of what popular, indeed educated, mythology has ascribed to Ricardo is a travesty of his meaning and intentions.[1] The case against the classical economists has often been based on the supposition that they wholeheartedly opposed the laws passed to protect the factory children, yet in 1833 McCulloch, who has been called the last of the classical economists, wrote to Ashley to tell him that the political economists were not necessarily against him, that he personally had been deeply impressed by the evidence about the ill-treatment of children which had been given before the select committee of the House of Commons over which Michael Sadler had presided, and that if he were a member of the House he would support the bill for their protection, though he 'would not interfere between adults and masters'. In fact an eminent economist, Torrens, did support Ashley's bill in the House of Commons.[2] But even leaving this special case on one side, it seems clear that the objects of the classical economists have been consistently misunderstood. It was their object to make an abstract study of the conditions which control one side of life on the supposition that one human motive, the pursuit of wealth, was all that need be considered. This was an intellectual exercise of the greatest value if the mechanics of society were to be understood; but to undertake it was not tantamount to an assertion that the desire for wealth was the only one that moved the hearts of men and women. Nor was the enquiry intended to

[1] See G. F. MacCleary, *The Malthusian Population Theory* (1953); Lionel Robbins, *The Theory of Economic Policy in English Classical Political Economy* (1952).

[2] Edwin Hodder, *The Life and Works of the Seventh Earl of Shaftesbury K.G.* (2 vols., 1886) Vol. I, pp. 157–8; J. T. Ward [op. cit., p. 63] pp. 411–14.

yield a code of laws which must for ever control human affairs, and could not be set aside even if the dictates of humanity required it.

Nevertheless the classical economists were themselves partially responsible for the fact that they were misunderstood. There can, for instance, be no doubt at all about the humanity of Malthus, but unfortunately now and again he produced a phrase or simile, like the notorious passage about 'nature's mighty feast', which could appear to be the expression of the most heartless brutality.[1] Lord Robbins admits that Ricardo's elliptical style and his abstract treatment of problems of deep human interest, such as the factors which determined the rate of wages, were at least in part responsible for a misconception about the spirit in which he viewed society; and the articles which McCulloch contributed between 1818 and 1837 to the *Edinburgh Review* suggest a conviction of personal infallibility, a habit of mind which some people were to find intolerable in economists, and an emphasis on the universal validity of the necessity for unrestricted competition, which some people would reasonably believe to be immoral.[2]

In fact the tone of McCulloch's articles suggests that, however unjust it might be to some of the eminent classical economists, the attack on the political economists in general was not altogether mistaken. This opinion is confirmed by the work of the publicists and politicians who took over the abstractions of the classical economists and turned them into dogma that was cruder, more absolute, more all-embracing, and more useful as ammunition in controversy. The first of these seems to be Mrs Marcet, who published her *Conversations in Political Economy* in 1816. In the thirties and forties she was followed by Harriet Martineau and men like John Macgregor; while from 1838 onwards political economy supplied Cobden with his most effective weapons in his fight for the repeal of the Corn Laws.

In whatever spirit it had originally been conceived political

---

[1] This can be found in T. R. Malthus, 'An Essay on the Principles of Population' (quarto edition, 1803). It was cut out from the 1807 edition, but it is available in J. M. Keynes, *Essays in Biography* (1933) p. 126.

[2] F. W. Fetter, *The Journal of Political Economy* (U.S.A.) Vol. LXI, No. 3, June 1953, 'The Authorship of Economic Articles in the *Edinburgh Review* 1802–47'. (I owe this reference to the kindness of Mr P. Sraffa.)

economy was in fact being drawn in to serve the controversial purposes of competitive capitalist society. The process can be recognized in the attitudes adopted towards this very problem of the legislation to protect children and 'young persons' in factories. Although McCulloch had sympathized with Ashley, Harriet Martineau believed that Ashley had been 'largely duped'. In 1837 Nassau Senior, recently professor of political economy at Oxford, a man who had apparently disapproved of excessive hours of labour for children, went on a tour of the factory districts. There he was obviously heavily indoctrinated by the factory owners, and on his return he published his opinion that a ten hour bill, such as Ashley and his friends were demanding, would be ruinous, that further restrictions on the hours observed in factories where 'young persons' were employed – that is on 12 hours a day for 5 days in the week, and 9 hours on Saturday – would not be safe, and that labour in a cotton factory was so easy and light that long hours were practicable, and not inhumane.[1]

There is an even more interesting later example of the kind of statements economists were making. In 1844 *The Edinburgh Review* printed an article on the labour of women and children. It admitted, frankly, the bad state of education and of living conditions in the factory districts, but it claimed that much of the agitation about the sufferings of the factory children was 'morbid' and it proposed as effective remedies for all their ills, unrestricted free trade and a universal system of secular education. Under unrestricted free trade 'according to the best informed of our practical economists', the field of employment would be capable of indefinite enlargement, thereby no doubt giving the working class the power to control the conditions of their work. Under a system of general secular education men and women would gain the necessary knowledge of 'the laws which regulate wages' and 'of the relations of population to subsistence'. It would also teach them to what colonies they might emigrate in the unlikely event of free trade not creating for them sufficiently advantageous conditions at home. Though this could not be known at the time the writer was one W. R. Greg, who was not only an economist, or at least a publicist who

[1] Nassau Senior, *Letters on the Factory Act as it affects the Cotton Manufacture addressed to the Right Honourable the President of the Board of Trade* (1837).

spoke in the name of political economy, but also a prominent Liberal manufacturer, who had, as it happened, been fined for overworking children in his factory.[1]

Thus was erected round the competitive capitalistic society of nineteenth-century Britain that curtain wall of close argument, dogmatic assertion, embattled prejudice and class interest, which went by the name of the 'laws of political economy'. If the classical economists had not erected it they had supplied many of the materials from which it was built and the authority of their name for its defence. Their methods and systems were not forgotten in its erection or wholly subordinated to prejudice or interest in its defence. If it had not been for their work this curtain wall would not have appeared so unassailable to so many men of good will.

The same mixture of abstract argument and social pressure that erected the wall, in the end made a breach in it. At the beginning of the third phase there was a change in the opinions of the economists. For instance in 1869 W. T. Thornton published his treatise *On Labour, its Wrongful Claims and Rightful Dues; its Actual Present and its Possible Future*, in which he criticized the doctrine of the wage fund, which was the foundation of the superstition that it was not possible either for trade union action or legislation to affect the rate of wages. The treatise was reviewed by J. S. Mill in the *Fortnightly Review*. Mill in general accepted Thornton's argument, saying with characteristic honesty: 'I must plead guilty to having, along with the world in general, accepted the theory without qualifications and limitations necessary to make it admissible.' It was an important admission, at a turning point in Mill's life, for there are intimations that in his last years Mill was a 'qualified socialist'.[2]

But the breach in the curtain wall was affected not so much by a development of doctrine as by the social and political changes of the time. It was the passing of the Second Reform Bill which made it necessary to give the protection of law to the

---

[1] *The Edinburgh Review*, Vol. LXXIX (January–April 1844) pp. 130–5. For the identification of its author, see Fetter [loc. cit., p. 292]. For Greg as an employer, see J. T. Ward [op. cit., p. 63] p. 202.

[2] J. S. Mill, *Dissertations and Discussions*, Vol. IV (1875) p. 43; Clapham, *Economic History* [op. cit., p. 18] Vol. II, pp. 482–3.

trade unions and their activities. And it was then that men and women in the upper classes had to accommodate themselves to the loss of the doctrines of the wage fund and of the inexorable settlement of wages by the laws of supply and demand. A profound change in current doctrine had been forced by a change in the distribution of wealth in society and the need to take account of the requirements of classes whose wishes had hitherto not been sufficiently considered. 'It was,' said Arnold Toynbee,

> the labour question, unsolved by the removal of restrictions, which was all that deductive Political Economy had to offer, that revived the power of observation. Political Economy was transformed by the working classes. The pressing desire to find a solution of problems which the abstract science treated as practically insoluble, drew the attention of economists to neglected facts.[1]

It is, however, significant for the history of social morality that, even though an effective breach was not made in the wall that encircled the minds of so many men till the third phase of the nineteenth century had well begun, the political economists had been under attack since early in the century. Christians and churchmen had been on both sides of this battle. Many Christians of all denominations were impressed by the cogency of the arguments of the economists. On the other hand there were always groups in the Church who rejected their arguments with the most severe anathemas. The existence of such men might be of importance to the Church when the breach was effected and the barriers were falling down.

The first of these critics were the evangelicals acting on the impulse which has already been suggested in an earlier chapter. The pioneer was Michael Thomas Sadler, a Leeds businessman of near Methodist origins and a strong Tory, who opposed both Catholic emancipation and the reform of Parliament. He attacked the doctrines of Ricardo as early as 1819, but it was in 1830 that he made his most extended assault on the economists in a book on the population problem. The book is prolix and confused, but it is not as ridiculous as Macaulay made it out to be in one of his destructive reviews. It does in fact make one

---

[1] Arnold Toynbee, *Industrial Revolution, a Reprint of Lectures on the Industrial Revolution in England, popular addresses, notes and other fragments* (1884) *with a new introduction by T. S. Ashton* (Newton Abbot, 1969) p. 10.

general point of considerable importance; but perhaps it is most remarkable for the severity of its attacks on the much misrepresented Malthus and his supposed repudiation of Christian charity. Sadler was, however, more important as a practical politician than as a theorist, and in 1829 he entered Parliament for Newark with the intention of opposing Catholic emancipation and of furthering certain social objectives, which had long been maturing in his mind.

He wished to introduce poor laws into Ireland at the expense of the Irish landlords. This would reduce suffering in Ireland and at the same time prevent the Irish poor from flooding into England and bringing down wages. He wished to protect the English agricultural labourer, whose lot he believed had steadily worsened in his lifetime owing to the practice of pulling down cottages and squeezing out smallholders, practices which he attributed to the introduction of the precepts of political economy into estate management; and he wished to protect the children in factories. He did not get very far towards achieving any of these objectives, but he took a step of considerable importance for the factory children. When in the autumn of 1831 he returned to Yorkshire he was pressed to take up the promotion of the legislation for which Richard Oastler was agitating, and when Parliament met again he obtained leave to introduce a bill to regulate the hours of labour of children and young persons. He proposed the bill's second reading in March 1832 in an eloquent speech of great length, which seems to have excited much interest, and which was reprinted as a pamphlet. To his great disappointment the bill was referred to a select committee, of which however he was chairman. Owing to the imminence of the general election of 1832 the work of the committee had to be hurried forward, and its report was very one-sided. But its effect on public opinion seems to have been important.[1]

This was, in fact, the beginning of a crusade invoking the sanctions of Christianity against an industrial system sanctioned by political economy, or what passed for political economy. There had been earlier attempts to protect the factory children,

[1] For Sadler's life, see R. B. Seeley, *Memoirs of M. T. Sadler* (1842). This needs to be supplemented by the article in Vol. XVII of the *D.N.B.*, pp. 594–8.

but they had been the sporadic efforts of benevolent individuals. This had greater popular support, greater continuity and greater significance. Sadler did not lead the movement for long. He lost his seat in Parliament in 1832 and never regained it, so that the ten-hours parson, G. S. Bull, invited another evangelical Tory, Lord Ashley, to take up the work. Ashley at that time knew nothing of the factory districts, though he may have received from an early mentor, Robert Southey, a distaste for manufacturers as men who did not respect the values of the old system. However, he accepted the task as a matter of duty, and thus involved himself in painful, frustrating and arduous work which would demand much of the rest of his life; for the defence of the children in the textile factories led to the defence of children employed in mines, in brickfields, in agriculture and so forth. Ashley's principles forbade that such as these should be at the mercy of the free competition of a ruthless capitalistic society.

There were, of course, many who did not share Ashley's religious and political views who also condemned the principles of free competition and the society which was the creation of a freely operating capitalist system, or who were at the least prepared for government to interfere with industry in particular matters. There were Owenites, Chartists and other men and women of advanced views, and there were those who may well have accepted in general the philosophy of the economists, but felt that certain things must be forbidden in the name of humanity. However, the principle on which Ashley based his life is unquestionable and significant. He acted as a Christian member of a Christian society in which the factory child, the ragged child and the lunatic had as much right to protection as any of those whom the competitive system favoured.

But the Christian society which Ashley assumed was an hierarchical one. He did his work as a Christian nobleman, and in the period that was to come, when many people would condemn the principles and results of a freely competitive capitalist society they would also condemn the principles of an hierarchical one. Therefore if the conception of a Christian society was to be acceptable it would have to be presented untrammelled by this legacy from the past.

It is, of course, also true that Ashley's religion was of an

unusually rigid and unaccommodating character, and that towards the end of his career his mind possibly stiffened and could
not adapt itself to the conditions of a rapidly developing situation. The intellectual issue is, however, probably not relevant.
What was needed in the middle of the century was a moral
condemnation of the society which seemed to have come into
existence through the operation of principles sanctioned by the
economists, and also of the system which had been inherited from
the inequalities of the past. As it happens an intellectual criticism of the work of the classical economists from a Christian point
of view was available. Richard Jones, at one time a clerical
fellow of Caius College, Cambridge, and subsequently, first from
1833 to 1835 a professor at King's College, London, and then
from 1835 till his death in 1855 a professor at Haileybury,
attacked Ricardo and his school for apparently asserting that
future developments in economic affairs could be deduced from
a relatively small number of preconceived principles. Such a
view, if it was what Ricardo had intended to maintain, implied
a deterministic view of human conduct which was incompatible
with the Christian doctrine of human responsibility, and Jones'
views were warmly supported by William Whewell, the master
of Trinity College, Cambridge. The insufficiency of the objectives
of the economists and their tendency to over-confident dog-
matism were also attacked in a sermon by Adam Sedgwick
which attained considerable notoriety in academic circles. But
none of this seems to have got far beyond academic circles. It
was intelligent and it was largely justified, but it does not seem
to have been what a very large section of the public needed.[1]

Much the same line of attack was adopted later in the century
by another clerical scholar, Archdeacon Cunningham, the
pioneer of the Cambridge school of economic history. Cunningham's studies convinced him that the principles of political
economy did not supply a satisfactory explanation of what
happened when applied to the facts of history and that the only
satisfactory method was to approach the facts first and then to
produce a general explanation, if there was one. He also thought
he saw how it was that the theory of the classical economists had

---

[1] The Rev. William Whewell, D.D., ed., *Literary Remains, consisting of Lectures and Tracts, of the late Rev. Richard Jones* (1859) and Adam Sedgwick,
A Discourse on the Studies of the University (Cambridge, 1833) p. 75.

stiffened into the all-embracing dogmatic code that was presented for men's acceptance in the middle of the century.
Cunningham's teaching may have assisted in the disintegration
in the assumptions of the economists after 1870; he was a close
associate of T. H. Green and Arnold Toynbee and, as early as
1879, he realized that the era of free competition and private
enterprise was passing, and that the *a priori* condemnation of
socialism did not hold water. But his intellectual independence
and percipience did not fit him to be the leader of a large body
of opinion. The men who moved public opinion in the nineteenth century were men whose approach was not primarily
intellectual and analytical, but moral and prophetical; men
who pronounced their condemnation on society, rather than
on a system of thought.[1]

Fortunately the emotional and moral climate of mid nineteenth century Britain was congenial to prophecy. At least three
prophets can easily be named whose judgement on British society
carried weight. They are Dickens, Carlyle and Ruskin; and to
these should probably be added the Frenchman Auguste Comte,
whose English followers the positivists, though relatively few,
played an important part in the intellectual life of their time.
None of these men were orthodox churchmen, two of them were
explicitly antagonists of Christianity, all were critics of the social
order of which the clergy were part. Many of the clergy were
perilously committed to that order and apt to view attacks upon
it with dislike and fear; indeed it seems probable that with some
men the old fear of revolution lingered on in some form, to be
revived in 1871 by the history of the Commune in Paris and the
shooting of the archbishop.[2] But it is impossible to erect barriers
against the communication of ideas, and all churchmen, even
the clergy, lived in a society in which men and women were
listening to these prophets.

For instance, Comte regarded his positivism as a substitute

---

[1] A. Cunningham, *William Cunningham Teacher and Priest* (1950); *The Contemporary Review*, Vol. XXXIV (December 1878–March 1879) pp. 245–60:
'The Progress of Socialism in England'; *The Wisdom of the Wise* (Cambridge, 1906) pp. 3–31, etc.

[2] See, e.g., *A Charge delivered to the Clergy and Churchwardens of the Diocese of
Bath and Wells at the general visitation held in April and May 1873 by Arthur
Charles Hervey D.D. Lord Bishop of Bath and Wells* (1873) pp. 29–30.

L

for Christianity; nevertheless there were close links between the positivists and some important churchmen. Llewellyn Davies, a clergyman and leading Christian, was related by marriage to two of the leading positivists, and seems to have lived on intimate terms with them. A second Christian Socialist, Tom Hughes, worked alongside the positivist Frederick Harrison in defence of the trade unions, and a third, Bishop Westcott, claimed that he gained his insight into social thought from an analysis he made of Comte's *Politique Positive* for the *Contemporary Review*. He said he found Comte to contain 'a powerful expression of many salient features of that which I had long held to be the true social embodiment of the gospel'.[1] This is no doubt an extreme case, but it is an example of the way in which the ideas even of those who rejected Christianity could find lodgement in the minds of churchmen, and from that point act as leaven which might ferment at least part of the lump.

Of the prophets who have been named Carlyle and Ruskin were most likely to influence churchmen; for the view of Comte that was most likely to commend itself to them was not as a source of inspiration or as an ally, but as an antagonist.[2] Dickens was, it is true, for most of his life after some sort a churchman, and indeed the clergy of the established Church do not come badly out of his novels; the heaviest blows of his lash were reserved for a certain nonconformist preacher. But Dickens was a singularly undogmatic Christian, and a singularly unecclesiastical churchman, and had in fact a standing, and reasonable, objection to clerical attitudes towards the education of the very poor. But in any case his influence was likely to be diffuse; a more clearly defined body of opinion and a more definite impact was likely to be received from his friend Thomas Carlyle.

It is not easy nowadays to appreciate the significance of Thomas Carlyle in the middle of the nineteenth century. The style has become an irritant. His attitude to many of his contemporaries suggests an unpleasing arrogance. Throughout his work there seems to be a tendency to scold without offering any

[1] B. F. Westcott, *Social Aspects of Christianity* [op. cit., p. 10] Preface, p. xii, and *Contemporary Review* (1867) pp. 399–421.

[2] e.g., see W. H. Fremantle, the *Contemporary Review* (1866) pp. 477–98.

practical help or suggestion, and there are elements in his teaching which, in the light of hindsight, have sinister implications. Nevertheless there can be no doubt about the value of his influence between about 1840 and 1860. *Sartor Resartus* helped men to see much of what was wrong in a Britain still stifled by corrupt survivals and callous shams. His *French Revolution* persuaded men to view the Revolution not so much as something to be fought and feared, but as a terrible soul-searching experience through which a nation of ordinary human beings had passed, and which had a profound moral significance for their brothers and sisters in other countries. And his three great tracts, *Chartism, Past and Present* and *Latter Day Pamphlets* brought vividly before men's minds the terrifying seriousness of what he called 'the condition-of-England question' and the utter inadequacy of the thought of 'the professors of the dismal science' of economics.

All of this made an effective impression on many of the men and women of the middle of the century, but after the first shock it tended to lead nowhere, and for Christians it developed objectionable characteristics. Carlyle passionately adhered to his own smoky theism and was openly contemptuous of Christianity, as formulated by the Church of England. Hort, the biblical scholar, believed that he had learned much from Carlyle; nevertheless he recognized why Carlyle hated Coleridge, 'whose influence he considers to be the one thing which still keeps intelligent men from abandoning the Church and her crucified Lord and formulae for the "Destinies", "Eternal Radiances", etc. etc.'. There were other disturbing tendencies in Carlyle's teaching. In 1846 J. B. Mozley, regius professor of divinity at Oxford, and Newman's brother-in-law, in a review of Carlyle's *Oliver Cromwell's Letters and Speeches* made the case that Carlyle valued power above all things. 'For him,' said Mozley, 'a naked monarchy of force includes all causes, all effects, within it; and we see the one essence into which all action, feeling, thought is resolvable.'[1] This tendency and Carlyle's racialism were to have tragic sequels in the days of Fascism and Nazism.

Carlyle's mantle was adopted by Ruskin, though in fact many of Ruskin's ideas actually derived from his work as an art

---

[1] J. B. Mozley, *Essays: Historical and Theological* (2 Vols., 1878) Vol. I, p. 231.
A. F. Hort, *Life and Letters of F. J. Hort* (2 vols., 1896) Vol. I, pp. 205–6.

historian, a department in which Carlyle did not take much interest. Ruskin's ideas can be seen taking shape in his *Seven Lamps of Architecture* published in 1849 and in the chapter on the nature of Gothic in the *Stones of Venice*, but they were not made clear to the public till he presented them in 1860 in the articles to the *Cornhill* which excited such indignation. He reproduced his *Cornhill* articles in 1862 in his book *Unto this last*. This book is certainly a turning point in the history of morals in the nineteenth century, but it presents this difficulty. Like all Ruskin's later works it is full of savage denunciations of the economists, whose work Ruskin quite clearly did not understand. He seems only to have started reading them seriously after he had formed his opinions, and then to have read them in a spirit of uncomprehending hostility. This is a pity for, if he had been more patient, he might have realized that many of the objects and values of John Stuart Mill were the same as his own. As a critic of other men's ideas Ruskin was often arrogant and obtuse. But as a prophet reminding a successful and self-satisfied society of values it was inclined to neglect, he was what the country needed.[1]

In 1862 there were many who were not prepared to take the lesson patiently. The exponents of the old school of political economy were still in arrogant possession of much of the ground. At first *Unto this last* sold sluggishly, and the writings with which he followed it were consistently vilified; indeed in 1863 a series of articles which he started in *Fraser's Magazine* suffered the same fate as his articles in the *Cornhill*. It was between 1870 and 1880 that his vindication began. In 1870 he began his visits to Oxford as Slade Professor which had so much influence on a number of undergraduates and prepared the way for the Oxford of T. H. Green and Arnold Toynbee. At about the same time *Unto this last* began to sell widely. Between publication and 1873 less than a thousand copies were sold; 'a few years later' after republication it was selling at the rate of 2,000 a year. The third phase had started, the professors of the dismal science were in full retreat, and it was Ruskin who had at least given form to the change. When in 1906 the first large body of labour members

[1] J. Ruskin, *The Seven Lamps of Architecture* (1849), particularly aphorism 33; *The Stones of Venice* (3 vols., 1851–3) Vol. 2, Ch. VI, particularly paras. X–XIV; *Unto this last* (1862). J. T. Fain, *Ruskin and the Economists* (Nashville, Tenn., 1956).

was elected to Parliament a journalist collected from them lists of books which had influenced them, and the work which appeared upon most lists was *Unto this last*.[1]

The message of Carlyle and Ruskin was inextricably fused with that of another prophet whose work was unmistakably Christian and specifically directed at the Church of England as an established Church. It will be remembered that in 1836 F. D. Maurice had become chaplain to Guy's Hospital. In 1840 he also became professor of English literature and history at King's College, London. In 1846 he resigned from Guy's and became chaplain at Lincoln's Inn. While in these posts a number of young men gathered round him who found that he gave them something that they did not seem to get from other religious leaders. One of these was Charles Kingsley, then a young country parson, who was with Maurice one of the pioneers of the Christian Socialists.

Maurice was an unusual man with an unusual past (see pp. 60, 78). The son of a Unitarian minister, he had been an expositor of Coleridge's ideas and a Liberal journalist. He had become a priest, but he was a priest who did not wish to undertake parochial work or to accept preferment, and who conceived that his mission was to 'Quakers, Unitarians and Socialists'. It might be expected that such a man would stand free from the traditions of the Church of England in a way that might be denied to a man whose ancestry and career had been those of a conventional clergyman of the Church of England. In addition to this it is clear that Maurice possessed that unusual charismatic gift which enables a man to draw disciples to him and probably to found an original tradition or a new school. Nevertheless it is important to recognize that the point from which Maurice's ideas developed is much the same as the position adopted by other churchmen immediately after the First Reform Act. The basic principles of his *Kingdom of Christ* are really identical with those expounded by Gladstone in his first book, and it seems probable that Archdeacon Denison would not have disagreed with what Maurice wrote in his pamphlet on education. That he travelled away from that point along a road which diverged from the highway chosen by

[1] Cook, *Ruskin* [op. cit., p. 280] Vol. II, pp. 13–14 and 55–7.

most churchmen was partly no doubt due to the fact that his past and his position did not commit him either to normal responsibilities or prejudices; but it was also due to a quality which was peculiarly strong in him and was probably one of the things that attracted so many young men. It was also a quality that was going to be the cause of much trouble and bewilderment.

This quality can be recognized in a series of addresses which he gave on the Lord's Prayer in the fateful year of 1848. They were a passionate assertion of the claims of spiritual realities, the importance of which he believed to transcend all earthly values. In Maurice's view the obligations imposed by the facts of a common creation, redemption and humanity must underlie all distinctions of property, rank or political function, if those things were to be justified. The values which derived from what was spiritual demanded the fealty of a lifetime; for overriding the claims of kings, or enthusiasts, or of anyone else, were the absolute demands of the City of God.[1] Other preachers might have said comparable things and believed them in a general way, or with qualifications. To Maurice these beliefs struck home with a particular force that permitted no qualifications. It was probably this that gave his teaching its peculiar attraction; it was probably this that made him refuse compromises on social or political matters that were acceptable to more earth-bound people, and indeed, were probably necessary if any practical policy was to be pursued.

While he was delivering these addresses Maurice's approach was tested by the course of events. The man responsible for this challenge was one J. M. Ludlow. Ludlow was the son of a colonel in the East India Company's service. He grew up and was educated in France, where his mother had settled after his father's death. His religion was derived from French Protestants, his ways of thought were French, and, after a brilliant career in French schools, he would have wished to have made his career in France; but in 1838 in supposed deference to his dead father's wishes he returned with his mother to England. There he lived a lonely and unhappy life. He became a skilled conveyancer, but he made few friends and could not come to terms with

[1] F. D. Maurice, M.A., Chaplain of Lincoln's Inn, *The Lord's Prayer. Nine Sermons preached in the Chapel of Lincoln's Inn in the months of February, March and April* (1848).

English society. He got to know Maurice through some charitable work he was doing, but he was not impressed.

In February 1848 there was a new revolution in France and Ludlow returned to look after the safety of his sisters who were still in Paris. He was deeply impressed by the early idealistic phase of the 1848 Revolution as he saw it in the streets of Paris, or studied it in contemporary French literature. When he returned to England he unburdened his soul in a letter to Maurice, possibly because he knew no other suitable person to whom he could write. It was a turning point for both of them. It added a new dimension to Maurice's thought. It led him to see clearly not only what had been wrong in the France of Louis Philippe, but what was wrong in the England of Queen Victoria, and how false and disastrous was the current notion that the iron law of competition necessarily governed men's relations with one another. Maurice's immediate sympathy gave Ludlow a friend, counsellor and father, such as he had never had. Through Maurice he gained friends, for whom his enterprise, his European experience and his intelligence provided an important focus for action.

Yet Ludlow's relationship with Maurice was never easy. Their minds were cast in different moulds. Maurice was uncertain, imprecise and groping, and he retained English prejudices which even in a spiritualized form were unacceptable to Ludlow. Ludlow's mind was clear, well-disciplined and precise. He was a Republican, a believer in social equality. He desired an active policy, whereas Maurice shrank from all secular organization, since what he desired was the spiritual reformation of society. As a result there was constant trouble between them. Maurice took sudden actions which embarrassed Ludlow, and expressed uncertainties which Ludlow could not understand. Ludlow rebuked Maurice in letters of great severity; but they were the letters of a son to a father, whom he loves and above all needs.

In the spring of 1848, however, their friendship was new and events went forward in such a way as for the moment to obscure their differences. On 10 April the Chartists held their monster meeting. Charles Kingsley came to London in great anxiety. He called on Maurice who was confined to his house with a heavy cold; Maurice sent him round to Ludlow, and the two young men set off with the ambitious intention of preventing blood-shed as the result of a clash between Chartists and the forces of order. Before they reached the meeting it had broken up peace-ably; but they were still anxious and that evening they met in Maurice's house and drew up a suitable proclamation. Two days later they met again with others and set in hand the series of pamphlets entitled *Politics for the People*. Thereafter there were further meetings and conferences with working men. New people joined the movement – Charles Mansfield, a chemist and a friend of Kingsley's who became a close friend of Ludlow, Tom Hughes, the author of *Tom Brown's School Days*, Vansittart Neale, a wealthy man, who spent a fortune trying to establish co-operative industry, Lloyd Jones, an ex-Chartist, Lord Goderich, subsequently the Liberal marquis of Ripon, then at a very radical stage of his career, and others.

The movement rather rapidly gained some impetus, and some notoriety. They started a reasonably influential paper, and began practical efforts to encourage the development of co-operation, that is, ownership of the capital required for ex-change or production by the consumers or the workers and not by private capitalists. With this object they developed co-opera-tive associations for tailors and seamstresses in London, and got in touch with the vigorous co-operative movement in the north of England. They helped to provide co-operators with a national organization, and to steer the act of 1852, the law which was necessary for the satisfactory working of co-operative societies, on to the statute book. They got in touch with the most import-ant trade union, the Amalgamated Society of Engineers, in its bitter struggle with the employers who wished to destroy it. They also tried their hand at developing co-operative industry.

It is probable that in much of what they were doing they were doomed to failure. Co-operative enterprise could be successful when it was organized by working-class consumers who knew each other and knew what they wanted: even so, when co-operative concerns expanded and employed labour who did not share the dividend, it began to look distressingly like a form of capitalism.[1] But co-operation was not likely to

---

[1] D. J. Vaughan, *Questions of the Day, Social, National and Religious* (1894) pp. 67–76; *Sermon preached on Easter Day 1877, on the occasion of the 9th Co-operative Conference held at Leicester* (1894).

succeed when it was the artificial product not of the workers themselves, but of upper-class idealists, and of idealists, moreover, who wished to impose a special form of Christian affinity upon it. It is therefore not surprising that, with the exception of two tailors' associations which survived for a considerable time, their co-operative industries were failures. Nor was the attempt to establish co-operative industry the policy which promised best results for the working class at that time. At that moment the most hopeful policy was to organize effective trade unions to protect workers in an industrial system which was securely in the hands of capitalism; and as an ultimate objective a publicly controlled industry was probably going to be a more practicable ideal than an industry controlled by those who worked in it.

The Christian Socialists' objectives were not only mistaken, they were also divided in aims among themselves. Ludlow and others wanted to work for democracy, but Ludlow wanted to impress on the democratic cause a definite Christian allegiance to which other men objected, and which indeed would never have been acceptable in the society which was taking shape in Britain in the second half of the nineteenth century. Maurice objected to democracy since he regarded the claim to sovereignty on the part of the people as a blasphemous contradiction to the sovereignty of God. He was also increasingly unhappy at his involvement in a secular agitation, and increasingly at odds with Ludlow, whom he could not persuade to understand him. There were other personal difficulties between members. Consequently when, in 1854, Maurice obstinately refused to accept a pamphlet by Goderich that favoured democracy, the group came to an end as a coherent whole. Maurice retreated into purely educational activities and devoted himself to the development of a working man's college in Red Lion Square, and after a moment's hesitation, when he realized that he could have had the reversion of the leadership, Ludlow followed his master.[1]

---

[1] The pioneer work on the Christian Socialists is that of C. E. Raven [op. cit., p. 29]. This is, however, outdated by T. Christensen, *Origin and History of Christian Socialism 1848–54* (Aarhus, 1962). See also N. C. Masterman, *John Malcolm Ludlow* (Cambridge, 1963); F. Maurice, *Life of Frederick Denison Maurice* [op. cit., p. 111], and Alec R. Vidler, *F. D. Maurice and Company* (1966).

It is, however, a mistake to end the story in 1854. For one thing the working man's college was an important venture, particularly since, as has been seen, it was copied in a great many places outside London. It was a step in the extension of higher education, if not always to working men, at least beyond the favoured circles that could go to such universities as existed in England at that moment. More important than this was the ever-widening realization on the part of an increasing number of people of that Christian challenge to the practice and principles of mid nineteenth-century society which Maurice and his friends represented. From early on the movement had attracted public attention, not all of it favourable. In 1851 there had been an unfortunate incident in a church in London which had led to Kingsley being inhibited from preaching in London for a short period. In 1853 an article in the *Quarterly* censored both Kingsley and Maurice as men of subversive tendencies. This led to an attempt to get Maurice condemned by the authorities of King's College. It failed in 1853, but was renewed in 1854 under cover of an attack on Maurice's views on eternal punishment, and Maurice was forced to resign. However, these attacks do not seem to have had an adverse effect on Maurice's influence, nor for that matter do they seem to have inhibited the circulation of Kingsley's pamphlets and books; indeed it is possible that they added to the interest men took in both of them. Certainly in the years that followed the influence both of Maurice and Kingsley continued to grow.

Maurice's influence seems to have been particularly strong at his old college, Trinity College, Cambridge. For instance two fellows of the college, J. Llewellyn Davies and D. J. Vaughan, who were the first translators of *Plato's Republic*, were his faithful disciples. Both were remarkable men in their own day; but historians seem to have missed their significance, probably because each of them spent most of his life as a parish priest. Davies served first in Limehouse, then in Whitechapel and then from 1856 to 1889 at Christchurch, Marylebone (see p. 255), probably barred from the promotion which his ability merited by his pronounced social views. Vaughan after a period in London was vicar of St Martin's in Leicester from 1860 to 1895, and master of Wyggeston College, Leicester, from 1860 to 1900. Two other fellows of Trinity who came under Maurice's influence, Westcott and Hort, the editors of the standard edition of the New Testament in Greek, are probably better known. As has been said Westcott, whose mind tended to move in ways which were different from those in which the minds of other people moved and which were not always intelligible to them, developed his social thought from an analysis of Comte; but he confirmed his views by reading Maurice on *Social Morality*. The progress of Hort's views can be followed in the extremely full letters published in his biography. It is an extremely interesting account for it shows what influence was exercised over a young scholar and priest in the middle of the century by Carlyle and Maurice and the Christian Socialists – the more interesting because Hort seems to have been an unusually intelligent man who was able to stand a little apart from his mentors and to criticize them.

Such men were themselves likely to influence others. As has been seen the most important function of Davies seems to have been to act as an effective controversialist in favour of Maurice's views and the position of the Christian Socialists, but he also contributed articles of considerable interest to the kind of serious periodical, such as the *Contemporary*, which was important in those days in the formation of opinion. Vaughan was the preacher of able and possibly influential sermons, many of which have been printed; he also founded and nourished a working man's college at Leicester, which still exists under the name of Vaughan College: but probably Vaughan's greatest importance in the development of opinion was his influence over his nephew, T. H. Green, who carried something of his social attitude back to Balliol. Hort was for a considerable period the parson of a country parish and it is probable that his influence on contemporary opinion was less than these others, though it seems to have become considerable in Cambridge after 1870. Westcott's influence was probably the most extensive of all these men. He was from 1852 to 1869 a master at Harrow, between 1869 and 1883 a canon of Peterborough and between 1883 and 1890 a canon of Westminster, where he became a popular preacher to large congregations. He was regius professor of divinity at Cambridge from 1870 to 1890, and from 1890 till his death in 1901 a notable bishop of Durham, deeply interested in the affairs of a large mining population.

It is said that while at Harrow Westcott's sermons influenced Charles Gore, then a boy in the school, who became, as did Westcott, a prominent member of the Christian Social Union. Another man who seems to have carried the ideals of Christian Socialism into school teaching was William Johnson Cory, who was a master at Eton from 1845 to 1872. He had as pupils Scott Holland and Stewart Headlam. Scott Holland seems to have learnt his social principles at Balliol rather than Eton, but Johnson Cory certainly started Stewart Headlam on his turbulent career, though in due course Headlam's ideas were more directly influenced by Maurice's teaching and he passed thence to political and economic positions more extreme than Maurice would have approved.

By no means all of those who were influenced by Maurice were in the academic profession or the Church. At the outset of her career Octavia Hill began her work under the aegis of Maurice and the Christian Socialists, though it was Ruskin who gave her her great chance. In several cases it seems to have been Kingsley's novels that provided the first impact. As a boy of 14 William Cunningham started reading *Alton Locke* and was so disturbed by it that it prevented him from sleeping and his mother took it away from him. He finished it when at the University of Edinburgh and in due course became ordained as a priest in the Church of England and came to Cambridge largely inspired by the hope of continuing Maurice's work in theology and politics. But the spell of Kingsley extended beyond the clergy of the broad church. It was said of H. C. Shuttleworth, who was ordained in 1873: 'though he was a red-hot Ritualist, the authors to whom he was most inclined were not Newman or Faber, but Ruskin and Kingsley', and that later Kingsley led him on to Maurice.[1]

How far this leaven worked among the clergy and laity of the established Church between 1854 and 1880 would be hard to say. The teaching of Maurice and the Christian Socialists was not the only stimulant for social thought in that period; there are, for instance, several interesting cases of priests learning the case for greater social justice where from time to time men of all ages have found it, in their bibles. But from whatever source the inspiration came it is clear that in this period an increasing number of individuals in the Church were learning to condemn

[1] G. W. E. Russell, ed., *H. C. Shuttleworth, a Memoir* (1903), pp. 11 and 39.

the morals and principles of mid nineteenth-century society. The movement seems to have been in some respects impeded by official indifference or opposition. Probably the most serious casualty from this cause was a very interesting man, T. C. Hancock. Hancock was drawn into holy orders by Maurice, but thereafter received no appointment worthy of his capacity, indeed for much of his career he received no appointment at all.[1] Stewart Headlam, also, wasted much of his career in frustrating conflicts with ecclesiastical authorities, though his influence, particularly through the Guild of St Matthew, was considerable. But on the whole the varieties of private patronage, the protections afforded by the parsons freehold and the mildness of episcopal discipline allowed the socialist clergy a liberty to express their views which is surprising when the nature of the established Church is taken into account.

In 1880 and the years that immediately followed it there was a general change in secular opinion. By that time the social thought of the third phase was taking on a more definite shape, and as a result Socialism, in its more concrete modern forms, became what it had not been before, a creed and a programme which was taken seriously by a number of Englishmen. It seems probable that the man who more than anyone else precipitated this change was the American social reformer Henry George, who came to England in 1882 to lecture. As has been said he was answered from the Liberal point of view by Arnold Toynbee, but he was attacked on the other flank by H. M. Hyndman, acting as a spokesman for the views of Marx. This seems to have been the first time that Marxist Socialism really attracted the attention of any large part of the British public, but from now on Marx's doctrine became a serious factor in the social thought of the country. Henry George's advent was, however, at most nothing more than a catalyst. The crisis of opinion in this decade was the result of the long-term intellectual and social developments that had produced the conditions of the third phase, given force and focus by the economic and political circumstances of that moment. Those circumstances produced a good

[1] See the article on Hancock by Stephen Yeo in *For Christ and the People*, ed. by Maurice B. Reckitt (1968). Hancock's own published sermons are entitled *Christ and the People* (1875).

deal of militant trade unionism, particularly among the un-skilled, who also caused the riots in Trafalgar Square that culminated in 'Bloody Sunday'. At the same time a number of Socialist societies came into existence. In 1881 Hyndman and others founded the Democratic Federation which became in 1883 the Social Democratic Federation. There was also William Morris' Socialist League. But the society that was most likely to attract the educated was not committed to Marxist theory or a Marxist programme. In 1882 a society had been founded by a group of people who hoped to further the reform of society by the regeneration of their own lives, but in 1884 it was converted to the possibly more practical programme of the systematic study of social conditions with a view to the reconstruction of society through Socialism attained by non-revolutionary means. These were the Fabian Socialists, and the kind of programme they sponsored was of a kind that relatively moderate opinion might accept.[1]

The revolution in thought that was taking place had its effect on the opinions of the clergy, as was probably inevitable. In 1909 Archdeacon Cunningham wrote a paper on 'Christianity and Socialism' describing the development of opinion as he had seen it since 1879 when he wrote his article in the *Contemporary Review* on the development of Socialism. He asserted that in 1879 Socialism had had hardly any footing in England at all. The ordinary newspaper reader regarded it as a craze which took possession of hysterical foreigners, but which had no attraction for the common sense of Englishmen; trade union policy, he said, was entirely uninfluenced by it in the days of the Junta; there was little sign that its doctrine had any hold on literary circles before the publication of the *Fabian Essays* in 1889. But he said of 1909,

> the world has moved since then; many measures which the last generation would have condemned as socialistic have been passed by Parliament; and, in any gathering of clergy and ministers, there are sure to be many who take a pride in declaring that they are Christian Socialists. It may be doubted whether any such change in public opinion occurred even at the Reformation itself.[2]

[1] On the origin of the Fabians, see A. M. MacBriar, *Fabian Socialism and English Politics 1884–1918* (Cambridge, 1962).
[2] W. Cunningham, *Journal of the Transactions of the Victoria Institute*, Vol. XLI

Such a change was obviously important, and it raises a question which by its nature brings my book to an end. What was the phrase 'Christian Socialism' going to mean in the future? One thing was already clear. It could no longer mean what it had meant to Maurice and his friends. They had hoped for the supersession of capitalistic industry by co-operative industry. They had hoped, Maurice especially, that this change would come about voluntarily and peacefully, and being middle class in origin and habit of life, however devoted they were and however ready to sacrifice their own comforts they had probably assumed the continuance, in some sort, of middle-class society. But the revolution on which they had pinned their hopes had not taken place. Many of them clung to their old beliefs. But the contrast between their speeches and other speeches made in the same period, and often in the same debate, or, for example, the contrast between the views of Bishop Westcott and the views of the miners in his diocese, shows that the world had moved away from them. What now seemed to be needed was a harsher revolution, a more complete expropriation, which would end in an industry and a society working under a more severe discipline than voluntary co-operation would ever produce.[1]

The paramount question was what kind of society would men have to accept? Marxist Socialism rejected Christianity and regarded the institutions which had fostered it as the result of the exploitation of the workers. Even a milder form of social democracy would be likely to be agnostic, and to call into existence all-embracing public services which would leave little room for voluntary actions and independent opinions. How then would Christianity fare under such a system? But even without Socialism that question was posed by the collectivist State. To that issue therefore I will devote my last chapter.

(1990) p. 70. On the development of Christian Socialist thought, see Peter d'A. Jones, *The Christian Socialist Revival 1877–1914* (Princeton, N.J., 1968).

[1] e.g. the speeches of T. Hughes and Westcott, *Church Congress* (Hull, 1890) pp. 319–44. See also G. F. A. Best, *Bishop Westcott and the Miners* (The Bishop Westcott Memorial Lecture, Cambridge, 1966).

I2

The New Leviathan

At his thirteenth general visitation, which took place in May and June 1867, John Sandford, archdeacon of Coventry, delivered a charge which was primarily devoted to social problems.[1] In it he commented on the things which the improvement of moral feelings in the country had accomplished since he was a boy. It had put down slavery. It had humanized the manners of all classes, and had put down duelling. It had tempered the severity of the law and diminished capital punishment. It had mitigated the horrors of war, and promoted kindly relations with people of other races 'as far as they are attainable'. It had taught the lesson that to conciliate rather than to coerce, to reclaim rather than to punish, was the true object for legislation. Above all it had of late enlarged men's views of the nature of Christian charity. It was now realized that in order to remedy what was amiss it was the duty of Christians 'to investigate the causes of calamity; to explore the sources of suffering; to ascertain what creates, and intensifies, and perpetuates poverty; what originates and propagates disease; what is the originator and the feeder of profligacy and of crime.' He therefore asked a devastating question:

> Why is it that, with a physical organization, a strength of character and will, an aptitude for work unrivalled by other nations, the industrial classes in England in mental culture, in manner of living, in much which makes and ennobles the man, still fall so short of what they might be?

He gave three answers to his question. The chief causes were in his view: intemperance, the 'foul and fetid dwellings of the

[1] J. Sandford *Social Reforms, or the Habits, Dwellings and Education of our People* (a Charge, 1867) pp. 6–7, 9.

people' and the poorness of popular education. For the results of intemperance he cited the evidence of magistrates, judges, prison chaplains and the like; for the wretched housing conditions he cited a good deal of diverse evidence which he was apparently prepared to supplement from his own knowledge, and for the inadequacy of popular education he drew on the third report of the Manchester and Salford Education Aid Society, which had provided a turning point in the comprehension of this problem. Very significantly, in each case he attributed these ills to a failure, or inadequacy, in the law. The licensing acts had failed to control the sale of liquor and the number of public houses. The sanitary act, presumably the act of 1866, had also failed – a government inspector, who offered evidence not admissible in the columns of a newspaper, had said that the act was only permissive and partial in its administration. The existing system of education could not do what was needed for the people. 'My matured conviction,' said Sandford,

> is that without an educational rate – without some form of compulsory attendance – without a recognition of religious differences which confessedly exist in this country, the comprehensive and effective education which our needs demand will never be attained.

In fact Sandford's answer to his question forced him to recognize that the country must adopt a collectivist policy if the working classes of England were ever to have a chance of becoming what they ought to become. He did not see, however, how far this would have to go, or fully understand what it would mean. As did many others at that time he believed that an effective improvement in working-class housing could be produced by self-supporting, profit-earning organizations, and he did not realize what results an increased reliance on the power of the State to provide general education for the people might have for the Church. 'I do not admit,' said he, 'that either the establishment of an educational rate, or a system of compulsory education, need interfere with the existing plan of combining religious and Church teaching with secular instruction.'

Both Sandford's vision, and his blindness, were shared by not a few of his contemporaries among eminent churchmen.

They also saw the need for the further development of collectivism, and they also misunderstood what it was likely to mean for the Church of England. Their failure sprang very largely from the fact that they gave the wrong answers to the most important questions which were raised by the development of collectivism. If the State was to be entrusted with this great increase in power it must be credited with sufficient moral authority to justify its use of power, and should be directed by a philosophy which should inform it what it could, and still more what it could not, do. Whence, then, should it get that authority, or who would give it that philosophy? These were questions which Maurice and Gladstone had asked in 1838 and 1839; the strange thing is that intelligent churchmen in 1868 tended to give much the same answers as Maurice and Gladstone had done thirty years before.

For in 1868 there appeared a collection of *Essays on Church Policy*. Except for J. B. Seeley and one other, the writers were clergymen, apparently broad church clergymen.[1] They faced the same issues as Sandford, but while Sandford had been conducting his visitation the Second Reform Act had been passed. The Church had therefore to face the probability of the development of democracy in the form of household suffrage. In these circumstances it seemed probable that of all issues the educational problem was going to be the most critical. The article on 'The Church and the education of the People' was written by the editor, W. L. Clay, incumbent of Rainhall, Lancashire, who had apparently been a school inspector.

Clay believed that the existing system of education would be replaced by a State system, independent of voluntary zeal and liberality though prepared to utilize such things where they existed. In such a system the position of the parish clergyman would undoubtedly diminish, and there might be trouble where a clergyman tried to cling to his old authority, or withdrew his school from the national system. But where the clergyman was sensible and played his part with discretion and tolerance he would still fill an important role. There was, said Clay, no general desire to extrude the clergy. 'It is only a clique of half-bred liberals afflicted, like Mr Lowe, with cleri-

---

[1] W. L. Clay, *Essays on Church Policy* [op. cit., p. 130]. My attention was called to this book by Dr Shannon's article [op. cit., p. 285].

cophobia, who desire to humiliate the clergy and oust them from their place in the education of the people.'[1] In other words Clay believed that collaboration between the Church and the democratic State was still possible, if only the clergy kept their heads. But in saying this he clearly underestimated the hostility to the clergy of the Education League and of Joseph Chamberlain, and also what was likely to be the extent of Chamberlain's influence with the new electorate.

Of the other articles, that by Seeley on the 'Church as a Teacher of Morality' is interesting, particularly in view of its conception of the 'nation' as a moral concept. But the most interesting article of all is that by Llewellyn Davies on the 'Voluntary Principle'. In this he discusses the duty of the established Church to collaborate with the State and protests against the high church or nonconformist view that such a collaboration was necessarily a degradation for the Church. Such a view was based on an indefensibly low view of the functions of the State. 'Is it right or desirable,' he asked,

> – is it in accordance with Christian doctrine – that the State should be treated as a purely human and un-Divine creation? Those who regard the Church as even less Divine than the State, may reasonably think of the State as purely human. But I cannot understand how any faith which recognizes the Church as a Divine Ordinance can help seeing in the State a Divine Ordinance also.

If, however, the State was also carrying out the purposes of God it could not be a degradation for the Church to be united to it. 'At the present time,' wrote Davies,

> there is a hope stirring in many loyal hearts that our national life may be wider, stronger, and higher in tone and aspiration. The theory that none but ignoble functions should be reserved to the State does not satisfy them. They think that a great people may aspire to act nobly and wisely as a people, and not only through casual voluntary combinations. The idea of a national Church is strictly in harmony with such hopes and aims, implying as it does that a Christian nation should publicly confess its Christianity.[2]

This assertion had implications which related both to the nature of the State and of the Church. On the one hand it ac-

---

[1] Clay [op. cit., p. 130] pp. 192 and 196–7.
[2] ibid., pp. 73–4 and 84.

cepted the fact that the activities of the State had a profound moral significance and suggested that that moral significance would be reinforced as the sphere of national policy became wider, 'and higher in tone and aspiration'. On the other hand it resisted the conception that a Church should be a restrictive self-regarding organization, shrinking from all taint of contact with secular affairs and primarily intent on imposing a narrow orthodoxy on its members.

This aspect of the matter naturally appealed to Maurice who had himself been the victim of orthodox bigotry. In September 1868 Maurice also dealt with the problem of Church and State in a series of eight letters to the *Daily News*. He regarded, he said, 'with intense horror the ecclesiastical tyranny which may creep in – which is creeping in – upon us under the name of religious liberty', and 'with extreme dislike the Erastian doctrines which are creating a reaction in favour of it'. For he believed 'a union of Church and State to be implied in the existence of each and to be necessary for the protection of moral freedom'. Their co-operation was in fact 'the co-operation of spirit with law'. The State's duty was to assert the law and conserve property; the Church's duty was to warn men that 'what you have is not your own, you are only trusted with it that you may do with it what it is right that you should do'. This might seem to allot a humble and subordinate role to the State but this was not Maurice's intention, for he said,

> that the State is not what Churchmen and Statesmen of different schools have declared it to be – a vulgar earthly institution, which might do the dirty work of the Church, paying its ministers, persecuting its foes or determining its teachings, but a sacred and divine institution bearing a witness for law and justice which the Church under no condition has borne or can bear.

The application of this formula depends on the interpretation of the words 'law and justice', which is not altogether clear. But in any case Church and State acting together, and Maurice believed they should never be disunited, must surely in his view have had sufficient moral authority for the tasks to be undertaken.[1]

The union between Church and State was after some sort

---

[1] Maurice, *Life* [op. cit., p. 111] Vol. II, pp. 584–6.

to be continued into the twentieth century, but as will be seen there were to be reasons why it might not be the operative factor in the nation's affairs that Llewellyn Davies hoped it would be. Nevertheless, even later in the nineteenth century men who foresaw the need for the much greater extension of the powers of the State also conceived that the process would be accomplished by the joint collaboration of Church and State. In 1891 and 1892 Westcott was already bishop of Durham. He fully realized what intolerable conditions existed in the country, and knew that they must be amended. 'There was a time,' said he in 1892, 'when economists would have said that such an effort was hopeless. Wider experience has taught us another lesson. The institutions of society and the motives of men which determine the facts summarily described as "economic laws" are liable to alteration.' A new era was beginning. 'The age of individualism,' he said in 1891, 'which began at the *Renaissance* seems to have done its work.'

> We are preparing for the fullness of corporate life in a higher form than that which characterized society in the middle ages. We acknowledge on all sides that a nation is something more than an arbitrary association of men who combine for their mutual advantage. We feel that a nation is no figure of speech, but a body of which all the citizens are truly members. . . . If, then, our nation is indeed a complete body, it must have an adequate spiritual organ; and such an organ is the National Church.[1]

Situated as he was as bishop in Durham, confronted by, and profoundly interested in, a large mining population almost all of whom were dissenters, many of them no doubt bitterly conscious of the harshness of their lot and resentful of the wealth of the Church, Westcott must necessarily have been conscious of some of the things which prevented the Church from performing the function which he had assigned to it. Indeed he clearly recognized something of the problem. Westcott's conception of an organic society involved the belief that different classes necessarily performed different functions, which implied a measure of inequality in opportunities and means corre-

---

[1] B. F. Westcott, *The Incarnation: A Revelation of Human Duties* (A Charge, 1892) pp. 22, 23. *The National Church and the Nation: A Speech, in Westminster Town Hall at the Annual Meeting of the Church Defence Institution May 14* (1891) pp. 3, 4.

sponding to inequalities of power, but he also believed that 'there is a wide agreement that the present distribution of wealth in England is unfavourable to the highest general well being of the country', and that, even if it might not be possible to change the distribution of wealth, 'at least we can endeavour to determine the causes which have produced and are continuing to produce a dangerous inequality, and to ascertain how they can be modified'.[1] One expedient that Westcott commended was for wealthy people to live a simpler form of life and not waste money on superfluities and luxuries, and to recognize that their wealth was not their own but given them for service. These rules of conduct he carried out in his own practice, and it is possible that a knowledge of this reached some of the mining community, for it seems to have been impossible to come into contact with him without feeling the great attraction of his personality. But whether any of this reconciled any considerable section of the mining community to a Church which drew so large an income from mining royalties must remain doubtful.

The same consideration affected the moral authority of the Church of England throughout the nation. However devoted were many of its ministers, however valuable their service, it was inescapably a rich man's Church. It was endowed with great wealth, much of which had come into the personal possession of those who had held high office in it, and in the middle of the century from time to time the large estates left by those who had been its bishops were noted in the press. Its priests tended to be recruited from one class in society, and to have been prepared for their work by an education which in normal circumstances was out of the reach of a poor man. Its congregations were often predominantly well-to-do, and their attitudes, even their charities, tended to be at best condescending. All this necessarily cut the Church off from a large section of society, particularly as the class consciousness inherent in the conditions of the third phase developed and progressively fewer people accepted an hierarchical order of society as a matter of course.

It is probable that churchmen did not recognize the full force of these considerations. After all, the unequal distribution of wealth and the extent of hereditary wealth and endowed

[1] Westcott, *The Incarnation* [op. cit., p. 319] pp. 19–22.

wealth had been a factor in English life from time out of mind. To many it seemed inevitable, and to be justified by the old conception that the greater the wealth the greater the service required, or by the commonplace that all wealth must be held as a trust for others. Against its wealth the Church could balance much devoted, and some very valuable, work in its parishes. Many of the social evils, which were in the last years of the century the subject of public discussion, had been for long recognized by the parochial clergy. Charles Booth had recognized how valuable was the knowledge which the clergy possessed of the lives of their people. The Socialist activities of the younger clergy showed how earnestly they were concerned with the evils of society. Meanwhile it had been the great privilege of certain bishops and priests of the established Church to mediate effectively in industrial strife.[1]

None of this, however, was likely seriously to modify the situation. If men object to inequalities of wealth they are not likely to be mollified by the services, or the charities, of those whom they believe to be over-endowed. Moreover in the crowded England of the last half of the century very many men and women must have had no contact at all with the parochial clergy, and no opportunity of judging the quality of their service. There is no doubt about the sincere commitment of the Socialist clergy, but their numbers were relatively small as compared with the whole body of the clergy. As the reports of a number of debates in the Church Congress, in the convocations and in more local gatherings of the clergy demonstrate, this number clearly by no means included all those who entertained sincere good will towards labour, and at least after 1880 most men seem to have rid themselves of the inhibitions which had been imposed by the old 'laws of political economy'. But sincere good will is not sufficient on its own and working-class leaders might be excused if they did not find it easy to identify themselves with middle-class Socialists and social reformers whose class, ways of thought and of speaking were so different from their own, and who inevitably tended to consider the

[1] This general attitude is reflected in Randall T. Davidson, D.P., 99th bishop, *A Charge delivered to the Clergy of the Diocese of Rochester, October 29, 30, 31, 1894* (1894) pp. 43–55. His quotation from Charles Booth is apparently from a *Speech on old Age Pensions*, made on 21 November 1892.

problems of the working classes very much from the outside.

It is true that in a number of cases the clergy were called in to arbitrate in industrial disputes, indeed by the end of the century a certain amount of intelligent thought had been given by some of them to the techniques which might make conciliation and arbitration successful.[1] But the significance of this can be exaggerated. An arbitrator is not a moral dictator imposing such terms on both sides as he considers to be morally just. He is rather a middle man trying to find an agreed settlement for a difficult situation – a settlement which must accord with the conditions which prevail at the moment, and in the circumstances which prevailed in the later nineteenth century one of those conditions was too often the acceptance of an unavoidable defeat for labour. In such circumstances all that the arbitrator could do was to try to modify the effects of that defeat.

Moreover, whatever the conditions of the settlement and whatever the position of the arbitrator, success required exceptional personal qualities. This seems to be demonstrated by the two most outstanding examples of successful arbitration of this period, Westcott's settlement of the miners' strike in 1892 and Mandell Creighton's services, as bishop of Peterborough, in resolving the lockout in the boot and shoe industry in Leicester and Nottingham in 1895. Westcott's success was clearly a triumph of character, Creighton's was the result of a careful analysis of the technicalities involved and prolonged patient diplomacy, during which he kept himself in the background as much as possible. It is significant that his advice to his clergy was that in trade disputes they should aim at benevolent neutrality, for they had not the knowledge to pronounce on such matters. They must try to alleviate the distress which would inevitably result from a dispute and do what they could to maintain the great principles of justice, and they must discover all that they could about conditions in their parishes. But they could do no more. Creighton himself was in fact a man of unusual intelligence and subtlety; what could happen when a clumsier, more rigid, mind addressed itself to this work can be seen in the much misrepresented activities of Frederick Temple

[1] See the contribution of W. Moore Ede, rector of Gateshead, to the meeting of the Church Congress at Nottingham (*Church Congress*, 1897) pp. 318–23.

as bishop of London during the strike in the London docks in 1889.[1] In fact the Church of England possessed neither the moral authority, nor, for that matter, the clarity of view, the impartiality or the knowledge to act as the spiritual guide of the nation in the industrial problems which were beginning to take up a large share of the nation's attention.

Meanwhile there remained the ancient adversaries of the Church. In a number of clerical biographies and other accounts of the situation in the last quarter of the century it is recorded that friendly relations were established between churchmen and nonconformists, and no doubt this was often true; but if it was true the fact demonstrates once again that it is the most vehement spirits who often mould a situation and completely dominate the record. The activities of the politically orientated dissenters, particularly their violent attacks on the elementary education bill of 1870, demonstrated clearly that an important section of the nation passionately rejected the spiritual authority of the Church of England. More than this, the modifications which they succeeded in making in the education bill successfully prevented any church school from gaining help from the rates, and so set in motion a process by which the church schools would be gradually squeezed out. The result of this was the continual erosion of the Church's influence and the increase of the power of a largely secular authority amply endowed from public resources.

The ever-increasing power of the State was therefore not going to conform to the old plan of Church and State, and still less would it accord with the old philosophy of the nonconformists. The nonconformists believed in the autonomous moral authority of free churches working within the framework of a State, to which they had denied all but the simplest responsibilities. In particular many of them had said explicitly that the State had no duty, and no right, to provide for the education of

[1] *Life and Letters of Mandell Creighton by his Wife* (2 vols., 1904) Vol. II, pp. 119–32. His advice to his clergy about trade disputes is quoted there from his primary *Charge* as bishop of Peterborough (Peterborough, 1894). The whole charge is well worth reading, particularly the section on the Church and society (pp. 19–28). For Temple and the dockers' strike, see Sandford, *Temple* [op. cit., p. 85] Vol. II, pp. 142–50.

M

children. That position could no longer be maintained, and by accepting the ideal of a State-provided compulsory system, with the proviso that the teaching must be 'undenominational', the nonconformists had accepted a principle which was clean contrary to their original principles and a practice which would serve to undermine their influence as effectively as it did that of the Church.

Therefore neither of the traditional political creeds were going to supply the guiding philosophy for the new State. Nor for that matter was much help to be gained from the professional philosophies which were being taught in the schools. There was some tendency at the turn of the century to commend German idealist philosophy, and in particular the philosophy of Hegel, as an explanation and justification for the new developments in the power of the State, but it may be doubted whether such philosophy would have been intelligible outside the circle of experts, and whether if intelligible it would have been acceptable. Other philosophies which dealt in the categories of 'self-regarding' and 'other-regarding' acts left ambiguities precisely where definition was wanted. In any case ordinary men were not very likely to look to professional philosophers for guidance: their philosophy was likely to be supplied by the general moral consensus of the inhabitants of Great Britain at any given moment, as generally interpreted by Parliament and put into effect by the appropriate ministers and civil servants.

This, in the nineteenth century at least, meant that the nation would still conceive itself to be a Christian nation, provided its Christianity was rather nebulously conceived and deprived of any effective dogmatic structure. It would also mean that in the late nineteenth century there would be an increasing sense of the moral importance of social reform, of the need to secure social justice for those to whom the existing order of society supplied less than their due as human beings. To this ideal the old principle of the sanctity of private rights would be, to a considerable extent, subordinated. How far this should go would obviously be a matter for opinion, and there would remain for a long time some very stout upholders of a generous conception of the inviolability of private rights; but the State in Britain had inherited a theory and a practice which would greatly assist the extension of its power whatever its basic philosophy. The theory was the Austinian conception of sovereignty, and the practice the use of the devices of delegated legislation, jurisdiction and administrative discretion.

According to the theory of Austin law must, in any country, be the responsibility of an identifiable sovereign body. The sovereign might be complex, that is it might consist of several institutions working in conjunction. It might only have an intermittent existence, as in those cases where the power to alter certain laws was reserved to a constituent assembly summoned according to prescribed form for that purpose. Or it might be unitary and continually in action. But whatever its nature the laws it made had absolute force; no right could be pleaded against it. This doctrine was at first a legal convenience, the necessity for which was indeed made clear by the course of sixteenth- and seventeenth-century history. Its implications were not generally realized during the earliest centuries of its acceptance, but obviously it was open to a much wider practical application than would have occurred to its earlier exponents.

In Britain this sovereignty was held to be the King in Parliament. This was originally a complex sovereign power, made up of King, Lords and Commons; but it was on the way to becoming unitary. By the middle of the nineteenth century the power of the monarch had been whittled away. The power of the House of Lords remained, as was demonstrated by the fate of the education bill promoted by the Liberal Government in 1906, but it was intermittent, arbitrary and decreasing in effectiveness. The sovereign power was coming to be concentrated in the House of Commons acting alone and legislating with authority to override anyone else's rights and privileges.

Thus was provided not only an inexhaustible reservoir of legislative authority to be used for the purposes of social reform but also a means by which executive power could be so armed for those uses that it was largely outside the restraints of the common law. These possibilities had been exploited relatively early in the nineteenth century. By the factory act of 1833 the factory inspectors were given power to frame regulations for the management of factories, to initiate complaints of any breach of these regulations, to try them and to punish the offenders. In 1834 the poor law commissioners were given power to promulgate regulations which would alter the framework and practice of government in the administration of the Poor Law, which was for many people the most important department of public policy, indeed the only department which affected their lives. Thereafter the development of these possibilities was slow and unpopular. Unwillingness to use them to the full delayed the formation of a satisfactory national system for public health till after 1866, and of education till after 1870. Nevertheless, as has been seen an increase of governmental responsibility was inevitable and the use of these powers became the commonplace of the English legal system, so much so that in his remarkable 'sketch of public law' in 1887–8 F. W. Maitland said that 'If you take up a modern volume of the reports of the Queen's Bench division, you will find that about half the cases reported have to do with rules of administrative law.'[1] A very formidable system of government was coming into existence and, as it took shape, traditionalists had cause to wonder whether its ways of working were in accordance with what they had believed to be the principles of the rule of law, and idealists whether all this was governed by the same spirit that they had hoped to conjure out of the unhappy chaos of nineteenth-century conditions.

For the nineteenth century is a period of many and diverse aspirations, and its sequel is not only significant for what did happen but also for what did not happen. Not every dream found its expression in the organization of the late nineteenth-century and twentieth-century State. The utopian schemes of early nineteenth-century social revolutionaries, the plans that were constantly generated by the fertile brain of Robert Owen, left not a wrack behind. Fortunately Bentham's pauper panopticons were never established. The idea of absolutely free trade, an industry untroubled by State interference and endorsed by a universal system of secular education which should teach everyone the truths of political economy and the importance of checks on the growth of population, were not carried to any logical conclusion. The belief treasured by so many diverse groups that the salvation of the victims of over-population, industrialism and other social pressures was to be

[1] F. W. Maitland, *The Constitutional History of England* (Cambridge, 1963, first edn., 1908) p. 505.

found in the establishment of large colonies of smallholders who should support themselves by spade husbandry, led only to meagre and unsatisfactory experiments. The Christian Socialists' hope that industry controlled by privately-owned capital would be replaced by industry using capital owned by those who were employed failed. Ruskin's Guild of St George never got off the ground.

Many of these schemes failed, at least in part, because those who promoted them made a number of different mistakes about the realities of the situation. The authors of the various early nineteenth-century utopian plans normally wildly misconceived the political possibilities of their own day, and the economic possibilities of any day. The benevolent potentialities of absolutely free competition were exaggerated. The reduplication of smallholdings was not the clue to the development of prosperity and happiness, even of those who lived in the countryside. In much of the countryside the only way to secure decent conditions for the labourers was to reduce the size of the labour force, to increase the amount of capital employed and to increase the size of the unit of production to make this practicable. The co-operative industry of the Christian Socialists was possibly ill organized and in many cases recruited unsuitable workers. Ruskin saw much that the ordinary businessman did not see, but he does not seem to have seen very clearly many of the inescapable realities of industry and trade.

In almost all of these schemes, however, there was one common cause for failure. They were idealistic schemes. They depended, at least in part, on the replacement of that ordinary human motive, the desire for wealth and material comfort, by higher motives – the desire to help others, the realization of other values than the enjoyment of better material conditions, as for instance the enjoyment of beauty or the exercise of sound craftsmanship, or of the delights of a wide culture. The sequel seems to demonstrate that though these motives were widely diffused in society, they were not generally strong enough to form the primary motive in social life.

It has been said that in every fat man there is a thin man struggling to get out. The analogy with English society in the nineteenth century is helpful. The ordinary society in Britain at that time can be reasonably compared to a powerfully-built fat man. The support of his body took up most of his energy and much of his thought. It did not occupy the whole of his mind, he could be humane, he could be sentimental, but his material needs were apt to claim priority in his efforts, and he devised a philosophy to prove that this must be so. Within him however there was a lean idealist whose ways of thought were different. There were always in nineteenth-century Britain men and women to whom material wealth meant little, and who were apt to dream of a society made up of people whose values were the same as their own. This was true of many of the revolutionary reformers and poets of the early nineteenth century; it was implicit in much of Carlyle's thought, though in his case from time to time uglier shapes appeared through the smoke. In Carlyle's *Past and Present* and in Pugin's *Contrasts* or Kenelm Digby's *Broad Stone of Honour* the dream took the curious form of nostalgia for the middle ages, a period in which it was believed that in place of the squalid materialism of the nineteenth century the dominant motives had been supplied by a vivid sense of the spiritual realities of the Christian faith and by the conception of chivalry.

The ambience of this particular idea was very wide. It was one of the factors which supplied the motive force for the Oxford Movement, and at that time inspired young people with the wish to pass their lives in fraternities and sororities in the worst places in the towns. It provided much of the furniture for Disraeli's novels, much of the thought of Young England, and can be detected in the idealism of the early Pre-Raphaelites. However, this exalted conception of what Britain might be was not confined to those who indulged in medievalism. It was present in the hope of a converted and Christianized Britain as conceived for instance by such evangelicals as Lord Shaftesbury. It lay behind Maurice's thought and the hopes of the Christian Socialists. Its most eloquent exponent was probably John Ruskin with his over-mastering realization of aesthetic values and his passionate desire for social justice. Through Ruskin it inspired William Morris, whose two fables *The Dream of John Ball* and *News from Nowhere* depend on two of the normal sources of inspiration for this way of thought, a return to the middle ages, though in this case it is in fact a more realistic view of the middle ages, and the revolutionary hope.

The existence of this ideal was of great advantage to nine-teenth-century Britain. It inspired lives of great devotion. It helped to support movements for practical reform. Its presence helped to purify the ideals of men who were in fact working for more material objectives, and was one, if only one, of the factors which helped to breach the curtain wall which the economists had erected around the old competitive society. But it was never realized. When all was done there appeared in the place of the original fat man not the lean, spiritually motivated man of men's dreams but another fat man, a better fat man no doubt, a happier fat man, with the fat in rather different places, but a man whose shape and motives bore a recognizable affinity to those of his predecessor.

The new man was also anxious to secure for himself the best possible standard of life in material things. This is a natural desire, it is important that the opportunity to gratify it should be as widely distributed as possible, but it is not quite the same type of motive as the idealists had hoped would dominate society. In order to achieve this high standard of living the new man realized, as his predecessor had done, that the nation must achieve the greatest possible material prosperity, even if this achievement was at the expense of those aesthetic values by which John Ruskin had set such store. And he was neither to gain, nor to maintain, what he wanted by a reliance on brotherly love or the absence of friction in a classless society. No doubt in the development of better conditions much personal idealism played an important part, but the sanction behind what was done was normally the coercive power of the democratic State, or effective trade union action. The result was a society by no means wholly devoted to material objectives, but it was not the society of which men had dreamed. William Morris's 'Nowhere' remained nowhere.

This contrast between aspiration and achievement, or at an earlier stage in political evolution between the ideal and the practical, was not peculiar to Britain. It seems to be reflected in the conflict between the anarchists and the Communists on the Continent, between Bakunin and Marx, or between a number of revolutionaries and the administrators of the State who emerged in Russia after the revolution. Before the Russian revolution it had emerged in George Sorel's *Réflexions sur la*

violence, with its attack on the comfortable parliamentary socialism of men like Jaurès and its commendation of the redemptive
effects of the adoption of revolutionary syndicalism, its acceptance of the apocalyptic conception of the general strike, and
the sanitary results of the appeal to some form of violence to
dissipate the miasma of bourgeois society. The same contrast
seems to be present in a conflict that sometimes appears between the ideals of student activists and their favourite philosophers and the objectives of ordinary trade unionists. In England
on the whole the conflict has been milder. The counterpart in
England of revolutionary syndicalism was guild socialism, with
its significantly medieval affinities. Of the contemporaries of
Sorel probably the most effective critics of what was taking
shape were irredeemably bourgeois thinkers such as Hilaire
Belloc in the *Servile State* (1912) and H. G. Wells in the *New
Machiavelli* (1911); and in due course, unfortunately, the issue
became confused with an issue that was very largely technical
and superficial.

The instruments by which in England the new State exercised its will were the legislative powers and the opportunities
for largely unrestricted executive action which Parliament
often delegated to ministers and subordinate bodies. Upon
these in the period after the First World War a fierce attack was
launched by eminent lawyers, the fiercest being *The New
Despotism* by Lord Hewart in 1929, and the most effective
criticisms being by Sir Carleton Allen, at one time professor of
jurisprudence at Oxford.[1] In some respects these attacks were
no doubt justified. Probably unavoidably, the system had
developed many of the characteristic vices of bureaucracy –
decisions made by anonymous civil servants, paper logic and
imaginary categories, the enforcement of regulations in defiance
of sense and humanity, blind and clumsy ruthlessness in the
actions of government. But the attackers seldom seemed to
have recognized the problem as a whole. They were apt to suggest that the system had been created by civil servants for the
convenience of civil servants and not adequately to consider
the difficulties presented by the urgent social needs which

---

[1] Lord Hewart, *The New Despotism* (1929). Sir Carleton Kemp Allen, *Law in
the Making* (Oxford, 1927); *Bureaucracy Triumphant* (1931); *Law and Orders*
(1945).

the system had been devised to satisfy. Moreover, they concentrated attention on such important but technical problems as whether it was right for Parliament to delegate such extensive powers, or the courts of law to be ousted from the control of ministerial decisions, or whether judicial or quasijudicial powers should be vested in special tribunals or ministerial discretion, and in so doing they diverted attention from the fundamental spiritual issues which the emergence of the new Leviathan inevitably raised.

Many of these issues only reached their full development after the period which this book is intended to discuss, indeed it may be guessed that in many cases that full development has not yet arrived. Nevertheless, what was happening in the third phase was in its way a culmination of two processes which had been going forward since 1830, and its nature throws some light on the significance of what took place in the intervening period. The two processes are the progressive disestablishment of the Church of England and the progressive secularization of society and the State.

The two processes have much in common, but it is important to recognize that they could differ in essentials and that the secularization of the State might have very different results from what had been desired by those who had wished for the disestablishment of the Church. The progressive disestablishment of the Church may be considered to have started with the results of the Reform Act of 1832, to have continued with the decline of the authority and prestige of the parish priest even in country districts, and to have been in large part completed by the replacement of the services he had supplied by the professional services supplied by the secular State. As a result of this process it might be said that the established Church had become little more than a crowned ghost sitting on the common grave of old Church and old King. But this result did not imply the triumph of religious Dissent. The principle of religious Dissent had been spiritual in conception – that men and women must be left free to attain their highest fulfilment unimpeded by the interference of any exterior authority, ecclesiastical or secular. The maintenance of that principle is not normally the result of the secularization of the State and society.

The secularization of the State is a process based on the principle that what are believed to be wholly secular objectives are the only possible results of organized public endeavour. The achievement of these ends is, however, deemed to be so important, and the organization required to attain them of necessity so all-embracing and powerful, that it presumes a concentration of authority intent on secular objects which may leave little scope for the observance of spiritual values, particularly of that spiritual value which is protected by the right to dissent. The development of this position was slow, unconscious and incomplete in the nineteenth century. It was not the result of the response to any theory, but rather of reluctant obedience to the dictates of necessity. If the State was to achieve those secular objectives which it became increasingly clear it must achieve, if it was to educate the people, supply a healthy environment in which they might live and regulate the conditions under which they worked, then it must take to itself sufficient authority to achieve these ends, and it could not allow its purposes to be impeded by the vagaries of the individual conscience or the eccentricities of private opinion. The working principle of the secular State was not to be respect for individual freedom but the necessity of compulsion.

This necessity cast its long shadow over the troubles of the Christian Socialists between 1848 and 1854. As has been seen (pp. 78–9), Maurice worked out a clearly conceived view of the relations of Church and State. They were complementary to one another. The State he said,

> though it deals with the outward life of man, is not, (as they call it) a secular body, but appeals to, and acts upon, the conscience of man in a way in which the Church cannot appeal to that conscience or act upon it, bears a witness for God which the Church cannot bear . . . the Church is necessarily a maimed and imperfect thing without the State not because it wants its revenue or its sword, but because God hath ordained an eternal connection with the law, which is embodied in the State, and the religious life-giving principle which is embodied in the Church.[1]

This view Maurice held till the end of his life, but it contained some unresolved problems. Supposing the law of the State did not embody the life-giving principle which is em-

[1] *The Kingdom of Christ* [op. cit., p. 78] Vol III, p. 106.

bodied in the Church, supposing the distribution of the property it protected was unjust, the principles it tolerated were contrary to precepts of Christianity, how far were the representatives of the Church permitted to go to rectify matters?

This issue presented itself to Maurice in 1848 when he received that letter from Ludlow that changed his life, when, as he told Ludlow, he realized 'better than I had ever done before, how hollow that material civilisation was, of which Louis Philippe had been the great promoter in France, and which we had been well inclined to adopt and to worship in England', and how much it was the duty of every man, 'but, above all of every clergyman' to strive to reassert Christian principles.[1] This realization brought him into the Christian Socialist movement, and thereby involved him in problems which he would have liked to avoid. Clearly the objects of that movement came well within his formula, but its operations very early began to cause trouble. For instance, the promotion of its objects might involve him in the possibly sordid manoeuvres of a nationwide political agitation from which he shrank after his experiences of the agitation on behalf of the National Society in 1838 and 1839. There was, however, a more fundamental difficulty. The development of the co-operative system might involve the method of compulsion sanctioned by an appeal to a secular authority which was other than the law of God that it was the duty of the Church to represent.

For it was suggested that a central organization should come into existence which should control by its superior authority the selfish propensities of individual co-operative societies. But Maurice could not believe that was in accordance with the spiritual principles of co-operation. Moreover there was another difficulty which has already been mentioned. Ludlow and others wished to invoke the principle of democracy, but, as has been said, Maurice believed that the people's claim to sovereignty involved the same blasphemy as that of which kings had been guilty, and he wondered whether, if the people claimed the power to cashier their rulers, they would not also claim the right to cashier Christ from being their King. In fact Maurice found himself in the tragic situation in which other

[1] F. D. Maurice, *Learning and Working* (Cambridge, 1855), 'Dedication to John Malcolm Ludlow', pp. v and vi.

spiritual leaders have found themselves. He had accepted a spiritual objective, but in order to attain it he was asked to assent to secular methods and to secular principles which seemed to be incompatible with its spirituality. His doubts, expressed in prolix and unhappy letters normally to Ludlow, pursued him through six years of frustration and misunderstanding, and in the end broke up the Christian Socialists as a coherent group.

At first sight Maurice's doubts may seem to be as perverse and unreasonable as his actions were sometimes unpredictable; but in fact the explanation seems to be a simple one. Maurice believed that motive was all-important. He believed that the reform of society, the improvement of the lot of the working classes, must come through the purification of the motives which guided society, a purification reflected in the co-operative ideal. He believed that such a purification was possible for he was sure that the assertion that the law which must govern society must be unceasing competition for material advantages was a lie. It was his task as a clergyman to encourage this purification of motive. It was not his task, and had never been his intention, to erect a system which merely exchanged one form of compulsion for another, one form of human sovereignty for another, with the sole object of improving certain people's physical conditions, however desirable that improvement might be.

If this was the source of Maurice's difficulties most of his friends and followers do not seem fully to have grasped the point. Nor do most of them seem to have recognized the problem which these difficulties should have revealed: that is, how far is it appropriate or legitimate to draw on spiritual authority to commend secular means in order to secure a secular objective? Strangely enough the one man who did realize this also seems to have believed that Maurice himself was as mistaken in this matter as the rest. As a young man F. J. Hort was greatly attracted by Carlyle and Maurice, and deeply interested in Christian Socialism. But fairly soon doubts began to occur to him. In February 1850, looking forward to the first issues of tracts on Christian Socialism, he was apparently prepared to be satisfied if they proposed merely an extension of what he called the 'benefit-society principle' to particular trades, 'provided they don't talk nonsense about people being fraternal and benevolent because they take part in a good investment for their money or labour. If', he added, 'they assert that Society itself and human relations should rest on the same principle, woe woe to them! So at least I feel.'[1] In July 1850 on a visit to London, he had an interesting conversation with Ludlow, in which he drew from Ludlow the admission that he believed wages must be regulated by the market price; thereby making, so Hort said,

a professed assailer of political economy doctrines entirely rest his support of one of the main elements of Socialism upon an assumed axiom of political economy, which goes on the assumption that selfishness is the law of men's actions! Again, I urged that I fully adopted the Christian principle of co-operation, but repudiated the socialistic scheme as substituting a mechanical for a moral co-operation, that I thought a real fellow-working was chiefly, if not only, possible under the old so-called 'competitive' machinery. To this he replied that practically, as men are selfish, mutual assistance and co-operation, springing from merely moral motives instead of from machinery are impossible.[2]

'Another strange confession!' said Hort. It was at least a significant confession. Like Maurice, Hort had uncovered the difficult and potentially dangerous contradiction at the heart of nineteenth-century idealistic thought. The selfishness and injustice of society as it existed in contemporary Britain was acknowledged and passionately condemned and men were anxious to create a more moral and happier society in its place. But it became increasingly clear that real social advances could only be secured by State compulsion, a process which was not likely to be of moral advantage to those who were coerced, nor even to those who benefited materially. It was not a contradiction that was likely to trouble most men's minds for the next thirty or forty years. Nor was it desirable that it should do so, for the most important lesson of those years was the morally stultifying results for large numbers of men and women of those conditions which the coercive power of the community alone could remove. Nevertheless the contradiction remained and, as the collectivist State became more formid-

[1] *Hort* [op. cit., p. 301] Vol. I, p. 130.
[2] ibid., Vol. I, p. 162.

able, and as a more radical, more secular, Socialism replaced Christian Socialism as an ideal, it became more obvious.

This possible cleavage between collectivism or Socialism and Christianity is reflected in a paper read in 1889 by D. J. Vaughan to a diocesan conference at the request of the bishop of Peterborough.[1] As might be expected of one who had been a Christian Socialist, Vaughan was sympathetic to collectivism and, up to a point, with Socialism. The points at which he differed from secular Socialism are interesting. He believed that its treatment of surplus value was based on a fallacy, though he admitted that was a technical point for economists to discuss. More important still, he believed it was apt to be based on a false, or at least an imperfect, view of human nature. Its exponents were either antagonistic to religion, or passed it by as a thing of no importance in the organization of society. 'And yet,' said Vaughan, 'it is beyond all question that our views of human society here and now, will be profoundly affected according as we believe that human nature is fundamentally animal or fundamentally spiritual.'

He also rejected the doctrine that 'property is robbery'.

> In the view of the Christian Church property is not robbery; but property is a trust, a responsibility, a moral danger to the possessor until the stewardship is fully recognized and diligently acted upon. Be the amount small or great it is essentially a trust, not an ownership, and must be used accordingly; though undoubtedly the larger the amount the greater is the responsibility. This is the Christian doctrine of property and had the Church always faithfully proclaimed it and acted upon it, we would come with cleaner hands now into the conflict with socialism.

Not every Christian would accept Vaughan's analysis of the problem of property; or rather there would be those who would accept Vaughan's view that property was a trust, while believing at the same time that there might be circumstances in which the statement that it was also the result of robbery was worthy of earnest consideration. The issue between materialistic and spiritual boundaries, is, however, one which anyone claiming the name of Christian must take seriously. It is inherent in the position adopted by W. Cunningham some

[1] D. J. Vaughan, *Questions of the Day* [op. cit., p. 306] pp. 251–60.

twenty years later – Cunningham would not become a member of the Christian Social Union because he did not believe that Christian law should be made the ultimate authority on social practice. It was not for the Church to advocate specific reforms, since presumably these must depend on the secular answers to purely secular problems, which should not be imposed by a spiritual authority; but he seems to have profounder objections than this to some Socialist teaching. He believed that the means by which Socialism proposed to attain its ends were not those of Christianity, since Socialism relied on compelling other people to do their duty and Christianity must endeavour to induce every man to do his own. He also believed that the objectives of Socialism and Christianity were different. For many Socialists the objective would be limited to securing for the mass of people the greatest material happiness in life on this earth, while Christians must necessarily take into account the claims of a life beyond.[1]

Cunningham was writing in the twentieth century and by that time the issue had become more urgent. The New Leviathan was already in existence and likely to grow. It was arming itself with the formidable weapons made available by the Austinian doctrine of sovereignty and the modern theory of the democratic State. Since the nation from which it derived its authority was heterogeneous in its religious beliefs or non-beliefs it was necessarily agnostic, except in a common acceptance of the great importance of material well-being. To gain its ends it necessarily resorted to methods of compulsion. Indeed, the dream of moral freedom ceased to seem significant to many of its advocates, since economists and psychologists were again tending to teach that human beings were in the grip of forces they could not control.

Clearly so formidable a creation would produce a great variety of moral problems for the individuals within its power. They might wish to direct their lives according to values which the State ignored, and, at least in certain matters, to be governed by organizations which did not draw their authority from the State or exist by its permission.

[1] A. Cunningham, *William Cunningham* [op. cit., p. 299] pp. 21–2 and 71. W. Cunningham, *Socialism and Christianity* (1910) pp. 12–14.

The issue was clearly of great importance for a Christian Church, but it could also affect the situation of members of other societies, such as trade unions, which might make their peculiar claims on the allegiance of men and women. The case for the autonomous rights of all societies within the State was made in an important book by an Anglican clergyman just before the first world war. The writer was J. N. Figgis, a distinguished Cambridge scholar and one-time pupil of Lord Acton and F. W. Maitland; indeed it was from Maitland's teaching about the medieval view of the State as a Community of Communities that his doctrine partly derived. When Figgis wrote his book *Churches in the Modern State* he had left Cambridge and, after a period in a Dorset parish, had become an Anglican monk in the Community of the Resurrection in the West Riding of Yorkshire.[1] Figgis' book is an effective attack on the legal conception that corporations within the State owed their entire existence to a law which drew its authority from the commands of an Austinian sovereign, and that the terms of this existence could be settled by that law without reference to their own inner life. It is an extremely cogent case. The way in which in Figgis' day the law had been brought to bear on certain spiritual issues was not easily to be defended, and apart from the technical legal issues the claims of the New Leviathan, with its blind assertion of overwhelming power, necessarily presented a serious problem to anyone who believed in spiritual independence.

It may be held, and this was no doubt Figgis' belief, that this problem was most serious for a Church which had been established and which was still bound to an agnostic State, whose policy it could not influence, by links which were both meaningless and dangerous. If this was so perhaps the time had come for the parting of the ways. This would seem to be the logic of Figgis' case, and it might also seem to be the lesson of the process which this book has tried to describe. Church and State had at one time been united; but since 1830, though formal disestablishment had been resisted, the course of events had gradually thrust them apart. It is possible that the tradition of

---

[1] J. N. Figgis, *Churches in the Modern State* (1913). It is interesting to compare this book with the adaptation of its ideas in H. J. Laski's *Studies in the Problem of Sovereignty* (New Haven, Conn., 1917).

the old unity had caused some Anglican incumbents to perform valuable services for the communities in which they lived. But that phase was over. Those services had been performed in the terms of an order of society which was now happily obsolete, and in any case they had not been adequate. It had been necessary for the legacy to pass into the hands of the secular State, and it could not be shared. The time had come to get rid of a pretence and break the bondage to a worldly secular society which could only damage the Church as a spiritual body.

Nevertheless it seems possible to conceive that history teaches a different lesson. One can make the case that the ties which bound the Church to the nation had been in some ways honourable bonds since they bound it to the service not of a congregation of the devout, but of a community of men and women as mixed and as varied as only a purely geographically defined community can be. It also seems possible that the Church had gained by being governed by a law administered in general by lay lawyers and not by theologians or ecclesiastics. This had created a situation in which there was room for a variety of opinions and for developments of doctrine and practice which might well have been snuffed out by a purely ecclesiastical authority. Evangelicals, tractarians and ritualists, broad churchmen and Christian Socialists had all taken advantage of this in their turn, and it would be hard to deny that without that variety the life of the Church would have been poorer and its witness narrower. In fact it might be suggested that the lesson which history taught was not that its establishment had been an encumbrance to the Church of England but that it had been, and was still, a privilege and an advantage.

In the twentieth century this was no doubt an old-fashioned view and it required an old-fashioned clergyman to express it. Figgis briefly noted in his book another book recently published by the then dean of Ripon, which he clearly did not consider particularly sensible. The dean was none other than W. H. Fremantle, once of Marylebone, and now an old man, for he was born in 1831. In his book Fremantle expressed the view that 'the condition of things established for more than a thousand years in England . . . where the nation as a whole, with all its powers, acts as a Christian Church . . . is the highest type of the Church'. Every person, he said, had some portion in building up the Kingdom of God, though some were marked off from others by their will to work in the joint cause and by a certain understanding of its purpose. He therefore deplored the smaller differences of ritual, or of opinion, which divided Christian from Christian, and man from man. The Church had other duties than the conduct of public worship and the public teaching of religion according to certain prescribed forms.

> To remove grievances, to raise the poor, to teach the young, to make taxation just to all, to bend the powers of the criminal law to the recovery of the erring members of the community, to train the people in a life which shall be clean, healthy, and orderly, to encourage international peace – these are the acts of the Christian body, by whatever name we call it, and the attempt to do the work of the greatest instrument of Christian progress by other than national means is nothing but an usurpation.[1]

Fremantle was clearly a man of consistent opinions. These were the principles on which he had run his parish forty years earlier. No doubt he underestimated the importance of the differences of opinion between Christian and Christian and Christian and non-Christian, but it is possible that others exaggerated their significance, and, at the least, it would be difficult to deny the social value of a system that had given Octavia Hill some of her first opportunities and provided for the apprenticeship of Samuel and Henrietta Barnett. In fact the contrast between the standpoint of Fremantle and Figgis seems to present the dilemma which is inherent in the history of the Church of England. Behind Fremantle in Marylebone stretched the long tradition of the Church of England parish, and it was on this tradition that Figgis had turned his back when he left his comfortable rectory at Marnhull in north Dorset to live in harsh conditions in a monastery on the edge of a smoky valley in industrial Yorkshire, because, as he told the parishioners whom he was leaving: 'I have come to see that if Christians are to convince the world of their seriousness they must be prepared to live as though they meant the creed which they profess.'[2]

[1] W. H. Fremantle, *Natural Christianity* (1911) pp. 89, 95, 99, 110, 130–1.
[2] M. G. Tucker, *John Neville Figgis* (1950) p. 14.

What he had come to see seems to present the issue between himself and Fremantle. How far had the commitment of the Church of England to the nineteenth-century hierarchical society in England and to the State in England prevented churchmen from living as though they meant the creed they professed? Or how far had it disclosed to them the true duties of a Christian body, the way to play their part in the building of the Kingdom of Christ? It cannot be denied that there was a heavy adverse balance. The life that Figgis left behind, the life that had been lived in Anglican vicarages, rectories, deaneries and bishops' palaces, had often been very comfortable. Those who had lived there had often been too amply rewarded, isolated by pride of class from the men to whom they were supposed to minister and integrated into a social system that was in many ways harsh and unjust. It might be hard to see any very close connection between such lives and the creed which those who lived them professed. On the other hand the lives of the clergy had by no means always been passed in pleasant places, and, wherever lived, the duties had often been hard and exacting. Indeed in many cases the devotion and the self-sacrifice had not only been great but enlightened by that sense of a personal comprehensive social responsibility, which perhaps was more a mark of Fremantle's theory of the Church than of that which Figgis might have sponsored.

It is however fruitless to try to make a comparison, and impossible to draw up a moral balance sheet equating what was good and what bad in the English Church in the nineteenth century. There does not yet exist sufficient comprehensive and systematic knowledge, and in any case moral balance sheets are without any meaning. Nor can any historian decide to what extent men were and ought not to have been the victims of the historical situation of which they were heirs. All that can be said is that the tradition and practice of nineteenth-century churchmen is well worthy of study and that it is important to consider it, with other elements, when considering the development of British ideas and institutions through the various phases of nineteenth-century history. Only by so doing will it be possible to understand the Britain which has resulted from the process, and only by so doing will it be possible to understand the Church of England.

Index